Commercial Law Aspects of Residential Mortgage Securitisation in Australia

Pelma Rajapakse • Shanuka Senarath

Commercial Law Aspects of Residential Mortgage Securitisation in Australia

palgrave
macmillan

Pelma Rajapakse
Griffith University
Brisbane, QLD, Australia

Shanuka Senarath
University of Colombo
Colombo, Sri Lanka

ISBN 978-3-030-00604-4 ISBN 978-3-030-00605-1 (eBook)
https://doi.org/10.1007/978-3-030-00605-1

Library of Congress Control Number: 2018968613

Cover illustration: krisanapong detraphiphat / Getty Images

This Palgrave Macmillan imprint is published by the registered company Springer Nature Switzerland AG.
The registered company address is: Gewerbestrasse 11, 6330 Cham, Switzerland

Foreword

In 1998, as a young academic, I wrote the first article warning of the macro-economic risks of securitisation transactions. During the late 1990s, the volume of issuance of asset-backed securities backed by all types of receivables and cash flows was increasing exponentially, year after year. There was also very little regulation or oversight of the transactions' structure, the credit quality of the underlying receivables, the value of the underlying collateral, as well as considerable uncertainty in governing law. Without much oversight, the financial services industry, which was making a great deal of money from these transactions, extolled the benefits of securitisation to both issuers and investors. Likening it to alchemy, securitisation enthusiasts failed to consider the possibility that the house of cards the industry was built on could ever come tumbling down. And tumble it did. The global financial crisis of 2007 saw the failure of financial institutions, extraordinary defaults by issuers, and loss contagion across the globe. Securitisation was "singled out for censure" as a significant contributor to the collapse of the financial markets.

Fast-forward ten years: the global economy has recovered and securitisation has had a resurgence to the point that it is currently a *ten-trillion*-dollar industry, begging the question of whether we have learnt anything from the failures and losses in the securitisation markets during the recent financial crisis. Which is why *Commercial Law Aspects of Residential Mortgage Securitisation in Australia* by Dr Pelma Rajapakse and Dr Shanuka Senarath is so important and so timely. Residential mortgage-backed securities, or RMBSs, are bonds or notes that are backed by residential mortgages or residential real estate loans. When the market for these securities falters or fails, entire neighbourhoods and even entire cities can lose billions of dollars in value. This loss of value has a direct impact on not only institutional market investors but also homeowners and families.

In their examination of the securitisation of residential mortgage loans in Australia, Drs Rajapakse and Senarath do a masterful job of elucidating the complexity of these transactions. In their methodical exploration of areas of regulatory gaps and careful identification of securitisation's negative externalities, they provide an important critical analysis. *Commercial Law Aspects of Residential Mortgage Securitisation in Australia* is an important reading for those who care about well-regulated and well-functioning public financial markets and recognise the contagion risks of market failure in the absence of oversight.

Maine Law Foundation Professor of Law
University of Maine School of Law
Portland, ME, USA

Fulbright Senior Scholar 2019
University of Melbourne
Melbourne, VIC, Australia

Lois R. Lupica

Preface

In a residential mortgage-backed security (RMBS) programme, a bank or other financial institution sells its rights in a pool of home loans to a special purpose vehicle (SPV), which pays for the asset pool by issuing fixed or floating rate bonds in the financial markets to institutional investors. The SPV finances the interest and principal payments under these bonds from the pooled home loan repayments. The SPV is a "special purpose" vehicle in the sense that it is established especially, and solely, for the purpose of acquiring the asset pool and issuing bonds against it.

In practice in Australia, the SPV itself is invariably structured as a trust, which holds the asset pool on behalf of the bondholders. Frequently, but not always in Australia, the income and security features of the asset pool are effectively split, so that the SPV retains the rights to the income from the asset pool but grants a charge or charges over the property in the asset pool in favour of a separate "security trustee", who holds these on behalf of the bondholders. In selling the asset pool to the SPV, the bank or financial institution removes those assets—subject to prudential regulator's approval—from its balance sheet for prudential regulation purposes. This has the effect of substantially reducing the bank's or institution's operating costs. For regulatory and tax purposes, it is important that the SPV is seen to be entirely independent of the originating bank or institution; that the sale to the SPV is seen as a "clean sale"; and the SPV is "insolvency-remote", in the sense that the asset pool cannot be put at risk by the insolvency of the SPV or the originating institution.

There is a dearth of both academic and practical literature on the legal and regulatory issues surrounding mortgage-backed securitisation programmes in Australia, as compared with overseas jurisdictions, such as the United States and the United Kingdom. Moreover, the descriptions of RMBS programmes overseas do not always accord with the way in which RMBS programmes are structured in Australia in practice. This book seeks to redress that imbalance.

To date, no comprehensive textbook or scholarly research book on mortgage securitisation law has been published in Australia. This book will make an excellent source of reference for both undergraduate and post-graduate students of business and finance law, academics, and legal practitioners in these areas. It is designed to provide the reader a comprehensive reference source on RMBS programmes, which can also be used by post-graduate students, academics, and professionals as a basis for further research on this topic.

Writing a monograph is a long venture if it was not for the encouragement, guidance, and support of many people. I am very much grateful to Dr Shanuka Senarath, who is a co-author for this book. Shanuka's personal willingness and commitment in editing the chapters have supported me for successful completion of this book project.

This book provides the most updated information on the law and the current practice of residential mortgage securitisation in Australia. I greatly acknowledge the guidance and support of my research supervisors, Dr Richard Copp, Dr Eduardo Roca of the Department of Accounting, Finance and Economics, Griffith University and Professor Justin Malbon of the School of Law, Monash University, Victoria.

I am grateful to Professor Lois R Lupica of the University of Maine School of Law, Portland, Maine, USA, for writing an explicit foreword for this book. Special thanks are due to Professor Fabrizio Carmignani, Head of the Department; Dr Jennifer Dickfos and Professor Brett Freudenberg, the Discipline Heads of the Department of Accounting Finance and Economics and Professor Don Anton, Director of the Law Futures Centre for their encouragement and support during the writing stages of this monograph. I gratefully acknowledge the resources and financial support provided by the Department of Accounting, Finance and Economics, and the Law Futures Centre of the Griffith Law School, at Griffith University.

The views and opinions expressed in the book belong solely to the authors, and any errors of omission that remain are the authors' responsibility. The law and practice are stated as at 31 October 2018.

Brisbane, QLD, Australia Pelma Rajapakse
Colombo, Sri Lanka Shanuka Senarath

Contents

Acronyms

AASB	Australian Accounting Standards Board
ACCC	Australian Competition and Consumer Commission
ACL	Australian Consumer Law
ADI	Authorised Deposit-taking Institutions
AFSL	Australian Financial Services Licence
APRA	Australian Prudential Regulation Authority
APS	APRA Prudential Standards
ASC	Australian Securities Commission
ASF	Australian Securitisation Forum
ASIC	Australian Securities and Investments Commission
ASX	Australian Stock Exchange
BIS	Bank for International Settlements
CCA	Competition and Consumer Act
CLERP	Corporate Law Economic Reform Program
FANMAC	First Australian National Mortgage Acceptance Corporation
FSI	Financial System Inquiry
FSRA	Financial Services Reform Act
GIC	Guaranteed Investment Certificate
GST	Goods and Services Tax
IMP	Independent Mortgage Provider
ISC	Insurance and Superannuation Commission
MBSs	Mortgage-Backed Securities
MIS	Managed Investment Scheme
MMSs	MGICA Mortgage Securities
RMBSs	Residential Mortgage-Backed Securities
SPV	Special Purpose Vehicle
TPA	Trade Practices Act

List of Legislation

Australian Securities and Investment Commission Act 2001 (Cth)
Banking Act 1959 (Cth)
Competition and Consumer Act 2010 (Cth)
Competition Policy Reform Act 1995 (Cth)
Consumer Credit Code 1996 (Cth)
Corporations Act 2001 (Cth)
Corporations Law (Cth)
Crimes Act 1958 (Vic)
Debits Tax Act 1982 (Cth)
Financial Services Reform Act 2001 (Cth)
Insolvency Act 1986 (UK)
Insurance Contracts Act 1984 (Cth)
Investment Company Act 1940 (US)
Land Tax Act 1915 (Qld)
Privacy Act 1988 (Cth)
Property Law Act 1974 (Qld)
Securities Act 1993 (US)
Statutory Instruments Act 1922 (Qld)
Trade Practices Act 1974 (Cth)
Trusts Act 1973 (Qld)

List of Cases

Abound Catering Conventions and Receptions Pty Ltd v National Australia Bank Ltd (unreported, VSC 26 October 1989).
Adams v Eta Foods Ltd (1987) ATPR 40-831.
Adams v Thrift [1915] 1 Ch 557.
Al-Nakib Investments (Jersey) Ltd v Longcroft [1990] 3 All ER 321.
Annand and Thompson Pty Ltd v TPC (1979) ATPR 40-116.
ASC v Nomura International Plc (1999) 17 ACLC 55.
Associated Broadcasting Services Ltd v Comptroller of Stamps (Vic) (1988) 88 ATC 4,359.
Association Broadcasting Services and Humes Ltd v Comptroller of Stamps (Vic) (1989) 89 ATC 4,646.
Attorney General for NSW v Australian Fixed Trusts Ltd (1974) 1 NSWLR 110.
Australian Consolidated Investments Ltd v Rossington Holdings Pty Ltd (1992) 35 FCR 226.
Australian Softwood Forests Pty Ltd v Attorney General for New South Wales (1981) 6 ACLR 45.
Bank of Barroda Ltd v Punjab National Bank Ltd [1944] AC 176.
Bellah v First National Bank of Hereford 495 F2D 1109 (5th Cir 1974).
Benlist Pty Ltd v Olivetti Australia Pty Ltd (1990) ATPR 40-043.
Blackpool Motor Car Co Ltd, Re, Hamilton v Blackpool Motor Car Co Ltd [1901] 1 Ch 77.
Brightlife Ltd, Re [1987] Ch 200 [1986] 3 All ER 673.
British India Steam Navigation Co v IRC (1881) 7 QBD 165.
Broad v CSD (NSW) (1980) 11 ATR 59.
Brockbank, Re, Ward v Bates [1948] Ch 206; [1948] 1 All ER 287.
BTR Plc and BTR Nylex Ltd, Re (1989) 23 FCR 553.

Burns Phillip Trustee Co Ltd v Commissioner of Stamp Duties (1983) 83 ATC 4,477.
Business Computers Ltd v Anglo African Leasing Ltd [1977] 1 WLR 578.
Cackett v Keswick [1902] 2 Ch 456.
Canham v Australian Guarantee Corporation Ltd (1993) 31 NSWLR 246.
Chiarabaglio v Westpac Banking Corporation (1989) ATPR 40-971.
Cleary and Ors v Australian Co-operative Foods Ltd (1999) ACSR 701.
Clenae Pty Ltd and Ors v ANZ Banking Group Ltd [1999] VSCA 35 (9 April 1999).
Collins Marrickville Pty Ltd v Henjo Investments Pty Ltd (1987) ATPR 40-782.
Commissioner of Stamp Duties (NSW) v Board (1980) 11 ATR 59.
Commonwealth Bank of Australia v Mehta (1993) 23 NSWLR 84.
Commonwealth Bank of Australia v Smith (1991) 102 ALR 453.
Cornish v Midland Bank [1985] All ER 513.
Crocco v Esanda Finance Co Ltd (1993) ASC 56-223.
Curtain Dream Plc, Re [1933] 1 Ch 1(CA).
Dacre, Re [1916] 1 Ch D 344.
David Securities Ltd v Commonwealth Bank of Australia (1990) 23 FCR 1.
Dawson v Great Northern and City Railway Co [1905] 1 KB 260 (CA 1904).
Dearle v Hall (1828) 3 Russ 1; 38 ER 475.
Demagogue Pty Ltd v Ramensky (1992) 39 FCR 31.
Derham Bros v Robertson [1898] 1 QB 765 (CA).
Diesel Motors Co v Kaye 345 NYS 2d 870 (1973).
Dixon v Winch [1900] 1 Ch 736 (CA).
DKG Contractors Ltd, Re [1990] BCC 903.
Duke Group Ltd (in liquidation) v Palmer (1999) SASC 97, (1991) 31 ACSR 213.
Edmonds v Blaina Furnaces Co [1887] 36 Ch D 215.
Email Ltd, Re (2000) 18 ACLC 708.
Endico Potatoes Inc v CIT Group Factoring Inc 67 F3d 1063 (1995).
Esanda Finance Corporation Ltd v Peat Marwick Hungerfords (1997) 188 CLR 241.
Escott v Barchris Construction Corp (283 F Supp 544, 1968).
Evergreen Valley Resort, Re 23 BR 659 (1982).
F & E Stanton, Re [1929] 1 Ch 160.
Fame Decorator Agencies Pty Ltd v Jeffries Industries Ltd and Ors (1998) 16 ACLC 1,235.
Feit v Leasco Data Equipment Corp (332 F Supp 544, 1971).
Forster v Baker [1910] 2 KB 636 (CA).
Fraser v NRMA Holdings Ltd (1995) 15 ACSR 590.
French's (Wine Bar) Ltd, Re [1987] BCLC 499.
Frith, Re [1902] 1 Ch D 342.
George Inglefield Ltd, Re [1990] BCLC 925.

Gilmore v Pool-Blunden and Ors (1999) SASC 186.
Gisborne v Gisborne [1877] App Cas 300.
Global Sportsman v Mirror Newspapers (1984) ATPR 40-463.
Government of Newfoundland v Newfoundland Railway Co [1888] 13 App Cas 199.
Group Four Industries Pty Ltd v Brosnan and Anor (1991) 9 ACLC 1,181.
Handevel Pty Ltd v Comptroller of Stamps (Vic) (1985) 62 ALR 204.
Harry Simpson and Co, Re (1964) 2 NSWLR 603.
Hedley Byrne and Co Ltd v Heller and Partners Ltd [1974] AC 465.
Heilbut, Symons and Co v Bucketton [1913] AC 30.
Henjo Investments Pty Ltd v Collins Marrickville Pty Ltd (No 1) (1988) 39 FCR 546.
Hill v Van Erp (1997) 188 CLR 159.
Hogan v Warterhouse (1991) 34 NSWLR 368.
Holroyd v Marshall 11 ER 999 (HL 1862).
Howard v Miller [1915] App Cas 318.
Jester-Barnes v Licenses and General Insurance Co Ltd (1939) 49 Ll L Rep 231.
Jones v Humphreys [1902]1 KB 10.
JW Broomhead Pty Ltd (in liquidation) v JW Broomhead Pty Ltd [1985] VR 891.
Karger v Paul [1984] VR 161.
Karmot Auto Spares Pty Ltd v Dominelli Ford (Hurstville) Pty Ltd (1992) ATPR 41-175.
Keen Mar Corporation Pty Ltd v Labrador Park Shopping Centre Pty Ltd (1989) ATPR 46-048.
Keighley, Maxsted and Co v Durant [1901] AC 240.
Kewside Pty Ltd v Warman International Ltd (1990) ATPR 46-050.
Khalaf Agalby v Darlington Commodities Ltd (1985) ATPR 40-535.
Kimberley NZI Finance Ltd v Torero Pty Ltd (1989) ATPR 46-054.
Knox v Mackinnon [1888] 13 App Cas 753.
Leigh Valley Trust Co v Central National Bank of Jacksonville 409 F2D 989 (5th Cir 1969).
Leitch and Ors v Natwest Australia Bank Ltd and Anor (unreported, 12 October 1995, Federal Court of Australia).
Lemon v Austin Friars Trust Ltd [1926] 2 Ch 1.
Levy v Abercorris Slate and Slab Co [1887] 37 Ch D 260.
Locker and Woolf Ltd v Western Australian Insurance Co Ltd [1936] 1 KB 408.
Lord Southampton's Estate, Re [1880] 16 Ch D 17.
Lovegrove, Re [1935] Ch 464.
Lumsden v Buchanan (1865) 4 Macq 950; 50 ER 350.
M K Hutchence and Ors (Trading as "INXS") v South Sea Bubble Co Pty Ltd (1986) 8 ATPR 40-667.
Maclanan v Stengold Pty Ltd (1991) ATPR 41-105.

Major's Furniture Mart v Castle Credit Corp 602 F 2d 538 (3rd Cir 1979).
MC Bacon Ltd, Re [1990] BCLC 324.
Mendelssohn v Normand Ltd [1969] 3 WLR 139.
Metropolitan Toronto Police Widows and Orphans Fund v Telus Communication Inc [2003] OJ No 128 (ONSC).
Muir v City of Glasgow Bank [1879] 4 App Cas 337.
NatWest Australia Bank Ltd Tricontinental Corporation Ltd (unreported, Supreme Court of Victoria, No. 2493 of 1990).
Newfoundland Government v Newfoundland Rly Co [1888] 13 App Cas 199.
Norman v Federal Commissioner of Taxation [illegible]
[illegible]; 50 ER [illegible] [1811] All ER Rep 587.
NRMA Ltd and Ors v Morgan (1999) 17 ACLC 1,029.
NV Slavenburg's Bank v International Natural Resources Ltd [1980] 1 All ER 955.
Oceanic Sun Line Special Shipping Co Inc v Fay (1988) 165 CLR 197.
Octavo Investments Pty Ltd v Knight (1979) 54 ALJR 87.
Olds Discount Co Ltd v John Playfair Ltd [1938] 3 All ER 275.
Olley v Malborough Court [1949] 1 KB 532.
Orion Finance v Crown Financial Mannt [1996] 2 BCLC 78.
Pappas v Soulac Pty Ltd (1983) 50 ALR 231.
Parker v Jackson [1936] 2 All ER 281.
Partridge v Equity Trustees Executors and Agency Co Ltd (1947) 75 CLR 149.
Pass v Dundas (1880) 43 LT 665.
Paula Brock v The Terrace Times Pty Ltd (1982) ATPR 40-267.
Permanent House (Holding) Ltd, Re (1989) 5 BCC 151.
Petera Pty Ltd v EAJ Pty Ltd (1985) ATPR 40-605.
Potts v Westpac Banking Corporation [1993] 1 Qd R 135.
Puxu Pty Ltd v Parkdale Custom Built Furniture Pty Ltd (1980) ATPR 40-171.
Rae v Meek [1889] 14 App Cas 558.
Reves v Ernst and Young US 110 S Ct 945 108 L Ed 2d 47 (21 February 1990).
Riedell v Commercial Bank of Australia Ltd [1931] VLR 362.
Ross v Warner (SD NY Dec 11 1980).
Rovell v American National Bank (Unreported, 21 October 1999: 7th Cir 1999).
Roxburghe v Cox [1881] 17 Ch D 520 (CA).
RWG Management Ltd v Commissioner for Corporate Affairs [1985] VR 385.
Saunders v Vautier (1841) 4 Beav 115; 49 ER 282.
Selangor United Rubber Estates v Cradock (No. 3) [1968] 1 WLR 1555.
Shepherd v Harris [1905] 2 Ch 310.
Shipman Boxboards Ltd, Re [1942] 2 DLR 781.
Smith v Hughes (1871) LR 6 QB 597.
Smith v Parks (1852) 16 Beav 115.
Snoid v Handley (198) ATPR 40-219.
Softley, Re, ex parte Hodgkin, (1875) LR 20 Eq 746.

Space Investments Ltd v Canadian Imperial Bank of Commerce Trust Co (Bahamas) Ltd [1986] 3 All ER 75.
Spurling (J) Ltd v Bradshaw [1956] 1 WLR 461; [1956] 3 All ER 121.
Steel Wing Co, Re [1921] 1 Ch 349.
Stephen v Barclays Bank Trust Co [1975] 1 All ER 625.
Sterling v TPC (1981) ATPR 40-212.
Stocks v Dobson [1853] 43 ER 411.
Stott v Milne [1884] 25 Ch D 710.
Taylors Industrial Flooring Ltd v M & H Plant Hire (Manchester) (1990) BCLC 216.
The Exhall Coal Company Ltd, Re (1866) 55 ER 970.
Thompson v London, Midland and Scottish Railway Co [1930] 1 KB 41.
Thornton v Shoe Lane Parking Ltd [1971] 2 QB 163.
Tolhurst v Associated Portland Cement Manufacturers Ltd [1902] 2 KB 660 (CA).
Tout and Finch Ltd, Re [1954] 1 All ER 127; [1954] 1 WLR 178.
TSC Industries Inc v Northway Inc 426 US 438 (1976).
Turner v Smith [1901] 1 Ch 213.
Universal Telecasters (Qld) Ltd v Guthrie (1978) 18 ALR 531.
Vickery, Re, Vickery v Stephens [1931] 1 Ch 572.
Vital Finance Corporation Pty Ltd v Taylor (1993) ASC 56-205.
WA Pines Pty Ltd v Hamilton (1981) WAR 225.
Ward, Re (1984) 55 ALR 395.
Warner v Elders Rural Finance Ltd (1993) 41 FCR 399.
Welsh Development Agency v Export Finance Co Ltd (1990) BCLC 148.
Westpac Banking Corporation v Potts (1992) Aust Torts Reports 81.
White v Blackmore [1972] 2 QB 651.
Wiestman v Katies Ltd (1977) ATPR 40-041.
Wilkins v Hogg (1861) 3 Giff 116; 66 ER 346.
Wilkinson v Feldworth Financial Services Pty Ltd (1999) 17 ACLC 220.
William Brandt's Son and Co v Dunlop Rubber Co Ltd [1905] App Cas 454.
William v Bartor [1927] 2 Ch 9.
Williams v Atlantic Assurance Co Ltd [1933] 1 KB 81.
Williams v Sorrell (1799) 4 Ves 389; 31 ER 198.
Winpar Holdings Ltd v Goldfields Kalgoorlie Ltd (2000) 18 ACLC 665.
World Series Cricket v Parish (1977) ATPR 40-040.
Worrall v Harford (1802) 32 ER 250.
York v Lucas (1985) 158 CLR 661.

List of Figures

List of Tables

CHAPTER 1

Introduction

1.1 Background

Financial product innovation has shown remarkable growth and competition over the past three decades as financial institutions have endeavoured to meet the diverse needs of borrowers and investors.[1] Notable product innovations during this period have included Eurobonds, currency and interest rate swaps, financial futures, options, and mortgage-backed securities.[2]

This development in financial innovation has been attributed to various legal, economic, and social factors,[3] including legal and regulatory rules,

[1] Financial innovation has been defined as the "development of a new product or process in the financial system for the purpose of improving operational effectiveness and efficiency": see R.E. Johnston, 'Technical Progress and Innovation' (1966) *Oxford Economic Papers* 158, 160.

[2] See generally, I. Cooper, 'Innovations: New Market Instruments' (1986) 2 *Oxford Review of Economic Policy* 1; T.S. Campbell, 'Innovations in Financial Intermediation' (1989) *Business Horizons* 70; E.J. Kane, 'Interaction of Financial and Regulatory Innovation' (1988) 78 *American Economic Review* 328; E.J. Kane, 'Impact of Regulation on Economic Behavior' (1981) 36 *The Journal of Finance* 355; M.H. Miller, 'Financial Innovation: The Last Twenty Years and the Next' (1986) 21 *Journal of Finance and Quantitative Analysis* 459; and H.T. Hu, 'New Financial Products, the Process of Financial Innovation and the Puzzle of Shareholder Welfare' (1991) 69 *Texas Law Review* 1237, 1276.

[3] See Sect. 2.4 of Chap. 2 for further discussion of the causes of financial innovation. For example, see also, Senarath, S. and Copp, R., 'Credit default swaps and the global financial

P. Rajapakse, S. Senarath, *Commercial Law Aspects of Residential Mortgage Securitisation in Australia*,
https://doi.org/10.1007/978-3-030-00605-1_1

taxes, technological improvements, increased efficiencies in collecting and processing information, increased interest rate volatility, higher disposable income, and more sophisticated investors in the market.[4]

Securitisation, which is one of the most significant innovations of the last 20 years,[5] is the process of converting illiquid but income-producing assets and receivables[6] that are not necessarily marketable into securities that can be more readily placed and traded in the capital markets. One example of the securitisation process, namely, residential mortgage securitisation, provides the focus for this book.[7]

crisis: reframing credit default swaps as quasi-insurance' (2013) 8 *Global Economy and Finance Journal*, 135.

[4] See also H.L. Baer and C.A. Pavel, 'Does Regulation Drive Innovation' (March 1988) *Economic Perspectives* 3, 6–11 (discussing the role of regulatory taxes—federal deposit insurance, reserve requirements, and capital requirements); S. Becketti, 'The Role of Stripped Securities in Portfolio Management' (May 1988) *Economic Review* 20; T.S. Campbell, (1989) 70–71; J.D. Finnerty, 'Financial Engineering in Corporate Finance: An Overview' (1988) 17 (4) *Financial Management* 14, 16; E.J. Kane, (1988) 332–333, which describes a dialectical relationship between regulation and financial innovation; M.H. Miller, (1986) 460. See also D. Thornton and C. Stone, 'Financial Innovation: Causes and Consequences', in K. Dowd and M.K. Lewis (eds.), *Current Issues in Financial and Monetary Economics* (Basingstoke: Macmillan, 1992) 23; D. Arner, 'Emerging Market Economies and Government Promotion of Securitization' (2002) 12 (2) *Duke Journal of Comparative and International Law* 505. S. Senarath., 'Securitisation and the global financial crisis: can risk retention prevent another crisis?', (2017) 18 *International Journal of Business and Globalisation*, 153; S. Senarath (2016), Not so "Bankruptcy-Remote': An insight into Sri Lankan Securitization Practices in a Post_GFC Context' (Paper presented at the MAC-MME conference, Prague, Czech Republic); Senarath, S. 'The Dodd-Frank Act doesn't solve the principal-agent problem in asset securitisation' (2017) *blogs.lse.ac.uk* (11 November 2018).

[5] See R. Pollsen, J. Hu and J. Elengical, 'A Record Year for Residential MBSs' (2002) *Mortgage Banking* 36; J.C. Shenker and A.J. Colletta, 'Asset Securitization: The Evolution, Current Issues, and New Frontiers' (1991) 69 *Texas Law Review* 1369, 1380; L. Alles, 'Securitisation's Bright Future: How Investment Science Brings Assets to Life' (2001) 2 *Journal of the Australian Society of Security Analysts* 28; P.A.U. Ali, 'Current Issues in Securitisation' (book review) (2002) 20 (4) *Company and Securities Law Journal* 243.

[6] The term "receivables" encompasses the receipt of loan repayments, including residential mortgage loans, car loans, credit card receivables, lease receivables, corporate trade receivables, and an ever-growing list of asset types.

[7] Securitisation is necessarily a topic replete with financial and economic jargon. An apology is made in advance to readers with financial economics training if they consider some of the explanations to be either trite or unnecessary. However, the primary target audience for the book is the legal fraternity who, it may be assumed, are largely unfamiliar with this financial and economic nomenclature. For this reason, explanations of financial or economic theory in the book are kept relatively uncomplicated, and unashamedly so.

Residential mortgage-backed securities (RMBSs) first attracted widespread attention in Australia in December 1986, with a A$50 million issue by the New South Wales government agency, First Australian National Mortgage Acceptance Corporation (FANMAC Ltd), which was used to purchase residential mortgages originated by co-operative housing societies.[8] Since then, the value of the market has grown considerably, reaching a peak of A$12.4 billion in June 1996,[9] before declining to A$8.1 billion in 1998, and rising to approximately A$10.2 billion in 2003.[10] Under the Commonwealth Government in 2004, the value of Commonwealth bonds issued in the Australian market has been significantly reduced since the late 1990s, as the government has sought to reduce its debt levels.[11]

Issuance of securities (including RMBSs, Commercial Mortgage Backed Securities (CMBSs), and other Asset Backed Securities (ABSs) reports its highest (since 2000) in 2007, reporting a total value exceeding $50 billion. Following the global turmoil in 2007, issuance of securities showed its lowest value (less than $20 billion) in 2008[12] (Fig. 1.1).

[8] Bankers Trust, 'Securitisation in Australia' (May 1999) *Asiamoney* 17; S. Lumpkin, 'Trends and Developments in Securitisation' (October 1999) *Financial Market Trends* 1; E. Carew, *Fast Money 4* (Sydney: Allen & Unwin, 1998) 200; and L.E. Dana, 'How the New Secondary Mortgage Market Works' (January 1985) *Law Institute Journal* 69.

[9] Standard and Poor's, *Credit Focus* (February 2000) 5–7.

[10] See generally, Standard and Poor's, *Australia and New Zealand ABS Performance Watch* (Melbourne, February 2004); Standard and Poor's, 'Australian Structured Finance Market Starts 2003 on a Positive Note' (April 2003) *Rating Direct* 3. See also, Anonymous, 'CBA Smashes Aussie MBS Records with $2.5 bn Global Hit' (March 2004) *Euroweek* 1.

[11] See, for example, *Commonwealth Budget Papers* for 2003/2004, Budget Paper No. 1, Statement 7: Budget Funding", 1–4; Press Release by the Hon Peter Costello, Federal Treasurer, 30 October 2002, on 'Review of the Commonwealth Government Securities Market' Federal Treasury, *Commonwealth Debt Management Review: A Review of the Commonwealth Government Securities Market*, Discussion Paper, October 2002; D. Bassanese, 'Financial Market Wins a Battle But Not the War' *Australian Financial Review*, 14 May 2003; Standard and Poor's, *An Investor Guide to Australia's Housing Market and Residential Mortgage-Backed Securities* (Melbourne, 2003) 9; and International Monetary Fund, 'Fiscal Improvement in Advanced Economies: How Long Will It Last?' *World Economic Outlook* (May 2002) 85. Monthly issues of the *Reserve Bank Bulletin* also show that the issuance of Commonwealth Government securities has fallen to historically low levels: see *Reserve Bank Bulletin*, various issues, Reserve Bank of Australia, Sydney, Table E.9—'Commonwealth Government Securities on Issue', 1986 to the present.

[12] Australian Securitisation forum, 'Market Snapshot' (2018) https://www.securitisation.com.au/marketsnapshot

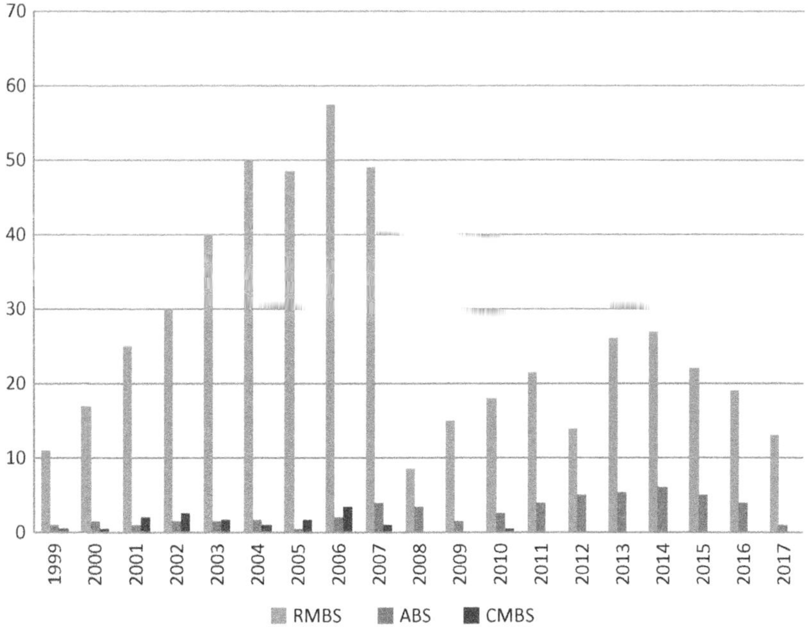

Fig. 1.1 Securitised issuance. (Source: Australian Securitisation Forum 2018)

However, the Australian securitisation market seems to be still rebuilding itself in the aftermath of the financial crisis. A notable feature of the post-crisis market is that CMBS, ABS, and other ABS did not follow the contraction suffered by RMBS, compared to the pre-crisis market figures.[13] Although the current government is committed to maintaining a Commonwealth bond market for risk management and other purposes, it is unlikely to increase government borrowing levels substantially in the foreseeable future, from either the domestic or international financial markets. This begs the question of whether, in order to maintain present living standards and national wealth, any future funding shortfall resulting from less Commonwealth borrowing would, other things being equal, need to be met by bond issues from the private sector. Since the corporate bond market in Australia lacks the depth of that in the United States or Europe,

[13] Chris Dalton, 'The Australian securitisation market 10 years on from the financial crisis, Australian Centre for Financial studies' (paper presented at the 22nd Melbourne Money and Finance Conference 10–11 July 2017, Melbourne, Australia).

one logical funding alternative is additional issues of mortgage-backed securities by the private sector. Securitisations that are based on residential mortgages, as distinct from non-residential (e.g. company) mortgages and charges, could provide a considerable source of funds in this regard.

Thus, to the extent that it is economically efficient, growth in the RMBS market in Australia is likely to continue to be important in the foreseeable future. In addition, the RMBS market provides additional opportunities for:

- Banks and other financial intermediaries, in terms of:
  - Funding
  - Off-balance sheet financing
  - Making non-liquid assets marketable
  - Additional fee revenue and interest income
  - Asset/liability management and liquidity management
  - Rapidly changing their level of exposure to housing loans
- Investors (such as fund managers), in terms of:
  - Further avenues for investment in new, innovative financial products
  - An ability to diversify into housing mortgages, which would otherwise be unavailable to them
  - Additional interest income[14]

There are two common forms of residential mortgage securitisation programmes in Australia. The first is a "bank" or "assignment" programme, so-called because it typically involves a bank[15] that assigns its mortgagee rights—for a price—to another entity. In a typical "bank" or "assignment"

[14] For an overview of these opportunities, see T. Valentine, G. Ford and R. Copp, *Financial Markets and Institutions in Australia* (Sydney: Pearson Education Australia, 2003) 71–72.

[15] Since 1996, most banks have been forced to establish RMBS programmes because of increasing competition in the housing loan market in Australia. While banks remain the major source of housing finance, non-bank lenders currently comprise more than one-fifth of all new lending. The success of the non-bank lenders is due in large part to product innovation, greater borrower accessibility through the introduction of mobile lenders, extensive origination networks, and the ability to securitise their housing loans through RMBS programmes. For more detail, see Standard and Poor's (2003) 18–19.

programme (illustrated in Fig. 1.2),[16] a housing loan provider, generally referred to as the originating bank,[17] "pools" selected housing loans and—for a price—transfers its rights under the relevant loan agreements to a special purpose vehicle (SPV), which then—again, for a price—issues notes or bonds to institutional investors. In Australia, the SPV is invariably structured as a trust.

In most bank or "assignment" programmes, the bank that originally issues the housing loans is the originator of the mortgages securing those housing loans—that is, the lending and mortgage originator roles are both embodied in the one organisation, which transfers its rights under the loan agreements to the SPV. However, in some other bank or "assignment" programmes, the lending bank is a separate entity from the mortgage originator, and it is the mortgage originator that transfers its rights as mortgagee to the SPV.

Relevant housing loan agreements are "pooled" according to specified criteria that perform a somewhat similar role to standard contract specifications in futures contracts. This is done to enhance the ultimate marketability of the lender's contractual mortgagee rights by making them as homogeneous as possible—for example, in terms of loan amount, outstanding tenure, type of security property (e.g. houses versus owner-occupied units), and interest-compounding period. The SPV, which may or may not be related to the bank or mortgage originator, pays an arm's-length price for the transferred rights, which is equal to their present value.

The rights transferred to the SPV (sometimes through a mortgage originator) include the lender's right to receive principal and interest repayments from the borrower, the lender's right to exercise its power of sale under the terms of the residential mortgage, and the lender's right to any mortgage insurance payout in the event of default by the borrower.

The SPV issues notes or bonds, usually in face values of $500,000, to institutional investors who, in return for investing in the issue, receive semi-annual interest until the expiry date of the facility, at which time the face value is returned to them. The price paid by investors reflects the present value of the periodic interest coupons and the face value. In

[16] Both forms of the residential mortgage securitisation process are discussed in detail in Chap. 3.

[17] The main originating banks in Australia include Macquarie Bank, Westpac, Commonwealth Bank, Citibank, St George Bank, and Adelaide Bank: see Standard and Poor's, *Structured Finance Australia and New Zealand* (Melbourne, 2000) 14. In this context, the originating bank will generally be the "sponsor" (or promoter) of the programme.

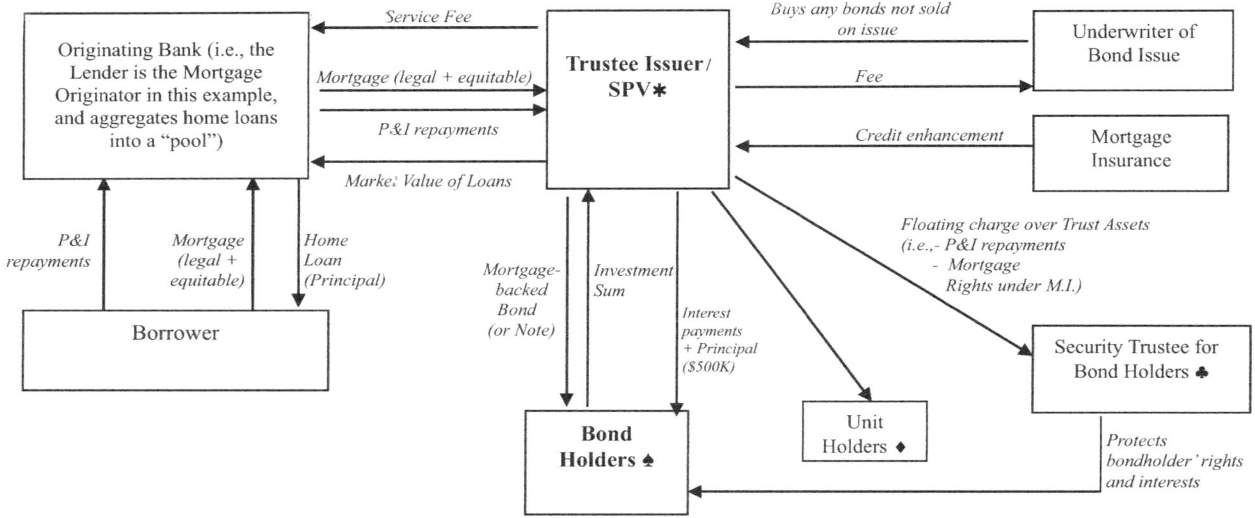

Fig. 1.2 Structure of typical assignment or "bank" programme. (∗Depending on the context, the issuer of the securities is also termed the special purpose vehicle (SPV), the Special Purpose Entity (SPE), or simply, the trustee; ♠ The bonds or notes are issued in a unit trust structure. The bonds themselves comprise principal and interest components. Usually, there are a number of classes of bondholders, whose rights vary with the class of bonds held. For example, Class A bondholders may have priority rights to interest or principal distributions over Class B bondholders; ♦ Unit holders in the trust are generally subsidiaries of the sponsoring bank and may be capital unit holders or income unit holders. Capital unit holders are those who hold capital units and are entitled, generally on winding up of the trust, to any residual trust capital or "corpus". Income unit holders are those who hold income units and are entitled to net trust income, if any exists, generally up to a maximum "token" amount (e.g. $1000) which is specified in the trust deed; ♣ The Security Trustee holds a floating charge over trust assets on behalf of the bondholders. The trust assets include the right to principal and interest repayments (ultimately, from borrowers on the initial housing loans), the right to exercise power of sale under those mortgages, and any rights to mortgage insurance payouts)

Australia, the notes or bonds are invariably issued by way of a trust, in which the issuer is the trustee for the bondholders.[18] The borrowers' principal and interest repayments act as an income "buffer" to help insulate the investor from the risk of default on the notes or bonds it has issued.

The notes or bonds issued are mortgage backed in the sense that if the issuer defaults on its obligation to pay interest (or ultimately the face value of the note) to the investor, a security trustee—in whom the legal rights under the pooled mortgages are vested—can exercise a power of sale over the secured residential properties and recover the monies owed. To the extent that the proceeds from the sale of the residential properties are insufficient to meet the outstanding debts to bondholders, the bondholders will rank as unsecured creditors in the event of a winding up of the trust.

The overall securitisation is profit driven, in the sense that at each stage of the process, income is generated for the relevant service provider. For example, the lender or mortgage originator earns revenue when it assigns (sells) its rights under the relevant loan agreements to the SPV. This represents a cost to the SPV, which is more than offset by the "all up" price at which it sells bonds or notes to the investors. Other stakeholders in the process also earn revenue from the services they provide. For example, the mortgage insurer earns premium income for providing insurance to the SPV in the event of loan default, and the fund manager earns fees for managing the SPV's investment portfolio.

In order to ensure that the mortgage loan receivables are sufficient to repay the bondholders on time, and to also make the bonds issued more attractive to institutional investors, various forms of "credit enhancement" methods are used. For example, a third-party lender may give a guarantee to the SPV, or the originator may agree to make a subordinated loan to the SPV. An alternative form of credit funding support may be provided by the issue of junior or subordinated (Class B) bonds by the trustee, payment of interest and principal in which they rank behind the senior (Class A) bonds issued by the SPV.

[18] For the purposes of this book, the term "bondholders" includes not only the holders of bonds but also the holders of notes. Both bonds and notes are negotiable instruments traded in the financial markets. The main differences between bonds and notes relate to their tenure, underlying cash flows, and pricing.

The SPV will generally have the issue of securities underwritten. Often the lead manager—typically, an investment bank—will underwrite the issue, relying on its network of institutional investors to purchase any unsubscribed securities. As an additional means of attracting investors, the RMBSs are risk and quality rated by ratings agencies such as Standard and Poor's or Moody's Investors.

The second common form of residential mortgage securitisation programme, and indeed the most prevalent in the financial market at the time of writing, is the so-called conduit programme. These programmes are typically established by the smaller regional banks, building societies, credit unions, and independent mortgage providers (IMPs)[19] that, individually, lack the asset size to sponsor an assignment programme in their own right (i.e. without the guarantee of a larger bank or credit institution). As a result, these institutions "warehouse" (or pool) their mortgages until they reach an aggregate value sufficient to back an RMBS issue, made either by the institution itself, or in combination with other smaller institutions. In order to make the bonds that the SPV issues more attractive to institutional investors, the smaller originators typically need to upgrade the quality of their bonds by obtaining the support of a larger bank as "guarantor". This "guarantee" may be variously described as a guarantee proper, or as a commitment on the part of the major bank to act as back-up servicer, standby credit facility provider, standby specialist servicer, liquidity facility provider, or Guaranteed Investment Certificate (GIC)[20] provider. This requirement is in addition to the usual mortgage insurance associated with bank or assignment programmes.

[19] An IMP is a third-party mortgage provider—that is, an institution that "originates" (or brings into existence) mortgages, usually as elements of mortgage loans—which is generally unaffiliated with the major banks. For example, IMPs in Australia include Aussie Home Loans Ltd, Australian Mortgage Securities Ltd, Interstar Securities Pty Ltd, RAMS Home Loans Pty Ltd, Macquarie Securitisation Ltd, and Resimac Ltd. The IMP or mortgage originator typically charges an origination fee, which is generally charged to the borrower to cover the costs of initiating the loan.

[20] A Guaranteed Investment Certificate is a certificate evidencing that a specified amount has been deposited at a trust company for a set time, usually five years, at a specified interest rate. Usually the certificate cannot be redeemed prior to maturity.

Inevitably, there can be many variations on the securitisation structures described here. However, for expository purposes, the structures illustrated in Fig. 1.2 and described earlier provide useful reference points for the legal analysis in other chapters of the book.

1.2 Objectives of the Book

Within the context of a public benefit approach, this book aims to evaluate, from a legal perspective, key commercial law aspects of the relevant legislation and regulation governing RMBSs in Australia, in order to:

1. Identify, in a qualitative manner,[21] those features of the existing law and regulation which:
   (a) *Facilitate* the development of the market for RMBSs in Australia
   (b) *Hinder* the development of the market for RMBSs in Australia
2. Suggest some key areas in which the current law and regulation relating to RMBSs in Australia could be reformed

The features of the existing law and regulation that facilitate and hinder the market will be evaluated using a "public benefit test" framework. This framework is similar to that used for the introduction of Commonwealth and State legislation pursuant to the *Statutory Instruments Act* 1992 (Qld) and the Commonwealth-State/Territory *Competition Principles Agreement* 1995.[22] This Agreement requires that legislation effecting

[21] But not in a social science sense, which typically involves surveys and interview etc.

[22] Pursuant to the *Statutory Instruments Act* 1992 (Qld), which is mirrored in every other State, and the *Competition Principles Agreement* dated 11 April 1995, between the Commonwealth and State and Territory governments, any legislation that is likely to impose appreciable costs on the community, or a section of it, is subjected to a Regulatory Impact Statement to determine whether the legislation is likely to be for the benefit of the public. The legislative review process is undertaken within the "public benefit test" framework, as required under the *National Competition Principles Agreement:* See National Competition Council, *National Competition Principles Agreement*, 11 February 1995 http://www.ncc.gov.au/publication.asp?publicationID=99&activityID=39

The "public benefit test" process involves (a) the identification of the restrictions on competition in the market, (b) an analysis of the effects of legislative restrictions, (c) an analysis of the costs and benefits, and (d) and the provision of appropriate recommendations. The approach adopted in such Regulatory Impact Statement is similar to that used in Chap. 8 of the book in the evaluation of the existing legislation and regulation governing RMBSs.

competition be reformed, unless it can be shown that the benefits of the restrictions to the public as a whole outweigh the costs—this is referred to as the "public benefit test".[23] Overall, the test involves an assessment of the economic, financial, and social benefits and costs associated with the current legislation and regulatory reform options. Chapter 8 of the book provides an analysis of the current law and regulation governing RMBSs based on the "public benefit test" approach adopted in accordance with the *Competition Principles Agreement*. Thus, in this book, the "public benefit test" framework is used as a guide to the legal analysis of regulatory factors that facilitate and hinder the RMBS market, rather than as a detailed economic evaluation or demonstration of the test.

The book finds that the current legislation and regulation governing RMBSs seems to be appropriate as it stands, in terms of the criteria expressed in the "public benefit test", used for evaluating legislation at Commonwealth and State levels. There are nevertheless significant potential moral hazard problems and risks inherent in the legislation. First, there is a risk that borrowers might find their homes sold out through no fault of their own, because of the actions and omissions of financial intermediaries of which they are unaware. As a result, the legislation or regulation should be amended to impose a requirement on banks to fully inform their borrowers about the risks and consequences of having assignment clauses in their home loan contracts and mortgages. Second, there is a need to reform the regulation in the foreseeable future to cater to unsophisticated investors in RMBS. Third, the risk-weighting of RMBS for capital adequacy purposes should be changed to a weighting less than the current 100%.

1.3 Scope of the Book

A number of caveats are apposite regarding the scope of this book. First, the scope of the book is limited to a *legal* analysis of the main commercial law and regulatory issues that typically arise in the securitisation of residential mortgages in Australia. The book does not address whether the

[23] For more details regarding the "public benefit test", see Queensland Treasury, *Public Benefit Test Guidelines: Approach to Undertaking Public Benefit Test Assessments for Legislation Reviews under National Competition Policy*, Brisbane, October 1999, http://www.treasury.qld.gov.au/office/knowledge/docs/ncp/public-benefit-test-guidelines.pdf pages 10–26, and Appendices 1–10 attached to the Public Benefit Test Guidelines. All other State governments have published similar guidelines based on cost-benefit analysis.

suggested reforms to the commercial law and practice governing RMBS issues would be economically efficient; whether the aggregate value of the benefits to the community of those suggested reforms would exceed their costs to the community in economic terms; or specific economic problems, such as the potential moral hazard problem inherent in bank or assignment programmes, which are identified in Chaps. 2 and 8.

Second, the book is limited to an analysis of the relevant *commercial* law and regulation governing RMBSs. Thus, the book does not address the income tax, capital gains tax, or GST issues surrounding RMBS programmes.

Third, as stated previously, the book focuses only on the commercial law and regulation governing RMBSs. It does not address in any detail the stamp duty and land tax considerations surrounding RMBS programmes or issues surrounding other transactions-based taxes such as Financial Institutions Duty and Bank Account Debits Tax. Nor are the rights and obligations of stakeholders under the recently enacted privacy legislation; insurance law aspects of RMBS issues; the law on the underlying negotiable instruments in RMBS issues; or the rights and liabilities of the key stakeholders in tort considered in detail in the following chapters.

1.4 Contributions Made by the Book

The book makes a number of contributions to the scholarly literature and to practice.

First, within the context of a "public benefit test" framework, the book seeks to critically evaluate, from a legal point of view, the impact and effectiveness of current law and regulation governing RMBSs in Australia. In so doing, it aims to provide guidance for the Federal government and its agencies such as the Australian Securities and Investments Commission, the Ministerial Council of Consumer Affairs, the Australian Prudential Regulation Authority (APRA), and the Reserve Bank of Australia.

Second, the book seeks to make a contribution to the formulation of law and public policy, by suggesting a number of reforms to the current law and practice surrounding RMBSs in Australia, as well as more effective ways of regulating the RMBS market in Australia. In part, these suggested reforms are based on the lessons learned from the experiences of overseas jurisdictions.

Third, there is a dearth of both academic and practical literature on the legal and regulatory issues surrounding RMBSs in Australia, as compared with overseas jurisdictions such as the United States and the United Kingdom. Moreover, the descriptions of RMBS programmes overseas do not always accord with the way in which RMBS programmes are structured in Australia in practice. This book seeks to redress that imbalance.

Fourth, to the extent that a scholarly legal literature about RMBS programmes exists in Australia, there are significant gaps in its coverage of key issues. For example, the current legal literature in Australia does not address in any significant detail issues such as the "true sale" of mortgagee rights to the SPV; the impact of the *Corporations Act* on RMBS issues and stakeholders; the impact of the recent Basel II proposals on the treatment of RMBSs for capital adequacy purposes; or the consequences for stakeholders of the mortgage originator or SPV becoming insolvent. The book seeks to fill these gaps in the existing literature.

1.5 Structure of the Book

Chapter 2 attempts to place RMBSs in a theoretical context by explaining the process of securitisation in general and of RMBS programmes in particular. The incentives for participants are outlined within a contractarian framework; and some of the key features that might characterise a theoretically optimal regulatory regime for RMBSs are suggested.

Chapter 3 outlines the mechanics, structure, and process of a typical residential mortgage securitisation in practice. In this chapter, a number of key issues that arise throughout the RMBS process are identified, which are further discussed in subsequent chapters.

Chapters 4, 5, 6, and 7 examine key legal and regulatory aspects of residential mortgage securitisation in Australia. Chapter 4 focuses on the origination process, and includes a consideration of the consequences for the originator of registering (as distinct from not registering) the residential mortgages used as security for the issue; the impact of Australia's capital adequacy guidelines on participants; and the *New Capital Adequacy Framework* and proposals for different regulation of asset securitisations recently propounded by the Bank for International Settlements (BIS).

Chapter 5 focuses on the transfer of the lender's (originator's) rights to the SPV. It includes a consideration of whether a transfer is a "true sale" of mortgagee rights; potential problems arising from the assignment of the lender's rights; issues involved in structuring an SPV; and the impact of the *Consumer Credit Code* on stakeholders when the lender's mortgagee rights are transferred.

Chapter 6 focuses in detail on the process of issuing RMBSs in Australia, and includes a consideration of the impact of the *Corporations Act*, as well as relevant aspects of trust law and contract law.

Chapter 7 outlines the consequences for stakeholders, if the mortgage originator (which would include the originating bank, in bank or "assignment" programmes) or subsequent assignee of its rights, becomes insolvent. From an economic point of view, the risk of such insolvency will (or should) already have been incorporated into the interest rates charged on the various stages of the RMBS programme. However, in this context, the law usually focuses not on these considerations, but on the consequences of mortgagee insolvency for borrowers and other stakeholders. Thus, this chapter considers the legal impacts of insolvency, both of an originator and of an SPV, including the position of secured creditors (e.g. the investors in the RMBSs themselves); whether particular transactions will be treated by the law as void or voidable because of insolvency; and the requirements of the rating agencies in relation to structuring an insolvency-remote issuer.

Chapter 8 provides an assessment of the current law and regulation relating to RMBS issues in Australia, focusing on those aspects of the law that respectively facilitate and impede the development of the RMBS market in Australia.

Finally, Chap. 9 presents the main conclusions and recommendations of the book, and suggests a number of areas in which further research is likely to prove fruitful.

Bibliography

Books and Book Chapters

Carew, E., *Fast Money*, Sydney: Allen and Unwin, 1998.

Thornton, D. and Stone, C., 'Financial Innovation: Causes and Consequences', in K. Dowd and M. K. Lewis (eds.), *Current Issues in Financial and Monetary Economics*, Basingstoke: Macmillan, 1992.

Valentine, T., Ford, G. and Copp, R., *Financial Markets and Institutions in Australia*, Sydney: Pearson Education Australia, 2003.

Journal Articles

Ali, P. A. U., 'Current Issues in Securitisation' (book review) (2002) 20 (4) *Company and Securities Law Journal* 243.

Alles, L., 'Securitisation's Bright Future: How Investment Science Brings Assets to Life' (2001) 2 *Journal of the Australian Society of Security Analysts* 28.

Arner, D., 'Emerging Market Economies and Government Promotion of Securitization' (2002) 12 (2) *Duke Journal of Comparative and International Law* 505.

Baer, H. L. and Pavel, C. A., 'Does Regulation Drive Innovation' (March 1988) *Economic Perspectives* 3.

Becketti, S. 'The Role of Stripped Securities in Portfolio Management' (May 1988) *Economic Review* 20.

Campbell, T. S., 'Innovations in Financial Intermediation' (1989) *Business Horizons* 70.

Cooper, I., 'Innovations: New Market Instruments' (1986) 2 *Oxford Review of Economic Policy* 1.

Dana, L. E., 'How the New Secondary Mortgage Market Works' (January 1985) *Law Institute Journal* 69.

Finnerty, J. D., 'Financial Engineering in Corporate Finance: An Overview' (1988) 17 (4) *Financial Management* 14.

Hu, H. T., 'New Financial Products, the Process of Financial Innovation and the Puzzle of Shareholder Welfare' (1991) 69 *Texas Law Review* 1236.

Johnston, R. E., 'Technical Progress and Innovation' (1966) *Oxford Economic Papers* 158.

Kane, E. J., 'Impact of Regulation on Economic Behavior' (1981) 36 *The Journal of Finance* 355.

Kane, E. J., 'Interaction of Financial and Regulatory Innovation' (1988) 78 *American Economic Review* 328.

Lumpkin, S., 'Trends and Developments in Securitisation' (October 1999) *Financial Market Trends* 1.

Miller, M. H., 'Financial Innovation: The Last Twenty Years and the Next' (1986) 21 *Journal of Finance and Quantitative Analysis* 459.

Pollsen, R., Hu, J. and Elengical, J., 'A Record Year for Residential MBS' (April 2002) *Mortgage Banking* (Washington) 36.

Senarath, S., 'Securitisation and the global financial crisis: can risk retention prevent another crisis?' (2017) 18 *International Journal of Business and Globalisation* 153.

Senarath, S., and Copp, R., 'Credit default swaps and the global financial crisis: reframing credit default swaps as quasi-insurance' (2015) 8 *Global Economy and Finance Journal* 135.

Shenker, J. C. and Colletta, A.J., 'Asset Securitization: Evolution' Current Issues and New Frontiers' (1991) 69 Texas Law Review 1369.

Working Papers, Magazines, Newspapers and Reports

Anonymous, 'CBA Smashes Aussie MBS Records with $2.5 bn Global Hit' (March 2004) *Euroweek* 1.

Bankers Trust, 'Securitisation in Australia' (May 1999) *Asiamoney* 17.

Bassanese, D., 'Financial Market Wins a Battle But Not the War' *Australian Financial Review*, 14 May 2003.

Commonwealth Treasury of Australia, *Commonwealth Budget Papers* for 2003/04, Budget Paper No. 1, Statement 7: Budget Funding, Canberra

Costello, P., 'Review of the Commonwealth Government Securities Market', *Commonwealth Debt Management Review: A Review of the Commonwealth Government Securities Market*, Discussion Paper, October 2002.

Dalton, C., 'The Australian securitisation market 10 years on from the financial crisis', Australian Centre for Financial studies (paper presented at the 22nd Melbourne Money and Finance Conference 10–11 July 2017, Melbourne, Australia).

International Monetary Fund, 'Fiscal Improvement in Advanced Economies: How Long Will It Last?' *World Economic Outlook* (May 2002) 85.

National Competition Council, *National Competition Principles Agreement*, 11 February 1995, http://www.ncc.gov.au/publication.asp?publicationID=99&activityID=39 (20 January 2002).

Queensland Treasury, *Public Benefit Test Guidelines: Approach to Undertaking Public Benefit Test Assessments for Legislation Reviews under National Competition Policy*, Brisbane, October 1999, http://www.treasury.qld.gov.au/office/knowledge/docs/ncp/public-benefit-test-guidelines.pdf (20 August 2003).

Reserve Bank of Australia, *Reserve Bank Bulletin*, Sydney (various issues).

Senarath, S. 'The Dodd-Frank Act doesn't solve the principal-agent problem in asset securitisation' (2017) *blogs.lse.ac.uk* (11 November 2018) http://blogs.lse.ac.uk/businessreview/2017/04/21/the-dodd-frank-act-doesnt-solve-the-principal-agent-problem-in-asset-securitisation/

Senarath, S., Not so "Bankruptcy-Remote': An insight into Sri Lankan Securitization Practices in a Post_GFC Context' (Paper presented at the MAC-MME conference 2016, Prague, Czech Republic).

Standard and Poor's, 'Australian Structured Finance Market Starts 2003 on a Positive Note' (April 2003) *Rating Direct* 3.

Standard and Poor's, *An Investor Guide to Australia's Housing Market and Residential Mortgage-Backed Securities* (Melbourne, 2003) 9.

Standard and Poor's, *Credit Focus*, Melbourne, February 2000.

Standard and Poor's, *Structured Finance Australia and New Zealand*, Melbourne, 2000.

Standard and Poor's, *Australia and New Zealand ABS Performance Watch,* Melbourne, February 2004.

Web Sites

Australian Securitisation Forum, 'Market snapshot' (2018) https://www.securitisation.com.au/marketsnapshot

CHAPTER 2

Towards Formulating a Conceptual Framework

2.1 Introduction

Based on microeconomic theory, this section attempts to construct a theoretical base to explain residential mortgage-backed securities (RMBSs), especially with a focus on RMBS programmes. Inter alia, given the fact that RMBSs are, in essence, a bundle of contracts, the inducements for participants are outlined within a contractarian framework,[1] and suggestions are made subjecting the regulatory regime to a "public benefit test" with reference to some of the key features that might characterise a theoretically optimal regulatory regime for RMBSs. Different stages of the securitisation process in Australia are analysed utilising the contractarian framework. The "public benefit test" is then used to identify the aspects of the current laws and regulations that facilitate and hinder the growth of the RMBS industry in Australia.

[1] Which is a subset of microeconomic theory.

P. Rajapakse, S. Senarath, *Commercial Law Aspects of Residential Mortgage Securitisation in Australia*,
https://doi.org/10.1007/978-3-030-00605-1_2

2.2 Securitisation Explained[2]

Securitisation is mostly defined by referring to the purpose, outcomes, or the process of securitisation.[3] On the other hand, there is no universally agreed uniform definition of securitisation. Professor Oditah states that "Securitisation is a buzz word lacking any technical meaning… a market usage which can mean different things to different people."[4]

The Oxford Dictionary of Economics defines asset securitisation as "The packaging of several non-marketable assets, such as mortgage loans, into bundles which are marketable." The same definition further states:

> [I]ndividual mortgages are not generally marketable because there is too much idiosyncratic risk in dealing with any one of them. A package of several similar mortgages reduces the riskiness, which allows the package to be marketed. The fact that mortgages are made marketable may enable them to be financed at lower interest rates.[5]

The Oxford Dictionary of Banking and Finance provides a definition of securitisation explaining the process of securitisation. This definition states that securitisation is "the process of turning assets into securities". The same definition further identifies securitisation as "Arrangement in which the originator sells a portfolio of assets, SPV [the issuer], who then finances the purchase by packaging the cash flows from these assets as tradable financial instruments [securities], which are sold to investors."[6]

As far as some textbook definitions of securitisation are concerned, Kothari in *Securitization: The Financial Instrument of the Future*, states

[2] This section provides a brief overview of the securitisation process. For a more comprehensive discussion of securitisation, see R. E. Kravitt and J. H. P. Johnston, *Securitization of Financial Assets* (2nd edition, N.Y.: Aspen Law and Business, 2002).

[3] Pelma Rajapakse, 'An Analysis of the Concepts of Mortgage-backed Securitization: An Economic and Legal Perspective, (2011) 10 *The Journal of Law and Financial Management* 22.

[4] Oditah Fidelis, *The Future for the Global Securities Market-Legal and Regulatory Aspects* (Oxford University Press, 1996) 84.

[5] This definition can be identified as a "purpose-based" definition. See John Balck, Nigar Hashimzade and Grath D Myles, *Dictionary of Economics* (Oxford University Press, 3rd ed., 2012).

[6] Barry Brindley (ed), *A Dictionary of Finance and Banking*, (Oxford University Press, 4th ed., 2008). For more alternative definitions on securitisation, see Cheng F Lee, Alice C Lee, and Gale, *Encyclopedia of Finance* (Springer, 2006).

that "Securitisation in its widest sense implies every process that converts a financial relation into a transaction."[7] Kothari further explains:

> It is taken to mean a device of structured financing in which an entity seeks to pool together its interest in identifiable cash flows over time, transfer the same to investors either with or without the support of future collaterals, and thereby achieve the purpose of financing. Thought the end-result of securitisation is financing, it is not "financing" as such because the entity securitizing its assets is not borrowing money but selling a stream of cash flows that was otherwise to accrue to it.[8]

An outcome-based definition of securitisation is provided in section 6(1)(a) of the *Privacy Act 1988* (Cth), which defines a "securitisation arrangement" as an arrangement:

> Involving the funding, or proposed funding, of (i) credit that has been, or is to be, provided by a credit provider; or (ii) the purchase of credit by a credit provider; by issuing instruments or entitlements to investors; and (b) under which payments to investors in respect of such instruments or entitlements are principally derived, directly or indirectly, from such credit.[9]

The securitisation process begins with a lender (e.g. a bank) granting a loan to a borrower. The bank or the loan provider equitably assigns or sells its rights (including mortgagee rights) on the asset on its books (e.g. mortgages, if the lending is for a house) to a special purpose vehicle (SPV).[10] These assets represent the borrowers' payment obligations (e.g. in case of a mortgage loan) or interest payments (e.g. in case of a student loan). The SPV funds the amount payable to the originator by issuing securitised bonds. The SPV then issues notes based on the assets to investors around the world. The initial lender will be (in most cases) appointed as the "servicer" to collect payments from the initial borrowers on behalf of the SPV. The service will transfer the collection to the SPV.[11] The

[7] V. Kothari, *Securitisation: The Financial Instrument of the Future* (Wiley Finance, 2006) 4.

[8] Ibid, 634–35.

[9] See *Privacy Act 1988* (Cth).

[10] This will be via a receivables purchase agreement, which will contain eligibility criteria for the receivables.

[11] In case of a default by the borrower, the service as the agent of the SPV may bring actions against the borrowers (e.g. mortgagors).

servicer will be paid a fee for her service. At the end of the process, those illiquid assets have turned into tradable, liquid debt securities. The principal and interest repayments by the initial borrower constitute a contingent receivable for the SPV (see Fig. 1.2). The investors who hold asset-backed bonds are paid by these incoming cash flows. As long as the net interest income exceeds the payments of interests and other costs, each stage of the process generates a profit.[12]

From a theoretical point of view, any income-generating asset can be securitised.[13] Inter alia, home mortgages, vehicle leases, commercial property mortgages, credit card receivables, TV rentals, student loans, health care receivables, telephone charges, bond portfolios, project finance loans, trade receivables, equipment leases, bank loans, film receivables, song royalties, tax receivables, lottery winnings, court settlements or it even could be debts to a sovereign nation.[14]

2.3 Mortgage-Backed Securities (MBSs)

Mortgage-backed securities (MBSs) are a particular form of asset-backed securities, which are based on mortgage loans. Residential mortgage-backed securities (RMBSs) are a particular type of MBS which are based on residential mortgages.

[12] For a detailed description of a securitisation programme, see in Kothari, above n 7; Sandaer A Davidson, Wolff L and Ching A, *Securitization: Structuring and Investment Analysis* (John Wiley & Sons 2003); Rajapakse, above n 3; Steven L Schwarcz and Adam D Ford, *Structured Finance: A Guide to the Principles of Asset Securitization* (Practising Law Institute, 2002); Steven Schwarcz, 'Parts are Greater than the Whole: How Securitization of Divisible Interests Can Revolutionize Structured Finance and Open the Capital Markets to Middle-Market Companies' (1993) *The Columbia Business Law Review* 139.

[13] Ajay Adhikari and Luis Betancourt, 'Accounting for Securitizations: A Comparison of SFAS 140 and IASB 39' (2008) *19 Journal of International Financial Management & Accounting* 73.

[14] Gregory R Salathé 'Reducing Health Care Costs Through Hospital Accounts Receivable Securitization' (1994) 80 *Virginia Law Review* 549; Joseph Hu, Robert B Pollsen and Jay Elengical, 'A Record Year for Residential MBS' (2002) 62 *Mortgage Banking* 365; Joseph C Shenker and Anthony J Colletta, 'Asset Securitization: Evolution' Current Issues and New Frontiers' (1991) 69 *Texas Law Review* 1369; Jay H Eisbruck, 'Blockbuster or Flop? The History and Evolution of Firm Receivables Securitization, 1995–2005' (2005) 11 *The Journal of Structured Finance* 11. S. Senarath., 'Securitisation and the global financial crisis: can risk retention prevent another crisis?', (2017) 18 *International Journal of Business and Globalisation*, 153.

However, RMBS programmes are simply an application of the securitisation principles discussed in our early discussion. Individuals borrow from their banks or independent mortgage providers (IMPs) in order to finance the purchase of a residence. It could be either for a home (to live in) or for investment purposes. The banks or IMPs then bundle such loans with similar characteristics into a "mortgage pool" and then sell (or in effect, transfer)[15] their legal rights in the pool (e.g. to receive repayments, and exercise power of sale as mortgagee over those residences included in the pool) to a third party, which are often established specifically to facilitate the RMBS programme.

As per our discussion elsewhere, the housing loan borrowers' principal and interest repayments eventually provide cash flow for these other intermediaries (third parties), and the value of the borrowers' mortgaged properties form a contingent receivable in the intermediaries' accounts. Using the incoming cash flows as revenue, the intermediaries then issue bonds to investors, who invest in financial markets. Provided their net interest income exceeds their interest and other expenses including transactions costs, at each stage of the process, each intermediary earns a profit.

In a classic RMBS bond issue, regular interest coupon payments are the income stream for the investor, together with the scheduled (and in some cases, unscheduled) repayments of the principal.

In some jurisdictions, for example, United States, RMBS programmes are either "pass-through" or "pay-through" in character. Pass-through programmes comprise issues of debt securities, such as bonds, in which the interest and principal repayments are "passed through" a trust to the investors on a scheduled "periodic payment" basis, at about the same time as they are received from the pool of initial borrowers.

On the other hand, pay-through issues may be debt securities or equity securities (e.g. ordinary shares). In the case of bonds, the interest and principal repayments are "paid through" a corporate SPV (not a trust) to the investors on a sometimes scheduled (regular), and sometimes unscheduled (irregular) basis, from the pool of initial borrowers.

In the case of shares, the principal and interest repayments made by the initial home loan borrowers are paid to a corporate SPV, which then pays them out again to investors in the form of dividend payments on the shares. These dividend payments may be regular,[16] or irregular, as in the case of dividends paid to ordinary shareholders. In this latter case, it would

[15] For example, by sub-participation.

[16] E.g. if the securities issued were preference shares that guarantee investors a regular dividend.

be unusual for the investors (ordinary shareholders) to receive their dividend payments at or about the same time as they are received from the pool of borrowers.

All of the RMBS issues so far in Australia have been debt issues. Most of these have been pass-through programmes in the sense described here, although some have had some pay-through characteristics.[17]

2.3.1 Risks Associated with a Securitisation Programme

Similar to many other financial transactions, a number of risks are associated with securitisation programmes. Inter alia, such risks include:[18]

- **Credit risk:** the risk associated with the default (or perhaps bankruptcy) of the borrower. In a securitisation programme, there is a risk that mortgages included in the asset pool (or a portion of those assets) may default. In case of a default, the usual action is that recovery actions will be taken. This may include sale of the mortgaged property. Some key concerns associated with default and foreclosures are the recovery rate (what is the ratio between the recovered amount and the due amount) and the recovery delay (the time taken since recognition of a default and actual recovery).[19]
- **Prepayment risk:** the risk that the borrower makes her payments before the due date. This incurs a loss of profit to the investors. In most jurisdictions, it is legal for a borrower to make payments before the due date (especially for residential mortgages). Prepayments are common especially when interest rates are lower.[20]
- **Delayed payment/slow payment risk:** this sort of risk is associated with the timing of payments. Delayed payments may not amount to defaults, but to a temporary delay in payments.[21]

[17] These programmes are discussed in greater depth in Chap. 3.

[18] This discussion is drawn from Kothari, above n 7, 195–196.

[19] Also see Mary E Barth, Gaizka Ormazabal, Daniel J. Taylor 'Asset Securitizations and Credit Risk' (2011) 87 *The Accounting Review* 423; Sharon S Yang, 'Securitisation and Tranching Longevity and House Price Risk for Reverse Mortgage Products' (2011) 36 *The Geneva Papers on Risk and Insurance – Issues and Practice* 648.

[20] In case of prepayment, the most likely option is to reinvest the sum of money received. Yet, it will have a number of repercussions on the smooth functioning of the securitisation programme. Kothari, above n 7, 105; Benjamin J Keys et al., 'Did Securitization Lead to Lax Screening? Evidence From Subprime Loans' (2008) 125 *Quarterly Journal of Economics* 307.

[21] See also Steven L Schwarcz, 'Structured Finance: The New Way to Securitize Assets' (1989) 11 *Cardozo Law Review* 607.

- **Servicer performance risk:** the risk that the servicer of the securitisation programme is unable, perhaps unwilling, to perform her duties as the servicer.[22]
- **Guarantor risk:** the risk that the guarantor may fail in performing its duties as the guarantor.
- **Liquidity risk:** the risk that the securitisation programme may face liquidity issues. This will mainly arise from a mismatch between maturities and payments. In other words, mismatches between cash inflows and outflows.
- **Legal risk:** the risk that a court ruling may adversely affect the functioning of the securitisation programme. For example, the possibility that a court may consider the transfer of assets to the SPV as a secured loan as opposed to a true sale and include in the originator's bankruptcy estate.[23]
- **Other risks:** other risks that may associate with a securitisation programme may include interest rate risk,[24] currency risk,[25] swap counterparty risk,[26] political risk,[27] sovereign risk/country risk,[28] exchange rate risk,[29] taxation risk,[30] and stamp duty risk.[31]

[22] In a typical securitisation programme, the trustee is capable of appointing an alternative service in case the existing servicer is no longer functioning. However, in most cases, the trustee can act as the servicer until a new servicer is appointed.

[23] Andreas A Jobst, 'Asset Securitisation as a Risk Management and Funding Tool: What Small Firms Need to Know' (2006) 32 *Managerial Finance* 731.

[24] See also Dwight Jaffee, 'The Interest Rate Risk of Fannie Mae and Freddie Mac' (2003) 24 *Journal of Financial Services Research* 5.

[25] Andreas A Jobst, 'What is Structured Finance? An Analysis of Derivatives, Securitization and Islamic Finance' (2006) 8 *The Securitization Conduit* (Reprinted in ICFAI Journal of Risk Management 2007).

[26] See David J Cummins and Philippe Trainar, 'Securitization, Insurance, and Reinsurance' (2009) 76 *Journal of Risk and Insurance* 463.

[27] Claire A Hill, 'Latin American Securitization: The Case of the Disappearing Political Risk' (1997) 38 *Virginia Journal of International Law* 293.

[28] Suhas Ketkar and Dilip Ratha, 'Recent Advances in Future-Flow Securitization' (2004) 11 *The Financer* 1. Also see Suhas Ketkar and Dilip Ratha, 'Securitization of Future Flow Receivables: A Useful Tool for Developing Countries' (2001) 38 *Finance and Development* 46.

[29] David J Cummins and Mary A Weiss, 'Convergence of Insurance and Financial Markets: Hybrid and Securitized Risk-Transfer Solutions' (2009) 76 *Journal of Risk and Insurance* 493; Alex Cowley and David Cummins, 'Securitization of Life Insurance Assets and Liabilities' (2005) 72 *Journal of Risk and Insurance* 193.

[30] Tamar Frankel and Joseph W LaPlume, 'Securitizing Insurance Risks' (2000) 19 *Annual Review of Banking Law* 203.

[31] See, Ian Ramsay, 'Financial Innovation and Regulation: The Case of Securitisation' (1993) 4 Journal of Banking and Finance Law and Practice 169. Also see, Senarath, S. and

2.3.2 Ringfencing

In order to create a "true sale", the SPV must be "ringfenced" from the mortgage originator. In other words, the SPV structure must be legally separated from the originating lender's reach. For a similar reason, the credit quality of the bonds issued by the SPV must be—and must be perceived by the regulatory authorities to be—separate and distinct from the credit quality of the selling bank or mortgage originator.[32]

2.3.3 On-Balance Sheet Financing Versus Off-Balance Sheet Financing

When calculating the level of capital, a bank is required to hold against the loan exposure, loans that are classified as "on-balance sheet" and "off-balance-sheet". For capital adequacy purposes, items are taken into account by the relevant regulatory authority—that is, the Australian Prudential Regulation Authority (APRA).

The calculation itself is risk-weighted, according to the perceived riskiness of the particular loan asset. For example, housing loans in respect of owner-occupied dwellings, which are on-balance sheet, are risk-weighted at 50% so that, for example, against a housing loan asset of $100,000, the originating bank will be required to hold a net capital of $50,000. In contrast, loans classified as "off-balance sheet" items are not taken into consideration by APRA for capital adequacy purposes, so that the bank need not hold any capital against that exposure. Banks and other financial institutions that are subject to prudential regulation requirements therefore face a direct incentive to convert on-balance sheet assets to off-balance sheet items.[33]

Copp, R., Credit default swaps and the global financial crisis: reframing credit default swaps as quasi-insurance (2015) 8 *Global Economy and Finance Journal*, 135.

[32] Deutsche Bundesbank, *Monthly Report*, July 1997, 56.

[33] For a more comprehensive discussion of capital adequacy requirements, see T. Valentine, G. Ford and R. Copp, (2003) Ch. 6. In addition, Reuven and Plautt have conducted an empirical study of substitutability between on- and off-balance sheet liquidity for the business sector. They argue that off-balance sheet contingent liabilities of financial institutions (e.g. loan commitments) serve as a substitute for on-balance sheet money and that off-balance sheet liquidity, like unused credit lines, should be taken account in determining debt-equity ratios for prudential regulation purposes. See G. Reuven and S. Plautt, 'Money Demand and Off-Balance Sheet Liquidity: Empirical Analysis and Implications for Monetary Policy' (1989) 1 *Journal of Accounting Auditing and Finance* 147. Also see the discussion

2.3.4 *Lack of Progression in the Australian RMBS Market*[34]

Some of the factors that may have contributed to the lack of development in the Australian RMBS market may include:

1. Historically low interest rates in recent years, and a ready supply of financial capital in the markets. These have to some extent acted as hindrances for banks and other financial institutions to convert their on-balance sheet assets to off-balance sheet items by securitising.
2. Poor understanding of the benefits and mechanics of asset securitisation generally, and RMBSs in particular, on the part of the smaller participants in the financial markets, such as some regional banks, building societies, and credit unions.
3. Disparity among terms and conditions in mortgages between banks and other mortgage providers, such as different prepayment penalties.[35] This heterogeneity has arguably hindered the suitability of home mortgage loans in Australia for securitisation purposes.
4. Availability of alternative funding sources, some of which (e.g. Commonwealth government securities[36]) might no longer be as prevalent in the future as they have been in the past.
5. Lack of specific legal and regulatory frameworks that facilitate securitisation.

We can predict that the RMBS market in Australia is likely to become deeper if and when interest rates increase and if a greater number of smaller financial institutions become more familiar with, and more involved in, RMBS issues. Additionally, the RMBS market will increase as legal and regulatory reforms are introduced to facilitate growth where this is perceived to be for the public benefit.

made in S. Senarath (2016), Not so "'Bankruptcy-Remote': An insight into Sri Lankan Securitization Practices in a Post_GFC Context" (Paper presented at the MAC-MME conference, Prague, Czech Republic); Senarath, S. 'The Dodd-Frank Act doesn't solve the principal-agent problem in asset securitisation' (2017) *blogs.lse.ac.uk* (11 November 2018).

[34] This discussion is adapted from I. H. Giddy, (February 2001) 5.

[35] See, for example, Standard and Poor's, 'Mortgage-Backed Criteria' *Structured Finance Australia and New Zealand* (Melbourne, 1999) 27, 28; Anon., 'The Issues Facing Global Australian RMBS' (June 2001) *Asiamoney* 55.

[36] See Chap. 1 for further discussion.

2.4 Incentives for Stakeholders

The securitisation process can be characterised as a series of contracts or agreements, from a commercial point of view. Stakeholders are motivated by each participant's desire for financial gain or profit.[37] For example, there are loan contracts between borrowers and the originating credit institution; contracts between the originating credit institution and other financial intermediaries to whom it assigns its mortgagee rights; and contracts between the SPV[38] and the institutional investors. There are also a number of side-contracts, such as those between the SPV and:

- Trust manager (perhaps we can call this the mortgagor) who manages the mortgage and other assets of the trust
- The "guarantor", liquidity facility provider,[39] and/or back-up servicer
- The mortgage insurer
- The credit rating agency (e.g. Standard and Poor's, or Moody's)
- The bank responsible for the collections account, if any
- The security trustee
- Any hedging providers (e.g. larger banks with whom the SPV engages in an interest rate swap)
- The custodian, if any, which provides documentation services (e.g. for loan contracts and mortgage documents)

From a theoretical perspective, asset securitisations such as RMBS issues may alleviate the agency costs of primary debt lending, by lowering the costs of monitoring borrower behaviour.[40] The reason is that if a "true

[37] In a broad sense, this even applies to the borrowers, who anticipate that ultimately the value of the property they have borrowed to purchase increases sufficiently to more than compensate them for their investment outlay and net borrowing costs.

[38] Strictly, these contracts are between the trustee issuer of the SPV and the bondholders.

[39] As noted earlier, these roles are described by a variety of different names.

[40] See B. Minton, T. Opler and S. Stanton, 'Asset Securitization Among Industrial Firms', Working Paper, Fisher College of Business, Ohio State University, Columbus Ohio, November 1997. Securitisations may also enable institutional investing firms to expropriate existing bondholders' or shareholders' wealth, although such expropriations are of less relevance in the present context: see B. Minton, T. Opler and S. Stanton, (1997) 6, 8–10; and J. Kensinger and J. D. Martin, 'Project Finance, Raising Money the Old-Fashioned Way' (1988) 1 *Journal of Applied Corporate Finance* 69; A. Borzi, 'Securitisation: It's Made Its Mark: How It Beat the Odds in the Eighties' (1991) (1) *Journal of the Australian Society of*

sale" has occurred, the originating lender's rights and obligations have been transferred to a legally separate entity.

Contractarian theory, which encompasses the agency theory often cited in the accounting and financial economic literatures,[41] provides a framework within which to analyse the incentives of the various stakeholders at each stage of, or contract in, the overall securitisation process.

In practice, RMBS issues offer the following incentives to each of the key stakeholder groups:

- For banks, IMPs, and other originating financial institutions, RMBS programmes provide additional opportunities for:

  - Off-balance sheet financing[42]
  - Fee income[43]

Security Analysts 7; R. Cutler, 'Remodelling the Mortgage' (1994) 64 (7) *Australian Accountant* 35; C. Dalton, 'Resurgence of Securitisation' (1992) 106(4) *Australian Banker (Melbourne)* 177.

[41] See, for example, M. Jensen and W. Meckling, 'Theory of the Firm: Managerial Behavior, Agency Costs and the Ownership Structure' (1976) *Journal of Financial Economics* 305. This article spawned a huge literature on agency theory and the role of agency costs in financial markets.

[42] The originator may have to raise extra capital to comply with risk-based capital adequacy guidelines and rules in order to support the total assets retained in the on-balance sheet. However, the need to do this may be avoided if the assets are sold via a securitisation. Because a securitisation is usually viewed for accounting purposes as a sale of assets/loan receivables rather than as financing, the originator does not record the transaction as a liability on its balance sheet. The proceeds from the sale of loan receivables are used to pay the originating (selling) institution's liabilities, so that (so long as APRA agrees) the originator's capital-to-assets ratio increases and, other things being equal, it has greater scope for borrowing. Its return on capital is also improved, because the originating (selling) institution has removed the liability from its balance sheet, but still retained the profit. For more details (albeit in the context of the United States and other countries overseas), see L. Bryan, 'The Risks, Potential and Promise of Securitisation' in L. T. Kendall (ed.), *Primer on Securitization* (Cambridge: MIT Press, 1996) Ch. 14; S. Din, 'Understanding Securitisation in the Context of Corporate Recapitalisations and Acquisitions' (2000) 15 (6) *Journal of International Banking Law* 128.

[43] For example, the originating institution may earn fees from the SPV for acting as "servicer" or "collections account" manager of the receivables. Fee income is desirable for three reasons: (1) it is independent of interest rates; (2) there is limited credit risk; and (3) it can be claimed as income immediately for accounting purposes. Traditionally, bank income was

- Transforming illiquid assets (i.e. home mortgage loans) into tradable securities[44]
- Arguably, the transfer of risk
- Obtaining additional liquidity[45]
- Reducing costs through economies of scale and scope[46]

- For institutional investors,[47] RMBS programmes provide additional opportunities for:

  - Diversification[48]

based on returns from loans and a lesser proportion from trading in government securities and currencies service fees and management fees. However, increased competition in conjunction with more volatile interest rates and costs has made reliance on spread income uncertain: see F. Oditah, (1996) 91–92. Indeed, a number of commentators predict that the future for financial institutions will involve moving away from the traditional role of financial warehouses, to concentrating primarily or even exclusively on being originators and servicers in return for fees: see T. Frankel, (1999) 145–146; J. C. Shenker and A. J. Colletta, (1991) 1395–1396. Such a system would allow lenders to continue the business of lending while sending much of the risk downstream in the securitisation process. In the United States, several banking institutions—NationsBank, the First National Bank of Boston, Wells Fargo, and Barnett Banks—have publicly embraced this strategy, by announcing the formation of "conduits" to enable the banks to originate various types of commercial mortgage loans and periodically securitise them through Wall Street underwriting firms: see Anon., 'Conduits Set Ambitious Goals for 1995' (February 1995) *Commercial Mortgage Alert* 6.

44 For example, assets can be liquefied at a rate based, not on the originating institution's credit quality, but on the inherent or enhanced credit quality of the assets themselves. Institutions with a below-investment grade credit quality can securitise their loans at the higher credit rating categories, making them easier to sell to investors. See S. L. Schwarcz, 'The Global Alchemy of Asset Securitization' (1995) 14 *International Financial Law Review* 30, 32.

45 For example, the originator raises capital immediately, rather than having to wait for the mortgage receivables to be repaid.

46 In addition, securitisation may be used by the originator in order to match the cash flows of its assets and liabilities. This is easier where the receivables are exactly used to repay the funding loan, because there is minimal mismatch in the timing of receipts and payments. Moreover, if the payments are structured on a pass-through basis, there is less risk of having to make repayments before the receivables are collected.

47 In Australia, as in the United States, mortgage securitisation market have attracted a large cross section of institutional investors, including banks, superannuation funds, and insurance companies: see for example, E. Carew, Fast Money 4 (Sydney: Allen & Unwin, 1998) 243; and Anon., *The Issues Facing the Global Australian RMBS* (June 2001) *Asiamoney* 55.

48 Mortgage pools reduce risk for investors by partial diversification, in that the pools hold loans of the same kind but diversify in terms of the borrower location, collateral, or various other factors. Moreover, investors that desire particular types of loans can buy shares in pools

- An investment that is tailored to investor preferences[49]
- An investment that is secured, over real property
- Investment at yields that tend to be attractive, compared with those of other debt instruments of similar risk[50]

In practice, Australian borrowers are not notified about the likelihood that their loans may be securitised, and the associated possible legal consequences. Stakeholders are therefore likely to face competing or inconsistent incentives, which in contractarian theory are resolved by achieving an equilibrium or balance between the various competing interests.[51] The precise point of this balance or equilibrium position depends directly upon the bargaining power of the various competing stakeholders, and is reflected in the pricing and terms of each contract made.

that hold such loans and, at the same time, diversify the risk from failure of any particular pool by holding the securities of different pools: see A. Finch, 'Securitisation' (1995) 6 *Journal of Banking and Finance Law and Practice* 247; and V. Kothari, *Securitisation: The Financial Instrument of the New Millennium* (Calcutta: Academy of Financial Services, 2003) Ch. 3.

Nor are investors the only stakeholders who benefit from the ability to diversify. The originator also has access to a wider range of funding sources. For example, securitisations by smaller regional banks, building societies, credit unions, or IMPs are sometimes a reaction to a tightening of bank credit—for example, banks may offer less credit or only offer short-term credit, or insist on onerous loan covenants, or additional security or guarantees: see G. Benston, 'The Future of Asset Securitization: The Benefits and Costs of Breaking Up the Bank' (1992) 5 *Journal of Applied Corporate Finance* 73. In these circumstances, an originating smaller regional bank, building society, credit union, or IMP may not itself have a credit standing for a bond issue, but the SPV could issue bonds secured on the mortgage receivables that have a higher rating than the originator (particularly if the financial guarantee of a larger bank is obtained). Hence, the originator diversifies its sources of funds, and is less reliant on traditional bank borrowings. Funding from international investors may also replace that of domestic banks.

[49] For example, investors looking for a high-grade (low-risk) investment can pick up senior or mostly "AAA"-rated instruments, while those looking for a greater risk and a commensurably higher rate of return, can opt for a instruments with a "BB+" credit rating (using the Standard and Poor's nomenclature).

[50] See Deutsche Bundesbank, *Monthly Report*, July 1997, 56; G. Benston, (1992) 72–74; and Financial Security Assurance Inc., *A Guide to Insured Asset-Backed Securities* (NY: FSA, 1999).

[51] A corporate firm is a "web of agency relationships": F. H, Easterbrook and D. R. Fischel, 'Corporate Control Transactions' (1982) 91 *Yale Law Journal* 698, 700. In reallocating funds between transacting parties, an agency problem arises between corporate managers and investors (shareholders), and between lenders and borrowers, because of the conflicting interests of the parties.

2.5 Regulation of Securitisation Market

2.5.1 Rationales Behind Regulation

As there are no external[52] or public good[53] effects, in terms of economic efficiency, this contracting process will be privately and socially optimal. Of these two, there is at least the potential for external effects, the chief externality being driven by moral hazard.[54] In this context, moral hazard would relate to the potential for banks or IMPs to approve housing loans too readily, in the belief that they can shift the risk (including the risk of liability for breach of contract)[55] to other legal entities.

Information asymmetry leads to this potential moral hazard problem. If, perhaps from a utopian point of view, in a market with perfect information, any information asymmetry between stakeholders would be reflected in the contract prices at each stage of the process. As we have identified elsewhere, the mortgagee rights of the originating bank or IMP are assigned in equity to the SPV.[56] The security trust deed sets the rights of

[52] An external effect is a benefit or cost falling on a third party or the community, who cannot pay or be compensated for it through the market mechanism: see D. A. Ipp and W. S. Weerasooria, (eds.), *Butterworths Business and Law Dictionary*, Sydney: Butterworths, 1997.

[53] A public good is a good for which property rights cannot be exclusively defined (i.e. it cannot be exclusively owned) and the provision of which to additional users costs nothing extra (i.e. its marginal supply cost is zero). For a more comprehensive explanation, see R. Pindyck and D. Rubinfeld, *Microeconomics* (5th edition, Englewood Cliffs NJ: Prentice Hall International, 2001) Ch. 15 and 17; and M. Obstfeld and K. Rogoff, *Foundations of International Macroeconomics* (Cambridge: The MIT Press, 1999) 407–427.

[54] In an insurance context, moral hazard is the risk that, when one party is fully insured and cannot be accurately monitored by an insurance company with limited information, its behaviour may change after the insurance has been purchased. It occurs when the party to be insured cannot influence the risk or magnitude of the event that triggers payment of the insurance: see R. Pindyck and D. Rubinfeld, (2001) Ch. 16. For a judicial discussion of the concept, see also *Locker and Woolf Ltd v Western Australian Insurance Co Ltd* [1936] 1 KB 408; and *Jester-Barnes v Licenses and General Insurance Co Ltd* (1939) 49 Ll L Rep 231.

[55] Transferring the risk to another legal entity would not, of course, necessarily relieve the bank or IMP of any liability in tort (e.g. for negligence or negligent misstatement). However, the principles of attributing such tortious liability is not only comparatively straightforward in this context, but have already been addressed in great detail (and recently) by others in the scholarly literature. See, for example, N. A. Katter, *Duty of Care in Australia* (Sydney: Law Book Company, 1999). For these reasons, liability in tort is explicitly excluded from the scope of this book.

[56] For example, in the Commonwealth Bank of Australia's home loan mortgage documentation, Clause 19.1 of the bank's standard terms and conditions of mortgage states, "We may

the SPV's security trustee relating to mortgages or trust assets. It provides that in the event of default, the bondholders have recourse to the mortgage pool and may direct the security trustee to appoint a receiver over the mortgaged assets, to sell or realise those assets, and/or to take relevant action to protect bondholders' interests.[57] However, most borrowers are oblivious to the risk that their homes (or investment dwellings) could be sold by downstream financial intermediaries who have purchased the bank's or IMP's mortgagee rights. This may arise, not due to a failure to pay on the part of the borrower, but as a result of some act or omission by a downstream financial intermediary in the supply chain.[58]

If borrowers are alerted to this risk and impart the information to others (thereby reducing the information asymmetry or gap between borrowers and originating lenders), the information becomes a public good. The reason is that no stakeholder can claim exclusive property rights to it.

It is an economic issue whether these risks are efficiently priced into all contracts included in the securitisation process. However, such an investigation is plainly beyond the scope of this book, and is best left to others with economic expertise. If such risks are *not* priced efficiently into all contracts in the securitisation process, there could be external costs that spill over into the community or at least that part of the community that borrows housing loans to finance the purchase of residences.

assign or otherwise deal with our rights under this mortgage or any Secured Agreement in any way we consider appropriate": see Commonwealth Bank of Australia, Consumer Land Mortgage, filed in the Queensland Land Registry as No. 700901021, and in the New South Wales Land Titles Office as No. 0671753. In comparison, Clause 18.1 of the National Australia Bank's standard home loan mortgage states, "The Bank may transfer or otherwise deal with the Bank's rights under this mortgage in any way the Bank considers appropriate. You agree that the Bank may disclose any information or documents the Bank considers necessary or desirable to help the Bank exercise this right": see National Australia Bank, *Home Mortgage Memorandum of Common Provisions* No. 704919519, Queensland.

[57] In the context of the book, the relevant clauses are set out in the securitisation programme conducted by the Macquarie Securitisation Ltd, *The PUMA Sub-Fund Series* - 2014: *Master Information Memorandum*, July, 2014, at pp 22 and 106. See also, *The PUMA Fund P-7: Master Information Memorandum*, Sydney, February, 2000, at paragraphs 6.2, 4.1 and 1.12.

[58] To the best of my knowledge, no borrowers have yet been forced to sell their mortgaged properties because of the fault of another party in the securitisation chain. However, there remains an appreciable risk based on moral hazard, and the fact that this risk has not yet materialised may be due more to rising house prices in recent years, than to any inherent safeguards in the existing regulatory or legal system.

From a societal perspective, it will be interesting to note precisely how the courts or the legislature will allocate these risks or, rather, the liability that flows from them. It is even conceivable that some different form of government regulation may ultimately be required to achieve net benefits to the public and "just" outcomes across all stakeholders. In either event, the courts will somehow be involved as arbiters in the risk allocation process—whether as adjudicators in the case of prospective plaintiffs (e.g. borrowers) who rely on the current state of the law or as interpreters of any new industry law or regulation that may be introduced by the legislature.

2.5.2 *The "Public Benefit Test"*

If economic efficiency is at least one of the objectives, with legislature intending to impose new legislation to govern the industry, either now or in the future, it seems clear (assuming) that the proposed legislative regime and its alternatives must be subjected to a social cost-benefit analysis, to compare and evaluate the alternative proposals with reference to the net social benefits that each is likely to yield.

Based on the National Competition Policy reforms of the early-mid 1990s,[59] the State and Commonwealth governments have been compelled to evaluate all new Acts of Parliament, and some subordinate legislation, in terms of economic cost-benefit analysis under the so-called public benefit test.[60]

Plainly, the specific costs and benefits of any proposed new industry regulation, and the stakeholders who bear them or to whom they accrue, will depend on the precise nature of the new regulation. It is impossible to foretell, with any precision, the nature or timing of any new regulatory regime. Nevertheless, some useful comment can be made about the general form that any such regulation would be *likely* to take.

[59] See, for example, the *Competition Policy Reform Act* 1995 (Cth); the Commonwealth-State *Competition Principles Agreement* signed April 1995 between the Commonwealth government, and all State and Territory governments; and the raft of legislation spawned by them by the Commonwealth and all State governments.

[60] See, for example, Queensland Treasury, *Public Benefit Test Guidelines: Approach to Undertaking Public Benefit Test Assessments for Legislation Reviews under National Competition Policy*, Brisbane, August 1999. All other State governments have published similar guidelines based on social cost-benefit analysis.

2.5.3 Optimal Regulatory Framework for Securities Market

Provided the social benefits outweigh the social costs, one way of helping a beneficial public good effect to evolve in the community could be to compel lenders by legislation to inform their borrowers about the risks of losing their residences once their loans are securitised, through no fault of their own.[61]

In a theoretical world in which all lenders securitised their housing loans, it would be difficult (from the point of view of consumer sovereignty) to see borrowers having any real difficulty if this was disclosed to them, perhaps at the time of the initial housing loan interview.[62] Of course, since in practice not all financial institutions securitise their housing loans, it is possible that borrowers would seek their housing finance from those other institutions whose loans do not expose borrowers to the risk of losing their residences because of a downstream intermediary's error or default.

However, from the point of view of producer sovereignty (and producer surplus), the mandatory disclosure of such risks is likely to be suicidal for those banks and IMPs that do securitise their loans by way of RMBS programmes, unless they were to offer borrowers a compensatory reduction in the housing loan interest rate or some other benefit.

[61] Disclosure can help reduce the cost of monitoring corporate managers' and borrowers' use of corporate assets for self-interested purposes. The modern literature on the firm recognises the importance of such agency problems: see M. C. Jensen, 'Agency Costs of Free Cash Flows, Corporate Finance and Takeovers' (1986) 74 *American Economic Review* 650. Moreover, rules mandating particular disclosures are common in principal-agent contexts: see, for example, P. G. Mahoney, 'Mandatory Disclosure as a Solution to the Agency Problem' (1995) 62 *The University of Chicago Law Review* 1047; P. Little, 'The Policy Underlying Financial Disclosure by Corporations and its Effect upon Legal Liability' (1991) 2 *Australian Journal of Corporate Law* 87; R. C. Merton, 'Financial Innovation and the Management and Regulation of Financial Institutions' (1995) 19 *Journal of Banking and Finance* 461; E. Ferran, and C. A. Goodhart, *Regulating Financial Services and Markets in the Twenty First Century* (Oxford: Hart Publishing, 2001) Ch. 1 and 2; and E. Roca, *Price Interdependence Among Equity Markets in the Asia-Pacific Region* (Aldershot, Hampshire: Ashgate Publishing, 2000) Ch. 4.

[62] Theoretically, there might be the risk of slightly higher interest rates on borrowers' housing loan facilities. However, in practice, any increase is likely to be relatively small. The precise extent of such an interest rate increase and the likely flow-on effects (e.g. to housing affordability and bank revenue) are best left to economic researchers with the requisite expertise. Such investigations are well beyond the scope of this book.

Ultimately, if the government does introduce new regulations governing the RMBS industry at some point in the future, it would not be surprising if the courts, after all claims on mortgage insurers have been settled or paid out, and left with limited resources for achieving a "just" outcome, resort to finding against the defendants with the "deepest pockets"—the banks. This would indeed be ironic if the banks have initiated securitisation programmes of this type in order to transfer the risk of precisely such an outcome to other entities.

2.6 Summary

This chapter identifies RMBS programmes from a theoretical point of view. In short, Borrowers, who seek funds from the financial markets, contract with banks or independent mortgage providers (IMPs), which sell the borrowers' secured loans to other financial intermediaries. The capital and interest repayments made by the borrowers provide cash flows that are ultimately received by these other intermediaries, with the value of the mortgaged property forming a contingent receivable in their accounts. Intermediaries, utilising these incoming cash flows as revenue, issue bonds to investors, who supply funds to the financial markets. At each stage of the process, each intermediary earns a profit, provided their net interest income exceeds their interest and other expenses (including transactions costs).

In reality borrowers are unaware of the fact that financial intermediaries have the right, under the mortgage securitisation agreement, to sell their home, without any default from the borrowers. Once some borrowers become aware of this risk and communicate it to others (thereby narrowing the information asymmetry between borrowers and lenders), there is the potential for a significant public good effect. Specifically, no stakeholder can claim the property rights to this information, which is—or becomes—a public good.

The next question that arises is the logical one: whether the industry needs to be regulated more closely and, if so, by whom? Assuming the provision of economically efficient and "just" outcomes to be the relevant policy objectives, the temptation to blithely prescribe industry regulation without a social cost-benefit, as operationalised in terms of a "public benefit test" analysis should be resisted. Nevertheless, some useful comment can be made about the form that any such regulation would be likely to take.

One way of facilitating a beneficial public good effect could be to mandate by regulation (provided the social benefits outweigh the social costs) that borrowers be informed about the risk of losing their residences, despite no default on their part. From the point of view of consumer sovereignty, it is difficult to see any real disadvantage to borrowers if this was disclosed to them at the time of the initial housing loan interview. However, from the point of view of producer sovereignty (and producer surplus), mandatory disclosure of such risks is likely to be suicidal for those banks and IMPs that securitise their loans in this manner, unless they offered borrowers a compensatory reduction in the housing loan interest rate or some other benefit.[63]

It would indeed be ironic if it were the banks, as the defendants with the deepest pockets, who ultimately became the entities held liable for any residual losses that result from RMBS programmes, when it was the banks who initiated RMBS issues in the belief that they would transfer risk to other parties. Adopting the contractarian framework, various stages of the securitisation process in Australia will be analysed in Chaps. 5, 6, and 7. Chapter 3 will set the stage for our analysis. In Chap. 8, aspects of the present law and regulation that facilitate and hinder the growth of the RMBS industry will be identified, based on the results of these analyses. Using results from the analysis, recommendations will be made in order to reform relevant legislation, and current practice relating to RMBS issues are provided in Chap. 9.

Bibliography

Books and Book Chapters

Black, J., Hashimzade, N. and Myles, M. D., *Dictionary of Economics*, 3rd edition, Oxford: Oxford University Press, 2012.

Brindley, B., (ed), *A Dictionary of Finance and Banking*, 4th edition, Oxford: Oxford: University Press, 2008.

Bryan, L., 'The Risks, Potential and Promise of Securitisation' in L. T. Kendall (ed.), *Primer on Securitization*, Cambridge: MIT Press, 1996.

Davidson, S. A., Wolff, L. and Ching A., *Securitization: Structuring and Investment Analysis,* New Jersey: John Wiley & Sons, 2003.

[63] Or, in the extreme, if there were no alternatives for borrowers in the market, because all current and prospective housing loan providers in the market were to securitise their loans without informing borrowers that they are doing so.

Ferran E. and C. A. Goodhart, *Regulating Financial Services and Markets in the Twenty First Century*, Oxford: Hart Publishing, 2001.

Fidelis, O., *The Future for the Global Securities Market-Legal and Regulatory Aspects*, Oxford: Oxford University Press, 1996.

Ipp, D. A. and Weerasooria, W.S., (eds.), *Butterworths Business and Law Dictionary*, Sydney: Butterworths, 1997.

Katter, N.A., *Duty of Care in Australia*, Sydney: Law Book Company, 1999.

Kothari V., *Securitisation: The Financial Instrument of the New Millennium*, Calcutta: Academy of Financial Services, 2003.

Kothari V., *Securitisation: The Financial Instrument of the Future*, Singapore: John Wiley & Sons, 2006.

Kravitt, R. E. and Johnston, J. H. P., *Securitization of Financial Assets*, 2nd edition, N.Y.: Aspen Law and Business, 2002.

Lee, C. F., Lee, A. C. and Gale, *Encyclopedia of Finance*, Springer, 2006.

Obstfeld, M. and Rogoff, K., *Foundations of International Macroeconomics* (Cambridge: The MIT Press, 1999.

Pindyck, R. and Rubinfeld, D., *Microeconomics*, 5th edition, Englewood Cliffs NJ: Prentice Hall International, 2001.

Roca, E., *Price Interdependence Among Equity Markets in the Asia-Pacific Region* Aldershot, Hampshire: Ashgate Publishing, 2000.

Schwarcz, S. L. and Ford, A.D., *Structured Finance: A Guide to the Principles of Asset Securitization*, N.Y.: Practising Law Institute, 2002.

Journal Articles

Adhikari, A. and Betancourt, L., 'Accounting for Securitizations: A Comparison of SFAS 140 and IASB 39' (2008) *19 Journal of International Financial Management & Accounting* 73.

Barth, M. E., Ormazabal, G. and Taylor, D. J., 'Asset Securitizations and Credit Risk' (2011) 87 *The Accounting Review* 423.

Benston, G., 'The Future of Asset Securitization: The Benefits and Costs of Breaking Up the Bank' (1992) 5 *Journal of Applied Corporate Finance* 73.

Borzi, A., 'Securitisation: It's Made Its Mark: How It Beat the Odds in the Eighties' (1991, 1) *Journal of the Australian Society of Security Analysts* 7.

Cowley, A. and Cummins, D., 'Securitization of Life Insurance Assets and Liabilities' (2005) 72 *Journal of Risk and Insurance* 193.

Cummins, D. J. and Trainar, P., 'Securitization, Insurance, and Reinsurance' (2009) 76 *Journal of Risk and Insurance* 463.

Cummins, D. J. and Weiss, M. A., 'Convergence of Insurance and Financial Markets: Hybrid and Securitized Risk-Transfer Solutions' (2009) 76 *Journal of Risk and Insurance* 493.

Cutler, R., 'Remodelling the Mortgage' (1994) 64 (7) *Australian Accountant* 35.

Dalton, C., 'Resurgence of Securitisation' (1992) 106(4) *Australian Banker (Melbourne)* 177.

Din, 'Understanding Securitisation in the Context of Corporate Recapitalisations and Acquisitions' (2000) 15 (6) *Journal of International Banking Law* 128.

Easterbrook, F. H. and D. R. Fischel., 'Corporate Control Transactions' (1982) 91 Yale Law Journal 698.

Eisbruck, J. H., 'Blockbuster or Flop? The History and Evolution of Firm Receivables Securitization, 1995–2005' (2005) 11 *The Journal of Structured Finance* 11.

Finch, A., 'Securitisation' (1995) 6 *Journal of Banking and Finance Law and Practice* 247.

Frankel, T. and LaPlume, J. W., 'Securitizing Insurance Risks' (2000) 19 *Annual Review of Banking Law* 203.

Jaffee, D., 'The Interest Rate Risk of Fannie Mae and Freddie Mac' (2003) 24 *Journal of Financial Services Research* 5.

Jensen, M. and Meckling, W., 'Theory of the Firm: Managerial Behavior, Agency Costs and the Ownership Structure' (1976) *Journal of Financial Economics* 305.

Jobst, A. A., 'Asset Securitisation as a Risk Management and Funding Tool: What Small Firms Need to Know' (2006) 32 *Managerial Finance* 731.

Jobst, A. A., 'What is Structured Finance? An Analysis of Derivatives, Securitization and Islamic Finance' (2006) 8 *The Securitization Conduit* (Reprinted in ICFAI Journal of Risk Management 2007).

Kensinger. J. and Martin, J. D., 'Project Finance, Raising Money the Old-Fashioned Way' (1988) 1 *Journal of Applied Corporate Finance* 69.

Ketkar, S. and Ratha, D., 'Recent Advances in Future-Flow Securitization' (2004) 11 *The Financer* 1.

Ketkar, S. and Ratha, D., 'Securitization of Future Flow Receivables: A Useful Tool for Developing Countries' (2001) 38 *Finance and Development* 46.

Keys B. J. et al., 'Did Securitization Lead to Lax Screening? Evidence From Subprime Loans' (2008) 125 *Quarterly Journal of Economics* 307.

Jensen, M. C., 'Agency Costs of Free Cash Flows, Corporate Finance and Takeovers' (1986) 74 *American Economic Review* 650.

Little, P., 'The Policy Underlying Financial Disclosure by Corporations and its Effect upon Legal Liability' (1991) 2 *Australian Journal of Corporate Law* 87

Mahoney, P. G., 'Mandatory Disclosure as a Solution to the Agency Problem' (1995) 62 *The University of Chicago Law Review* 1047.

Merton, R. C, 'Financial Innovation and the Management and Regulation of Financial Institutions' (1995) 19 *Journal of Banking and Finance* 461.

Minton, B., Opler, T. and Stanton, S., 'Asset Securitization Among Industrial Firms', Working Paper, Fisher College of Business, Ohio State University, Columbus Ohio, November 1997.

Rajapakse, P., 'An Analysis of the Concepts of Mortgage-backed Securitization: An Economic and Legal Perspective, (2011) 10 *The Journal of Law and Financial Management* 22.

Ramsay, I., 'Financial Innovation and Regulation: The Case of Securitisation' (1993) 4 Journal of Banking and Finance Law and Practice 169.

Reuven, G. and Plautt, S., 'Money Demand and Off-Balance Sheet Liquidity: Empirical Analysis and Implications for Monetary Policy' (1989) 1 *Journal of Accounting Auditing and Finance* 147.

Robert, J. H., Pollsen B, and Elengical, J., 'A Record Year for Residential MBS' ([illegible]) [illegible] *Mortgage Banking* 365.

Salathe, J. R., 'Reducing Health Care Costs Through Hospital Accounts Receivable Securitization' (1994) 80 *Virginia Law Review* 549.

Schwarcz, S. L., 'Parts are Greater than the Whole: How Securitization of Divisible Interests Can Revolutionize Structured Finance and Open the Capital Markets to Middle-Market Companies' (1993) *The Columbia Business Law Review* 139.

Schwarcz, S. L., 'Structured Finance: The New Way to Securitize Assets' (1989) 11 *Cardozo Law Review* 607.

Schwarcz. S. L., 'The Global Alchemy of Asset Securitization' (1995) 14 *International Financial Law Review* 30.

Senarath, S., 'Securitisation and the global financial crisis: can risk retention prevent another crisis?' (2017) 18 *International Journal of Business and Globalisation* 153.

Senarath, S. and Copp, R., 'Credit default swaps and the global financial crisis: reframing credit default swaps as quasi-insurance' (2015) 8 *Global Economy and Finance Journal* 135.

Shenker, J. C. and Colletta, A. J., 'Asset Securitization: Evolution' Current Issues and New Frontiers' (1991) 69 Texas Law Review 1369.

Yang, S. S., 'Securitisation and Tranching Longevity and House Price Risk for Reverse Mortgage Products' (2011) 36 *The Geneva Papers on Risk and Insurance – Issues and Practice* 648.

Working Papers, Magazines, Newspapers and Reports

Anon., 'Conduits Set Ambitious Goals for 1995' (February 1995) *Commercial Mortgage Alert* 6.

Anon., 'The Issues Facing Global Australian RMBS' (June 2001) *Asiamoney* 55.

Bundesbank, *Monthly Report*, July 1997.

Carew, E., *Fast Money*, Sydney: Allen and Unwin, 1998.

Deutsche Bundesbank, *Monthly Report*, July 1997.

Financial Security Assurance Inc., *A Guide to Insured Asset-Backed Securities*, N.Y.: FSA, 1999.

Macquarie Securitisation Ltd, *The PUMA Fund P-7: Master Information Memorandum*, Sydney, February, 2000.

Macquarie Securitisation Ltd, *The PUMA Sub-Fund Series*—2014: *Master Information Memorandum*, Sydney, July, 2014.

National Australia Bank, *Home Mortgage Memorandum of Common Provisions* No. 704919519, Queensland.

Queensland Treasury, *Public Benefit Test Guidelines: Approach to Undertaking Public Benefit Test Assessments for Legislation Reviews under National Competition Policy*, Brisbane, August 1999.

Senarath, S. 'The Dodd-Frank Act doesn't solve the principal-agent problem in asset securitisation' (2017) *blogs.lse.ac.uk* (11 November 2018) http://blogs.lse.ac.uk/businessreview/2017/04/21/the-dodd-frank-act-doesnt-solve-the-principal-agent-problem-in-asset-securitisation/

Senarath, S., Not so "Bankruptcy-Remote': An insight into Sri Lankan Securitization Practices in a Post_GFC Context' (Paper presented at the MAC-MME conference 2016, Prague, Czech Republic).

Standard and Poor's, 'Mortgage-Backed Criteria' *Structured Finance Australia and New Zealand* (Melbourne, 1999).

CHAPTER 3

Structuring and Issuance in Residential Mortgage Securitisation

3.1 Introduction

This chapter provides an overview of the manner in which a typical Australian residential mortgage-backed security (RMBS) programme is conducted in practice. As part of the analysis, this chapter focuses on the nature of affairs in the RMBS industry together with an analysis of existing laws and regulations that facilitate and hinder the growth of the industry. However, this chapter also focuses on mechanics and procedural aspects of an RMBS programme, together with some practical concerns of a typical RMBS programme.[1]

3.2 Structuring Mortgage Securitisation Programme

In practice, when it comes to an RMBS programme, the originator (who seeks to raise cash) may select suitable home loans with the intention of utilising them as the basis for issuing mortgage-backed bonds to the institutional investor market. As we have noted in our previous discussion, these home

[1] Such as the structure of the RMBS programme; procedural aspects of the mortgage origination process; the establishment of the SPV and the transfer of the lender's rights to it; the issuance of the mortgage-backed bonds; the credit enhancement mechanisms that are available; and related operational aspects, such as the appointment of a fund manager or other ancillary service providers.

P. Rajapakse, S. Senarath, *Commercial Law Aspects of Residential Mortgage Securitisation in Australia*,
https://doi.org/10.1007/978-3-030-00605-1_3

loans represent borrowers' payment obligations to the originator. Also, as discussed earlier, there are two types of RMBS programmes in Australia—namely, bank or "assignment" programmes, and conduit programmes.

3.2.1 *Bank or "Assignment" Programmes*

Typically, in an "assignment" programme, the lender (a bank or an independent mortgage provider [IMP]) will pool similar residential loans (which remain recognised as assets on the balance sheet) and makes an equitable assignment of its rights in that asset pool to a special purpose vehicle (SPV). This assignment will include its mortgagee rights (in respect of the supporting security properties).[2] For larger banks, the mortgage originator will be the lender, which sponsors the programme; however, essentially, this need not be the case. Smaller players, such as regional banks, credit unions, building societies, or IMPs, may seek to obtain the support of a larger bank to "sponsor" the intended securitisation programme.

Through the issue of securitised bonds, the SPV funds the amount owed as consideration for the equitable assignment. In practice, the SPV appoints the original lender as the "servicer" and/or the "fund manager"[3] (who is responsible for the continuing management of the loans and supporting security[4]) of the securitisation programme.

3.2.2 *Conduit Programmes*

The most common form of RMBS programme in Australia is conduit programmes. Financial intermediaries, such as regional banks, that lack the asset size to sponsor an assignment programme, without the credit support of a larger bank or other facility provider, typically tend to establish conduit programmes.

[2] See generally, T. Robinson, 'Securitisation Update,' *Seventh Annual Credit Law Conference*, BLEC, Melbourne, September 1997.

[3] Generally, the fund manager is appointed by the trustee to administer and manage the mortgage pool, invest liquid funds, and liaise with bond investors and underwriters.

[4] Examples of bank RMBS programmes in Australia include Citibank Pty Ltd's *Securitised Australian Mortgage Trust 2003*; AMP Bank Ltd's *Progress 2003 Trust*; and Suncorp Metway Bank Ltd's *Apollo 2003 Trust*: see Standard and Poor's, 'RMBS CDO Activity Leads Australian Securitisation Issuance Growth in 2003', *Credit Ratings Commentary and News* (Melbourne, July 2003).

These smaller institutions may pool (perhaps we can call it "warehouse") their mortgages until they reach an aggregate value sufficient to back a bond issue. The bond issue will be made either by the institution itself or in combination with other smaller institutions. The support of a larger bank or other facility provider is generally obtained since the bonds issued by the smaller originators would not be sufficiently attractive to institutional investors, without the support of a larger institution. On the other hand, however, the support of a larger bank or institution tends to upgrade the quality of the smaller originators' bonds, with the "guarantee" provided by the bigger institution. This "guarantee" may take the form of a formal guarantee, but more usually, the larger bank agrees (in exchange for a fee) to act "back-up servicer", "standby credit facility provider", "standby specialist servicer", or "liquidity facility provider" for the issue.[5]

3.2.3 "Pass-Through" Versus "Pay-Through" Structures

Pass-through and pay-through are among commonly discussed securitisation structures in literature. Whether the programme is a bank or conduit programme, as discussed earlier,[6] an RMBS programme can also be structured on a "pass-through" or "pay-through" basis. In "pass-through" issues, the principal repayments are "passed through" to the investor at about the same time as they are received from the pool of initial borrowers according to an agreed (e.g. monthly) repayment schedule,[7] whereas in

[5] By way of example, Macquarie Bank Ltd's PUMA Fund operates one of the largest conduit programmes in Australia: see M. B. Johnson, 'Oz Securitisation Gathers Pace' (March 2001) *Asiamoney* 47, 48; Anon., 'PUMA Securitisation Pioneer' (May 1999) *Euroweek* 19, 20. This programme is sponsored by the fund manager, Macquarie Securitisation Ltd, which is a subsidiary of Macquarie Bank Ltd. In this particular programme, as well as acting as sponsor and fund manager, Macquarie Securitisation Ltd acts as servicer, and there is a separate mortgage manager. Perpetual Trustee Australia Ltd acts as trustee of the fund: see Macquarie Securitisation Ltd., *Master Information Memorandum, PUMA Sub-Fund Series 2014* (Sydney, July 2014) particularly at pp 67–68.

[6] For a more detailed discussion, see T. Frankel, *Securitization: Structured Financing, Financial Assets Pools, and Asset-Backed Securities* (Boston: Little Brown & Co, 1991) Ch 6; and M. Boolean, 'Mortgage Securitisation in the United Kingdom' in C. Stone, A Zissu and J. Lederman (eds.), *Asset Securitisation Theory and Practice in Europe* (London: Euromoney, 1991) Ch 42.

[7] As explained in Chap. 2, "pass-through" issues are issues of debt securities, such as bonds, in which the interest and principal repayments are "passed through" a trust to the investors on a scheduled "periodic payment" basis, at about the same time as they are received from the pool of initial borrowers. More specifically, the principal and interest repayments by

"pay-through" issues,[8] the "principal" repayments are paid to the investor at any time, and not necessarily as they are received from the pool of borrowers.[9] A pass-through structure is the most basic structure in securitisation. In a pass-through, the SPV is a mere distributing vehicle.[10] This represents

home loan borrowers are collected and paid into a "warehouse" fund on a scheduled basis (most commonly, on a monthly basis), and paid out to bondholders on a scheduled basis (most commonly, quarterly or semi-annually, although the frequency of payment depends largely on the cash flow management requirements of the Issuer and fund manager). In this context, the "warehouse" fund is a fund, usually in the name of the programme sponsor, and is established for the purpose of temporarily holding an asset until a downstream intermediary (e.g. the trustee of the SPV) is ready to receive it. See I. Ramsay, 'Financial Innovation and Regulation: The Case of Securitisation' (1993) *Journal of Banking and Financial Law and Practice* 169, 171 for further discussion.

[8] As noted earlier, "pay-through" issues may be debt securities (e.g. bonds) or equity securities (e.g. ordinary shares). In the case of *bonds*, the interest and principal repayments are "paid through" a corporate SPV (not a trust) to the investors on a sometimes scheduled (i.e. regular), and sometimes unscheduled (irregular) basis, from the pool of initial borrowers.

In the case of ordinary *shares*, the principal and interest repayments made by the initial home loan borrowers are paid to a corporate SPV, which then pays them out again to investors in the form of dividend payments on the shares. These dividend payments may be regular (e.g. if the securities issued were preference shares that guaranteed investors a regular dividend), or irregular, as in the case of dividends paid to ordinary shareholders. In this latter case, it would be unusual for the investors (ordinary shareholders) to receive their dividend payments at or about the same time as they are received from the pool of borrowers.

[9] In those jurisdictions where pay-through programmes are used, such the United States, a sponsor's decision to structure its programme as a "pass-through" or "pay-through" programme will depend on programme costs, investor preferences, and the treatment of type of programme under prevailing corporate and tax laws. The type of programme chosen will be the product of a trade-off between these sometimes-competing considerations. For example, the sponsor may choose to save on programme costs by issuing just one class of securities to one type of investor, rather than different classes of securities to multiple classes of investors. It would choose a pass-through programme, rather than a pay-through programme. While this is cheaper, the sponsor foregoes the additional net revenue it might earn from a pay-though programme in which it would be able to access a wide range of potential investors with different preferences in terms of risk, liquidity, and investment horizon.

Alternatively, the sponsor's target investors might prefer that the regular (e.g. monthly) home loan repayments from borrowers are reconfigured into different (e.g. quarterly or semi-annual) payment streams. By contrast, investors might prefer, for asset/liability management purposes, that the incoming regular home loan repayments of principal and interest are reconfigured so that, in terms of the bonds issued by the SPV, the principal is paid at maturity in one "bullet payment", rather than, for example, on a "reducing principal" basis over the term of the bond facility.

[10] It is noteworthy that even in a pass-through structure there could be junior and senior note structures similar to a typical pay-through structure. In such a securitisation programme,

a key difference between the two types of issues and has obvious cash flow management implications[11] for the SPV in meeting its obligations to bondholders.

Most RMBS programmes in Australia have had a "pass-through" structure. However, there are RMBS programmes with "pay-through" characteristics. For example, at least in the United States, different tranches of securities for different classes of investor are normally reserved for pay-through programmes, and yet, Macquarie Bank's PUMA programme, which is expressed as a pass-through programme,[12] also provides different tranches of securities.

As far as Australian and overseas RMBS programmes are concerned, there are at least two other differences. First, although some participants in the RMBS markets in Australia use the terms "pass-through" and "pay-through" interchangeably, in a strict sense, there are no pay-through *equity*-based RMBS programmes in Australia. That is, all the RMBS

junior notes will be subordinated to senior notes. We will be discussing some practical examples of a pay-through structure with subordinated junior notes in Chap. 7.

[11] Cf. also I.H. Giddy, 'Alternative Forms of Asset-Backed Securities', delivered at *Workshop on Asset-Backed Securities*, New York University, 2001, 2–4, who notes, in a US context:

> A basic premise of the pass-through structure is that reconfiguration of the cash flows is not permitted [under US tax law], as it would cause the trust to be deemed a taxable entity. Instead of being taxed directly, the trust's tax liabilities flow through to the holders of the pass-through certificates. Pass through payments should match the incoming payments on the assets. Imputed or actual principal and interest payments from payer may not be re-characterised, as would be the case, for example, with discount or premium prices paid for loan pools. The interest portion of a payment stream may be divided, for example, among investors and the servicer, or to support credit enhancement, but principal must be passed through to repay investors as received. Thus, in a pass-through security, the economics of the debt instrument issued [are] essentially the same as [those] of the underlying asset or asset pool... [In contrast], investors in a pay-through are no longer [equitable] owners in underlying assets; they have simply invested in a bond backed by some assets. Therefore, the issuing entity can manipulate the cash flows without tax consequences, hence the use of the pay-through structure for CMOs which manipulate the incoming cash flows into separate payment streams. Thus pay-through securities may be structured so that asset cash flows can be reconfigured to support forms of debt unlike those of the underlying assets.

In the market nomenclature, "CMOs" are collateralised mortgage obligations—a basic form of pay-through mortgage-backed security used in the United States.

[12] See, *Master Information Memorandum PUMA Fund P-7*, paragraph 2.

programmes in Australia to date have comprised *debt* issues—a fact explained, at least in part, by the current market regulation in Australia. Pay-through securities that are issued as ordinary shares in Australia would need to comply with the fundraising and security disclosure provisions set out in Ch. 6D of the *Corporations Act*,[13] which can be more burdensome and complex (and therefore it will be costly to comply with in practice) than those applicable to simple public debt issues.[14]

In the Australian context, all the SPVs (so far) have been structured as trusts, in contrast to corporate issuers. This is also largely due to the current market regulations. Under the *Corporations Act*, it may be no cheaper for banks and other financial institutions to structure an SPV as a company since, in many cases in practice, a corporate SPV that issued public debt would need to set up a trust for the debenture holders.[15] In such conditions, it is perhaps understandable that banks and other financial institutions would see little value in issuing RMBSs through a corporate SPV *and* trust, when they can do so through a trust.

3.3 Mortgage Origination

3.3.1 The Process of Mortgage Origination

The securitisation process begins with an intended borrower making an application for a loan. This loan could be, inter alia, a home loan mortgage, a commercial property mortgage, or a vehicle lease. Once the lender receives an application for a loan, assessors of the lender will evaluate the loan application. If the application is approved, then the lawyers (also called solicitors/barristers in Australia and United Kingdom) of the lender will prepare the relevant documents while taking steps to grant the loan. Invariably, it is a condition of the home loan contract that the loan be insured,[16] either by a bank subsidiary insurance arm, or by an independent insurer. Once the loan is approved, subject to the requirements of the

[13] Sections 710–723 of Ch. 6D of the *Corporations Act*.

[14] Specifically, those debt securities that fall within the definition of "debentures" in section 9 of the *Corporations Act*, and which are regulated by Ch. 2 L of the Act. See Chap. 6 of this book for further details.

[15] See, for example, section 283AA of the *Corporations Act* and Chap. 6 of this book.

[16] For example, one of the conditions might be that the borrower maintains full replacement home owner's insurance on the mortgaged property.

National Credit Code and other relevant legislation, the bank's solicitors prepare and settle the mortgage and loan documentation.

There are two main forms of origination process when it comes to an IMP.[17] In practice, some IMPs document the details of the borrower's loan application and forward it to a bank for approval. Such IMPs in fact act as "spotters" for the larger banks, and the origination fee they receive is more or less a "spotter's fee". The rest of the origination process is conducted mainly by the bank similar to the discussion earlier. Other IMPs more or less proceed similar to a bank, although small banks follow an origination procedure that is similar again to that used by the banks. In the next step, the IMP transfers the mortgages to an SPV in return for a purchase price payable on the sale.

3.3.2 The Originator in the Capacity of the Servicer

In practice, the SPV typically appoints the originator as the servicer of the RMBS programme. The originator collects the mortgage repayments on behalf of the SPV in return for a service fee. Typically, the servicer collects these mortgage receivables in a separate escrow or trust account,[18] from which collections are drawn by the SPV. The SPV utilises these funds either to fund immediate interest payments to its bond investors or to reinvest the money, so that it can pay bond investors at a later date. In the event of default by the mortgagors, the servicer will, as the agent of the SPV, ultimately bring an action—perhaps foreclosure—against the mortgagors.[19]

3.3.3 Substitution of Residential Mortgages

In practice, in a typical mortgage securitisation, RMBS issues are structured in such a way to allow the mortgage pool to be "topped up" with new substitute mortgagers at the initial issue of the securities. There are

[17] For example, RAMS Home Loans Ltd, Wizard Loans Pty Ltd, or Aussie Home Loans Ltd.

[18] This escrow account is set up to absorb any losses from the housing loan defaults or repayment shortfalls.

[19] See, for example, see *Master Information Memorandum, PUMA Sub-Fund Series 2014 at p 75.*

two main reasons behind this. First, to supplement the cash flow needed by the trustee-issuer to fund the RMBS issue,[20] and second, to extend the lifespan of the issue, if required.[21]

The trustee/issuer will utilise "principal collections",[22] which mainly comprise the proceeds of mortgages. There are two key issues pertaining to mortgage substitution. The first is with regard to the quality of the substitute mortgages, and the second is the impact of substitution in the event of the originator's or issuer's insolvency. The quality of the new mortgages must be comparable with that of the old to avoid jeopardising the rating of the bonds issued. Accordingly, the original lender must provide similar warranties in respect of the replacement mortgages as were given in respect of the original mortgages placed in the pool.[23] In the event of a breach of warranty, the original lender is required to repurchase the recalcitrant mortgage.[24] The second issue relates to insolvency. There could be a legal risk of the substitution of mortgages into the mortgage pool being regarded as a transaction at an under-value or as a preference in the event of the issuing vehicle's or the originator's insolvency.

In those RMBS issues where mortgage substitution is not permitted, the issuer's exposure to unanticipated adverse future events may be limited if the issuer is able to redeem the bonds issued.

3.3.4 *Monetary Advances*

Some RMBS programmes also permit the trustee-issuer to make further advances to existing borrowers in the pool. However, in some cases, if the borrowers meet normal credit assessment guidelines and are approved by a relevant mortgage insurer, the trustee-issuer could make a subsequent

[20] Some mortgages that comprise the initial pool will be discharged or enforced earlier than expected, so that the trustee/issuer may miss out on cash flow needed to fund the RMBS issue. The realisation or redemption value to the trustee/issuer in such a situation will reflect the expected foregone repayments from housing loan borrowers, but not any unexpected cash flows (e.g. from unanticipated interest rate changes).

[21] The substitution of mortgages can be used to extend the life of a bond issue, making RMBSs more attractive for certain investors and allowing the issuer to spread the recovery of its initial expenses over a longer period, which may be useful for the issuer in managing its tax liabilities.

[22] For example, in the context of the PUMA programme, which allows the substitution of mortgages, see *Master Information Memorandum, PUMA Fund P-7*, paragraph 4.7.3.

[23] Ibid.

[24] Id, paragraph 5.2

advance to a mortgage borrower.[25] Such advances are typically funded by the trustee-issuer from the principal collections of the fund.[26]

In a practical sense, perhaps, it may be advantageous for the issuer to finance the further advance out of the earnings of redeemed mortgages, given that this can have the same consequence as the substitution of mortgages—it can maintain the income flow to the issuer and prolong the life of the issue, if required.[27] On the other hand, the originator must generally either make the advance on the security of a new second mortgage that ranks behind the original mortgage held by the issuer, for the originator to fund the further advance. Or re-acquire the mortgage from the vehicle in exchange for cash or investments or substitute mortgages, if permitted, with the result that the mortgage on which the further advance is made ceases to form part of the backing for the issue.

In order to affect the transfer of the amplified debt created by the further advance, a separate agreement between the originator and issuer is not generally required. The original agreement—perhaps we could call it mortgage origination deed—typically is worded broadly in order to transfer the originator's present and future rights.[28] The effect of an agreement to sell future property rights has been analysed in *Holroyd v Marshall*[29] in the following way:

> A contract which engages to transfer property, which is not in existence, cannot operate as an immediate alienation merely because there is nothing to transfer.
>
> But if a vendor ... agrees to sell ... property, real or personal, of which he is not possessed at the time and he receives the consideration for the contract, and afterwards becomes possessed of property answering the descrip-

[25] Id, paragraph 4.8.1.

[26] These include principal receipts in respect of mortgages of the fund; payments under the lender's mortgage insurance policies in respect of principal outstanding under mortgages; and any compensation received from a mortgage manager for outstanding principal under any mortgage.

[27] For further detail, see S. Gangwani, 'MBS Structuring: Concepts and Techniques' (1998) 1 *The Securitization Conduit* 26, 32.

[28] P. Murray and B. Hadaway, 'Mortgage-Backed Securities: An Investigation of Legal and Financial Issues' (1986) 11 *Journal of Corporation Law* 203, 210.

[29] (1862) 10 HL Cas 191, 211; [1861] All ER Rep 414, 418 as explained in *Tailby v Official Receiver* (1888) 13 App Cas 523; [1886–90] ALL ER Rep 486 HL; and D. Campbell (ed.), *International Asset Securitisation and Other Financing Tools* (N.Y.: Transnational Publishers, 2000) Ch. 8.

> tion in the contract, there is no doubt that a Court of Equity would compel him to perform the contract, and that the contract would, in equity, transfer the beneficial interest to the … purchaser immediately on the property being acquired.

Therefore, when an originator makes a further advance on a mortgage that has been securitised, the debt that the originator acquires will be transferred automatically to the issuing vehicle in accordance with the sale agreement. On the same principle, it would also become subject to the trustee issuer's security.

3.4 Setting Up a Special Purpose Vehicle

A special purpose vehicle (SPV) is a legal entity that has been set up for a specific (and limited) purpose by another entity, known as the sponsoring firm. An SPV can take the form of a corporation, trust, partnership, subsidiary company of the originator, or a limited liability company. In Australia, the larger SPVs are established as master trusts. An SPV is established not only to offer securities to the market but also to ensure the bankruptcy-remoteness of the RMBS programme. Larger SPVs comprise two classes of trust funds—namely, warehouse funds and sub-funds. Both these trust funds create a pursuant to the trust deed for the Master Trust. A warehouse fund is used to originate housing loans funded by a single investor, called a "warehousing investor", in preparation for a securitisation in the future. The purpose of a sub-fund is to issue bonds or notes, and to use the sale proceeds from the issue of those securities to acquire housing loans from a warehouse fund or other mortgage originator. Each warehouse fund and sub-fund is a separate and independent trust within the Master Trust fund, and in keeping with equitable principles proscribing the commingling of trust funds, the assets and liabilities of each fund are segregated from those of every other warehouse fund or sub-fund.[30]

The trustee-issuer of the Master Trust fund issues bonds, such as RMBSs, pursuant to provisions in the trust and a sub-fund notice. Again, consistent with equitable principles about the commingling of trust funds, the assets of the Master Trust cannot be used to meet the liabilities of any

[30] Macquarie Bank's PUMA programme is one such Master Trust fund in Australia: see *Master Information Memorandum, PUMA Fund P-7*, paragraph 2.

other trusts, and none of the assets of other trusts are available to meet the liabilities of the Master Trust fund.[31]

Eventually, beneficial interest in the SPV is held by the capital and income unit holders. The capital and income unit holders are only entitled to receive payments or distributions subject to prior ranking entitlements described under the general priority of payment under the trust deed.[32]

3.5 Transferring Lender's Rights

When the process of mortgage origination and the structure of the SPV is in operation, the rights of the original mortgagees must be transferred to the SPV in a manner that is legally effective and commercially practical. A legal or equitable assignment can be utilised for a transfer of mortgagee rights from a mortgage originator to a third party.[33] In terms of an effective legal assignment, the mortgagee's rights would be vested absolutely in the SPV. Under an equitable assignment, the SPV would be recognised in equity as having acquired those mortgagee rights, but not in law—in law, the transferor would remain their legal "owner", holding the mortgagee rights on bare trust for the SPV as trustee for the bondholders.[34]

Smaller banks and IMPs typically equitably assign their mortgages to a "warehouse trust fund" or "sub-fund" administered by a larger bank, which also sponsors the RMBS programme. In such a case, the instrument

[31] See, for example, *Master Information Memorandum, PUMA Fund P-7*, paragraphs 4.17, 7.4. See also K. N. Klee, and B. C. Butler, 'Asset-Backed Securitization, Special Purpose Vehicles and Other Securitization Issues' (2002) 35 (2) *Uniform Commercial Code Law Journal* 23. S. Senarath (2016), Not so '"Bankruptcy-Remote": An insight into Sri Lankan Securitization Practices in a Post_GFC Context' (Paper presented at the MAC-MME conference, Prague, Czech Republic); Senarath, S. 'The Dodd-Frank Act doesn't solve the principal-agent problem in asset securitisation' (2017) *blogs.lse.ac.uk* (11 November 2018).

[32] For instance, in the context of Macquarie Bank's PUMA Fund, the ultimate beneficial interest is held by the fund manager Macquarie Securitisation Ltd as capital and income unit holder. See, *Master Information Memorandum, PUMA Sub-Fund Series 2014*, at p 21.

[33] These concepts, and their relevance to RMBS issues, are discussed in more detail in Chap. 5.

[34] In the context of the Macquarie Bank's PUMA programme, see, *Master Information Memorandum, PUMA Fund P-7*, paragraphs 5.1–5.3.

of assignment provides that the transfer is to be perfected or completed in particular circumstances,[35] such as the mortgage originator entering into administration or going into liquidation.[36]

In the case of Australian mortgagees, rights in all RMBS programmes in practice are sold by way of legal assignment to the SPV that issues the RMBSs. The SPV then becomes the "lender of record" for these housing loans and ultimately receives all repayments from borrowers. In purchasing the mortgages in this way from the originator at their market value, the trustee or security trustee of the SPV becomes, in law, the mortgagee of the residential properties in the pool.[37]

It is crucial that the assignment is structured such that mortgages in the pool are distinct from insolvency risks associated with the originator. To utilise the US idiom that has found its way into the Australian market classification, the assignment or transfer is structured so as to be "bankruptcy-remote"[38] to achieve investor acceptance in the capital market securities.[39] Usually bankruptcy-remoteness is achieved by ensuring that the assignment or transfer constitutes a "true sale" by the originator to the SPV. Given that the sale is perceived to be "arm's length" at a valid market price, and its timing is at least six months before any stakeholder insolvency, afterward even if the mortgage originator becomes insolvent, the mortgaged properties in the pool will generally, under insolvency law, be insulated from other assets of the originator that may be used to satisfy its creditors.[40] The separation of

[35] See D. Glennie and E. Bouter, *Securitisation* (London: Kluwer Law International, 1998) 4–5.

[36] The consequences of the mortgage originator becoming insolvent are discussed in further detail in Chap. 7.

[37] While the trustee (or security trustee, if any) of the SPV holds the legal title to the residential mortgage loans, investors in the RMBSs acquire a concomitant beneficial interest by paying a price for the loan receivables equal to their present value. This present value reflects the rate of return the trustee-issuer wants to offer to the investors and must be lower than the inherent rate of return of the loan receivables if the overall transaction is to be profitable.

[38] Insolvency-remote in this context means that the SPV is unlikely to be adversely affected by a bankruptcy of the originator. Such insolvency issues are discussed in Chap. 7. See also T. J. Gordon, 'Securitization of Executory Future Flows as Bankruptcy-Remote True Sales' (2000) 67 (4) *The University of Chicago Law Review* 1317.

[39] L. R. Lupica, 'Circumvention of the Bankruptcy Process: The Statutory Institutionalization of Securitization' (2000) 33 *Connecticut Law Review* 199.

[40] G. Engel and A. Koslow, 'Securitization Advise for Asset-Based Lenders', in J. Cunningham (ed.), *Asset Based Financing* (N.Y.: Practising Law Institute, 1996) 479.

the originator from the mortgaged assets generally also enables funds to be raised at less cost, through securities issued by the SPV, than if the originator were to raise funds in its own right.[41]

The SPV may pay surplus income from the mortgage receivables, which is not needed to repay the loan securities, to either the originator so that the originator takes the profit (e.g. as servicing fees), or to the programme sponsor, or perhaps even both.

3.6 The Fund Manager

An administrator, also referred as the fund manager, is appointed in order to manage the fund assets on behalf of the trustee-issuer, and to exercise the trustee-issuer's rights and powers and discharge its obligations, if required.[42] Depending on the nature of the RMBS programme, the extent of role of the fund manager may vary. The fund manager is often required to make payments on behalf of the issuer—this includes payments to investors in its RMBSs through authorised paying agents,[43] gathering interest and principal payments from mortgagors, administering investments and borrowings, discharging loans and related securities on redemption, monitoring arrears, and ensuring the safe custody of title deeds and documents. Regular detailed reports are required to be submitted to rating agencies. The trustee-issuer generally executes a management deed[44] outlining the scope of the fund manager's duties.[45]

[41] Bankers Trust, 'Securitisation in Australia' (May 1999) *Asiamoney* 17, 18; Standard and Poor's, (July 2003); and A. Finch, 'Securitisation' (1995) 6 *Journal of Banking and Finance Law and Practice* 247, 262.

[42] For example, in the context of the PUMA programme, Macquarie Securitisation Ltd is typically appointed as fund manager: see, *Master Information Memorandum, PUMA Fund P-7*, paragraph 7.3.

[43] The fund manager is typically authorised to withdraw funds from the issuer's bank accounts for these purposes.

[44] See, for example, *Master Information Memorandum, PUMA Sub-Fund Series 2014, p 99.*

[45] This management deed may entrust the fund manager with other powers. For example, in Macquarie Bank's PUMA programme, the fund manager retains the legal right to reset the interest rate and take enforcement proceedings: see, *Master Information Memorandum, PUMA Fund P-7*, paragraph 5.2. However, the fund manager is itself subject to fiduciary obligations with regard to the manner in which it exercises these powers: see, for example, *Master Information Memorandum, PUMA Fund P-7*, paragraphs 4.1–4.5. Moreover, the trust deed does not typically extend to authorising the fund manager to sell mortgages or release them without the security trustee's authorisation: see, for example, *Master Information*

However, as we have noted earlier, the role and responsibilities of the fund manager depend on the nature of the programme. For example, in some RMBS programmes, these roles are split along functional lines. Thus, the fund manager is appointed only to manage the assets and any liabilities of the trust fund and make payments to investors. For example, a collection manager will be appointed by the trustee-issuer to collect housing loans repayments. A servicer may be appointed to monitor arrears and discharge loans and securities on final payout of the loan. A custodian might be appointed to ensure safe custody of title deeds and related documents.

To the extent authorised by the trustee-issuer, the fund manager acts in the capacity of a disclosed agent[46] of the trustee[47] and, provided it acts within the bounds of its authority, is not liable to bondholders or others for the debt issued by the trustee of the SPV.

The fund manager is required to regularly report to the trustee-issuer as part of its duties, during the life of the RMBS issue. In order to perform its obligations, the fund manager is generally entitled to a comprehensive range of regular information about the fund. These include copies of quarterly or monthly management accounts, details of further advances and substitutions, where permitted, cash flow projections, arrears figures and enforcement action being taken, movements of title deeds and other documents, and the issuer's audited annual financial statements.

3.7 Credit Enhancement

Once the SPV, the issuing entity, has been established, the issuer needs to structure the classes of securities, while achieving the intended credit ratings. This is the point where credit rating agencies enter into the process by awarding ratings to the bonds based on securitised assets. Credit enhancement is used to arrive at the targeted rating of the bonds. In this manner, credit enhancement fills the gap between the actual quality of the

Memorandum, PUMA Fund P-7, paragraph 5.2. Furthermore, upon the occurrence of certain events specified in the management deed, the fund manager's appointment can be terminated and a new manager appointed. Those circumstances include the commencement of winding up of the fund manager, and the appointment of a receiver to the fund manager: see, for example, *Master Information Memorandum, PUMA Fund P-7*, paragraph 7.1.

[46] See, for example, S. Fisher, *Agency Law* (Sydney: Butterworths, 2000) Chaps. 4 and 9.

[47] E.g. in entering contacts on behalf of the trustee.

underlying assets and the intended ratings.[48] The ratings agencies usually require that the structure of an RMBS programme be, so far as is practicable, free from financial risks.[49] Particularly for smaller banks and IMPs, the ratings of the bonds issued—and therefore the net cost of funding an RMBS issue—are directly dependent on the credit enhancement they can shelter. Key methods used to enhance the credit quality of RMBSs issued in Australia include mortgage insurance, subordinated bond structures, and cash reserves.[50]

3.7.1 *Mortgage Insurance as a Means of Credit Enhancement*

In reality, the lenders' mortgage insurance policies[51] provide full insurance coverage of the principal and interest outstanding on the mortgage loans acquired by the SPV. Each mortgage insurance policy generally includes

[48] David Jones, 'Emerging problems with the Basel Capital Accord: Regulatory Capital Arbitrage and Related Issues' (2000) 24 *Journal of Banking & Finance* 35; Samantha Menzies, 'Increased Scrutiny' (2015) 5 *Australian Securitisation Journal* 12.

[49] Standard and Poor's, 'Mortgage-Backed Criteria' (1999) *Structured Finance Australia and New Zealand* 38–39; L. Hsu and C. Mohebbi, 'Credit Enhancement in ABS Structure' in F. J. Fabozzi (ed.), *Accessing Capital Markets Through Securitization* (Pennsylvania: FJA Associates, 2001) 35. These risks include credit risk, liquidity risk, and revenue risk. Credit risk is the risk of loss resulting to the issuer if a home loan borrower defaults. Liquidity risk is the risk of delay between the receipt of funds from the home loan borrower, and the due date for payment of interest on the securities and other expenses. Revenue risk can be subdivided into "interest rate differential" risk (i.e. the risk that the interest payments being made by the home loan borrowers will be insufficient for the issuer to make the interest payments due on the RMBSs issued) and re-investment risk (i.e. the risk that the rate of return on the issuer's liquid funds will be less than that which is due on the securities issued). Each of these risks can be minimised or managed by various mechanisms, including interest rate futures, options, and swaps. A detailed discussion of these instruments is beyond the scope of this book. However, for a broad overview of these risk management tools in an Australian context, see, for example, G. Pierson et al., *Business Finance* (Sydney: McGraw-Hill, 2002); S. Bishop et al., *Corporate Finance* (Sydney: Pearson Education, 2000); or R. Bruce et al., *Handbook of Australian Corporate Finance* (5th edition, Sydney: Butterworths, 1997).

[50] Other methods include over-collateralisation (discussed separately below) and, as noted earlier, third-party guarantees. For a detailed discussion of credit enhancement methods, see L. Hsu and C. Mohebbi (2001) 35.

[51] For example, Commercial Union Australia Mortgage Insurance Corporation Ltd (CUAMIC); Housing Loan Insurance Corporation (HLIC); MGICA Ltd; Sun Alliance and Royal Mortgage Insurance Ltd: *Master Information Memorandum, PUMA Fund P-7*, paragraph 8.

cash flow cover entitling the SPV to receive scheduled payments of principal and interest for a maximum period of two years, in respect of mortgage loans, which are more than 30 days delinquent.[52] However, lenders' mortgage insurance will typically not cover losses that occur as a result of, among other things, fraud by the trustee, originator, manager, or their agents; a right of set-off by the borrower against the trustee; or the re-opening of "unjust" mortgages (as defined by section 70 of the *National Credit Code*).[53]

One potential disadvantage of mortgage insurance is that the ratings of RMBSs issued can be downgraded if the insurer's ability to pay out on claims is threatened.

3.7.2 *Structural Credit Enhancements*

Another form of credit enhancement identified in the overseas literature,[54] and perhaps sometimes used in Australia, is to divide the RMBSs on issue into senior and junior securities. When the credit enhancement comes from the structure of the liabilities, it is referred as structural enhancement—especially in securitisation when there are different asset classes with different priorities of payment, where junior classes provide protection to senior asset classes.

Accordingly, structural credit enhancement essentially applies to the senior notes but not the subordinated notes. The repayments from the home loan borrowers are first used to pay interest on these senior bonds, which have a claim over the entire cash flow to get paid first.[55] Being lower risk, these senior bonds are characterised by a relatively low rate of return.

Let us say for an asset structure comprising Class A, Class B, and Class C, the most junior class will provide protection from default to the B and A classes. On the other hand, the B class provides enhancements to the A class. In this manner, receivables are used to pay senior securities first, making them the safest asset class. Next comes the mezzanine class and then the junior class. The last class, referred as "toxic waste" in finance jargon is similar to equity holders in a company, who are exposed to the

[52] See, for example, *Master Information Memorandum, PUMA Fund P-7*, paragraph 6.1.
[53] Ibid, The *Consumer Credit Code* is also discussed in further detail in Chap. 5.
[54] See, for example, L. Hsu and C. Mohebbi, (2001) 35, 37.
[55] See, for instance, *Master Information Memorandum, PUMA Fund P-7*, paragraph 4.5.

risk of losing capital and interest. As a result, senior classes may gain a higher (e.g. AAA) rating and yield a lower interest rate (see, e.g. Fig. 1.2). Lower classes get comparatively lower rating and thus gain comparatively higher yield. As far as structured credit enhancement is considered, in contrast to other forms of enhancements, it is a re-allocation of risk at the cost of other classes. On the other hand, other methods provide credit enhancement to the entire transaction.[56]

3.7.3 *Cash Collaterals*

A third method of credit enhancement[57] is for the sponsor, usually via the SPV, to hold a specific cash reserve to address liquidity risk. In this way, liquid funds are available in the event of a delay between the trustee-issuer receiving funds from the home loan borrowers and having to make payments to bondholders.

In simple terms, cash collaterals refer to the cash retained by an SPV. For cash collaterals to be effective as a means of credit enhancement, cash collaterals should be subordinate to the interests of the investor. Cash collaterals can be gained in several ways—retaining a portion of funding by the SPV at the beginning or as a subordinated loan at the beginning. On the other hand, retention of excess profits can build up cash collaterals. In this manner, cash collaterals can be both credit enhancement as well as liquidity enhancement. For example, let us consider a pool of residential mortgages worth $100 million. The originator transfers it to the SPV. The SPV then raises $100 million and transfers only $90 million to the originator. The remaining $10 million is the cash collateral that acts as credit enhancement.[58]

[56] Sandaer A Davidson, Wolff L and Ching A, *Securitization: Structuring and Investment Analysis* (John Wiley & Sons 2003).

[57] Again, see, for example, L. Hsu and C. Mohebbi (2001) 35.

[58] For example, Macquarie Bank's PUMA Fund holds a cash reserve known as a "principal cash balance": see, *Master Information Memorandum, PUMA Fund P-7*, paragraphs 6.4 and 4.4.7. On each issue date, a certain amount of the proceeds of the issue of bonds is held as a principal cash balance, which is invested in authorised investments other than mortgages: see, *Master Information Memorandum, PUMA Fund P-7*, paragraph 7.5. The fund manager determines the amount to be held as the principal cash balance from time to time. Provided this does not result in a downgrading in the rating of the PUMA bonds, the principal cash balance must not at any time be greater than 2% of the then principal balance of all the bonds: *Master Information Memorandum, PUMA Fund P-7* paragraph 4.4.7. If the collec-

3.8 Issuance of Securities

3.8.1 *"The Bonds"*

RMBSs are bonds secured by a portfolio of mortgages over residential property. The bonds themselves are typically collateralised by a portfolio of security properties held in the mortgage pool, sometimes in addition to contractual "debt recourse" obligations, mortgage insurance, guarantees, or a combination of these risk-reduction[59] methods. Indeed, the bonds are usually over-collateralised.[60] They are typically structured in Australia as corporate bonds or commercial paper, with interest being at a fixed or variable rate, generally paid quarterly or semi-annually, and principal being paid at maturity of the bond facility,[61] which is usually after a term of up to 35 years in Australia.[62] This cash flow structure tends more to suit the

tions on housing loans, and any other collections, on a particular payment date are insufficient to meet the expenses of the fund, including interest on the bonds, then the principal cash balance is used to pay those expenses.

[59] Or strictly, risk-transfer methods.

[60] The value of the collateral in mortgage-backed securities is the liquidation value of the underlying security properties. There are a number of reasons for over-collateralising bonds. First, the cash flow from the residential loans accrues first to the originator, and only then to the pool and ultimately to bondholders. Therefore, there is a risk that balance available from the mortgage pool may not keep pace with the issuer's obligations in relation to principal and interest payments on the bonds. Second, additional collateral protects bondholders against defaults on individual loans and against any decline in the market value of the security properties between valuation dates. Third, originators typically prefer this arrangement over higher-paying yields to investors as compensation for higher default risk and possible depreciation in the value of security properties. Payments on the excess collateral are reinvested and returned to the originators when the bonds are paid off: see C. Pavel, 'Securitization' (Jul-Aug. 1986) *Economic Perspective (Federal Reserve Bank of Chicago)* 16, 18. The value of the collateral is reviewed regularly and, when appropriate, re-valued to the market value of the pooled assets. The issuer may be required to "top up" the value of the collateral during the life of the bond issue to cover any prepayments or defaults.

[61] See F. Fabozzi, (ed.), *The Handbook of Mortgage-Backed Securities* (Massachusetts: Probus Publishing Co, 1995) Ch. 16, 263.

[62] For example, bonds issued by the trustee of Macquarie Bank's PUMA Fund are structured as pass-through debt securities, issued by the trustee-issuer as floating rate or fixed rate bonds: see, *Master Information Memorandum, PUMA Fund P-7*, paragraphs 2 and 4.3. The bonds are secured by residential mortgages and other "authorised investments" in the Fund. Bonds will initially be issued in minimum parcels of a least $1,000,000, although each bond has a denomination (or face value) of $10,000. Bonds issued by the trustee of the PUMA Fund are offered to professional investors and accordingly do not need to comply with the disclosure provisions relating to investors in section 708 of the *Corporations Act*. See, *Master*

requirements of institutional investors, many of whom prefer quarterly or semi-annual payments to the monthly principal and interest payments produced by residential mortgage loans.[63]

3.8.2 *Issuance of Securities*

The process of issuing the RMBSs typically commences with the trustee-issuer authorising a lead manager and/or a co-manager to sell some or all of the bonds in the primary market. The co-manager is usually required to underwrite the entire issue, although both the co-manager and the lead manager are involved in the marketing and distribution of the bonds to

Information Memorandum, PUMA Fund P-7, paragraphs 1.8 and 1.10. For a further discussion, see Chap. 6.

The bonds are issued in multiple series, with each series giving investors different rights. A series may comprise three classes of bonds: (1) senior bonds, (2) subordinated bonds, and (3) fast prepayment bonds. Principal repayments on senior and subordinated bonds are made on quarterly coupon interest payment dates, and on fast prepayment bonds, they are made on monthly coupon interest payment dates. As a general rule, interest and principal payments on senior and fast prepayment bonds rank ahead of those payments on subordinated bonds: see, *Master Information Memorandum, PUMA Fund P-7* paragraphs 4.3.5–4.3.7, 4.8. Senior bonds in each series are divided into tranches, and bear floating or fixed rate coupon interest. Subordinated bondholders are generally subordinated in favour of senior and Fast Prepayment bondholders in relation to both interest and principal. Fast prepayment bonds bear monthly payments of floating rate coupon interest and principal and convert to senior bonds if they are not fully repaid by the first quarterly coupon interest and payment date. These bonds are issued to assist in the funding of redraws of prepaid principal by borrowers and principal increases and further advances on the mortgage loans.

The bonds are typically issued in the form of registered securities. The actual debt obligation is constituted in a separate document from the security itself. In the separate document, the issuer promises to pay the investors, who from time to time appear on a register as a holder of the relevant security. Each bondholder is issued with a "Bondholder Acknowledgement" under which the trustee-issuer acknowledges that the bondholder has been entered in the register as the holder of particular bonds. See, *Master Information Memorandum, PUMA Fund P-7*, paragraphs 4.12 and 4.13.

[63] The payment of principal and interest on the bonds themselves is not dependent upon the cash flow of the underlying loan assets. Housing loan repayments typically comprise principal and interest (to reduce the risk of borrowers' default), but such payments are said to be inconvenient for institutional investors, since the capital and income components of the repayments must be separated for different tax treatments, and the frequency of repayments does not generally match the frequency of payments under the trustee-issuer's own obligations to investors: see F.J. Fabozzi, 'Mortgages', in F.J. Fabozzi (ed.), *The Handbook of Mortgage-Backed Securities* (Massachusetts: Probus Publishing Co, 1995) 9–10.

investors. Conditions on secondary market sales by initial investors are generally contained in the documentation governing primary market sales.[64]

After issuance, the bonds are uploaded to (or electronically lodged in) the Austraclear system,[65] and Austraclear Ltd becomes the registered holder of the bonds.[66] In Australia, virtually all RMBSs are issued as registered securities under the *Corporations Act*.[67]

3.9 Balance Sheet Concerns of RMBSs

Assuming Australian Prudential Regulation Authority (APRA) grants regulatory relief, as demonstrated in the following Table (Table 3.1), the cash raised by an RMBS issue does not usually require an offsetting liability to be shown on the originator's balance sheet. From the originator's view point, the cash represents proceeds of the sale of mortgage receivables to the SPV.

[64] For instance, under Macquarie Bank's PUMA programme, the bondholders are entitled to transfer their bonds in the secondary market subject to the following conditions:

- The offer for sale or invitation to purchase of the bonds is not an offer or invitation that requires disclosure under Part 6D.2 of the *Corporations Act*.
- The transfer must be made in compliance with Part 6D.2 of the *Corporations Act*.

The bonds are only purchased or sold by execution and registration of a Transfer and Acceptance in the prescribed form: see *Master Information Memorandum, PUMA Fund P-7*, paragraphs 4.12–4.15. The Bond Transfer and Acceptance Form must be duly stamped (if applicable), executed by the transferor and the transferee, and lodged for registration, together with a Bondholder Acknowledgement under which the trustee-issuer acknowledges that the bondholder has been entered in the register as the holder of securities.

The trustee-issuer may refuse registration of the Bond Transfer and Acceptance if it is not duly executed or if it would result in a contravention of terms of the trust deed or relevant legislation. The trustee-issuer is not, under the conditions of the bond issue, bound to provide reasons for any refusal of registration.

Upon receipt of the transfer and acceptance form, the trustee-issuer registers the transferee in the Register of Bond Acceptance Transfers, which under the conditions of the bond issue constitutes passing of title in the bond to the transferee. Until this occurs, the trustee can recognise only the transferor as the holder, and all payment notices are made in the interim to the transferor.

[65] Secondary market trades are effected by book entry transfers in the Austraclear system, rather than physical delivery of particular bond certificates.

[66] See, *Master Information Memorandum, PUMA Fund P-7*, paragraph 4.19.

[67] See Chap. 6 for further detail.

Table 3.1 Balance sheet impact of securitising assets of ABC Bank

Assume, for expository purposes:			
Assets	*Liabilities*	*Equity*	*Ratio*
Receivables $100[a]	Debt $100	Equity $100	Debt/equity = 1/1
Equipment $100			
1. If ABC Bank borrows $100, secured by its receivables, its ratio of debt to equity deteriorates:			
Assets	*Liabilities*	*Equity*	*Ratio worse*
Cash $100	Debt $200	Equity $100	Debt/equity = 2/1
2. But if ABC Bank sells $100 of its receivables (e.g. to an SPV):			
Assets	*Liabilities*	*Equity*	*Ratio unchanged*
Cash $100	Debt $100	Equity $100	Debt/equity = 1/1
Equipment $100			
3. And if ABC Bank then uses (e.g.) $90 of its cash to pay off some of its debt, its ratio of debt to equity dramatically improves:			
Assets	*Liabilities*	*Equity*	*Ratio improved*
Cash $10	Debt $10	Equity $100	Debt/equity= 1/10
Equipment $100			

[a]For simplification purposes, mortgage receivables are recorded as $100: This diagram is based on S. L. Schwarcz, *Structured Finance* (N.Y.: Practising Law Institute, 1993) 2. See also S. Senarath, 'Securitisation and the global financial crisis: can risk retention prevent another crisis?' (2017) 18 *International Journal of Business and Globalisation*, 153

The Table assumes that the receivables are sold at face value

3.9.1 *Off-Balance Sheet Exposure*

Provided that the originator is a bank or another financial institution that is required to maintain a minimum balance of risk-based capital under the capital adequacy guidelines,[68] securitisation permits the originator to sell mortgage loan assets[69] in respect of which it would otherwise be required to maintain capital. Assigning its rights as mortgage lender therefore, where other factors remain constant, reduces the bank's regulatory compliance costs, and its overall cost of funds.

[68] See Chap. 4 for a discussion of capital adequacy requirements for Authorised Deposit-taking Institutions (ADIs).

[69] I.e. loans reflected as assets on its balance sheet.

On the other hand, an originator may be restricted by its indenture covenants from incurring or securing debt beyond a specified level. Securitisation may enable the originator to nevertheless raise cash in such a way that it complies with these covenants, since the originator is selling assets, rather than incurring additional debt.

3.10 Summary

This discussion has examined the mechanics in structuring a residential mortgage securitisation programme in Australia. They can be summarised as[70]:

(i) Origination: making or purchasing mortgage loans.
(ii) Transferring the loans to a special purpose vehicle (SPV): in Australia, this SPV is invariably structured as a trust, whose funds comprise the principal and interest repayments from the initial housing loan borrowers, as well as the prices paid by investors for the mortgage-backed bonds it issues.
(iii) Arranging for the credit enhancement: various means, including mortgage insurance, senior-subordinated debt structures, cash reserves, over-collateralisation, and third-party guarantees.
(iv) Regulatory compliance: including arrangements for regulatory relief from APRA for capital adequacy purposes.
(v) Issuing the RMBSs.
(vi) Operating and managing the trust fund: includes the mortgage pool.
(vii) Seeking to influence secondary market sales of RMBSs already issued.

From theoretical and practical perspectives, a number of key issues arise throughout this processes that are addressed further in subsequent discussion. These key issues include the impact of capital adequacy requirements for prudential supervision purposes, including whether the current risk-weighting of RMBSs is appropriate, how a "true sale" of mortgagee rights to the SPV is to be effected, and how

[70] For a description of the various structures of securitisation transactions, see D. C. Bonsall (ed.), *Securitisation* (London: Butterworths, 1990) Ch 1; R. S. Borod (ed.), *Securitization – Asset-Backed and Mortgaged- Backed Securities* (Boston: Brown, Rudnick, Freed & Gesmer, 1995); and J. C. Shenker and A. J. Colletta, (1991).

the potential problems arising from the assignment of such rights are to be minimised or eliminated; how an SPV is to be structured so that it is "insolvency-remote"; consequences of any one stakeholder (or a number of them) in the chain becoming insolvent; together with techniques of minimising the risk of such insolvency for other participants.

Bibliography

Books and Book Chapters

Bishop, S. R., Crapp, H. R., Faff, R. W. and Twite, G. J., *Corporate Finance*, 4th edition, Sydney: Pearson Education, 2000.

Bonsall, D. C. (ed.), *Securitisation*, London: Butterworths, 1990.

Boolean, M., 'Mortgage Securitisation in the United Kingdom' in C. Stone, A. Zissu and J. Lederman (eds.), *Asset Securitisation Theory and Practice in Europe*, London: Euromoney Publications, 1991.

Borod, R. S. (ed.), *Securitization, Asset-Backed Securities and Mortgage-Backed Securities*, Boston: Brown, Rudnick, Freed & Gesmer, 1995.

Bruce, R., McKern, B., Pollard, I. and Skully, M., *Handbook of Australian Corporate Finance*, 5th edition, Sydney: Butterworths, 1997.

Campbell, D. (ed.), *International Asset Securitization and Other Financing Tools*, N.Y.: Transnational Publishers, 2000.

Davidson, S. A., Wolff, L. and Ching, A., *Securitization: Structuring and Investment Analysis*, New Jersey, John Wiley & Sons 2003.

Fabozzi, F. J. (ed.), *The Handbook of Mortgage-Backed Securities*, Massachusetts: Probus Publishing Company, 1995.

Fisher, S., *Agency Law*, Sydney: Butterworths, 2000.

Frankel, T., *Securitization: Structured Financing, Financial Asset Pools, and Asset-Backed Securities*, Boston: Little Brown & Co, 1991, v I and v II.

Glennie, D. and Bouter, E., *Securitisation*, London: Kluwer Law International, 1998.

Hsu, L. and Mohebbi, C., 'Credit Enhancement in ABS Structure', in F. J. Fabozzi (ed.), *Accessing Capital Markets Through Securitization*, Pennsylvania: FJA Associates, 2001.

Pierson, G., Brown, R., Easton, S. and Howard, P., *Business Finance*, 8th edition, Sydney: McGraw-Hill, 2002.

Schwarcz, S. L. and Ford, A. D., *Structured Finance: A Guide to the Principles of Asset Securitization*, N.Y.: Practising Law Institute, 2002 (Loose-Leaf Service).

Journal Articles

Engel, G. and Koslow, A., 'Securitization Advice for Asset-Based Lenders', in J. Cunningham (ed.), *Asset Based Financing*, N.Y.: Practising Law Institute, 1996.

Gangwani, S., 'MBS Structuring: Concepts and Techniques' (1998) 1 *The Securitization Conduit* 26.

Gordon, T. J., 'Securitization of Executory Future Flows as Bankruptcy-Remote True Sales' (2000) 67 (4) *The University of Chicago Law Review* 1317.

Jones, D., 'Emerging problems with the Basel Capital Accord: Regulatory Capital Arbitrage and Related Issues' (2000) 24 *Journal of Banking & Finance* 35.

Klee, K. N. and Butler, B. C., 'Asset-Backed Securitization, Special Purpose Vehicles and Other Securitization Issues' (2002) 35 (2) *Uniform Commercial Code Law Journal* 23.

Lupica, L. R., 'Circumvention of the Bankruptcy Process: the Statutory Institutionalisation of Securitization' (2000) 33 *Connecticut Law Review* 199.

Menzies, S., 'Increased Scrutiny' (2015) 5 *Australian Securitisation Journal* 12.

Murray, P. C. and Hadaway, B. L., 'Mortgage-Backed Securities: An Investigation of Legal and Financial Issues' (1986) 11 *The Journal of Corporation Law* 203.

Ramsay, I. M., 'Financial Innovation and Regulation: the Case of Securitisation' (1993) 4 (3) *Journal of Banking and Finance Law and Practice* 169.

Senarath, S., 'Securitisation and the global financial crisis: can risk retention prevent another crisis?' (2017) 18 *International Journal of Business and Globalisation* 153.

Shenker, J. C. and Colletta, A.J., 'Asset Securitization: Evolution' Current Issues and New Frontiers' (1991) 69 Texas Law Review 1369.

Working Papers, Magazines, Newspapers and Reports

Giddy, I. H., Asset Securitization: A Cost-Benefit Analysis, Stern School of Business, New York University, 2001, http://www.giddy.org/abs-hypo.htm

Robinson, T., 'Securitisation Update,' *Seventh Annual Credit Law Conference*, BLEC, Melbourne, September 1997.

Standard and Poor's, 'RMBS, CDO Activity Lead Australian Securitisation Issuance Growth in 2003', *Credit Ratings Commentary and News,* July 2003.

Johnson, M. B., 'OZ Securitisation Gathers Pace' (March 2001) *Asiamoney* 47.

Anonymous, 'PUMA Securitisation Pioneer' (May 1999) *Euroweek* 6.

Macquarie Securitisation Ltd, *The PUMA Fund P-7: Master Information Memorandum*, Sydney, February, 2000.

Macquarie Securitisation Ltd., *Master Information Memorandum, PUMA Sub-Fund Series* 2014, Sydney, July 2014.

Bankers Trust, 'Securitisation in Australia' (May 1999) *Asiamoney* 17.

Finch, A., 'Securitisation' (1995) 6 (4) *Journal of Banking and Finance Law and Practice* 247.

Senarath, S. 'The Dodd-Frank Act doesn't solve the principal-agent problem in asset securitisation' (2017) *blogs.lse.ac.uk*. http://blogs.lse.ac.uk/businessreview/2017/04/21/the-dodd-frank-act-doesnt-solve-the-principal-agent-problem-in-asset-securitisation/

Senarath, S., Not so "Bankruptcy-Remote': An insight into Sri Lankan Securitization Practices in a Post_GFC Context' (Paper presented at the MAC-MME conference 2016, Prague, Czech Republic).

Standard and Poor's, 'Credit Ratings on Mortgage-Backed Securities', *Structured Finance Australia and New Zealand*, Melbourne, 1998.

CHAPTER 4

Mortgage Origination

This chapter focuses on three key concerns—namely, "security" as a concept that relates to the securitisation process, legal consequences for various stakeholders of registering that security and thus it is available to be searched on public records, and the likely impact of Australian Prudential Regulation Authority's (APRA) capital adequacy guidelines on various stakeholders. The above legal and regulatory concerns arise in the mortgage origination process and are examined with a view of assessing their impact upon the growth of the residential mortgage-backed security (RMBS) market.

4.1 A Mortgage as "Security"

For our discussion, a residential mortgage is identified as a transfer of an interest in property by a housing loan borrower to a mortgage originator as security for the repayment of the housing loan. A mortgage is thus created by the borrower, as mortgagor, transferring rights over the security property to the originator, as mortgagee, whom it provides with rights against the mortgaged property, including the right to sell the security property, as well as the right to enforce against the mortgagor's promise to pay.

English law recognises a security as "real" or "personal". Australian law too recognises this fundamental difference. The concepts of the mortgage, lien, and charge are said to have their roots in the Roman law

P. Rajapakse, S. Senarath, *Commercial Law Aspects of Residential Mortgage Securitisation in Australia*,
https://doi.org/10.1007/978-3-030-00605-1_4

transactions of *fiducia* (the basic mortgage), *pignus* (possessory security), and *hypotheca* (hypothecation or charge).[1] Personal securities can be classified into "choses in action" and "choses in possession". Choses in possession refers to the intangible rights over property that are enforceable by legal action, are generally more relevant for our discussion, except at the point of the borrower's redemption of the mortgage (e.g. upon early payout of the loan), or where the security trustee exercises its rights as mortgagee in possession.[2]

There is a plethora of scholarly legal writing on the fine distinctions between "property", "proprietary", and "ownership" interests attributed to the concept of "security". The search for the "proprietary" interest in a security has largely been resolved on the test of whether, once the relevant *res* has been identified, the attendant rights are rights *in rem* or rights *in personam*.[3] Salmond contends that the principle of "ownership" is based on the relative rights of competing stakeholders,[4] while Sykes has extended this theory by arguing that these rights are conglomerations of rights in a composite sense, capable of both individual and separate existence, and alienation.[5]

In the Australian context, in RMBS programmes, all mortgages comprising the mortgage pool are registered on each property's certificate of title, under the Torrens system. This creates a statutory charge over the

[1] E. I. Sykes and S. Walker, *The Law of Securities* (5th edition, Sydney: LBC, 1993) 16–18. See also T Frankel, *Structured Financing, Financial Assets Pools and Asset-Backed Securities* (Boston: Little Brown Co., 1991) 232–235; and D. Everett, 'Securities Over Receivables', in M. Gillooly (ed.) *Securities Over Personality* (Sydney: The Federation Press, 1994) 55.

[2] See Chap. 7 for further details.

[3] It has been argued, albeit in a US context, that the affiliated or extended meaning of "security" as described, for example, in section. 92(2) of the *Corporations Act,* is consistent with the notion of a "security" in the general law sense, where a justifiable or real link can be established between the instruments and the subject security property (the *res*) to which a proprietary interest may be traced. If this interpretation is accepted, a mortgage-backed security (based on mortgages of real property interests) may be one example of a derivative "security", in the sense that existence of the financial "security" is dependent on and flows from the security transaction and is incapable of an existence apart from the mortgage. Other statutes also define tradable investment instruments, such as bonds, notes, stocks, and shares, as "securities". For further discussion, see Frankel, above n 1, 230; and cf. Sykes, who considers personal guarantees to fall short of qualifying as a "security" in the absence of the *res* to which resort could be made: see. Sykes and Walker, above n 1, 11.

[4] J.W. Salmond, *Jurisprudence* (12th edition, London: Sweet & Maxwell, 1966) 246.

[5] Sykes and Walker, above n 1, 7–8.

security property for the right to repayment of the loan on the originating mortgagee. The borrower is thus liable to repay the principal together with interest, and obey positive[6] and negative[7] covenants.

4.2 Consequences of Registering a Mortgage

Subject to the mortgagee's statutory charge, under the Torrens system, the borrower of a registered mortgage remains the legal owner of the property, holding an equity of redemption—that is, a right to redeem[8]—recognised in equity.

Hence the mortgagor does not lose her legal ownership of the mortgaged property, and the mortgagee has neither possession of, nor legal title to, the security property. When the debt is repaid, the mortgage will be released. A clear title reverts back to the mortgagor.

Under the Torrens system, if a mortgage is not registered, only an equitable interest in the security property is created for the mortgagee. In Australia, state legislation with regard to property requires an equitable mortgage (an interest in land) to be in writing[9] or created by an equitable assignment. The only substantive requirement of a valid equitable assignment is that there is an expressed (and written[10]) intention to assign.

As far as Australian RMBS issues are concerned, the mortgage originator is identified as the holder of the registered mortgage while any subsequent (equitable) assignees such as the trustee-issuers are equitable mortgagees on the certificate of title. If the borrower defaults, the lender has the right to exercise its power of sale, foreclose,[11] appoint a receiver,

[6] For instance, to maintain the property in proper repair, and to pay any rates and taxes.

[7] For example, to prevent the deterioration of the property, nuisance and, in some deeds of mortgage, to not part with possession.

[8] That is, a right to "buy back" the property—in other words, to pay off a mortgage on the property, so that the equitable interest and legal estate merge. "Clogs" on this right to redeem, such as extinguish it or delay it for an unreasonable time, are now generally covered by the unconscionability provisions of the *Trade Practices Act* 1974 (Cth) and the consumer credit legislation: see Chap. 5 for further detail.

[9] See section 11 of the *Property Law Act* 1974 (Qld), which is based on the original English *Statute of Frauds*, and which is replicated in all Australian States.

[10] Again, see section 11 of the *Property Law Act* 1974 (Qld).

[11] This effectively extinguishes the borrower's equity of redemption, so that legal ownership of the security property passes to the mortgagee.

and enter into possession, as well as sue personally to enforce the mortgagor's contractual obligation to repay the loan obligation.[12]

Neither previous authorities nor scholarly literature related to RMBS in Australia discuss the subject of priority between competing mortgages, which is a standard fare in most exegeses of the law of mortgages.[13] However, it is reasonable to predict that a contest of priorities between competing mortgages might arise in the future, in at least two situations in Australia

It is reasonable to predict that a borrower might, wittingly or perhaps unwittingly, grant a *registered* mortgage[14] in future that granted to the originator, to another lender who has acted bona fide and is unaware that rights under the earlier registered first mortgage have been assigned in equity to the trustee-issuer. In such a situation, it is likely that a contest might arise between the equitable assignee of the mortgagee and the subsequent registered mortgagee. However, at a glance, it might seem that the holder of the later registered interest may take priority over the earlier equitable unregistered interest.[15]

The above discussion ignores the fact of the originator's earlier registered first mortgage, of which the second registered mortgagee *must* have been aware, provided it was noted on the certificate of title of the property at the time the later mortgage was granted.[16] Henceforth, a legal analysis that would make sense would be that the first registered mortgagee has effectively subrogated its rights to the trustee-issuer, who would replace

[12] In practice in Australia, equitable mortgagees seek to reserve equivalent powers to those of a legal mortgagee.

[13] Cf. The subject of priority contests between competing mortgages has arisen in the literature overseas, where the markets are already much more mature than in Australia, although there it is perceived to be a procedural issue, more than one of substantive rights: see, e.g. Frankel, above n 1, 231–232.

[14] See, e.g. *Land Title Act* 1994 (Qld), section 178, which confers priority on registered securities over unregistered, and later registered securities.

[15] For example, in *Dearle v Hall* (1828) 3 Russ 1; 38 ER 475, it was held that an assignee of a debt may lose priority to a later equitable assignee who was first to give notice to the debtor, and who gave valuable consideration without notice of the earlier assignment.

[16] That is, although the rule in *Dearle v Hall* plainly applies to a priority contest between competing (purely) equitable assignment interests, it is doubtful whether it applies to an assignment of a debt secured by a *registered* mortgage in Australia. For further elaboration, see Sykes and Walker, above n 1, 405, 803. Moreover, section 62 of the *Land Title Act* 1994 (Qld) would seem to override the rule in *Dearle v Hall*. The express conferral of legal and equitable interests by this section allows the rule to be distinguished, as the rule may only apply to competing equitable assignments: Sykes and S. Walker, above n 1, 803.

the first registered mortgagee and would take priority over the holder of the later registered interest, who must have been aware of the earlier registered mortgage.[17]

It is always possible that a borrower might grant an *unregistered* mortgage to another bona fide lender, later in time to that granted to the originator, who is unaware of any equitable assignment to the trustee-issuer. Hence, back again, a concern about priority contest may occur between the trustee-issuer *qua* the equitable assignee, and the second unregistered mortgagee. Yet, contest of this nature should be resolved comparatively effortlessly—either (a) on the maxim that where the equities are equal, the first in time prevails or, more correctly, (b) consistent with the foregoing analysis—that the first registered mortgagee has effectively subrogated its rights to the trustee-issuer, who thereby stands "in the shoes" of the first registered mortgagee to take priority over the holder of the later unregistered interest, which must have had knowledge, either actual or constructive, of the earlier registered interest.[18] However, priority contests, similar to what we have discussed, are likely to arise at some distant point in the future.[19]

4.3 Guidelines for Capital Adequacy

A bank, in general, accepts deposits, on behalf of her customers. Yet, however, from a traditional viewpoint, all IMPs are not deposit-taking institutions. As noted in our previous discussion, some IMPs act more or less as "spotters" for bigger banks, and the origination fee they receive is effectively in the nature of a "spotter's fee". Hence, IMPs of this kind do not accept deposits in a traditional banking sense.

In the context of Australia's prudential supervision requirements, the above classification becomes significant. As far as Australian prudential

[17] It would be open to argument that the later mortgagee would or should know of the practice (certainly, that of the major banks) that all mortgages may be assigned, and that it has therefore borne a risk of which it ought to have been aware. However, such cases are likely to turn on the facts, and in the absence of distinguishing facts, it is submitted that the foregoing analysis is more correct as a general proposition.

[18] Other types of priority contests are likely to be resolved along conventional lines, as discussed, for example, in Sykes and Walker, above n 1, 454–464.

[19] For example, when the market in Australia has matured to the point where each of a number of originators might, without knowledge of the others' existence, take *un*registered mortgages over the same security property, or group of security properties. Indeed, it is difficult to imagine priority problems arising, under the current Torrens system, unless both security interests were unregistered.

supervision is concerned, banks and those IMPs that act as deposit-taking institutions, perhaps in a traditional banking sense, are recognised as "Australian Deposit-taking Institutions" (ADIs).

4.3.1 Towards Capital Adequacy Guidelines

Based on Bank for International Settlements (BIS) concordat of 1988, also known as the Basel Accord I, Australia has derived the capital adequacy requirements to which ADIs in Australia are subjected to.[20] Even though the Basel Accord forms minimum standards, it is open to each jurisdiction to adopt their own, arguably more stringent requirements, to their financial systems. The Basel Accord(s), however, intends to strengthen the stability of the international banking system and to establish a reliable global framework with the view of diminishing competitive inequalities among global banks. In 1999, the BIS decided to introduce a new capital adequacy framework to replace the existing guidelines. As part of their effort, BIS issued a consultative paper with the title "A New Capital Adequacy Framework" in June 1999, the Basel Accord II, and with the view of setting conclusive recommendations in the future.[21]

Based on the above guidelines, the Australian Prudential Regulation Authority (APRA) developed their own risk-based capital guidelines which attempt to make capital requirements more profound to variances in credit risk, reflect off-balance sheet exposure, and minimise disincentives to holding liquid and low-risk assets. These guidelines are as follows: APS 111 *Capital Adequacy: Measurement of Capital*, APS 112 *Capital adequacy: Standardised Approach to Credit Risk*, and APS 120 *Prudential Standard Securitisation*. The sole intention of these guidelines is to equip ADIs with adequate capital to meet their credit risk. The APRA has issued a harmonised set of prudential standards covering all banks and other financial intermediaries (ADIs).

As per the Basel Accord, capital comprises two elements—namely, "Tier 1 Capital" (also known as Common Equity), "Tier 1 (additional)

[20] Capital adequacy regulation of banks and other financial institutions in Australia, as in many countries, is based on international guidelines issued by the Basel Committee on Banking Supervision. The Basel Committee, which comprises central banks and bank supervisory agencies from other countries, operates under the auspices of the Bank for International Settlements (BIS) and consults widely with supervisory agencies in other countries and with industry on prudential matters.

[21] See BIS Home Page: http://www.bis.org

Capital" and Tier 2 Capital. Table 4.1 presents a summary of the main elements of capital. Generally, each definition of capital includes a specific combination of a certain number of a bank's ordinary shares, preferred

Table 4.1 Definition of capital[a]

Tier 1 (Common Equity) Capital[b]
Paid-up ordinary shares.[c]
Paid-up mutual equity interests.[d]
Retained earnings.
Undistributed current year earnings.[e]
Accumulated other comprehensive income and other disclosed reserves.
Minority interests arising from the issue of ordinary shares to third parties by a fully consolidated subsidiary.[f]
Tier 1 (Additional) Capital[g]
Instruments issued by an ADI that are not included in common equity Tier 1 Capital[h]
Instruments issued by a fully consolidated subsidiary of the level 2 group and held by third parties.[i]
Regulatory adjustments applied in the calculation of Additional Tier 1 Capital in accordance with Attachment D of Prudential Standard.

[a]This Table is extracted from APS 112—*Capital Adequacy: Standardised Approach to Credit Risk* http://www.apra.gov.au

[b]Tier 1 Capital includes the uppermost quality components of capital. APS 111 identifies four parameters that should be satisfied in order to identify capital as Tier 1 Capital. Accordingly, (a) provide a permanent and unrestricted commitment of funds, (b) are freely available to absorb losses, (c) do not impose any unavoidable servicing charge against earnings, and (d) rank behind the claims of depositors and other creditors in the event of winding-up of the issuer

[c]Attachment B of APS 111 identifies criteria that should be met for paid-up ordinary shares to be considered as Tier 1 Capital

[d]Attachment K of APS 111 identifies criteria that should be met for paid-up mutual equity interests

[e]Attachment K of APS 111 identifies criteria that should be met for paid-up mutual equity interests

[f]Calculated in accordance with Attachment C of APS

[g]Additional Tier 1 Capital comprises high-quality components of capital that satisfy the following essential characteristics: (a) provide a permanent and unrestricted commitment of funds, (b) are freely available to absorb losses, (c) rank behind the claims of depositors and other more senior creditors in the event of winding-up of the issuer, and (d) provide for fully discretionary capital distributions

[h]Instruments issued by an ADI that are not included in Common Equity Tier 1 Capital and meet following criteria will be inclusion in Additional Tier 1 Capital: (a) the criteria for inclusion in Additional Tier 1 Capital set out in Attachment E of this Prudential Standard; (b) for instruments classified as liabilities under Australian Accounting Standards, the loss absorption requirements set out in Attachment F of this Prudential Standard; and (c) the requirements for loss absorption at the point of non-viability set out in Attachment J of this Prudential Standard

[i]Calculated in accordance with Attachment C of this Prudential Standard where (a) the instruments would, if issued by the ADI, meet the criteria in Attachment E of this Prudential Standard; (b) instruments classified as liabilities under Australian Accounting Standards meet the loss absorption requirements set out in Attachment F of this Prudential Standard; and (c) the instruments meet the requirements for loss absorption at the point of non-viability set out in Attachment J of this Prudential Standard

shares, contingency and other financial reserves, allowances for loan or lease losses, minority interests in equity accounts of consolidated subsidiaries, and other financial instruments. Furthermore, capital is regularly reduced by any outstanding goodwill and by certain other applicable adjustments.

As we already know, risk-weighting of the capital-to-assets ratio suggests that the higher the level of asset risk, the greater is the level of capital backing required. Assets are grouped among four risk-weighting categories that range from 0% to 100%. This categorisation is based on the credit risk of the assets. Table 4.2 depicts the risk-weighting and the assets within each category.

For assets assigned a risk-weighting of 0%, ADIs do not need to hold any capital. For assets with 100% risk-weighting, ADIs need to hold capital on a one-to-one basis. Based on other risk weight categories (e.g. 20% and 50%), ADIs should hold capital, correspondingly reduced capital, associated with each risk weight category.

The calculation of an ADI's "risk weighted assets" involves assigning its assets and certain off-balance sheet items (e.g. standby letters of credit, guarantees, and commitments to lend or purchase) to broad risk categories. Each category has been assigned a corresponding percentage factor intended to reflect the credit and other risks associated with it (Table 4.3). An ADI's total risk-weighted assets are equal to the sum of the items in each risk category, weighted according to the category's corresponding percentage.

On a portfolio basis, the risk-weightings reflect broad guidelines about the likely credit risk of each category of borrower. However, the mythology provides no detailed description (as in a method) to assess the credit risks associated with individual borrowers. Under these guidelines, each bank is required to assess every counterparty's credit risk individually and, then, allocate the amount of capital to cover that risk accordingly. Finally, price transaction such that they reflect the risk.

4.3.2 *Risk-Weighting of RMBSs and Consequences of Guidelines*

Prudential Standard APS 120—*Securitisation* came into effect in January 2018 with the objective of ensuring that deposit-taking institutions adopt prudent practices to manage the risks associated with securitisation and also to ensure that adequate regulatory capital is held against

Table 4.2 Risk weights[a]

Zero weight
Notes and coins
All Australian dollar balances and other Australian dollar claims on the Reserve Bank of Australia.
Gold bullion held in the ADI's own vaults or on an allocated basis by another party to the extent that it is back by gold bullion liabilities.[b]
All Australian dollar claims on the Australian government.
Claims on overseas central governments and state or regional governments, State or Territory Governments in Australia (for credit rating category 1).
Cash items in the process of collection.[c]
Claims on overseas central governments and state or regional governments, State or Territory Governments in Australia (for credit rating category 2).
Claims on international banking agencies and multilateral development banks (for credit rating category 1).[d]
Claims (other than equity) on ADIs and overseas banks, being claims with an original maturity of three months or less (for credit rating category 1, 2, and 3).
Claims (other than equity) on ADIs and overseas banks with an original maturity of more than three months (for credit rating category 1).
Claims (other than equity) on Australian and international corporate counterparties (including insurance and securities companies) and commercial public sector entities (for credit rating category 1).
Claims on local governments and non-commercial public sector entities in Australia and overseas (for credit rating category 1).
Margin lending against listed instruments on recognised exchanges that is not deducted from capital as required under APS 111.
50% risk
Claims on overseas central governments and state or regional governments, State or Territory Governments in Australia (for credit rating category 3).
Claims on local governments and non-commercial public sector entities in Australia and overseas (for credit rating category 2).
Claims on international banking agencies and multilateral development banks (for credit rating category 2, 3, and unrated).
Claims (other than equity) on ADIs and overseas banks, being claims with an original maturity of three months or less (for credit rating category 4 and 5).
Claims (other than equity) on ADIs and overseas banks with an original maturity of more than three months (for credit rating category 2, 3, and unrated).
Claims (other than equity) on Australian and international corporate counterparties (including insurance and securities companies) and commercial public sector entities (for credit rating category 2).
100% risk
Claims on overseas central governments and state or regional governments, State or Territory Governments in Australia (for credit rating category 4, 5, and unrated).

(*continued*)

Table 4.2 (continued)

Claims on local governments and non-commercial public sector entities in Australia and overseas (for credit rating category 3, 4, 5, and unrated).
Claims on international banking agencies and multilateral development banks (for credit rating category 4 and 5 unrated).
Claims (other than equity) on ADIs and overseas banks with an original maturity of more than three months (for credit rating category 4 and 5).
The unsecured portion of any claim[e] (other than loans or claims secured against eligible residential mortgages in paragraph 14 of APS 111) that is past due for more than 90 days and/or impaired. Where specific provisions are less than 20% of the outstanding amount of the past due claim or impaired asset.
Claims (other than equity) on Australian and international corporate counterparties (including insurance and securities companies) and commercial public sector entities (for credit rating category 3, 4, and unrated) [f]
All claims (other than equity) on private sector counterparties (other than ADIs, overseas banks, and corporate counterparties).
Investments in premises, plant and equipment, and all other fixed assets.
Claims on all fixed assets under operating leases.
All other assets and claims not specified elsewhere.

[a]Refer to APS 112 *Capital adequacy: Standardised Approach to Credit Risk* (July 2018) http://www.apra.gov.au

[b]Gold bullion held on an unallocated basis by another party, though backed by gold liabilities, is weighted as a claim on the counterparty unless a lower risk weight is approved by APRA

[c]E.g. cheques, drafts, and other items drawn on other ADIs or overseas banks that are payable immediately upon presentation and that are in the process of collection

[d]APS 112—Attachment E

[e]For the purpose of defining the secured portion of past due claims, eligible collateral, guarantees, and credit derivatives will be the same as those recognised for CRM purposes as set out in Attachments F, G, and H of this Prudential Standard

[f]APS 112—Attachment E

the associated credit risk.[22] An ADI, who is the originator of securitised assets, may exclude the underlying exposures in the calculation of its Regulatory Capital for credit risk under Prudential Standard—APS 112 Capital Adequacy or Prudential Standard APS 113, provided that operational requirements identified in APS 120 are met.[23] Accordingly, the ADI must ensure that significant credit risk associated with the underlying pool of exposures has been transferred to third partie(s).[24] As part of

[22] Prudential Standard APS 120—Securitisation, objectives.

[23] Prudential Standard APS 120. Operational requirements are detailed in Attachment A—Operational requirements for regulatory capital relief.

[24] Prudential Standard APS 120—Securitisation, Attachment A.

Table 4.3 Off-balance sheet business[a]

Direct credit substitutes	**Credit Conversion Factor**
Direct credit substitutes	100
Performance-related contingencies	50
Trade-related contingencies	20
Lending of securities or posting of securities as collateral	100
Assets sold with recourse	100
Forward asset purchases	100
Partly paid shares and securities	100
Placements of forward deposits	100
Note issuance and underwriting facilities	50
Other commitments	
Commitments with certain drawdown	100
Commitments[b] with original maturity of:	
One year or less; or	20
Over one year	50
Commitments that can be unconditionally cancelled at any time without notice or that effectively provide for automatic cancellation due to deterioration in a borrower's creditworthiness	0
Irrevocable standby commitments provided under APRA-approved industry support arrangements	0

[a]Refer to APS 112 *Capital adequacy: Standardised Approach to Credit Risk* (July 2018) http://www.apra.gov.au

[b]E.g. undrawn formal standby facilities and credit lines

this requirement, an originating ADI and any member of a group to which an ADI belongs must not hold or fund the acquisition of more than 20% of the non-senior securities issued in the securitisation, or more than 20% of any tranche of non-senior securities issued in the securitisation; hold (or fund) the acquisition of non-senior securities and hold (fund or provide) other loss positions or credit enhancements, which represent more than 20% of the loss cover provided in the securitisation to support senior securitisation exposures.[25] However, APS 120,

[25] Prudential Standard APS 120—Securitisation, Attachment A. However, if there are two or more originators of the underlying pool in a securitisation, an originating ADI must apply the tests based on the proportion of assets originated by the ADI to the total amount of assets in the pool. Also, it should be noted that ADI must sell non-senior securities issued in the securitisation to third parties. An originating ADI must not repurchase non-senior securities once sold. And the originating ADI may purchase securities issued in a securitisation,

in its scope, states that except where otherwise provided, this Prudential Standard applies to all roles undertaken by—and investments of—an ADI in a securitisation. This Prudential Standard applies whether the exposures in the pool have been on an ADI's balance sheet, originated by an ADI into the pool without being first on the ADI's balance sheet, or originated by any other entity.[26]

There are clear guidelines given in APS 120 for a special purpose vehicle (SPV). Accordingly, the SPV must be a corporation, trust, or other entity organised for a specific purpose; and the purpose of the SPV must be clearly defined as facilitating securitisation and the activities of the SPV must be limited to those associated with the securitisation.[27] The ADI should not own or hold a material direct, indirect, or beneficial interest in any share capital, including ordinary shares or preference shares, of an SPV where the SPV is a corporation.[28]

In this manner, APS 120 intends to maintain separation between ADI and assets originated and securitised by the same. Capital relief is also available for ADI(s) maintaining guidelines given in APS 120. This seems to be a positive development in contrast to capital adequacy requirements in the past, especially in contrast to pre-GFC capital adequacy requirements for asset securitisation in Australia. However, the concept "true sale" seems missing from APS 120. Instead, the word "arm's length" has been used in the text. However, as we have discussed earlier, a number of measures have been taken in APS 120 to detach assets from its originator. As per the knowledge of authors, these guidelines haven't been tested in courts until now in Australia. If courts, for some reason, decide to claw-back trust assets in case of originators' bankruptcy, the sole purpose of "detachment" would have no value at all.[29]

provided: (a) the purchase is conducted on an arm's-length basis and on market terms and conditions; (b) the ADI has no pre-existing obligation to undertake the purchase; and (c) the purchase does not give effect to a call option other than a clean-up call that complies with paragraph 6(c) of this Attachment.

[26] Prudential Standard APS 120—Securitisation, paragraph 8.

[27] Prudential Standard APS 120—Securitisation, paragraph 14.

[28] Prudential Standard APS 120—Securitisation, paragraph 14. This is further extended towards not holding any indirect or beneficial interest in any share capital in the trustee where the SPV is a trust; restrictions on SPV's name; limitations on directors representing ADI on SPV's board of directors, restrictions on ADIs' employees acting as trustees, etc.

[29] It is the view of the authors that we should consider court decisions taken in major asset-securitising jurisdictions in terms of the above discussion on claw-back. In 2009, a landmark case has been reported in the US named as *Re General Growth Properties*. The above decision

4.3.3 *Risk-Weighting of RMBSs in Overseas Jurisdictions*

That APRA in Australia adopts the "fall back" approach for the purpose of the risk-weighting of RMBSs is noticeably different from other prudential regulators in overseas jurisdictions. If regulatory capital relief is not obtained by prudential regulators overseas, their "fall back" positions are that RMBSs are risk-weighted are as follows for some other countries:

- **France:** 50%[30]
- **England and Canada**: 50%, subject to certain conditions[31]
- **Japan:** 50% with further concessional risk-weightings of 0–20% if the issue is appropriately credit-enhanced[32]
- **United States:** between 0 and 50%, based on the risk of the RMBS programme sponsor and other stakeholders providing credit enhancement[33]

by the US bankruptcy Court in New York questions the future of securitisation, while demonstrating that the SPV structure will not always shield these entities from becoming intertwined in bankruptcy with a troubled parent company.

[30] See G. S. Marc, 'French Securitisation Law and Practice' (1998) 1 *The Securitisation Conduit*, 10, at which Marc notes that, like Australia, Germany at this stage remains at 100%.

[31] In the case of the UK, see the Bank of England's guidelines on *Loan Transfers and Securitisations*, cited in P.R. Wood, *Law and Practice of International Finance* (London: Sweet & Maxwell, 1995) 63; and Notice BSD/1992/6, November 1992. This Notice was replaced by more detailed guidelines issued by the UK Financial Services Authority (FSA) in June 1998: see the FSA Web site at http://www.fsa.gov.uk. L. Stuart, and G. Old, 'The FSA Rules for Securitisation and Loan Transfers—A User's Guide' (2000) 15 (9) *Journal of International Banking Law* 211. In the case of Canada, see the guidelines of the Office of the Superintendent of Financial Institutions in Canada, at http://www.osfi-bsif.gc.ca; F. G. Thompson, 'An Overview of Current Issues and Trends in the Canadian Securitization Market' (1994) 37 *Private Investments Abroad* 81.

[32] See the Bank of Japan's capital adequacy guidelines, cited in E.J. Park, 'Allowing Japanese Banks to Engage in Securitisation' (1996) 17 *Pennsylvania Law Journal* 723, 728; H. Kanda, 'Securitization in Japan' (1998) 8 (2) *Duke Journal of Comparative and International Law* 359; B. Railton, et al., 'Securitisation Legislation in Japan and Thailand' (2002) 17 (1) *Journal of International Banking Law* 12; Y. Shimada, and S. Itoh, 'Japanese Asset Securitization: A Guide for Practitioners' (1997) 38 *Harvard International Law Journal* 171.

[33] See the Federal Reserve Board's capital adequacy guidelines, cited in A. M. Hodgkin, 'Bank and Thrift Regulatory Considerations', in R. S. Borod (ed.) *Securitization: Asset-Backed and Mortgage-Backed Securities* (Boston: Brown, Rudnick, Freed & Gesmer, 1994) 2–9. For an alternative discussion on capital adequacy and related issues, see, in general, S. Senarath., 'Securitisation and the global financial crisis: can risk retention prevent another crisis?', (2017) 18 *International Journal of Business and Globalisation*, 153; S. Senarath

As we have already noted, international prudential regulation is inspected by the Bank for International Settlements (BIS).[34] A number of standing committees and organisations have been set up by the Bank over the last 40 years to help monitor and influence the international financial system and world financial stability, and come up with international "best practice" in the regulation of international financial markets. The Basel Committee on Banking Supervision is one of these, established in 1974 by the Governors of the G10 central banks.[35]

The Basel Committee uses its significant inspiration to formulate guidelines and "best practice" standards[36] with the view that those standards will be implemented, although they will be adapted to each jurisdiction by their central banks.

The Basel Committee, in 1988, recommended the introduction of a new prudential requirement by central banks to be implemented by the end of 1992—namely, a risk-based capital-to-assets ratio of 8%,[37] which formed the basis for Australia's current system of capital adequacy. The Committee in June 1999 issued a proposal for a new capital adequacy framework that will overwrite the 1988 Accord, so-called Basel Accord II.

For fully secured residential housing loans, the current Australian risk-weighting of 50% reflects, and is in line with, a Basel II recommendation in 2001.[38] Based on the consultative paper issued in April 2003,[39] the BIS proposed that the relevant risk-weightings be further reduced; hence, after 2008, lending that is fully secured by mortgages on residential properties would be risk-weighted at 35%,[40] and henceforth, mortgage securitisations in general would be risk-weighted as follows[41] (Table 4.4):

(2016)., 'Not so "Bankruptcy-Remote": An insight into Sri Lankan Securitization Practices in a Post_GFC Context' (Paper presented at the MAC-MME conference, Prague, Czech Republic); Senarath, S. 'The Dodd-Frank Act doesn't solve the principal-agent problem in asset securitisation' (2017) *blogs.lse.ac.uk* (11 November 2018).

[34] Which is an international organisation based in Basel, Switzerland, whose role, since its establishment in 1930, has been to foster international financial cooperation and acts as bank to the central banks of member countries.

[35] The so-called G10 (or "Group of Ten") central banks comprise those of Belgium, Canada, France, Germany, Italy, Japan, the Netherlands, Sweden, Switzerland, the United Kingdom, and the United States.

[36] These are subject to the formal approval of the Governors of the G10 central banks.

[37] Referred as the Basel Capital Accord.

[38] BIS, *Basel Accord II New Framework* (1988) Annex 2, paragraph 21.

[39] BIS, *Basel Accord II Consultative Paper* 3 (abbreviated by the Basel Committee to "CP3") (April 2003).

[40] Ibid, Annex 9, paragraph 14.

[41] Ibid, paragraphs 526–529.

Table 4.4 Long-term category (Basel II proposal)

External credit assessment	*AAA to AA-*	*A+ to A-*	*BBB+ to BBB-*	*BB+ to BB-*	*B+ and below or unrated*
Risk weight	20%	50%	100%	350%	Deduction

Basel II has not specifically discussed and distinguished between mortgage securitisations and RMBSs. Australian RMBS issues are characteristically rated AA- or above,[42] suggesting that the "fall back" position for ADIs that are unable to obtain regulatory capital relief after 2008 would be that their RMBSs be risk-weighted at 20%. Therefore, even if regulatory capital relief was not obtained from APRA, the ADI would, as a "fall back" position, have to provide less capital cover for the RMBS issue than it would for home loans secured by the same mortgages. This is exactly the converse of the current position and leads to the question whether RMBSs may be significantly less risky than residential mortgage loans[43] and whether the current risk-weightings are appropriate at all.[44]

4.4 Summary

As far as the Australian context is concerned, typically the originator is identified on the certificate of title as the holder of the registered mortgage, and any subsequent assignees are known as equitable mortgagees. If the initial borrower defaults, the mortgagee has the right to exercise its power of sell, rights to foreclose, appoint a receiver, enter into possession, and the right to sue personally to enforce the borrower's loan contract. While priority contests between mortgagees in the context of an RMBS programme are conceivable at present, under the current Torrens system, it is unclear as to how to identify priority concerns, unless both security interests were unregistered.

[42] Standard and Poor's, *Structured Finance Australia and New Zealand* (Melbourne, 1999) 17.

[43] Common sense suggests that this is likely where a smaller or regional ADI is utilising a larger, well-known sponsor to upgrade the quality of its RMBSs.

[44] As noted earlier, a financial risk assessment of RMBS programmes is plainly beyond the scope of this book. Nevertheless, this represents a fruitful area for future research.

In Australia, for capital adequacy concerns, a typical residential mortgage loan is risk-weighted at 50%. However, RMBSs based on the same residential mortgages may be risk-weighted at zero, provided that regulatory capital relief has been obtained from APRA. In any case, provided APRA does not grant regulatory capital relief, the RMBSs may be weighted at up to 100% for capital adequacy purposes, depending on the extent of credit enhancement and disclosure to investors. However, as far as recent Basel II proposals, presence of insurance for investors of RMBS, overseas regulation (with 50% risk weight for RMBS) are concerned, the direction and extent of this disparity in the risk-weightings is somewhat surprising. Furthermore, the above disparity naturally creates commercial incentives, due to current regulation. Accordingly, ADIs will have the incentive to use their residential mortgage loans to issue RMBSs, and institutions may have the incentive not to invest in the RMBSs.

Considering the Basel II recommendations, it can be suggested that the Australian authorities would consider reducing the risk-weighting for RMBSs. There need to be more in-depth estimation of the appropriate weighting for RMBSs, which is beyond our discussion.

Bibliography

Books and Book Chapters

Frankel, T., *Securitization: Structured Financing, Financial Asset Pools, and Asset-Backed Securities*, Boston: Little Brown & Co, 1991, v I and v II.

Gillooly, M. (ed.), *Securities over Personality*, Sydney: The Federation Press, 1994.

Salmond, J. W., *Jurisprudence*, 12th edition, London: Sweet & Maxwell, 1966.

Sykes, E. I. and Walker, S., *The Law of Securities*, 5th edition, Sydney: Law Book Company, 1993.

Wood, P. R., *Title Finance, Derivatives, Set-Off, and Netting*, London: Sweet & Maxwell, 1995.

Journal Articles

Hodgkin, A. M., 'Bank and Thrift Regulatory Considerations', in R. S. Borod (ed.), *Securitization: Asset-Backed and Mortgage-Backed Securities*, Boston: Brown, Rudnick, Freed & Gesmer, 1994.

Kanda, H., 'Securitization in Japan' (1998) (8) (2) *Duke Journal of Comparative and International Law* 359.

Marc, G. S., 'French Securitisation Law and Practice' (1998) 1 *The Securitisation Conduit* 10.

Park, E. J., 'Allowing Japanese Banks to Engage in Securitization: Potential Benefits, Regulatory Obstacles, and Theories for Reform' (1996) 17 *University of Pennsylvania Journal of International Economic Law* 723.

Railton, B., Kinami, N. and Lawden, J., 'Securitisation Legislation in Japan and Thailand' (2002) 17 (1) *Journal of International Banking Law* 12.

Senarath, S., 'Securitisation and the global financial crisis: can risk retention prevent another crisis?' (2017) 18 *International Journal of Business and Globalisation* 153.

Shimada, Y. and Itoh, S., 'Japanese Asset Securitization: A Guide for Practitioners' (1997) 38 *Harvard International Law Journal* 171.

Stuart, L. and Old, G., 'The FSA Rules for Securitisation and Loan Transfers – A User's Guide' (2000) 15 (9) *Journal of International Banking Law* 211.

Thompson, F. G., 'An Overview of Current Issues and Trends in the Canadian Securitization Market' (1994) 37 *Private Investments Abroad* 81.

Working Papers, Magazines, Newspapers and Reports

Standard and Poor's, 'Credit Ratings on Mortgage-Backed Securities', *Structured Finance Australia and New Zealand*, Melbourne, 1998.

Australian Prudential Regulation Authority, Prudential Standard APS 112 – Capital Adequacy: Standardised Approach to Credit Risk, July 2019, https://www.apra.gov.au (11 November 2019).

Australian Prudential Regulation Authority, Prudential Standard APS 111 – Capital Adequacy: Capital Adequacy: Measurement of Capital, January 2018, https://www.apra.gov.au (11 November 2019).

BIS, *Basel Accord II New Framework* (1988) Annex 2, http://www.bis.org (15 October 2004).

BIS, *Basel Accord II Consultative Paper* 3 (April 2003), http://www.bis.org (15 October 2004).

Senarath, S. 'The Dodd-Frank Act doesn't solve the principal-agent problem in asset securitisation' (2017) *blogs.lse.ac.uk* (11 November 2018). http://blogs.lse.ac.uk/businessreview/2017/04/21/the-dodd-frank-act-doesnt-solve-the-principal-agent-problem-in-asset-securitisation/

Senarath, S., Not so "Bankruptcy-Remote': An insight into Sri Lankan Securitization Practices in a Post_GFC Context' (Paper presented at the MAC-MME conference 2016, Prague, Czech Republic).

Web Sites

BIS Home Page, http://www.bis.org
APRA Home Page, http://www.apra.gov.au
Financial Services Authority Home Page, http://www.fsa.gov.uk
Government of Canada The Office of the Superintendent of Financial Institutions home page, http://www.osfi-bsif.gc.ca

CHAPTER 5

The Legal Process for Transferring Mortgagee's Rights to the Special Purpose Vehicle

5.1 Introduction

In the process of transferring the mortgagee's rights to an special purpose vehicle (SPV),[1] banks as well as other financial institutions should ensure to take steps to constitute the transfer a "true sale".[2] A true sale is believed to bring about a number of advantages. Among them, regulatory capital relief from the Australian Prudential Regulation Authority (APRA) for Authorised Deposit-taking Institutions (ADI), insolvency-remoteness of

[1] Commonly referred as Special Purpose Entity (SPE) or Financial Vehicle Corporation (FVC) or Trustee. In some jurisdictions, different names are used to refer to the same. For example, in Japan, the term Special Purpose Association (SPA) or Special Purpose Company (SPC) is used. See Roy B True, 'Risk and Insolvency Issues in Japanese Asset Securitization' (1996) 28 New *York University Journal of International Law and Politic* 505. Also called single purpose entity (SPE), see Pearce Forrest, 'Bankruptcy-Remote Special Purpose Entities and a Business's Right to Waive its Ability to File for Bankruptcy' (2012) 28 *Emory Bankruptcy Developments Journal* 507.

[2] Referred as a "clean sale", especially in overseas literature. Also, the term "Clean sale" has been used in the APRA Capital Adequacy Guidelines. A "true sale" is one which will prevent the property becoming part of the seller's bankruptcy estate in a bankruptcy subsequent to the sale. A true sale is at the very heart of legal issues in securitisation. Provided a securitisation programme is based on a true sale, the investors get a legal right over the receivables. In contrast, if it is not a true sale, investors may be either at par with unsecured lenders, or even worse. Schwarch, Steven L, 'Structured Finance: The New Way to Securitize Assets' (1989) 11 *Cordozo Law Review* 607.

P. Rajapakse, S. Senarath, *Commercial Law Aspects of Residential Mortgage Securitisation in Australia*,
https://doi.org/10.1007/978-3-030-00605-1_5

the trust assets from its originator's bankruptcy, tax advantages, and consistency in terms of law of trusts and equity are prominent.

A "true sale" or perhaps what we call a "clean sale" is essential for an SPV to distance itself from the originator. A true sale is needed to avoid any risk of having commercial (or any other) obligation to support the liquidity of the programme or the market value of securities issued, or perhaps to make good any losses suffered by investors.

Mortgage assets that are subjected to an equitable assignment that consist of the mortgagee's rights under the mortgage, relevant security property insurance policies, and mortgage insurance policies, and the originator's interests in any contracts it may have with solicitors, valuers, or other professionals in connection with the origination of the mortgages.

This chapter discusses the manner in which the originator's rights together with the underlying collateral can be transferred to the trustee-issuer. Also, this section deals with those legal concerns that arise with the same. These issues include the extent to which the transfer of mortgagee rights to the SPV is a "true sale" in contrast to a mere financing arrangement, the manner in which an SPV is structured in Australia to effect a "true sale", and the impact of the *National Credit Code* (NCC) on RMBS issues, with specific reference to legislative provisions of Queensland.

5.2 What Is a "True Sale"?

In a typical securitisation transaction, a future payment stream is legally separated from the entity originated by the right to receive payments. This "legal separation" is crucial in order to make sure that even if the originator becomes bankrupt, in a future point of time, the creditors of the originator are not capable of reaching the said future income stream. This future payment stream, in turn, is dedicated to make payments to the investors in the capital markets, to whom the RMBSs are issued.[3]

In order to constitute a "sale", the originator would normally transfer all of its rights, titles, and interests in the payment stream. The transfer would be made to a "bankruptcy-remote" third party. The idea is to make

[3]Schwarcz, above n 2. See also Joseph C Shenker and Anthony J Colletta, 'Asset Securitization: Evolution, Current Issues and New Frontiers' (1990) 69 *Texas Law Review* 1369.

a complete separation of the income stream from its originator. Such a "sale" which results in isolating trust assets from accessibility of the debtor's estate under bankruptcy law can be identified as a "true sale".[4]

In determining a "true sale", courts have failed to adhere to a uniform criteria.[5] Yet, some key factors that may constitute a true sale can be identified by looking into key case authorities and also literature published in different jurisdictions.[6] Accordingly, the following factors have been identified as instrumental in drawing the line between a true sale and a financing contract (also called as a secured loan). The manner in which such factors are categorised into subgroups also differs extensively in literature.[7]

(a) *Nature of the "Recourse" Status*

The extent to which the transferee has the ability to recourse from the transferor has been discussed in many authorities as a key concern in determining a "true sale". Yet, the mere existence of a recourse provision would not prejudice the true sale nature of the transaction. If there exists a recourse provision, then the courts would look into the nature of the recourse provision and the true nature of the transaction. Emphasis will be

[4] See, e.g. the discussion on "true sale" made in Schwarcz, above n 2.

[5] On the one hand, courts exhibit ambiguity in determining factors of a true sale, while on the other hand, courts depict lack of uniformity in "re-characterizing" a sale contract.

[6] In determining authorities, we have confined to common law jurisdictions—namely, the United States, Canada, and United Kingdom.

[7] Following articles have been taken into consideration in order to make the above classification. Steven L Schwarcz, 'Structured Finance: The New Way to Securitize Assets' (1990) 11 *Cardozo Law Review* 607; Schwarcz, above n 2; Peter V Pantaleo et al., 'Rethinking the Role of Recourse in the Sale of Financial Assets' (1996) 52 *The Business Lawyer* 159; Kravitt J Brown and M Platt, *Securitization of Financial Assets* (vol. 1) (Aspen Publishers, 2006). Pelma Rajapakse and Naomal Gunawardena 'Assignment of mortgage loans to a special purpose vehicle in securitisation in Sri Lanka: With some reference to Australian Securitisation Programs' (2013) 28 *Banking and Finance Law Review* 475; S. Senarath., 'Securitisation and the global financial crisis: can risk retention prevent another crisis?', (2017) 18 *International Journal of Business and Globalisation*, 153; Senarath, S. and Copp, R., Credit default swaps and the global financial crisis: reframing credit default swaps as quasi-insurance (2015) 8 *Global Economy and Finance Journal*, 135; S. Senarath (2016)., Not so "'Bankruptcy-Remote': An insight into Sri Lankan Securitization Practices in a Post_GFC Context" (Paper presented at the MAC-MME conference, Prague, Czech Republic); Senarath, S. 'The Dodd-Frank Act doesn't solve the principal-agent problem in asset securitisation' (2017) *blogs.lse.ac.uk* (11 November 2018).

paid on legal rights, economic consequences of the transaction, including inter alia, risk assumed by each party, and also guarantees given by the transferor.[8]

Pantaleo et al.[9] categorise recourse into four categories. Accordingly, (a) recourse for un-collectability,[10] (b) recourse to provide an agreed rate for returns including agreements to eliminate fluctuations,[11] (c) protection from reduced yields,[12] and (d) recourse for representation and warranties not relating to credit quality.

(b) *Right to Repurchase and Rights for Collection of Surpluses*

If the agreement contains provisions such that the "seller" is capable of repurchasing or redeeming a property, such provision will be evidence for a secured transaction as opposed to a true sale.[13] On the other hand, some judgements suggest that presence of rights for collection of surpluses is an indication of a secured loan.[14]

(c) *Pricing Mechanism*

If the agreement is such that pricing is based upon fluctuating interest rates (e.g. what we find in commercial loans), it is more of an indicative of a secured loan.[15] If the SPV purchases the assets based on a pre-agreed discounted rate, and the agreed rate is such that it would not be changed later based on the actual costs, such a transaction would be more likely a true sale.[16]

[8] For a detailed description, see *Major's Furniture Mart v Castle Credit Corp*, 602 F 2d 538 (3rd Cir, 1979). A detailed discussion on the validity of recourse provisions and also the validity of investor agreements on not to seek recourse provisions has been discussed in Chap. 5.

[9] Pantaleo, above n 7.

[10] *Re Grand Union Co*, 219 F 353 (2nd Cir, 1914*) Major's Furniture Mart v Castle Credit Corp, 602 F 2d 538 (3rd Cir, 1979).*

[11] *Re Sprint Mortgage Bankers Corp*, 164 BR 224 (Bankr EDNY, 1994).

[12] *Merchants' Transfer & Storage Co v Rafferty*, 48 F 2d 540 (2d Cir, 1931).

[13] Schwarcz, above n 2.

[14] *Evergreen Valley Resort, Inc*, 23 B.R. 659, 661–61 (Bankr. D.Me.1982); *Re Nixon Mach Co*, 6 BR 847, 854 (Bankr ED Tenn, 1980).

[15] *Home Bond Co v McChesney, 239 US 568 (1916)*; *Dorothy v Commonwealth Commercial Co*, 116 NE 143 (1917).

[16] Schwarcz, above n 2.

(d) *Administration and Control of Accounts*

The nature of control over collection of payments has been identified as a factor that decides between a true sale and a secured loan. Such controls include the ownership of books, records, and also may include inter alia, having the right to control the conduct of the servicer (collection agent), ability to impose collection policies, and make notices to the borrowers to make payments.[17]

(e) *Intent of the Parties/Nature of Documentation*

The courts would not hesitate to place weight on the intention of the parties of the transaction, especially when the parties are sophisticated, in deciding whether a particular transaction is a true sale or a finance arrangement. Courts will look into transaction documents in order to figure out the true intention of the parties.[18] Yet, distinction should be made from the fact that courts would not blindly follow the "label" given by parties to define their transaction but the true intention of the parties.[19]

[17] In a securitisation programme, the originator would be appointed as the collection agent in most cases, especially for practical convenience. Mere appointment of the originator as the collection agent would not jeopardise the "sales treatment" given to the transaction. If the originator acting as the servicer acts as the same as other servicers, receives a fee for her services, and the transferee (in this case, the SPV) has the right to remove the originator from the position of the servicer to make sure that the appointment of the initial originator as the collection agent would not pose a threat to the true sale nature of the transaction. Schwarcz, above n 2. See also *Lloyds & Scottish Fin Ltd v Cyril Lord Carpets Seles Ltd* [1979] 129 NLJ 366; *People v Service Inst Inc*, 421 NY Supp 325 (1979).

[18] Brown and Kravitt, above n 7.

[19] This has been discussed in a number of authorities including in *Major's Furniture*. However, exceptions are not rare. *Metropolitan Toronto Police Widows and Orphans Fund v Telus Communications Inc* [2003] 30 BLR 128. Adopting a literal interpretation, the Supreme Court of Ontario decided all agreements with clear written evidence of intention of parties to have a true sale as "true sales". For a discussion on the emphasis paid by courts for the language used, see, generally, Stephen I Glover, 'Structured Finance Goes Chap. 11: Asset Securitization by Reorganizing Companies' (1992) 47 *The Business Lawyer* 611.

(f) *Irrevocability*

"Irrevocability" is very closely related to the concept of "recourse" discussed earlier. If the ownership of the assets that has been transferred to the issuer (SPV) contains a provision which enables the transferee to hand over the transferred assets back to the transferor, that would be a clear indication of a finance arrangement.[20]

(g) *Notice to Third Party*

Notice to the third party (more precisely the notice of transfer), the borrower, would be a crucial factor in determining between an equitable assignment and a true sale. If the borrower has been notified, it would be a clear indication that reflects the intention of the parties.[21]

(h) *Accounting and Tax Treatment*

If the accounting and tax treatment to a transaction is a "sale", it would also be indicative in determining the intention of the parties.[22] For example, if the tax treatment for a transaction is a sale, it would be more likely that the profit or loss for the particular transaction would be determined at the point of the transaction and taxed at the same time.[23]

5.3 Accounting Considerations

The key issue in accounting for securitisations is "de-recognition". In other words, whether a transaction should be treated as a sale (de-recognise)[24] of assets or as a secured borrowing. Depending on whether a transaction is accounted for as a sale or as a secured borrowing, the financial statement

[20] Rajapakse and Gunawardena, above n 7.

[21] Rajapakse and Gunawardena, above n 7. However, it should be noted that mere "notice to borrower" would not constitute a true sale. Yet, such notice would be an indication of the parties and would be evidence of a true sale.

[22] Ibid.

[23] Vinod Kothari, *Securitization: The Financial instrument of the Future* (John Wiley & Sons, 2006).

[24] If the asset is de-recognised, the transferor will have no further involvements with the transferred asset.

effects may be quite significant.[25] The significance lies with the fact that if the transaction accounts for a sale, the assets are removed from the balance sheet, and simultaneously, a loss or a gain will be recognised. If it is a secured borrowing, the asset essentially remains in the balance sheet and the borrower recognises a liability for the proceeds from the transfer.[26]

Two general approaches exist to addressing the de-recognition issue—namely, the "predominant-characteristic paradigm" and the "financial components paradigm".[27] As far as the predominant-characteristic paradigm, also referred as "risks and rewards" approach, is concerned, the characteristics of the transaction will determine the accounting. This essentially means if all, or perhaps the majority, of risks and rewards of ownership are retained by the transferor, then the asset is not considered to have been sold. Hence, the transaction is recognised as a secured borrowing. If, on the other hand, the majority of the risks and rewards of ownership have been transferred to the transferee, then the transaction is regarded as a sale. Hence, the entire asset is removed from the balance sheet. In the financial components paradigm, also known as the "control approach", assets can be divided into components. De-recognition will be identified for a particular component of an asset, based on the extent to which the control of a component is surrendered. For example, if the transferor retains a portion of the underlying cash flows and sells the remainder of the interests in the SPV, the transferred asset is de-recognised and a new component, the retained interest, is recognised.[28] The other significant concern in accounting for securitisation is whether or not the securitisation vehicle should be consolidated. This concern is essentially interrelated to the above concern since a sale transaction followed by a consolidation of the transferee will inevitably "nullify" the effect of the sale.[29]

[25] Katherine Schipper and Teri Lombardi Yohn, 'Standard-setting Issues and Academic Research Related to the Accounting for Financial Asset Transfers' (2007) 21 *Accounting Horizons* 59.

[26] Ajay Adhikari and Luis Betancourt, 'Accounting for Securitizations: A Comparison of FASB 140 and IASB 39' (2008) 19 *Journal of International Financial Management & Accounting* 73.

[27] Raymond E Perry, 'Accounting for Securitizations' (1993) 7 *Accounting Horizons* 71.

[28] Adhikari and Betancourt, above n 26. Some scholars have identified the financial component paradigm as a significant improvement compared to the risk and reward approach, as far as accounting for securitisation is concerned. See, for example, Jason Kravitt, 'Introduction to Securitization' (1988) (Working paper) http://www.securitization.net/knowledge/accounting/fas125.asp

[29] In scholarly literature, consolidation has been identified as a critical consideration in securitisation. See Eugene A Imhoff Jr 'Asset Securitization: Economic Effects and Accounting Issues' (1992) 6 *Accounting Horizons* 5. A detailed discussion on devastating effects of consolidation on securitisation has been discussed in Chap. 5: Insolvency considerations for securitisation (see Sect. 5.6 *Re General Growth Properties Inc*).

The originator would prefer if the transaction is treated as a sale for accounting purposes, hence the assets can shift off-balance sheet, and a loan treatment for taxation purposes, so that the gains will not be taxed immediately. If the transaction is a sale, then the books will consider the originator has sold some assets (receivables) and gained a loss/profit by doing so. On the other hand, if the transaction is treated as a loan treatment, then the assets will remain in the books and (balance sheet) of the originator. Thus, it is clear that the nature of "sale" is the key concern of the accounting consideration of securitisation. The nature of recourse, control of the asset, and so on are prime concerns of all accounting standards relating to securitisation.[30] For the purpose of this section, we will consider the following accounting standards:

- FASB 13
- FASB 77
- FASB 125
- FASB 140
- IAS 39

5.3.1 *Financial Accounting Standards Board Statement No. 13*

Financial Accounting Standards Board (FASB) Statement No. 13 on Accounting for leases (hereinafter FASB 13) is one of the earliest statements of accounting dealing with principles of securitisation.[31] The statement distinguishes between receivables assigned with recourse and without recourse. Accordingly, a subsequent sale of the receivables of the lease property will not negate the treatment given to the lease initially. For a sale without recourse to profit or loss on the sale will be accounted at the time of the sale. Accordingly, it was obvious that receivables that have been sold without recourse will constitute a "sale" and vice versa.

[30] See Kothari, above n 23.

[31] *Statement of Financial Accounting Standards No. 13*, (November 1976), Financial Accounting Standards Board.

5.3.2 *Financial Accounting Standards Board Statement No. 77*

Until 1983, the common belief was that sale of receivables without recourse can only constitute a true sale. Financial Accounting Standards Board (FASB) Statement No. 77 (hereinafter FASB 77) deals with assignment of receivables with recourse based on "predominant characteristics approach". A transaction is considered as a bona fide true sale if it meets certain criteria. A transfer of receivables with recourse shall be recognised as a sale if all the following conditions are met:

- The transferor surrenders control of the future economic benefits embodied in the receivables. Control has not been surrendered if the transferor has an option to repurchase the receivables at later date.[32]
- The transferor's obligation under the recourse provisions can be reasonably estimated.[33]
- The transferee cannot require the transferor to repurchase the receivables except pursuant to the recourse provisions.[34]

If any of the conditions is not met, the amount of the proceeds from the transfer of receivables shall be reported as a liability. FASB 77 thus contains an "all or non-approach". If the transaction consists of features of a sale, the entire asset will be treated as a sale and will be removed from books or *vice versa*. With sophisticated financial transactions, there are situations where some components of an asset remain with the buyer while some remain with the seller.[35]

[32] *Financial Accounting Standards Board Statement* No. 77, (1983) Financial Accounting Standards Board [5(a)].

[33] See Ibid, [5(b)], where it states:

> Lack of experience with receivables with characteristics similar to those being transferred or other factors that affect a determination at the transfer date of the collectability of the receivables may impair the ability to make a reasonable estimate of the probable bad debt losses and related costs of collections and repossessions. A transfer of receivables shall not be recognized as a sale if collectability of the receivables and related costs of collection and repossession are not subject to reasonable estimation.

[34] Ibid, [5(c)].

[35] See Kothari, above n 23, 770.

5.3.3 *Financial Accounting Standards Board Statement No. 125*

In 1997, FASB 77 was replaced by Financial Accounting Standards Board Statement No. 125 (FASB statement No. 125: accounting for transfers and servicing of financial assets and extinguishment of liabilities). Much of the focus of this statement was on off-balance sheet financing and acted as the most comprehensive accounting standard for securitization by the time.[36] This Statement provides accounting and reporting standards for transfers and servicing of financial assets and extinguishments of liabilities. These standards are based on an application of a "financial components approach" that is focused on control.[37] Based on this approach, after a transfer of financial assets, an entity recognises the financial and servicing assets it controls and the liabilities it has incurred, de-recognises financial assets when control has been surrendered, and de-recognises liabilities when extinguished. In this manner, FASB 125 provides consistent standards for distinguishing transfers of financial assets that are sales, from transfers that are secured borrowings.

Paragraph 9 of the FASB 125 states that a transfer of financial assets in which the transferor surrenders control over those assets is accounted for as a sale to the extent that consideration other than beneficial interests in the transferred assets is received in exchange. The transferor has surrendered control over transferred assets if and only if all the following conditions are met:

- The transferred assets have been isolated from the transferor's bankruptcy estate. In other words, beyond the reach of the transferor and its creditors in the event of bankruptcy of the transferor.[38]
- Either (a) each transferee obtains the right (free of conditions that constrain it from taking advantage of that right) to pledge or exchange the transferred assets or (b) the transferee is a QSPE (Qualified Special Purpose Entity) and the holders of beneficial interests in that entity have the right (free of conditions that constrain them from taking advantage of that right) to pledge or exchange those interests.[39]

[36] Kothari, above n 23, 765.

[37] See the summary of the *Financial Accounting Standards Board Statement* No. 125 (1983) Financial Accounting Standards Board.

[38] Ibid, [9(a)].

[39] Ibid, [9(b)].

- The transferor does not maintain effective control over the transferred assets through (a) an agreement that both entitles and obligates the transferor to repurchase or redeem them before their maturity or (b) an agreement that entitles the transferor to repurchase or redeem transferred assets that are not readily obtainable.[40]

The consideration received for the sale is taken into account in determining a true sale. If the consideration is merely the beneficial interest of the asset, then the transfer would not account as a sale.[41] Further, the legal isolation of the asset is crucial in identifying a true sale.[42] In this manner, FASB 125 provides provisions such that sale treatment is given to the extent the components of risk are transferred.[43]

5.3.4 *Financial Accounting Standards Board Statement 140*[44]

Financial Accounting Standards Board Statement No. 13 (FASB 140) replaces FASB Statement No. 125. FASB 140 revises the standards for accounting for securitisations and other transfers of financial assets and collateral. FASB 140 also deals with certain disclosures requirements. However, FASB 140 contains most of Statement 125's provisions without reconsideration. Following a "financial components"[45] approach that focuses on control, the FASB 140 is to provide accounting and reporting standards for transfers and servicing of financial assets and extinguishments of liabilities. FASB 140 recognises the financial and servicing assets of controls and the liabilities it has incurred, derecognises financial assets when control has been surrendered, and derecognises liabilities when extinguished.[46] The financial standard draws the line between a bona fide sale and a secured borrowing.[47]

[40] Ibid, [9(c)].
[41] Ibid, [12].
[42] Ibid, [119].
[43] Kothari, above n 23, 770.
[44] *Financial Accounting Standards Board Statement* No. 140, (September 2000) Financial Accounting Standards Board.
[45] Refer to the discussion on financial components approach at the beginning of the chapter.
[46] According to this statement, a liability can be derecognised if and only if either (a) the debtor pays the creditor and is relieved of its obligation for the liability or (b) the debtor is legally released from being the primary obligor under the liability either judicially or by the creditor.
[47] This section has been drawn from the actual FASB 140.

As far as a transfer of assets receives a consideration (other than beneficial interest) and provided the transferor has surrendered the control of the asset, the sale treatment can be gained. Paragraph 9 of FASB 140 states that the transferor is considered to have surrendered control over transferred assets if and only if all the conditions are met. The three-fold test to determine whether the transfer of asset in a securitisation will be accounted for sale under FASB 140 requires the following conditions to be met:

- The transferred asset is isolated from the transferor's bankruptcy estate. In other words, beyond the reach of transferor's creditors in the event of bankruptcy of the transferor.[48]
- Beneficial interest holders (the transferee or Qualified Special Purpose Entity (QSPE)) can freely pledge or exchange the transferred assets or beneficial interests.[49]
- The transferor does not maintain effective control over the asset. This is either (a) an agreement that both entitles and obligates the transferor to repurchase (or redeem) before their maturity or (b) the ability to unilaterally cause the holder to return specific assets, other than through a clean-up call.[50]

If these three conditions are met, the transferor is allowed to consider the transfer as a "sale". This will invariably remove the asset from the transferor's books. A gain or a loss is recognised based on the difference between the allocated basis for the sold components and the sales proceeds. In contrast, if any of these components are not met, the transfer receives a "secured borrowing" status.

FASB 140 employs a financial components approach. A financial component approach allows financial assets to be sliced into many components. FASB 140 contains special consolidation provisions for SPVs that meet specific requirements.[51] The key concern is that a QSPE should not be consolidated in the transferor's financial statements.

Under FASB 140, an SPE is a QSPE if the SPE meets the following criteria. Accordingly, (a) the SPV must be demonstrably distinct from the

[48] *Financial Accounting Standards Board Statement* No. 140, (September 2000) Financial Accounting Standards Board [Para 9(a)].

[49] Ibid, [9(b)].

[50] Ibid, [9(c)].

[51] Adhikari and Betancourt, above n 26.

transferor,[52] (b) activities permitted to the SPV are significantly limited and specified in the documentation. Changes to such provision are possible only with the approval of the majority of the beneficial interest holders,[53] (c) an SPE can only hold passive financial assets (With some exceptions), and (d) an SPE sells or disposes her non-cash financial assets only in response to automatic response to conditions.[54]

However, if the transferee is not a QSPE, but a trust or a similar entity, and remains some sort of continuous involvement, the transferor should evaluate consolidation via FASB interpretation Number 46R (FIN 46R).

5.4 Judicial Interpretation of "True Sale"

The key fulcrum of securitisation is the sale of the asset by the originator to a bankruptcy-remote SPV, where obviously the legal issues start arising. Whether this transfer of assets is a "true sale" or a mere financial arrangement is a key concern in a securitisation arrangement. If the transaction constitutes a true sale, then the assets become the property of the SPV. Then the assets can be taken off from the originator's balance sheet. Most importantly, bankruptcy of the originator cannot affect the assets any longer.

5.4.1 *The United Kingdom*

In a significant number of cases elsewhere in the United Kingdom, the courts have re-characterised intended securitisation transactions as collateralised borrowings. In the case *Re Curtain Dream Plc*,[55] a "sale" was re-characterised as a secured loan arrangement. It was held that for a transaction to be re-characterised, it is not necessary that the parties' agreement should be shown to be a sham intended to mask their true agreement. It is sufficient that the agreement does not fall into the legal category within which the parties have sought to place it.[56]

[52] *Financial Accounting Standards Board Statement* No. 140, (September 2000) Financial Accounting Standards Board [Para 36].

[53] Ibid, [37]–[38].

[54] Ibid, [39]–[45].

[55] [1990] BCLC 925.

[56] *Welsh Development Agency v Export Finance Co Ltd* (1992) BCLC 148.

(a) *Re George Inglefield Limited*

In this English case, the originator is an organisation that sold goods on a hire purchase basis to its customers. The trader (the initial originator) then sold her hired goods together with their account receivables to a financier. Even though these sale arrangements are not notified to customers, the receivable transactions were done as absolute assignments. In this case, Romer J introduced three conditions that constitute a true sale in [illegible] to a financing agreement. His Honour stated that in determining the nature of a securitisation transaction, consideration must be given to the entire document, giving emphasis to the difference between a sale and a secured sale.

- First, the ability of a seller of receivables to repurchase the assets sold will indicate financing rather than a true sale: in a sale transaction, the vendor is not entitled to get back the subject matter of the sale by returning to the purchaser the money that has transacted between them. In the case of a mortgage or charge, until it has been foreclosed, the mortgagor is entitled to get back the subject matter of the mortgage or charge by returning to the mortgagee the money that has been paid.
- Second, in a true sale, the purchaser is more likely to have the right to claim the profits made by the assets acquired: if a mortgagee realises the mortgaged property for a sum that is insufficient to repay the mortgagor, the mortgagee is entitled to recover from the mortgagor any balance; in contrast, in a sale and purchase contract, the purchaser has to bear losses suffered on a subsequent sale of the asset.
- Third, in a true sale, the buyer should be able to realise the profits: if a mortgagee realises the subject matter of the mortgage for a sum (which is higher than the repayment), mortgagee should account to the mortgagor for any surplus. In a sale and purchase contract, any profit realised by the purchaser is credited to the purchaser's account.[57]

(b) *Orion Finance v Crown Financial Management*

In this case, the court decided that just mere presence of one of the above factors decided in *Re George Inglefield Limited* would not dispute a

[57] *Re George Inglefield Limited* [1933] Ch. 1, 23.

true sale. For example, a transaction can exist with the option of repurchase. However, in *Orion Finance v Crown Financial Management*, courts did not establish a clear ruling.

> No single one of these features may be determinative. The absence of any right in the transferor to recover the property transfer inconsistent with the transaction being by way of security; but its existence may be inferred, and its presence may not be conclusive. The transaction may take the form of a sale with an option to repurchase, and this is not to be equated with a right of redemption merely because the repurchase price is calculated with reference to the original sale price together with the interest since the date of the sale. On the other hand, the presence of a right of recourse by the transferee against the transferor to recover a shortfall may be inconsistent with a sale; but it is not necessarily so, and its absence is not conclusive. A security may be without recourse. Moreover, the nature of the property may be such that it is impossible or at least very unlikely that it will be realised at either a profit or loss. Many financing arrangements possess this feature. The fact that the transferee may have to make adjustments and payments to the transferor after the debts have been got in from the debtors does not prevent the transaction from being by way of a sale.[58]

(c) *Welsh Development Agency v Export Finance*

In the case of *Welsh Development Agency v Export Finance Co Ltd*, a transaction which appears to be a financing transaction, but documented as a sale of goods, was considered as a sale. In this case, the court referred to "external" and "internal" routes to the construction of commercial documents. Dillon J stated that:

> [B]ut the question can also arise where, without any question of sham, there is some objective criterion in law by which the court can test whether the agreement the parties have made does or does not fall into the legal category in which the parties have sought to place their agreement. As to whether the authorities established conclusively what was to count as a charge: In my judgment there is no one clear touchstone by which it can necessarily and inevitably be said that a document which is not a sham and which is expressed as an agreement for sale must necessarily, as a matter of law, amount to no more than the creation of a mortgage or charge on the property expressed

[58] *Orion Finance v Crown Financial Management* [1996] 2 BCLC 78.

> to be sold. It is necessary therefore to look at the provisions in the master agreement as a whole to decide whether in substance it amounts to an agreement for the sale of goods or only to a mortgage or charge on goods and their proceeds.[59]

It is obvious that intention of the parties is a key component in English tradition in identifying whether a transaction is a true sale or a financing arrangement.[60]

5.4.2 *Canada*

(a) *Metropolitan Toronto Police Widows and Orphans Fund v Telus Communications Inc (BC Tel's case)*

In this case, the court paid attention to the criteria that draw the line between a true sale and a finance transaction. The emphasis was on the fact whether the originator intends a genuine sale of assets to the SPV. Accordingly, (a) the intention of the parties to the transaction; (b) the actual wording of the contract. Particularly, the exact words used in the contract. Whether it contains references to a loan, security, or perhaps the repayment of principal or interest on a loan; (c) the actual conduct of the parties; and whether it was in BC Tel's interest to structure the transaction as a sale or a secured loan; (d) BC Tel's true interest to structure the transaction as a sale or secured loan; (e) the transfer of ownership and risk. Also, the recourse provisions (f) the right to claim (any) surplus; whether seller has been appointed as the servicer; (g) whether the seller retained the right of redemption with respect to the assets sold (which was identified as the ultimate test to be applied in order to determine the characterisation of the transaction).[61]

However, it should be stated that there is no "bright line test" in order to determine the extent to which the seller as the servicer may retain the

[59] *Welsh Development Agency* vs. *Export Finance Co Ltd*; CA 1992.

[60] Kothari, above n 23, 588. Also see Anne-Marie Neagle, 'Re-characterisation Risk in Securitization and other Structured Finance Transactions in Expansion and Diversification in Securitization', cited in Jan Job de Vries Robbé, *Securitization Law and Practice: In the Face of the Credit Crunch* (Kluwer Law International, 2008).

[61] [2003] OJ No 128. (ONSC) http://www.canli.org/on/cas/2003 (20 January 2004) paragraphs [40–41].

credit risk with regard to the assets that have been sold. In the BC Tel's case citing the English judgement, *Welsh Development Agency v Export Finance Company Ltd*,[62] the courts decided that even though no real risk passed from the seller to the purchaser, the transaction was however a sale.

5.4.3 *The United States*

In contrast, the position adopted by the US courts in the oft-cited decision of *Major's Furniture Mart v Castle Credit Corp*[63] is that the parties' intention is not, at least in the United States, a primary factor in determining whether a securitisation transaction involves a "true sale" or a secured loan. In that case, the respondent argued that the language of the agreement expressly referred only to sales and purchases, and on that basis, the parties did not intend to effect a security transfer. The court responded that it was not bound by the nomenclature that the parties applied to their relationship. The nature of the agreement is properly governed by the business activities of the parties. The court emphasised the fact that there was full recourse to the seller and noted the following elements of recourse provided by the plaintiff, Major's Furniture Mart:

- The plaintiff retained all conceivable risks of not being able to collect on these accounts.
- The plaintiff warranted that the customers met the criteria set forth by the defendant.
- The plaintiff performed credit checks to ensure that the criteria were met.
- The plaintiff guaranteed that the accounts were fully collectible.
- The plaintiff was to indemnify out of a reserve account for losses sustained due to customer default.
- The plaintiff was to repurchase any account that remained in default for more than 60 days.[64]

In the circumstances, it was held that the true nature of the transaction was such that the legal rights and economic consequences of the agreement bore a greater similarity to a collateralised borrowing than to a "true sale".

[62] [1992] BCLC 148.
[63] 602 F 2d 538 (3rd Cir 1979).
[64] 602 F 2d 538 (3rd Cir 1979). See also J. Lindsay and C Thomson, (1997) 21. A similar approach was adopted in *Re Evergreen Valley Resort* 23 BR 659 (1982).

The court adopted a similar economic, as opposed to an intention-based, approach to the question of true sale in *Endico Potatoes Inc v CIT Group Factoring Inc*[65]. In particular, the court focused on the level of risk transferred to the purchaser. In a sale or assignment of loan receivables, there is always a risk that the obligor—the initial borrower in this context—will not pay. The court held that if this risk was not fully and finally transferred to the SPV, a true sale had not occurred and the transaction was, in effect, a secured loan.

In adhering to this strict view (which, incidentally, is the same as that adopted by APRA for Australian capital adequacy purposes), it will be noted that this US decision is at variance with some of the English and Canadian authorities, which have held that even full recourse back to the originator is not incompatible with a concept of a legal sale.[66]

5.4.4 *Summary of Overseas Decisions*

Even though there a number of authorities deciding between a true sale and financing transaction for the purpose of insolvency, for most modern securitisation transactions, such facts do not form a part of the transaction. English cases and those arising from the British Commonwealth, including Canada, tend to honour the expressed intention of the parties than the real practice.[67] In the case of the United States, there are some judgements that ignore the expressed word(s) and re-classified a transaction as a secured loan. Anyhow, there are other tempting factors that may result in differing decisions, for example, capital market differences between jurisdictions, which include the fact that different capital markets are subject to different rules, the age of the judicial decisions, and the level at which the case was decided in the court hierarchy. Therefore, the cases are not easily

[65] 67 F3d 1063 (1995).

[66] [2003] O.J. No 128 (ONSC) paragraphs [50–51]. Indeed, in the English decision of *Welsh Development Agency* discussed earlier, the court found that although no real risk had passed from the seller to the purchaser, the transaction was nonetheless one of sale. Dillon LJ in that case emphasised that there was no clear touchstone for determining whether an agreement is really a sale or a secured transaction. For further discussion, see S. L. Schwarcz, *Structured Finance: A Guide to the Principles of Asset Securitization* (New York: Practising Law Institute, 1994) 28. In addition, see the Canadian decision of *Metropolitan Widows' Fund*, also noted earlier.

[67] See, for example, *Welsh Development Agency v Export Finance Company Ltd* [1992] BCLC 148; *Metropolitan Toronto Police Widows and Orphans Fund v Telus Communication Inc* [1996] 2 BCLC 78.

harmonised, and which factors are relevant and which should be given greater weight are open to interpretation. This uncertainty in the judicial treatment prompted some to quip that a court could flip a coin and finds support in the case law for either characterisation—"true sale" or secured loan.[68]

5.4.5 *Australia*

Thus far, there is no reported case in the Australian context that decides between a purported sale and a secured loan in a securitisation transaction or, perhaps to be more specific, in an RMBS programme. The Australian *Corporations Act*, which incorporates Australian accounting standards, provides some important comments that can be used in constituting a true sale in the Australian context.

In the Australian context, the use of a trust structure in mortgage securitisation paves the way for off-balance sheet treatment for accounting purposes. However, the trustee company should be a non-related or a subsidiary of the originator. Thus, it is vital that the originator does not hold a majority interest in the trustee company for the purposes of the Australian accounting standard on consolidation.[69]

Under the current law, the mortgage originator is prohibited from claiming ownership interest in the SPV or vice versa. Hence, a test to determine consolidation is (a) whether the SPV is part of another entity and (b) who controls the entity.

AASB 1024 defines "Control" accordingly: "the capacity of an entity to dominate decision making, directly or indirectly, in relation to the financial and operating policies of another entity ..."[70] Hence control depends on substance rather than form.

[68] R.D. Aicher and W.J. Fellerhoff, 'Characterisation of a Transfer of Receivables as a Sale a Secured Loan Upon Bankruptcy of the Transferor' (1991) 65 *American Banking Law Journal*. 181,183. For further discussion on the preconditions for a "true sale" of mortgage assets, see T. E. Plank, 'The True Sale of Loans and the Role Recourse' (1991) 14 *George Mason University Law Review* 287, 315; M. Oates, 'RBA Guidelines on Funds Management and Securitisation' (1994) 10 (3) *Australian Banking Law Bulletin* 23.

[69] See I. Plater, 'Accounting and Tax for Off-Balance Sheet Financing' *IIR Conference*, Sydney, September 1992, 6–12; and M. J. Cohn, 'Asset Securitization: How Remote is Bankruptcy Remote?' (1998) 26 (4) *Hofstra Law Review* 929.

[70] AASB, 'AASB Adoption of IASB Standards by 2005', August 2004, http://www.aasb.com.au

Provided that accounting standards form part of the corporations law in Australia, in drawing the line between a true sale and a secured loan, Australian courts can adopt a "substance over form" approach.

5.5 Assignment of the Originating Mortgagee's Rights

Under general law, a debt or other chose can be assigned via two methods—namely, legal assignment and equitable assignment.[71] It is the practice of Australian RMBS programmes to assign the originating mortgagee's rights in equity. There are a number of reasons for this.

For an assignment to be held valid at law, such an assignment should be absolute.[72] It also should be in writing and should be for the whole of the debt. It should be notified in writing to the debtor.[73] If an assignment fails to comply with any of those, such an assignment will be classified as an equitable assignment, in contrast to a true sale.[74]

[71] Contractual rights, being choses in action as opposed to things in possession, were not assignable at common law without the consent of both parties to the original contract. The courts of equity, however, did give effect to assignments of choses in action. Perhaps the most significant feature of the division between the common law and equity was the almost complete refusal by the courts of law to recognise equitable rights, titles, and interests. Each system, law, and equity devised its own procedural rules and remedies, resulting in substantive differences in the approaches of the two jurisdictions. For a discussion of the divisions between, and subsequent fusion of, the courts of common law and equity, see R.P. Meagher et al., *Equity Doctrines and Remedies* (4th edition, Sydney: Butterworths, 2002) 36–41.

[72] In other words, the assignment of mortgagee rights should not be by way of a charge.

[73] *Jones v Humphreys* [1902]1 KB 10; *Forster v Baker* [1910] 2 KB 636 (CA); *In re Steel Wing Co Ltd.* [1921] 2 Ch 349. A legal assignment operates from the date on which notice is given to the underlying debtor to transfer (a) the legal right to the debt, (b) the legal and other remedies for the same, and (c) the power for the assignee to give a good discharge for the debt without the concurrence of the assignor. For more detail, see H. Saban, *Corporate Debt Securitisation* (Singapore: Butterworths, 1994) 42; M. Ono, 'Unique Aspects of Japanese Securitization Relating to the Assignment of Financial Assets: A Comment on Raines and Wong' (2002) 12 (2) *Duke Journal of Comparative and International Law* 469.

[74] See sections 199–200 of the *Property Law Act* 1974 (Qld). Difficult and unresolved issues may arise as to whether consideration is necessary for the effectiveness of an equitable assignment. However, a detailed discussion of these issues is not only beyond the scope of this book, but would be entirely moot since, in an RMBS context, the SPV as equitable assignee does provide consideration: it pays the originating mortgagee a sum equal to the present value of the mortgagee's rights and obligations.

Section 199 of the *Property Law Act* 1974 (Qld) complies with requirements of legal assignment of a debt by way of a deed. Such an assignment may claim priority rights over all existing equities of the assignor.[75]

An assignment may transfer only rights but not obligations.[76] Without the consent of the debtor, it is not possible to assign obligations to a third party, even though this concept is often misunderstood.[77] When it comes to residential mortgage securitisation, it is only the originating mortgagee's rights[78] that can be assigned.

There are a number of practical concerns arising with a legal assignment:

- A legal assignment that accompanies a notice will eliminate the originator (assignor) from the transaction, since the mortgage together with mortgagee's rights are now vested in the trustee-issuer (assignee), with direct recourse to the borrower.
- A legal assignment deals with the transfer of an "entire loan", as there is no legal basis at law for a legal or absolute transfer of *part* of a loan.[79] In this manner, a legal assignment cannot transfer any obligation for the trustee-issuer to provide further funds in a loan facility where the loan has not yet been fully drawn down by the borrower.
- As we have already noted, to be recognised at law, notice of the assignment should be given to the initial borrower. In practice,

[75] See also *Newfoundland Government v Newfoundland Rly Co* (1888) 13 App Cas 199 (PC); *Smith v Parks* (1852) 16 Beav 115; *Re Tout and Finch Ltd* [1954] 1 All ER 127; [1954] 1 WLR 178.

[76] Thereby effecting a novation. In the context of securitisation, a novation involves a tripartite arrangement whereby the two parties to an original contract, the originator and the debtor, agree with an SPV that the SPV shall become a substitute for the originator, and thus assume the originator's rights and obligations under that contract and in the creation of a new contract between the SPV and the debtor.

[77] See *Tolhurst v Associated Portland Cement Manufacturers Ltd* [1902] 2 KB 660, 668 (CA). Neither at law nor in equity could the burden of a contract be shifted from the shoulders of a contractor onto those of another, without the consent of the contractee: per Lord Collins MR. In an Australian context, see also B. E. Salter, *An Overview of the Legal Issues Relevant to Securitisation in Australia* (Sydney: Clayton Utz, February 2000) 5.

[78] Strictly, it is the mortgagee's "rights, title and interest" that are assigned.

[79] *Encyclopaedia of Forms and Precedents*, v 4, 566. This is the case in all Australian jurisdictions except Western Australia: see section 20(3) of the *Property Law Act* 1969 (WA). In the other Australian jurisdictions, however, an assignment of part of a loan is recognised in equity: see *Williams v Atlantic Assurance Co* [1933] 1 KB 81 and *Re Steel Wing Co* [1921] 1 Ch 349.

> mortgage originators (i.e. banks) prefer assignment in equity in contrast to law, so that the customers are not aware of the fact that their mortgages have been securitised (due to commercial incentives).[80]

An equitable assignment, in which only the beneficial interests will be transferred, retaining the legal title with the transferor, has positive advantages for an originator desiring to securitise its mortgage interests which, in part, mirror the disadvantages of a legal assignment.[81] An equitable assignment must be in writing[82]; there needs to be evidence suggesting that the originator (assignor) intends to transfer its interest immediately and irrevocably to the SPV (as assignee). This will usually be by a deed.[83] However, it has

[80] Standard and Poor's, *Structured Finance Australia and New Zealand* (1999) 40; and B. Taylor, 'Assignments of Securities in Corporate Re-Financing' (1998) 13 *Australian Banking and Finance Law Bulletin* 141–155. In some jurisdictions, the giving of notice to the underlying mortgagors will be a necessary formality in the transfer of mortgages. In most European systems, for example, the Spanish Civil Code provides compulsory notice to the debtor in order to effect the transfer. Similarly, in France, Luxembourg, Italy Japan, South Korea, the giving of notice to the debtor is a formal requirement: J. Borrows, 'Legal and Regulatory Issues' in D. C. Gardner (ed.), *Securitisation* (London: Euromoney, 1997) 15; P. R. Wood, *Title Finance Derivatives, Securitisation, Set-Off and Netting* (London: Sweet & Maxwell, 1995) 53.

[81] *Holroyd v Marshall* 11 ER 999 (HL 1862); and *Howard v Miller* [1915] App Cas 318 (PC). Like a legal or absolute assignment, an equitable assignment does not operate to transfer obligations from the originator to the issuer. An equitable assignment will, however, transfer all rights of the originator in the loan or part thereof to the issuer, since a transfer of part of a right or chose in action is permissible under an equitable assignment: see *Jones v Humphreys* [1902] 1 KB 10 and *Williams v Atlantic Assurance Co Ltd* [1933] 1 KB 81. This in effect gives the SPV/assignee recourse to the borrower in equity, albeit only to the extent of the beneficial interest in that part of the loan assigned, and only when the originator/assignor (or the owner of the legal title) is joined as a party to a claim. See *Derham Bros. v Robertson* [1898] 1 QB 765 (CA); *William Brandt's Son and Co v Dunlop Rubber Co Ltd* [1905] App Cas 454; L. B. Klein, 'Legal Issues Relating to Participation in Bank Loans', in J. Lederman (ed.), *The Commercial Loan Resale Market* (Columbus, Ohio: McGraw-Hill Education, 1991) 357, 385. Issues relating to sub-participations are not discussed here as they are beyond the scope of this book.

[82] The assignment of equitable interests has historically been regulated by statute. For example, section 9 of the *Statute of Frauds* 1677 required all "grants and assignments" inter vivos of "any trust or confidence" to be in writing, signed by the assignor. For any assignment to be valid, it had to be in writing from the beginning. See H. A. J. Ford and W. A. Lee *Principles of the Law of Trusts* (Sydney: Law Book Company, 2004) Ch. 3.

[83] *Norman v Federal Commissioner of Taxation* (1963) 109 CLR 9, 29.

been discussed that a letter has been held to be sufficient.[84] It is noteworthy that in an equitable assignment, notice to the borrower is not mandatory, for the assignment to be effective in equity.[85]

5.5.1 *The Problem of Notice*

As we have already discussed in Chap. 2, a moral hazard concern occurs since no notice is given to home loan borrowers notifying that the mortgagee rights to their loans have been assigned to another party. This may result in implications for economic efficiency. From a strict legal point of view, neglecting (or perhaps, deliberately failing) to notify borrowers of a risk that their houses may be sold without a default (fault) from the borrower would seem at the least to be unconscionable.[86] In *Canham v Australian Guarantee Corporation Ltd*, Kirby P stated:

> The ultimate theory behind the philosophy of truth in lending ... is that disclosure ... will help to ensure honesty and integrity in the relationship (where one party is normally disadvantaged and even vulnerable); promote informed choices by consumers; and allow the market form financial services to operate effectively.[87]

[84] *Re Ward* (1984) 55 ALR 395.

[85] This is not to say that notice of the assignment to the debtor is unimportant. It could be highly significant in at least two situations in practice—first, where there are competing assignments of the same mortgage (in effect, this boils down to a priority problem, already discussed in Chap. 4); and second, where the borrower purports to pay off his or her loan to the assignor/originator, unaware that its mortgagee rights have been assigned, and obtaining the originator's purported discharge of the debt: *Stocks v Dobson* [1853] 43 ER 411. If a borrower were to pay the originator, which then became insolvent immediately after receiving the payment but prior to paying the SPV, the SPV would have no recourse against the debtor: see R. Derham, *Set-Off* (2nd edition, Oxford University Press, 1996); The SPV would then need to either claim that the originator received the payment in trust for the SPV, or claim against the originator's estate, in common with other creditors. (This might occur, for example, if the SPV was unable to establish a proprietary right to the payment received, or trace its proprietary interest in the payment into the hands of the originator).

[86] Indeed, there would seem to be an appreciable future risk of litigation against the banks, IMPs, and/or sponsors for contravention of the "unconscionable conduct" provisions of the *Competition and Consumer Act* 2010 (Cth).

[87] (1993) 31 NSWLR 246, 254; and (1993) ASC 56227, 58354.

There could be a number of possible concerns if borrowers are not given notice of the assignment.[88] While not informing borrowers of the assignments may be expedient for the banks, it is contrary to the conventional wisdom on mortgage transfers. For instance, according to at least one leading text:

> [T]he transfer of a mortgage is an unsafe investment, unless the mortgagor concurs or joins in the transfer as a party to the transaction ... if a transferee makes the initial mistake of not obtaining the concurrence of the mortgagor, it is vital that notice of the transfer should at once be given.[89]

Despite the fact of whether a transfer is legal or equitable, it is sensible for a transferee of a mortgage to grant notice to the borrower that their mortgage has been transferred to a third party. The main risk that is likely to occur is that, provided notice is not given and the mortgagor continues to make payments to the assignor/originator, the mortgagor cannot be obliged to remit those payments to the SPV.[90] In the real world, this concern is addressed by paying the mortgage borrowers' repayments directly into the trustee-issuer's bank account; thus, payments do not pass through the originator's hands.[91] Using modern technology, it is always possible for computer systems to be programmed such that payments divert and direct debits to the appropriate account. Yet, this arrangement could not be implemented with mortgage payments made by cheque, without informing borrowers in some sense (even if only by virtue of the account details on their bank statements).[92]

[88] These potential problems tend to exist in all common and civil law jurisdictions. See generally, Wood, above n 80, 52–53.

[89] E. Cousins, *The Law of Mortgages* (2nd edition, London: Sweet & Maxwell, 1989) 384–386.

[90] *Williams v Sorrell (*1799) 4 Ves 389, 31 ER 198; *Norrish v Marshall* (1821) 5 Madd 475, 56 ER 977 [1814] All ER Rep 587; *Re Lord Southampton's Estate* [1880] 16 Ch D 178; *Parker v Jackson* [1936] 2 All ER 281.

[91] *Master Information Memorandum, PUMA Fund P-7* (2000) paragraph 5.2.

[92] The lack of notice to borrowers also exposes the banks to the risk of litigation. Nor should the banks be unaware of this risk. For example, the foreign currency lawsuits of the early 1990s were largely a result of management in the major banks failing to inform their borrowers of the potential risks involved in non-traditional borrowing. See, for example, *Clenae Pty Ltd and Ors v ANZ Banking Group Ltd* [1999] VSCA 35 (9 April 1999); *David Securities Ltd v Commonwealth Bank* [1990] 23 FCR 1; *Chiarabaglio v Westpac Banking Corporation* (1989) ATPR 40–971; and *Leitch and Ors v Natwest Australia Bank Ltd and Anor* (unreported, 12 October 1995, Federal Court of Australia) per Cooper J.

Further, the failure to notify the borrower of the assignment may permit the borrower to set off claims that he or she has against the originator, against obligations he or she owes to the originator. Under general law, an assignee whether legal or equitable, takes "subject to equities" which means that the SPV/assignee should be in no better position vis-à-vis the debtor than the originator/assignor was prior to the assignment.[93] If the borrower is notified of the transfer, any future right to set off will be lost.[94] Therefore, set-off rights will remain and be binding on the assignee, to the extent that they arise out of the same contract that gives rise to the loan asset.[95]

Set-off rights are fundamentally important to bank or assignment programmes, for two reasons. Banks mainly are deposit-taking institutions. It is more likely that borrowers will also maintain deposits or perhaps trading accounts with their banks. Hence, they are entitled to set off their deposits against their debt obligations to the bank.[96]

Provided that the SPV/assignee has given notice to the borrower of the transfer of the loan,[97] the borrower loses future right to set off claims, yet will retain any rights or equities accrued up to the date on which he or she received the notice.[98] Also if a bank fails to honour its commitment towards the borrower to whom the mortgages were granted, damages that the borrower incurs may be set off against the borrower's loan obligation.[99]

If the mortgagor agrees not to exercise any right of set-off against the originator under general law in the originator's mortgage documentation, the risk of an SPV not receiving its anticipated income due to right of set-off exercised by a mortgagor against the original mortgage lender can be minimised.[100] Any such agreement will be valid under normal

[93] *Dawson v Great Northern and City Railway Co* [1905] 1 KB 260 (CA 1904); and *Re Harry Simpson and Co* (1964) NSWLR 603, 605.

[94] Under general law, once notice of assignment has been given, the debtor cannot do anything to take away or diminish the rights of the assignee as they stood at the time of the notice *Roxburghe v Cox* [1881]17 Ch D 520, 526 (CA); see generally Derham, above n 85.

[95] *Business Computers Ltd v Anglo African Leasing Ltd* [1977] 1 WLR 578 (Ch).

[96] For a detailed discussion, see M. Wormell, 'Securitisation and Set-Off' (1998) 9 *Journal of Banking and Finance Law and Practice* 181.

[97] Or, for example, in the context of US law, once contractual privity is established between the borrower and the SPV.

[98] *Diesel Motors Co v Kaye* 345 NYS 2d 870, 875 (1973): S. L. Schwarz (1993) 30–31; T. Frankel, (1991) paragraph 7.23.

[99] *Government of Newfoundland v Newfoundland Railway Co* [1888] 13 App Cas 199 (PC).

[100] Borrows, above n 80.

circumstances until such time as a mortgagor became insolvent. The operation of insolvency set-off might then result in the reduction of the trustee-issuer's income in respect of a particular mortgage.[101]

5.5.2 *Avenues for the SPV to Enforce Its Rights Other than as Equitable Mortgagee*

Suing on the Debt

Just like any other loan secured by collateral, a housing loan comprises two elements. The first is a personal contract for payment of the debt; and second, an interest in the debtor's property as security for the payment of the debt. In a typical RMBS programme, both are normally transferred together in equity.

If the trustee-issuer permits a commingling of its own funds with those of the originating bank, in a bank or assignment programme,[102] the SPV's proprietary interest may be lost.[103] Hence, any dispute between the SPV and the originating bank will need to be resolved based on the debtor-creditor relationship.

[101] See generally, Wood, above n 80. Because of the competing claims that could arise and which could be set off against each other, it is clearly prudent for mortgages in favour of the originator's employees to be excluded from the pool of mortgages that make up the backing for an issue of RMBS. The same argument can be made for the exclusion of mortgages in favour of persons who are depositors with the originator. However, an originator that is authorised to take deposits (e.g. a bank or building society) might find it difficult to implement this, especially if its general policy is only to grant mortgages in favour of its own depositors. Moreover, a mortgagor who is originally unconnected to the originator might become one of its employees or depositors. When considering the seriousness of this risk arising from the operation of equities, however, it is important to bear in mind that equities exercisable by individual mortgagors are likely to give rise only to isolated problems in specific cases. Since such isolated incidents are unlikely to undermine the value of the trustee-issuer's earnings to any significant extent, they can therefore be viewed as being relatively limited importance in practice.

[102] It is difficult to see, in the absence of ineptitude and perhaps negligence, how commingling of funds could occur in a conduit programme. There would appear to be more scope for this to occur in a bank programme where the trustee-issuer is essentially a subsidiary or other entity related to the originating bank.

[103] Standard and Poor's, *Structured Finance in Australia and New Zealand* (Melbourne: 1999) 73.

Remedies for Breach of Trust[104]

The legal title to the residential mortgages on trust for the trustee-issuer will be held by the originator or the security trustee under an equitable assignment. This trust extends to all rights and claims, including accrued interest, arising out of the mortgages.[105] If the originator fails to dispatch funds to the issuer, it would be in breach of trust as well as the originator would be in breach of its contractual obligations under the terms of the mortgages.

The claim for breach of trust may play a crucial role if the originator becomes insolvent. This is mainly due to the fact that the trustee-issuer might then be able to trace the money that should have been transmitted to it to obtain satisfaction of its claim in priority to the originator's unsecured creditors.[106]

If the trust property is so mixed with other property, the right to trace is lost. The originator will become untraceable. Thus, the issuer's only claim against the originator would be a personal claim for breach of trust.

Implications

One of the main concerns in assignment programmes, in terms of legal and prudential aspects, is the fact whether sufficient risk and reward have been transferred from the originator to the trust. This is in order to establish that a "true sale" of the mortgagee's rights has occurred. As we have already discussed, if the originating bank retains influence over assets or the originator retains a right to share in any profits of the SPV, it will less likely to be classified as a true sale. Provided that there is no "true sale" involved, mortgaged loans assigned will lose their off-balance sheet status for regulatory and accounting purposes and will be re-characterised as

[104] It is interesting that, as discussed earlier, in Australian RMBS programmes, the originator's mortgagee rights are assigned in equity to an SPV. In this way, the originator as the holder of a legal (and initially equitable) interest in residential mortgages purports to vest an equitable interest in those mortgages in the SPV by assignment. However, purely from the perspective of trust law, the equitable interest could equally well be vested in the SPV by the originator, at law, making a declaration of trust. The difference between the two mechanisms would be that while both would convey an equitable interest to the SPV, the equitable assignment would result in a constructive trust, whereas the declaration of trust would create an express trust. See Ford and Lee, above n 82, paragraph 3180. The reason why most RMBS programmes in Australia utilise the equitable assignment route, rather than an express trust, is that it is perceived to be simpler and less costly.

[105] Standard and Poor's, *Structured Finance in Australia and New Zealand* (1999) 73.

[106] See Borrows, above n 80.

on-balance sheet secured loans. This will create significant consequences inter alia for a financial institution's capital adequacy and taxation obligations. Since there are no Australian cases dealing with this matter and also available few cases that have been decided overseas are somewhat inconsistent, it is difficult to determine a "true sale".

5.6 Establishing a Special Purpose Vehicle

In a typical Australian RMBS programme, the SPV takes the form of a unit trust. The unit trust will hold an equitable interest in the underlying residential mortgages on behalf of the beneficiaries. The unit trust also receives and disburses income through to the RMBS investors and unit holders. In Australia, the unit trust structure involves the appointment of an established, independent trustee company to act as trustee.

Generally, unit holders are subsidiaries of the bank or the sponsor.[107] In most Australian RMBS programmes, the trust has two separate classes of capital and income beneficiaries.[108]

Those who hold capital units are entitled to a distribution of the corpus of the trust estate (if any remains), after all the obligations of the trustee to the creditors of the trust are met.[109] On the other hand, the holders of the income units are entitled to receive distributions of net trust income (if any) after the day-to-day expenses of the trust are met.[110]

Generally, the trustee also acts in the capacity of the issuer of the RMBSs. Institutional investors, typical investors of RMBSs, are rank as secured creditors of the unit trust. The trustee typically grants a charge over the mortgages of the trust to a security trustee, who agrees to hold that charge for the benefit of certain secured creditors.[111] If the trust were to be wound up, the security trustee would be required to ensure that the assets of the trust were distributed according to the law governing corporate trustees.[112]

[107] See, for example, Macquarie Securitisation Ltd's *PUMA Master Fund P-7*, in *Master Information Memorandum, PUMA Fund P-7 and Master Information Memorandum, PUMA Sub-Fund Series 2014, p 58.*

[108] I.e. those beneficiaries that hold units representing an interest in the capital of the trust, and those that hold units representing an interest in the net income of the trust up to a maximum, after all interest and principal payments have been made to the RMBS investors.

[109] Macquarie Securitisation Ltd in the context of Macquarie Bank's *PUMA Master Fund P-7*, in *Master Information Memorandum, PUMA Fund P-7*, paragraph 4.6.

[110] Such as interest obligations on the RMBSs, and fees and expenses.

[111] E.g. the bondholders, or the interest rate risk manager.

[112] For further discussion, see Chap. 6.

5.7 Impact of the *National Credit Code*

Recent reforms to consumer credit law have resulted in a single national consumer credit regime governed by National Consumer Credit Protection Act 2009 (Cth) (NCCP), which includes the *National Credit Code* (Code) as Schedule 1 to the Act. The NCC replaces previous state-based consumer credit codes and the *Uniform Consumer Credit Code* (UCCC) and it continues to apply to the conduct of Australian credit licence holders. ASIC is responsible for administering the NCCP.

The NCC applies to credit contracts entered into on or after 1 July 2010 where:

- The lender is in the business of providing credit.
- A charge is made for providing the credit.
- The debtor is a natural person or strata corporation.
- The credit is provided for personal, domestic, or household purposes.
- To purchase, renovate, or improve residential property for investment purposes, or to refinance credit previously provided for this purpose.[113]

As far as the Code is concerned, the prime concern in the industry has been the issue of whether the SPV and the originator may be classed as a "credit provider" and whether the SPV is therefore subject to the responsibilities imposed on credit providers by the Code. If the transaction is classified as a "providing credit" in contrast to a true sale, responsibilities of the SPV include the provision of:

- Complete pre-contractual disclosure of details pertaining to credit contracts to borrowers and guarantors[114]
- Regular account statements and notices[115] (there may include notices of any changes in the interest rate, and account-keeping fees and charges)[116] so that borrowers are aware of the current state of their loan accounts

[113] Section 5, NCC. The NCC does not apply to certain loans, including: low-cost, short-term credit (less than 62 days), insurance premiums paid by instalments, bill facilities, and staff loans.

[114] See especially, sections 14–16 of the Code.

[115] See sections 33–36 of the Code.

[116] See also A. Duggan and E. Lanyon, *Consumer Credit Law* (Sydney: Butterworths, 1999) Ch. 11.

- Key rights to borrowers, such as
  - The right to negotiate a variation of loans on the grounds of temporary hardship (e.g. illness, unemployment)[117]
  - A right to apply to court or a tribunal to reopen unjust transactions[118] and review unconscionable interest and other charges[119]

[117] See section 72. Debtors who are unable to meet their repayment obligations because of substantial hardship caused by circumstances such as unemployment or illness may apply to the credit provider for extension of time, or postponement, or reduced payment arrangements. These provisions apply only if the debtors can reasonably expect to meet their obligations if these variations are granted. A debtor may apply to a court if the provider refuses to agree to a variation.

[118] See sections 76. A debtor, mortgagor, or guarantor may apply to a court for a determination on whether a credit contract is unjust: sections 76–78. If this is proven, the contract may be reopened and appropriate remedies granted. The meaning of "unjust" is very wide. Under section 204, it includes "unconscionable, harsh or oppressive" credit contracts, and could go further. For example, it is not inconceivable that a credit contract might be found to be unjust if it breaches the moral standards that the community expects from business operators. The court must consider "the public interest", and all the circumstances of the case, in a manner reminiscent of the factors considered under the unconscionability provisions of the *Competition and Consumer Act* 2010 (Cth). The court also has wide powers to reopen an unjust transaction. Those orders include relieving the debtor or guarantor of his or her payment obligations.

Section 81 of the Code enables the court to join as parties to proceedings, additional persons who have an interest in the profits of the mortgage or a beneficial interest in a mortgage, and to make orders affecting the persons if the court holds the mortgage to be unjust: *Crocco v Esanda Finance Co Ltd* (1993) ASC 56, 223. It is conceivable that, if the court holds the residential loan contracts in an RMBS programme to be unjust, the court could join the trustee of the SPV as a party to the proceedings, and make an order concerning the trustee which, while not explicitly, could indirectly impact adversely on the interests of bondholders in the sense that the trustee would seek indemnification from the trust fund. It is also conceivable that an originating lender might join the trustee of the SPV and seek a contribution from it for compensation payable. For further discussion, see T. Robinson, 'Securitisation Update', *Seventh Annual Credit Law Conference* (Melbourne: BLEC, 1997) 4.

[119] In practice, an application fee is generally payable by the mortgagor to the Originator/Servicer. Section 78 of the Code provides that upon the application of a debtor or guarantor, the court may declare an establishment fee or charge to be unconscionable and annul or reduce the fee or charge. Section 78(3) provides: "In determining whether an establishment fee or charge is unconscionable, the Court is to have regard to whether the amount of the fee or charge is equal to the credit provider's reasonable costs of determining an application for credit and the initial administrative costs of providing the credit or is equal to the credit provider's average reasonable costs of those things in respect of that class of contract." While there is no formal definition of "establishment fee or charge" in the Code, section 78(3) indicates that it is the fee imposed for determining the application, together with the initial administrative costs of providing credit. While section 78(3) does not strictly compel credit

- A right to protection against enforcement of unfair loan agreements by the lender[120]

In a practical sense, implementing the above with all borrowers in a mortgage pool, including performing necessary statutory responsibilities, involves significant costs. Under the provisions of the Code, failure by the credit provider to perform its responsibilities may involve civil[121] and/or criminal[122] liability for itself and for any linked supplier[123] who is also deemed a "credit provider" for the purposes of the Code.

providers to ensure that their establishment fees or charges exceed the credit provider's costs, it plainly creates considerable incentive for the credit provider to do so when read together with the other provisions in section 78. Under these other provisions, credit providers who do not relate establishment fees to reasonable costs run the risk of actions by debtors and guarantors for court orders. Section 19 of the Code also gives the debtor the right to terminate the credit contract before credit has been provided.

[120] See Pt. 5 of the Code.

[121] A debtor or guarantor in a relevant residential mortgage loan may apply to court regarding a possible breach of any of the key requirements of the Code: sections 112–114. If the breach is proven, the credit provider may lose all the interest charges owing on the mortgage loan. Alternatively, if it is a continuing credit contract, the credit provider could lose all interest charges for the period ordered, which could be significant if the interest is compounded, for example, on a monthly basis. Where the debtor's or guarantor's loss is greater than the amount of outstanding interest charges, the credit provider may be ordered to pay compensation to the actual loss.

The extent of any civil liability might even depend upon who makes the application for the imposition of these civil consequences. If it is the debtor, then the size of the penalty can be significantly greater than that would be the case if the credit provider or the "State Consumer Agency"—i.e. in Queensland, the Office of Fair Trading—brought the application. The credit provider is subject to a maximum fine of $500,000 for each key contravention under the Code.

In terms of other forms of civil liability, Division 1 Pt. 6 of the Code provides that a court may order the credit provider to make restitution or pay compensation to any person affected by a contravention, other than one for which a civil penalty is specifically provided for in the Code. This could conceivably extend to securitised bondholders. In addition, a credit provider's failure to comply with certain requirements in connection with a mortgage or guarantee may result in the mortgage or guarantee (or particular provisions of those documents) being ordered void or unenforceable.

[122] The commission of an offence under the Code exposes the credit provider, and officers of a corporate credit provider who aid and abet the commission of that offence, to monetary penalties. The level of penalty varies with the contravention, but the maximum penalty currently provided for in the Code is $10,000.

[123] In terms of the liability of such a linked credit provider, a credit provider may become "linked" to a loan contract if a supplier of goods and services regularly refers its customers to that credit provider or has a contract, arrangement, or understanding with the credit provider.

5.7.1 *Credit Provider in an RMBS Programme*

A credit provider is defined as "a person that provides credit and includes a prospective credit provider"[124] in the Code. In section 3, the term "Credit" is defined as;

> For the purposes of this Code, 'credit' is provided if, under a contract:
>
> (a) payment of a debt owed by person (the debtor) to another (the credit provider) is deferred; or
> (b) one person (the debtor) incurs a deferred debt to another (the credit provider).[125]

In practice, almost all mortgage originators,[126] except in the case of independent mortgage providers (IMPs) who effectively act as spotters for the banks or larger mortgage providers,[127] are credit providers under this definition and are therefore subject to the responsibilities imposed on credit providers by the Code.

Section 188 of the Code deals with a vital concern. Once the originator's mortgagee rights have been assigned in equity to the SPV, the real concern is whether the credit provider is the originating lender or the trustee-issuer, for the purpose of the Code. Section 188 says:

> (1) If the rights of a credit provider under a credit contract, mortgage or guarantee are assigned or pass by law to another person, this Code from then on applies to that other person, and does not impose any further obligation on the credit provider.

For example, an agent for a bank often arranges home mortgage finance for clients of a building company, which sells house and land packages. The bank might be classified as a linked credit provider to the building company on the basis of these dealings. This linked credit provider might become liable under sections 127–128 for misrepresentations or breaches of contract by the supplier, if it is not commercially worthwhile to sue the supplier (e.g. because it is insolvent or in liquidation).

[124] See Schedule 1 of the Code.

[125] According to section 3(2), the amount of credit is the amount of the debt actually deferred, excluding interest and certain other charges under the contract.

[126] For further discussion of the mechanics of mortgage origination, see the preceding chapters, or Robinson, above n 118.

[127] In the case of those IMPs that effectively act as "spotters" for the banks or larger mortgage providers (see Chap. 3), the initial lender, not the IMP, will normally be the credit provider for the purposes of the Code. After assignment, the issues relating to who is the relevant "credit provider" for the purposes of the Code—i.e. the initial lender or the SPV—are the same as set out below.

(2) The debtor, mortgagor or guarantor has and may exercise the same rights in respect of the credit contract, mortgage or guarantee against the assignee as the debtor, mortgagor or guarantor has against the credit provider.
(3) Subsection (1) does not apply while the credit provider continues to receive payments from the debtor ...

Accordingly, we can argue that these provisions imply that after their housing mortgage has been assigned in equity to an SPV, the borrowers/mortgagors would hypothetically have the same rights against the trustee-issuer (assignee) as they had against the originating bank or IMP (i.e. assignor)[128] who made the loan to them.[129]

As noted in our previous discussion, especially in practice, notice of the assignment is not generally granted to debtors. It is more likely that borrowers may not normally be aware that an assignment has taken place. More likely, borrowers would continue to make repayments to their initial credit provider (i.e. the bank). This implies that the originator remains the "credit provider" for the purposes of the Code in contrast to the SPV.[130] This is, of course, a line of argument that the banks and sponsors of RMBS issues would have considerable incentive to employ, should any cases on point be litigated.[131]

[128] Section 188(2); Robinson, above n 118. Borrowers/mortgagors would also acquire the usual rights under general law against the equitable assignee that result from equitable assignment: see Meagher, above n 71, paragraphs 699, 6100, 6101; and A. J. Duggan, *Regulated Credit: The Sale Aspect* (Sydney: Law Book Company, 1986) paragraph 12.32. For example, if the originating bank or IMP (assignor) imposed excessive charges on the mortgagor in contravention of the Code, the mortgagor would be able *ex facie* to assert a right to recover the amount of the excess from the SPV (assignee). Similarly, the mortgagor may potentially have rights, actionable directly against the SPV (as assignee), in respect of misrepresentations or misleading conduct by the originating bank or IMP, either at common law or under legislation such as the *Competition and Consumer* 2010 (Cth).

[129] In short, they may sue the trustee-issuer of the SPV as assignee of the originating mortgagee's rights. By itself, section 188(1) is plainly a statutory gloss on the equitable rule that obligations cannot be assigned: see Chap. 4 for more detail.

[130] By virtue of section 188(3) of the Code.

[131] A counter-argument is that, in this situation, while the borrowers are continuing to make post-assignment repayments to the bank or IMP as credit provider from the borrowers' perspective, the bank or IMP is receiving the repayments as *agent* from the SPV's (assignee's) perspective. However, the problem with this counter-argument is that the borrowers are not given notice of the assignment, so that the bank or IMP would appear to be acting as agent for an *undisclosed* principal. According to the doctrine of the undisclosed

For a typical RMBS programme, the originator remains the credit provider as long as she continues to receive repayments from the mortgagors, as far as the effect of section 188 is concerned. When such repayment comes to an end, the trustee-issuer of the SPV should essentially become the credit provider, and assume the attendant responsibilities under the Code.[132]

However, based on the addition to the Code in 1998, in any event, under the section 192,[133] the Code allows stakeholders to grant indemnities in respect of civil and criminal liability under the Code. As we have discussed earlier, in a practical sense, the trustee-issuer is not liable for

principal, it is arguable that the originating bank or IMP remains liable as the credit provider, not only on the basis of section. 188(3), but also at common law. See, for example, *Keighley, Maxted and Co v Durant* [1901] AC 240, 261; *Vital Finance Corporation Pty Ltd v Taylor* (1993) ASC 56–205, 58,179–58,182; D. W. Greig and J. L. R. Davis, *The Law of Contract* (Sydney: Law Book Company, 1987) 1001–2; and S. Fisher, *Agency Law* (Sydney: Butterworths, 2000) Ch. 10.

[132] The effect is more likely to be of intellectual curiosity than of practical significance since, if borrowers are never notified of the assignments to the SPV, in the normal course of events they will continue making repayments on their loans to their originating lender until the loans are paid off. After that point, there should, in general, be no practical concern with whether the SPV or the originator is the relevant "credit provider" under the Code.

[133] Section 192 of the code states;

(1) An indemnity for any liability under this Code is not void, and cannot be declared void, on the grounds of public policy, despite any rule of law to the contrary.
(2) The liabilities to which this section applies include the following:
    (a) a liability for any criminal or civil penalty incurred by any person under this Code;
    (b) a payment in settlement of a liability or alleged liability under this Code;
    (c) a liability under another indemnity for any liability under this Code.
(3) This section is subject to subsection 191(2).
(4) This section does not derogate from any other rights and remedies that exist apart from this section.

In short, the section allows any stakeholder who is potentially liable under the Code to obtain an indemnity from another person, who may themselves in turn obtain an indemnity from anyone except the borrower or guarantor. In general, rights and remedies under general law are preserved. Section 192 allows a credit provider to contract out of liability for a criminal penalty under the Code. At common law, such an agreement would be void as contrary to public policy, but section 191(2) displaces this rule. It provides that an indemnity from any person for any liability under the Code is not void on the ground of public policy. The provision also validates indemnities obtained retrospectively.

compliance with the Code. Also, it is reasonable to assume that trustee-issuer does not strictly need an indemnity against liability potentially arising under it. Yet, an order of a court of law (perhaps a tribunal) may still be made under section 76,[134] and it would be indiscreet if trustees did not obtain an indemnity from the credit provider against such liability.

However, such indemnities are needed to establish a clean sale. Were it not for provision for indemnities, it is more likely that the trustee-issuer of the SPV would not be obtaining "clean" mortgagee rights, for which it gave good consideration when those rights were assigned to it in equity.

Henceforth, it is common for trustee-issuers to obtain indemnities not only from originators[135] but also from originating banks or IMPs to obtain similar indemnities from their agents, for trustee-issuers to obtain indemnities from their fund managers, usually to a pre-specified limit,[136] and thereafter from the trust assets,[137] and for the security trustee to obtain indemnities from the trustee-issuer.

5.7.2 Payments in Advance for Housing Loans

One of the main cash flow management complications that a lender may face is early payouts, (prepayments) of loans by borrowers. Anyhow, even in a sophisticated age with information technology and financial engineering, prepayment can lead to a number of "confusions" with a lender's operating budgets since prepayments can disrupt with the

[134] See the foregoing discussion in relation to unjust loan contracts.

[135] See, for instance, in the context of Macquarie Bank's RMBS programmes, *Master Information Memorandum, PUMA Fund-P7*, paragraph 5.3 (c) and 8.3 (c) and *Master Information Memorandum, PUMA Sub-Fund Series* 2014, pp 102–105. Perhaps interestingly, the APRA does not regard this as a contravention of its prudential regulatory guidelines in relation to the assignment being a "true sale", presumably because indemnities in respect of liability under the *National Credit Code* are not regarded as granting the SPV recourse back to the originator in respect of its primary debt obligations (which is the main thrust of the prudential requirements).

[136] For example, under the Management Deed of the Macquarie Securitisation Program *PUMA Fund P-7*, the Fund Manager has agreed to indemnify the trustee-issuer against any civil liability under the Code up to a maximum of $500,000: see, *Master Information Memorandum, PUMA Fund-P7*, paragraph 5.8.3.

[137] See, for instance, *Master Information Memorandum, PUMA Fund-P7*, paragraph 5.8.2, and 8.10.

timing and duration of interest income,[138] principal repayments, and expenses that the lender has carefully scheduled and factored into its cash flow management algorithms.

In the context of RMBS issues, a prepayment can drag the SPV, as equitable assignee of the originating mortgagee's rights, to a similar position to that of the traditional lender. The conventional way that lenders deal with borrowers' prepayment of loans is to levy an early prepayment charge, which generally equates to the capitalised value of the estimated net interest and fees foregone.

Under legislative provisions of the Code, the mortgagor-borrower or guarantor is not only entitled to pay out the loan contract at any time but also entitled to make partial prepayments at any time and should be granted credit for the same. In contrast to traditional lenders, RMBS programme sponsors are not capable of prohibiting prepayments ahead of time. To deal with the issue, perhaps as a solution, the RMBS programme sponsors tend to impose a fee on a partial prepayment or in case of an early payout,[139] which is legal under the Code, with regulations on the level of the fees that can be charged.[140]

The fee that will be imposed on a prepayment will be based on the costs and loss of income associated with reinvestment of the prepaid principal from the date of prepayment to that of the final scheduled payment under

[138] Duration, in this context is defined in a financial engineering sense, as a measure of the average time at which payments are made, weighted by the size of the payments: see B. Hunt and C. Terry *Financial Institutions and Markets* (3rd edition, Melbourne: Thomson Publishing, 2002) 192; and T. Valentine, G. Ford and R. Copp *Financial Markets and Institutions in Australia* (Sydney: Pearson Education, 2003) 173–182.

[139] The issue here is the fact whether an early termination or prepayment fee can take in to account not only the administrative costs of the SPV, but also of other parties. E.g. servicer. To the extent that these costs are generally reflected in those of the SPV itself, the answer would appear to be in the affirmative, for reasons similar to those set out here.

[140] Section 78 states, upon the application of a debtor or guarantor, a fee or charge payable on early termination of a credit contract, or for a prepayment of an amount under a credit contract, can be declared unconscionable and be annulled or reduced. s 78(4) states: "For the purposes of this section, a fee or charge payable on early termination of the contract or a prepayment of an amount under the credit contract is unconscionable if and only if it appears to the court that it exceeds a reasonable estimate of the credit provider's loss arising from the early termination or prepayment, including the credit provider's average reasonable administrative costs in respect of such a termination or prepayment."

the loan.[141] Such costs are generally covered by mortgage insurance policies, in the event that the sponsor makes significant losses.[142]

5.8 Summary

As far as case law of Australia is concerned, there is no decided case (so far) that draws the line between a true sale and a secured loan in terms of an RMBS programme. Offshore case law, which is rather conflicting and ambiguous, provides bit of a guidance towards drawing the line.

On the other hand, provided that accounting standards form part of the Australian Corporations Law, we can argue that it is more likely that Australian courts would investigate into substance of the transaction while taking account of all of the circumstances of the case, and check whether the mortgage originator owns or controls the SPV, or vice versa. The mere "expressed intention" of parties to the transaction, depicted in the documentation, will have very little, or perhaps no importance in deciding between a true sale and a secured loan. Hence a mere title "residential mortgage-backed securitisation" is unlikely to establish a true sale transaction.

In the case of an Australian RMBS programme, the originating mortgagee's rights are regularly assigned to the SPV in equity, provided that an equitable assignment involves fewer formalities in contrast to a legal assignment. Provided the intention to assign is manifested in writing, the originator or the SPV need not inform the borrower about the assignment, for an equitable assignment to be valid. Also, in terms of cost concerns, the originator and the SPV tend to prefer an equitable assignment over a legal transfer.

Unit trust structure is the generally used structure of an SPV in Australia. In a unit trust, beneficiaries hold units representing equitable interests in the underlying residential mortgages. The income generated from these mortgages, in the form of borrowers' repayments, is received

[141] See, for example, in the context of Macquarie Bank's PUMA Fund, *Master Information Memorandum, PUMA Fund-P7*, 40–41 and *Master Information Memorandum, PUMA Sub-Fund Series* 2014, p 74.

[142] In fairness to the banks and other IMPs, home loan borrowers are often also entitled to redraw on previously prepaid principal amounts (generally, without penalty): see, for example, *Master Information Memorandum, PUMA Fund-P7*, paragraph 8.3 (f).

by the SPV and disbursed to the RMBS investors, perhaps called bondholders. If any excess income exists, it will be distributed among unit holders. These bond holders could be, and most likely they will be, subsidiaries of the programme sponsor.

As far as the NCC is concerned, the main question that occurs with regard to RMBS programmes in Australia is whether the SPV as well as the originating lender can be identified as a "credit providers" under the Code, with all the associated errands that role implies. Even though the Code has aroused curiosity in the industry, its impact is rather illusory than real. In a practical sense, borrowers are not aware of the assignment of their loans, and will continue to make their repayments, until the loans are paid off. As far as the provisions of the Code are concerned, as long as borrowers continue to pay their repayments to the originator, and the transfer is not notified to the borrower, the SPV will not be regarded as the "credit provider" and hence escape liability of unjust or unconscionable conduct unless a court order orders otherwise. However, even then, the Code allows the SPV to be indemnified in respect of such liability, and such indemnities are in practice a prerequisite to the equitable assignment occurring in the first place.

Bibliography

Books and Book Chapters

Aicher, R. D. and Fellerhoff, W. J., 'Characterisation of a Transfer of Receivables as a Sale of Secured Loan upon Bankruptcy of the Transferor' (1991) 65 *American Banking Law Journal* 181.

Brown, J. Kravitt and Platt, M., *Securitization of Financial Assets* (Aspen Publishers, 2006).

De Vries Robbé, Jan Job, *Securitization Law and Practice: In the Face of the Credit Crunch* (Kluwer Law International, 2008).

Derham, R., *Set-Off*, 2nd edition, Oxford University Press, 1996.

Duggan, A. J., *Regulated Credit: The Sale Aspect*, Sydney: Law Book Company, 1986.

Fisher, S., *Agency Law*, Sydney: Butterworths, 2000.

Ford, H. A. J. and Lee, W. A., *Principles of the Law of Trusts*, Sydney: Law Book Company, 2004.

Greig, D. W. and Davis, J. L. R., *The Law of Contract*, Sydney: Law Book Company, 1987.

Kothari, Vinod, Securitization*: The Financial Instrument of the Future* (John Wiley & Sons, 2006).

Meagher, R. P., Gummow, W. M. C. and Lehane, J. R. F., *Equity: Doctrines and Remedies*, 4th edition, Sydney: Butterworths, 2002.

Saban, H., *Corporate Debt Securitisation*, Singapore: Butterworths, 1994.

Salter, B., *Legal Changes Affecting the Structure of Securitisation Programmes*, Discussion Paper, Sydney: Clayton Utz, 1993.

Schwarcz, S. L., *Structured Finance: A Guide to the Principles of Asset Securitization*, N.Y.: Practising Law Institute, 1993.

Valentine, T., Ford, G. and Copp, R., *Financial Markets and Institutions in Australia*, Sydney: Pearson Education Australia, 2003.

Journal Articles

Adhikari, Ajay and Betancourt, Luis, 'Accounting for Securitizations: A Comparison of FASB 140 and IASB 39' (2008) 19 *Journal of International Financial Management & Accounting* 73.

Borrows, J., 'Legal and Regulatory Issues' in D. C. Gardner (ed.), *Securitisation*, London: Euromoney, 1997.

Forrest, Pearce, 'Bankruptcy-Remote Special Purpose Entities and a Business's Right to Waive its Ability to File for Bankruptcy' (2012) 28 *Emory Bankruptcy Developments Journal* 507.

Klein, L. B., 'Legal Issues Relating to Participation in Bank Loans', in J. Lederman (ed.), *The Commercial Loan Resale Market*, Columbus, Ohio: McGraw-Hill Education, 1991.

Lindsay, J. and Thomson, C., 'Accounting and Tax Issues' in D. C. Gardner (ed.), *Securitization*, London: Euromoney, 1997.

Oates, M., 'RBA Guidelines on Funds Management and Securitisation' (1994) 10 (3) *Australian Banking Law Bulletin* 23.

Ono, M., 'Unique Aspects of Japanese Securitization Relating to the Assignment of Financial Assets: A Comment on Raines and Wong' (2002) 12 (2) *Duke Journal of Comparative and International Law* 469.

Pantaleo, V Peter, Edelman, Herbert S., Feldkamp, Frederick L., Kravitt, Jason, McNeill, Walter, Plank, Thomas E., Morrison, Kenneth P., Schwarcz, Steven L., Shupack, Paul and Zaretsky, Barry, 'Rethinking the Role of Recourse in the Sale of Financial Assets' (1996) 52 *The Business Lawyer* 159.

Perry, Raymond E., 'Accounting for Securitizations' (1993) 7 *Accounting Horizons* 71

Plank, T. E., 'The True Sale of Loans and the Role of Recourse' (1991) 14 *George Mason University Law Review* 287.

Plater, I., 'Accounting and Tax for Off-Balance Sheet Financing', *IIR Conference*, Sydney, September 1992.

Rajapakse, Pelma and Gunawardena, Naomal, 'Assignment of Mortgage Loans to a Special Purpose Vehicle in Securitization in Sri Lanka: With Some Reference to Australian Securitization Programs' (2013) 28 *Banking and Finance Law Review* 475.

Schipper, Katherine and Yohn, Teri Lombardi, 'Standard-setting Issues and Academic Research Related to the Accounting for Financial Asset Transfers' (2007) 21 *Accounting Horizons* 59.

Schwarcz, Steven L., 'Structured Finance: The New Way to Securitize Assets' (1989) 11 *Cardozo Law Review* 607.

Senarath, S., 'Securitisation and the global financial crisis: can risk retention prevent another crisis?' (2017) 18 *International Journal of Business and Globalisation* 153.

Senarath, S. and Copp, R., 'Credit default swaps and the global financial crisis: reframing credit default swaps as quasi-insurance' (2015) 8 *Global Economy and Finance Journal* 135.

Shenker, C. Joseph and Colletta, Anthony J., 'Asset Securitization: Evolution' Current Issues and New Frontiers' (1991) 69 *Texas Law Review* 1369.

Taylor, B., 'Assignment of Securities in Corporate Refinancing' (1998) 13 (10) *Australian Banking and Finance Law Bulletin* 141.

True, Roy B., 'Risk and Insolvency Issues in Japanese Asset Securitization' (1996) 28 *New York University Journal of International Law and Politic* 505.

Working Papers, Magazines, Newspapers and Reports

Senarath, S., 'The Dodd-Frank Act doesn't solve the principal-agent problem in asset securitisation' (2017) *blogs.lse.ac.uk* (11 November 2018).

Senarath, S., Not so "Bankruptcy-Remote': An insight into Sri Lankan Securitization Practices in a Post-GFC Context' (Paper presented at the MAC-MME conference 2016, Prague, Czech Republic).

Kravitt, Jason, 'Introduction to Securitization' (Working paper, 1988) http://www.securitization.net/knowledge/accounting/fas125.asp

Imhoff Jr, Eugene A., 'Asset Securitization: Economic Effects and Accounting Issues' (1992) 6 *Accounting Horizons* 5.

Financial Accounting Standards Board, *Statement of Financial Accounting Standards No. 13* (November 1976).

Financial Accounting Standards Board, *Financial Accounting Standards Board Statement No. 77* (December 1983).

Financial Accounting Standards Board, *Statement of Financial Accounting Concepts No. 6* (December 1985).

Financial Accounting Standards Board, *Financial Accounting Standards Board Statement No. 125* (June 1996).

Financial Accounting Standards Board, *Financial Accounting Standards Board Statement No. 140* (September 2000).

Standard and Poor's, *Structured Finance Australia and New Zealand*, Melbourne, 1999.

Macquarie Securitisation Ltd, *The PUMA Fund P-7: Master Information Memorandum*, Sydney, February, 2000.

Macquarie Securitisation Ltd, *The PUMA Sub-Fund Series* 2014, *Master Information Memorandum*, Sydney, July, 2014.

Robinson, T., 'Securitisation Update', *Seventh Annual Credit Law Conference*, Melbourne: BLEC, September 1997. http://blogs.lse.ac.uk/businessreview/2017/04/21/the-dodd-frank-act-doesnt-solve-the-principal-agent-problem-in-asset-securitisation/

Web Sites

Superior Court of Justice (ONSC), http://www.canli.org/on/cas/2003

AASB Home Page, http://www.aasb.com.au

CHAPTER 6

Law and Regulation of the Issue of Mortgage-Backed Securities

6.1 Introduction

In our previous discussion, we have identified the manner in which mortgage originator assigns the mortgages and mortgagee rights to a special purpose vehicle (SPV), the nature of trustee-issuer of the SPV, and how it issues residential mortgage-backed securities (RMBSs) (typically in the form of bonds or notes) to investors. It is noteworthy at this point that for the purposes of the *Corporations Act* 2001 (Cth),[1] these RMBSs are in practice invariably characterised as "debentures", the requirements of which mandate a trust structure for SPVs that issue RMBSs in Australia.

However, the income received by the SPV, originating from the loan repayments made by the initial housing loan borrowers, acts as a cash inflow against which the trustee-issuer's obligations under the RMBS issue are offset.

The most significant investors in RMBSs in Australia include the authorised deposit-taking institutions (ADIs), and the insurance and superannuation funds.[2] Such investors are apparently sophisticated in

[1] See sections 9 and 92. Debt instruments that cannot be characterised as "debentures" under the Act automatically fall within the ambit of the Managed Investment Scheme ("MIS") provisions of the *Corporations Act*.

[2] Standard and Poor's, 'RMBS, CDO Activity Lead Australian Securitisation Issuance Growth in 2003' *Credit Ratings and Commentary* (Melbourne, 16 July 2003) 5.

P. Rajapakse, S. Senarath, *Commercial Law Aspects of Residential Mortgage Securitisation in Australia*,
https://doi.org/10.1007/978-3-030-00605-1_6

their knowledge of such investments, in contrast to the average small individual investor. Due to their greater experience and expertise, issuers of securities to sophisticated investors are not subject to the same onerous disclosure requirements under the *Corporations Act* as are issuers of securities to "average" individual investors.

6.2 Regulation of Trustees

Provided that the debt securities underlying an issue are characterised as debentures (and they invariably are in practice), the appointment of a trustee is prerequisite to any issue.[3] This trust provides a mechanism for investor protection, and sets in place a legal structure, which establishes a nexus between the issuer and fund manager, the holders of the debt instruments or debentures, and third parties.

Section 283 AC of the *Corporations Act* provides that the trustee must be a body corporate and the body corporate must be one of the types mentioned in this section. The trustee company may be appointed without leave of the court, provided the proposed trustee is not disqualified for being:

- A shareholder beneficially holding shares in the borrowing company.
- A creditor of the borrowing company.
- A guarantor of the borrowing company.
- A party related to a company, which is not itself disqualified, or to the borrowing company: section 283AE(2). Broadly, the bodies corporate that meet the requirements include Australian banks, life insurance companies, public trustee companies, and approved bodies corporate of a similar character.

Section 283AE of the *Corporations Act* provides for the retirement and replacement of trustees to be effected pursuant to the terms under the debenture or by appointment. The issuer may also apply to the court to

[3] See section 283AA of the *Corporations Act*. Because the *Corporations Act* is examined in some detail in Sect. 6.3, this section of the chapter outlines provisions of that Act only insofar as they are relevant to explaining the trust law aspects of RMBS programmes in Australia. See also, P. Rajapakse, '*Corporations Act* and Trust Aspects of Asset Securitisation in Australia', in D. Campbell (ed.), ***International Asset Securitisation and Other Financing Tools*** (N.Y.: Transnational Publishers Inc., 2000) 66–75.

replace a trustee that has been wound up or deregistered or refuses to act as trustee.[4] Notice of appointment in the prescribed form must be lodged with the ASIC within two weeks of the appointment.[5]

6.2.1 Trustee: Rights, Obligations, and Duties

In practice, the rights and obligations of a trustee to an RMBS issue are derived from the general law relating to trustees, and from the trust deed and other instruments executed in connection with the issue. While some of the most important duties and powers of trustees under general law are noted, they have been discussed in depth elsewhere in the literature, and this book does not consider them in any significant detail.[6] Duties of trustees are well known and need not be expanded in detail here; two duties do merit some clarification in the context of RMBSs. These are the trustee's duties of due care and diligence; the trustee's duty not to discriminate between bondholders of the same class; and the trustee's duty not to profit from position or engage in other conflicts of interest.

Trustees' Duty of Care and Diligence

In a securitisation programme, trustees are statutorily obliged to exercise due care and diligence to satisfy themselves not only that the pooled mortgage repayments from the home loan borrowers and any other permissible income of trust are sufficient to repay the amounts lent to the trust by bondholders as they become due, but also that all necessary arrangements for investor protection, and all procedural and documentary requirements for the valid issuance of the RMBSs have been complied with.[7]

Section 283DB of the *Corporations Act* states that any provision in a trust deed is void if it would have the effect of exempting a trustee from a

[4] *Corporations Act*, section 283BD.

[5] *Corporations Act*, section 283BC.

[6] For a more comprehensive discussion of these aspects of trust law, see generally, H. A. J. Ford and W. A. Lee, *Principles of the Law of Trust* (Sydney: Law Book Company, 2004) paragraphs 14000–14080; and K. R. Ayers, 'Limiting Trustee Liability to Lenders' (1996) *New Zealand Law Journal* 181. Also see, in general, S. Senarath (2016), Not so "'Bankruptcy-Remote': An insight into Sri Lankan Securitization Practices in a Post-GFC Context" (Paper presented at the MAC-MME conference, Prague, Czech Republic); Senarath, S. 'The Dodd-Frank Act doesn't solve the principal-agent problem in asset securitisation' (2017) blogs.lse.ac.uk (11 November 2018).

[7] *Trusts Act* 1973 (Qld) sections 21–24; *Trusts Act* 1925 (NSW) sections 14–14C; *Trust Act* 1958 (Vic) sections 6–8.

breach of trust involving a failure to show due care and diligence. If the deed permits, the bondholders may, by at least a three-quarter majority (in nominal value terms), release a trustee from liability, but this could only in relation to a past event.[8] However, the trust deed may not ease a trustee of the duty to refrain from fraud or deliberate wrongdoing: section 283DA.[9]

Bondholders of the Same Class Should Not Be Discriminated

It is a paramount duty for a trustee to act impartially between the various beneficiaries of the trust.[10] However, in an RMBS framework, there is often more than one class of RMBSs.[11] In this scenario, the trustee's general duty not to discriminate is typically clarified by the trust deed, in order to make it explicit that the trustee is permitted to consider only the interests of the superior class of securities, where there might otherwise be a conflict between these interests and those of another class of bondholders. Generally, the beneficiaries, bondholders, and other immediate stakeholders all consent to this arrangement when they sign the relevant documentation "up front" (e.g. in the case of bondholders, at the time they purchase the bonds).

Duty Not to Engage in Conflicts of Interest or Profit from the Position as Trustee

As decided in *Hogan v Waterhouse,* a trustee may not benefit from his position as a trustee or profit from trust property.[12] This can be viewed as a specific example illustrating the general prohibition on a trustee occupying a position in which there is a conflict between its own personal interests and its duties as a trustee. Insofar as this requires a trustee to act gratuitously, this duty is, however, invariably modified in commercial trust deeds, such as those relating to issues of mortgage-backed securities, so as to permit the

[8] See sections 283DB(1)(c)(d), and 283DB(2).

[9] *Wilkins v Hogg* (1861) 3 Giff 116, 120, 66 ER 346, 348; *Pass v Dundas* (1880) 43 LT 665, 666; *Knox v Mackinnon* (1888) 13 App. Cas 753, 765 (HL); *Rae v Meek* (1889) 14 App Cas 558, 572. (HL). See also T. Frankel, *Securitization: Structured Financing* (Boston: Little Brown & Co, 1991) paragraphs 14.2–14.3.

[10] R. D. Ellis, 'Securitisation Vehicles: Fiduciary Duties and Bondholders' Rights' (1999) 24 *The Journal of Corporation Law* 296, 310.

[11] For example, where the lower tier subordinated bonds are included as a form of credit enhancement for the main tier senior bonds. See, for example, *Master Information Memorandum, PUMA Fund P-7,* paragraph 4.5 and *Master Information Memorandum, PUMA Sub-Fund Series* 2014, pp 16, 22–23.

[12] (1991) 34 NSWLR 368; *William v Bartor* [1927] 2 Ch 9.

trustee to be paid, usually by the issuer, for its services. In *Space Investments Ltd v Canadian Imperial Bank of Commerce Trust Co (Bahamas) Ltd*, Lord Templeman stated that "although as a general rule a trustee is not allowed to derive benefit from trust property, that general rule may be altered by the express terms of the trust instrument. One illustration is an express provision in a settlement which permits a trustee to charge and deduct from trust money remuneration for the services of the trustee."[13]

6.2.2 Discrepancy of Trustee Obligations

Ordinarily, a trustee is bound and entitled to use its own judgement and need not consult with or accede to the wishes or demands of the beneficiaries of the trust. Nevertheless, trustees are obliged to obey the terms of their trust deed.[14] Otherwise, section 283DB of the *Corporations Act* provides that the terms can be varied only with the consent of all the beneficiaries of the trust, or the court. It would be practically impossible for a trustee to obtain the consent of all of the bondholders, in the context of an RMBS issue.

In anticipation of the possibility that the terms of the trust may prove too restrictive or otherwise inappropriate during the life of the issue, and because obtaining the court's consent is often cumbersome and costly, a typical trust deed will make provision for its modification—and also the modification of the terms and conditions of the bonds themselves—by agreement between the trustee-issuer and the security trustee. Investors in the RMBSs generally consent to this modification mechanism when they agree to purchase the bonds. Limits are imposed on this power of modification so that, for example, the security trustee and the issuer can only consent to changes which will not materially prejudice the interests of the bondholders, which are of a minor, formal, or technical nature, or which are necessary in order to correct a manifest error or maintain the rating of the bonds.[15]

[13] [1986] 3 All ER 75, 77 per Lord Templeman.

[14] *Gisborne v Gisborne* (1877) App Cas 300; *Karger v Paul* [1984] VR 161. It might be thought that the trustee could be removed if all of the trust beneficiaries, acting together, seek its removal or replacement: *Saunders v Vautier* (1841) 4 Beav 115, 49 ER 282; *Re Brockbank* [1948] Ch 206, [1948] 1 All ER 287; *Stephen v Barclays Bank Trust Co* [1975] 1 All ER 625, 637. However, in the context of an RMBS programme, the beneficiaries are in fact normally entities controlled by the SPV, so that this situation would rarely, if ever, arise.

[15] See, for example, *Master Information Memorandum, PUMA Fund P-7*, paragraph 7.2.

Also a typical trust deed makes provision for the trustee and the fund manager to make other changes to the trust deed, provided these are sanctioned by a specified proportion of the bondholders at bondholders' meetings, generally on a special resolution of bondholders.[16] Such special resolutions of the bondholders cannot alter the priorities applying in relation to the fund,[17] nor can they be used to alter the coupon interest payable on the bonds, the coupon interest payment dates, or the final maturity date of the bonds.

6.2.3 *Trustee Powers Under the Trust Act*

As we have already understood, the powers of the trustee are governed by the trust deed itself and the *Trusts Act* 1973 (Qld), with the statutory provisions applying insofar as they are not inconsistent with the express provisions of the trust deed. These address the scope of the trustee's activities, the investment of trust funds, and the management of trust liabilities,[18] including:

- The power to hold and control the title deeds to security properties.[19]
- The power to enter into hedge agreements, standby arrangements, and subordinated borrowings.[20]

[16] Sections 283EA and 283 EB of the *Corporations Act.*

[17] The order of priorities under the trust deed is as follows: The proceeds from the enforcement of the charge must be applied first, for payment of all fees incurred to the performance by the trustee of his or her powers; second, for payment of all other outgoings in relation to the fund; third, for payment of any securities having priority over the charge; fourth, on payment of moneys owing to the secured creditors.

[18] See generally, sections 12(1), 21, 57, 76, 77, 80, and 96 of the *Trusts Act* 1973 (Qld).

[19] For example, the Standard and Poor's rating agency requires that the trustee secure custody of all the title deeds and charge certificates in respect of registered mortgages: see Standard and Poor's *Credit Review: International Structured Finance,* April 1991, 51; and also *Master Information Memorandum, PUMA Fund P-7,* paragraph 7.1 and *Master Information Memorandum, PUMA Sub-Fund Series* 2014, pp 99–100. In fact, ensuring the security of title deeds may not only be a practical necessity (and a rating requirement), but can also be a legal obligation because of the general duty imposed on trustees to exercise the same care and control in respect of trust property as they would do in respect of their own: see *Trusts Act* 1973 (Qld) sections 21–24; and *Partridge v Equity Trustees Executors and Agency Co Ltd* (1947) 75 CLR 149. In an RMBS issue, the title deeds and related documents will typically be held by a third-party depository. This practice is generally stipulated by the trust deed, which also authorises the payment of associated fees or expenses out of the income of the trust property. The trust deed may even go further, and purport to exclude the trustee from liability in respect of losses incurred in connection with such deposits: see H. Saban, *Corporate Debt Securitisation* (Singapore: Butterworths, 1994) 77–78.

[20] See generally, for example, *Master Information Memorandum, PUMA Fund P-7,* paragraphs 7.2 and 7.3.

- The power to employ the necessary agents.[21]
- The power to apply to the court for directions regarding matters in connection with the performance of the trustee's functions, or any matters touching on the interests of bondholders.[22]

Additional powers given under the deed typically bestow on the trustee power to act on the advice or information supplied by lawyers, accountants, bankers, auctioneers, valuers, brokers, surveyors, and other experts; exercise or desist from exercising any discretion vested in it as trustee; determine on a conclusive and binding basis all questions and doubts relating to the trust deed as between itself, the holders of the instruments,

[21] The trust deed will invariably contain provisions entitling the trustee to appoint agents to conduct the day-to-day administration of the trust on its behalf. Under general law, a trustee must take the requisite degree of care when exercising a power conferred by a trust deed to appoint an agent; and there is some authority to the effect that the trustee will not be liable for an agent's defaults, where the trustee can show that it acted in good faith and with sufficient care when choosing and supervising the agent: *Shepherd v Harris* [1905] 2 Ch 310. Interestingly, however, this begs the question of how the agent's default occurred in the first place, and many commentators consider that this does not relieve the trustee of its primary duty of care in appointing and supervising its agents: see P. Jones, 'Delegation by Trustees, A Reappraisal' (1990) 22 *The Modern Law Review* 381, 395; and P.V. Baker, *Snell's Equity* (London: Sweet & Maxwell, 1990) 266, in which it is argued that the liability of a trustee for any loss no longer depends on reasonableness, but merely on whether it acted in good faith.

To attempt to remove doubt, an express power to appoint agents may be included in securitisation trust deeds, requiring the trustee to exercise care in choosing an agent, but purporting to relieve it of any supervisory obligation thereafter: see, for example, *Master Information Memorandum, PUMA Fund P-7*, paragraph 7.1. The trust deed will provide that a trustee is not liable for the acts, receipts, neglects, or defaults of any banker, broker, or other person with whom any trust money or securities may be deposited, nor for the insufficiency or deficiency of any securities, nor for any other analogous loss (*Re Vickery, Vickery v Stephens* [1931] 1 Ch 572, 582), unless the same happens through its own wilful default. However, the validity of such clauses is very much debateable. Although it has been held in *Re Vickery, Vickery v Stephens* [1931] 1 Ch 572, 582 that wilful default in this context requires either a consciousness of negligence or breach of duty, or recklessness in the performance of that duty, this decision has been criticised, and may be out of line with earlier cases in which wilful default was also held to encompass unconscious failure by a trustee to exercise the requisite care. See for instance, P. Jones (1990) 395. Mortgage securitisation trust deeds therefore generally include an express indemnity to allow a trustee to be reimbursed for losses: see, for example, *Master Information Memorandum, PUMA Sub-Fund Series*, 2014, p 102.

[22] Section 283EC of the *Corporations Act*.

and all persons claiming through them; employ, delegate to, and pay for agents, solicitors, and other consultants with regard to the execution and exercise of the trusts, powers and discretion under the deed.[23]

6.2.4 *Nature of the Relationship Between the Trustee and Bondholders*

In the Australian context, the relationship in practice between the trustee of an SPV and the bondholders who invest in RMBSs is not one of trustee and beneficiaries. The true beneficiaries of the SPV—that is, the principal trust—are the unit holders, which are invariably entities controlled by the SPV itself (and often by the sponsoring bank or an Independent Mortgage Provider—IMP). The real relationship between the trustee and the bondholders is one of trustee and secured creditors, where the security for the bonds held by the investors is ultimately the residential mortgages of the initial home loan borrowers, whose mortgages have been pooled and assigned by their originating bank or IMP. This means that the bondholders have recourse to the mortgage pool, irrespective of the trustee's right of indemnity against it.[24]

Investment Powers of Trustee

The relevant legislation in Queensland, New South Wales, and Victoria permits trustees to invest in mortgage-backed securities in the context of the trustee's investment powers and the scope of fund management.[25] For example, with respect to Macquarie Bank's PUMA Trust Fund, the trustee's primary investment policy is to invest in residential property mortgages. The trust deed specifies that the residential property mortgages must be registered as first legal mortgages over freehold land, or over

[23] See, for example, Master Information Memorandum, PUMA Fund P-7, paragraph 7.1.

[24] See, *Master Information Memorandum, PUMA Fund P-7*, 2000, paragraphs 1.12 and 4.1.

[25] Cf. The position of trustees of *client* trusts, who invest in RMBSs. Amendments to the *Trusts Acts* in the various States have facilitated sales of RMBSs, insofar as trustees of client trusts are now permitted to invest in RMBSs, whereas previously they were limited to investing in certain low-risk, "authorised" investments, such as government bonds: see section 24 *et seq* of the *Trusts Act* 1973 (Qld); and A. Finch, 'Securitisation' (1995) *Journal of Banking and Finance Law and Practice* 247, 272–273. Formerly, trustees were restricted to investing in certain listed "authorised investments: see, for example, P. Collinson, 'Trustee Investments Status for Mortgage-Backed Securities' in *Conference on Impediments to the Securitisation of Housing Mortgages*, Proceedings (Canberra: AGPS, 1988) 96–104.

leasehold land with a lease term at least 15 years longer than the term of the loan secured by the mortgage. However, the trustee is permitted, under the trust deed, to also invest in cash; bonds, debentures, stock, or treasury bills of the Commonwealth of Australia or any State or Territory Government; the debentures or stock of any Commonwealth, State, or Territory public statutory authority where the repayment of principal and the payment of interest is guaranteed by the Commonwealth or the State or Territory Government; notes or other securities of the Commonwealth of Australia or any State or Territory Government; deposits with, or the acquisition of certificates of deposits issued by an Australian bank; and bills of exchange accepted or endorsed by an Australian bank.[26]

Trustee's Right of Indemnity from the Trust Property

As we already know, debts of a trust create personal liability on the trustee as if they were its own.[27] For the purposes of implicating trust liabilities, the law does not characterise the trustee as incurring liabilities only in a representative capacity. A trustee may avoid exposing its personal estate to trust liabilities if the trust creditors agree to this.[28] The exclusion must be express and unequivocal, particularly as the tendency seems to be to interpret such clauses against the trustee. This is the basis for the limitation on liability endorsed on debt instruments issued by trustees under mortgage securitisation programmes. The trustee purports, with these clauses, to limit its liability on the issued bonds to the particular fund to which they relate, so that its personal assets will not be exposed to the risk that, at maturity, there may be insufficient funds available to meet the debt obligations then falling due. Typically, the deed contains a clause stating that the trustee does not issue the debt securities personally, but only in its capacity as trustee. Strictly speaking, this statement does not correctly reflect the legal position, for it is clear that the trustee is personally liable on the debt

[26] See, *Master Information Memorandum*, PUMA Sub-Fund Series 2014, p 100.

[27] *Octavo Investments Pty Ltd v Knight* (1979) 54 ALJR 87, 89. That is, the debts incurred by a trustee on behalf of a trust are classified as its own, as if they were incurred by the trustee on its own account: D. G. Glennie and E. C. De Bouter, *Securitisation* (London: Kluwer Law, 1998) Ch. 1, 5.

[28] See, *Lumsden v Buckanan* (1865) 4 Macq 950; and see H. Saban (1994) 78; and R. Hughes, 'The Right of a Trustee who Carries on Business to Indemnify out of Trust Property' (1991) *Australian Business Law Review* 5. Merely contracting as trustee will not be sufficient to achieve this: *Muir v City of Glasgow Bank* (1879) 4 App Cas 337; and see B. Taylor, (1998) 268–272.

securities. The trustee's liability to bondholders is limited to those amounts that are available to be applied to the RMBSs in accordance with the trust deed. Such clauses seek to ensure that the trustee's personal assets are not exposed to the risks of the mortgage securitisation, and that the bondholders have rights against the trustee commensurate only with the trustee's own (legal) ability to debit the trust assets for these amounts.[29]

Anyhow, the trustee is not expected to abide by the liabilities of a trust itself without compensation—the trustee generally has a right of indemnity[30] against the trust assets for expenses and liabilities properly incurred in administering the trust.[31] This right of indemnity arises from three sources. First, a trustee has a right in equity to indemnify itself from the trust estate for properly incurred trust liabilities. Second, the trustee's right in equity to be reimbursed for legitimate expenses is reflected in section 72 of the *Trusts Act* 1973 (Qld), which expressly provides that a trustee may reimburse itself or pay out of the trust property all expenses incurred in or about the execution of its trusts or trust powers. Third, the documentation underlying most mortgage securitisation schemes usually also provides for the trustee to reimburse itself from the trust property for trust liabilities. For example, in the case of Macquarie Bank's PUMA Fund, the trustee-issuer is indemnified out of the assets of the trust for any liability incurred by the trustee-issuer in performing its duties, although this indemnity does not extend to liabilities arising from the trustee-issuer's fraud, negligence, or wilful default. This right of indemnity is secured by an equitable charge—perhaps we could call this a lien—over the trust property. This lien entitles the trustee to retain the property until the right of indemnity has been satisfied and, if need be, to sell it.[32]

However, the right of a trustee for indemnification from the trust assets for properly incurred trust liabilities is subject to a critical limitation. The

[29] See, for example, *Master Information Memorandum, PUMA Sub-Fund Series 2014*, p 100.

[30] See *J.W. Broomhead Pty Ltd (in liq) v J.W. Broomhead Pty Ltd* [1985] VR 891. Theoretically, a trust creditor's primary remedy is against the trustee personally and its estate. Where the trustee's personal estate is insufficient, a trust creditor can then proceed against the trust's assets derivatively by subrogation to the trustee's rights of indemnification for the trust's debts. See R. P. Meagher, W. M. C. Gummow and J. R. F. Lehane, *Equity Doctrines and Remedies* (4th edition, 2002) Ch. 9.

[31] *Worrall v Harford* (1802) 32 ER 250, 252; and B. Taylor, (1998) 268–270. See, *Master Information Memorandum, PUMA Sub-Fund Series* 2014, p 100.

[32] *Re The Exhall Coal Company (Ltd)* (1866) 55 ER 970; and *Stott v Milne* (1884) 25 Ch D 710.

actual value or quantum of the right is not calculated simply on the amount of the properly incurred trust liabilities, but after taking into consideration all of the trustee's liabilities to the trust estate on other matters.[33] Thus, for example, if the trustee has committed a breach of trust so that it is personally liable to reimburse the trust estate, the indemnity in respect of the properly incurred trust debts will be accordingly reduced.[34]

Implications for Bondholders and Creditors

The fact that their debts are secured ultimately against the residential mortgages of the initial home loan borrowers, and the fact that the trustee is personally liable for a trust's debts as if they were its own[35] (albeit subject to a right of indemnity) offer some comfort to the bondholders in the capacity of creditors in RMBS issues. However, in order to circumvent the risk that the trustee may be tempted to engage in a conflict between its own interest and its duty to pay interest (and ultimately the principal) to the bondholders, and to further secure the trust's payment obligations to bondholders and other secured creditors, the trustee-issuers in RMBS programmes typically charge their trust assets in favour of an independent security trustee.

6.2.5 The Security Trustee

In general, the security trustee holds the benefit of the security, for example, say the rights to the assigned mortgages, and the instruments containing the trustee-issuer's covenants on trust not only for the bondholders but also for the persons to whom obligations are owed by the trustee-issuer, such as providers of liquidity facilities or start-up[36] facilities. In other words, the security trustee acts as trustee on behalf of the secured creditors.

Typically, the charge granted by the trustee-issuer in favour of the security trustee is a floating charge, registered with ASIC, over all of the trust

[33] *Re Frith* [1902] 1 Cg D 342, 345; *Re Dacre* [1916] 1 Ch D 344.

[34] *Re Johnson* (1880) 15 Ch D 548, 555. In other words, a balance must be struck between what is due by way of compensation to the trust estate and what is due to the trustee by way of indemnity and only if that balance is in favour of the trustee can it recover from the estate and then only to the extent of that balance: *RWG Management Ltd v Commissioner for Corporate Affairs* [1985] VR 385, 398.

[35] *Octavo Investments Pty Ltd v Knight* (1979) 54 ALJR 87, 89.

[36] This might include the originator, for example.

assets.[37] This floating charge secures the moneys owing to the bondholders, the redraw facility providers, the liquidity facility providers, any other standby letter of credit providers, and any interest rate swap providers.[38]

The trustee-issuer typically agrees not to dispose of the assets of the trust that are subject to the floating charge, except in accordance with the trust deed. If the trustee-issuer does dispose of any trust assets, including mortgage loans, other than in accordance with the trust deed, the person who acquires the property takes it free of the floating charge. The floating charge granted over the assets crystallises (i.e. in effect, it becomes a fixed charge) upon default,[39] the definition of which normally includes any dealing by the trustee-issuer with a trust asset. As with the trustee-issuer, the security trustee's liability to the secured creditors (i.e. its beneficiaries) is constrained by the security trustee's right of indemnity from the assets of the trust. A typical trust deed contains express indemnities from the trustee-issuer in the security trustee's favour, and specifically provides that the security trustee is not obliged to act on the instructions of bondholders unless it is indemnified to its satisfaction by them. Again, however, this limitation will not apply where the security trustee limits its right of indemnity as a result of its fraud, negligence, or wilful default.[40] In the context of the PUMA Fund, it sets out the following events of default: (a) if the trustee does not pay in full any moneys payable to bondholders; (b) if the trustee defaults in performing any obligation to bondholders, or to the security trustee under the security trust deed; (c) if any warranty in relation to the fund made by the trustee is proved to be untrue; (d) if the trustee breaches any undertaking given to the security trustee; (e) if any (other) event of insolvency occurs in relation to the fund; and (f) if any event of crystallisation occurs.

In the event of default, the secured creditors may direct the security trustee by special resolution to appoint a receiver over the trust assets, to sell and realise the assets or take other relevant action, consistent with the trust deed, to protect their interests.

[37] For example, the security trustee appointed in respect of Macquarie Bank's PUMA Fund is Perpetual Trustee Company Ltd: see, *Master Information Memorandum, PUMA Sub-Fund Series*, 2014, p 102.

[38] In the context of Macquarie Bank's PUMA Fund, these parties are collectively known as the "secured creditors" of the Fund. For more detail on the security trust deed for the PUMA Fund, see, *Master Information Memorandum, PUMA Sub-Fund Series*, 2014, p 107.

[39] See, *Master Information Memorandum, PUMA Sub-Fund Series*, 2014, p 108.

[40] See, for example, *Master Information Memorandum of PUMA Sub-Fund Series*, 2014, p 108.

The trust deed may also contain provisions permitting the security trustee to enter into contracts or other arrangements with the trustee-issuer, notwithstanding its fiduciary relationship with the bondholders. These provisions operate as a qualification to the general rule that the trustee-issuer cannot enter into a conflict between its duty and its personal interest, and bondholders and other immediate stakeholders consent to such arrangements when they sign the relevant documentation at the time of initially purchasing the RMBSs.

6.3 Legislative Requirements as per the *Corporations Act*

Despite the fact whether it is pass-through or pay-through, all RMBS transactions are subject to the *Corporations Act 2001 (Cth)*. The *Corporations Act* affects RMBS programmes in three principal ways. First of all, it regulates the structure of RMBSs; then, it imposes a number of disclosure requirements on RMBS issues; and finally, it regulates participants in the Australian RMBS industry.[41]

6.3.1 *Structure of RMBSs*

In theory, RMBS issues can be based on equity and debt instruments. An investor in an equity security issued through a residential mortgage-backed securitisation structure holds a beneficial interest in the underlying mortgage pool. Although the instrument may be described as a bond or note, in real terms, an investor receives a unit in a unit trust, entitling it to a share of the income and capital of the trust assets. The unit is structured to replicate the qualities of a debt instrument. Steps will be taken in order to ensure that investors receive, on nominated dates, an amount equivalent to interest (i.e. a distribution of income) and a repayment of principal.

The SPV issue instruments known as bonds, notes, or commercial paper, under a debt security. In contrast to equity securities, investors do not have an ownership interest in the underlying mortgage pool. Instead,

[41] See generally, Clayton Utz, *A Guide to the Law of Securitisation in Australia* (Sydney: Clayton Utz, 2004); B. J. McWilliams, 'Companies and Securities Impediments to Mortgage Securitisation' in *Conference on Impediments to the Securitisation of Housing Mortgages, Proceedings and Conference Papers* (Canberra: AGPS, 1988) 96–104. Senarath, 'Securitisation and the global financial crisis: can risk retention prevent another crisis?', (2017) 18 International Journal of Business and Globalisation, 153.

they hold a promise by the SPV to pay interest and principal. This is typically combined with a security interest over the securitised mortgages through a charge given by the SPV to a security trustee for the benefit of investors. These debt securities can be structured on a pass-through basis and as floating rate or fixed rate securities.

The First Australian National Mortgage Acceptance Corporation (FANMAC) Trusts issue is the only equity issue in Australia to date[42] made in the early 1990s. The NSW government funded (a highly publicised) social housing scheme with fixed rate mortgages for low-income borrowers, which was known as the "HomeFund" scheme.[43] One of the principal problems with the early FANMAC Trusts issues was the nature of the underlying asset pool, the residential mortgages to low-income earners, in particular, the way the loans were marketed to borrowers. The loans provided for low interest rates in the early years of the loans, gradually lifting to higher fixed rates. When borrowers experienced the "payment shock"[44] as the full rates of interest came into effect, combined with a recession and higher unemployment, there were multiple defaults. Additionally, because the fixed rates were higher than the prevailing interest rates at the end of the concession period, mortgagors began redeeming their loans and switching to normal variable-rate mortgages. The FANMAC pass-through mortgage-backed securities fundamentally passed the prepayment and default risks on to investors. The issue ultimately failed, in part because of lack of servicing capacity on the part of the borrowers under the scheme, and in part because the FANMAC issues limited investors' rights of recourse to the underlying asset pool. However, the NSW government was eventually forced to step in to compensate both borrowers and investors.[45]

Perhaps in part because of the failure of the FANMAC-HomeFund issue, as well as the fact that guidelines of many institutional investors such as Insurance and Superannuation Commission (ISC) favour debt securities over equity securities whose market yields can be readily compared

[42] FANMAC Ltd was incorporated in 1985, with the NSW government a 26% shareholder and the balance held by private investors. For further details, see B. Taylor, 'The Enforceability of Debt Securities Issued by Trustees in Securitisation Programs' (1998) 26 *Journal of Banking and Finance Law and Practice* 261.

[43] B. Salter, 'Changes to the Law Relating to Securitisation' *Discussion Paper*, Clayton Utz, Sydney, 1993, 2; A. Boyd, 'Securitisation market shrank 14% last year', *Australian Financial Review*, 24 February 1994, 30.

[44] See E. Ferran, *Mortgage Securitisation: Legal Aspects* (London: Butterworths, 1992) 10.

[45] See, for example, R. Bruce, B. McKern, I. Pollard and M. Skully, *Handbook of Australian Corporate Finance* (5th edition, Sydney: Butterworths, 1997) 257.

with those of semi-government note stock for portfolio management purposes,[46] all RMBS issues since the late 1980s in Australia have been confined to debt instruments.[47]

Characterisation of RMBSs as Debentures

As per sections 9 and 92 of the *Corporations Act*, the debt securities underlying RMBS issues are, in practice, invariably characterised as "debentures"; section 9 of the *Corporations Act* simply ascribes to the term "securities" that meaning given it by section 92. Section 92(1) of the *Act* defines "securities" to include[48]:

(a) *Debentures, stocks or bonds issued or proposed to be issued by a government*
(b) *Shares in, or debentures of, a body*
(c) *Interests in a managed investment scheme*
(d) *Units of such shares*
(e) *An option contract within the meaning of Ch. 7 of the Act*[49]

[46] See Standard and Poor's, *Structured Finance in Australia and New Zealand* (Melbourne, 1999) 5.

[47] B. Taylor, (1998) 261, 263. Historically, another factor that supported the use of debt securities, rather than equity securities, was that the restrictions on life insurance companies acquiring interests in trust schemes under section 39 of the previous *Life Insurance Act* 1945 (Cth) did not apply to acquisition of debt securities issued by trustees. In the current *Life Insurance Act* 1995 (Cth), there is no similar provision to section 39. It has also been argued that debt instruments better reflect investor expectations, as securitisation investments are structured to provide a debt risk and return, with an intended low risk and return: see J. B. Tevis, 'Asset-Backed Securities: Secondary Market Implications and Regulation' (1991) 23 *Pacific Law Journal* 135, 142.

[48] The definition does not cover a futures contract or an excluded security. An "excluded security" is defined in section 9 of the *Corporations Act* and is basically any share, debenture, or prescribed interest in retirement village schemes.

[49] In comparison, the definition of "security" in the United States *Securities Act* 1933 perhaps more helpfully sets forth a number of examples of what constitutes a security: See generally, T. Frankel, (1991) 130–131. However, even in the United States, it has been left to the courts to refine the definition in order to determine whether a particular instrument is a "security" for the purposes of Federal securities laws. For example, in *Leigh Valley Trust Co v Central National Bank of Jacksonville* 409 F2D 989 (5th Cir 1969), the US Court of Appeal applied a literal reading of the statute and found that a loan sub-participation *was* a "security" for the purpose of the *Securities Exchange Act* 1933. (A sub-participation refers to the sale of part of the loan held by the lender to a third party on a non-recourse basis. Sub-participation may take two forms: a funded sub-participation and a risk sub-participation. For a detailed discussion of this topic, see T. Frankel, (1991) Ch 11; J. P. Carver, 'The

Section 9 of the *Corporations Act* defines a "debenture" in relation to a body to mean:

> [A] chose in action that includes an undertaking by the body to repay as a debt money deposited with or lent to the body. The chose in action may (but need not) include a charge over property of the body to secure repayment of the money.[50]

However, while this definition of debenture specifically provides that a debenture need not be secured by a charge over the body's property, this does not accord with the public's understanding of the word. In commercial practice, a debenture is a debt instrument by which the issuing company borrows from investors, who are paid quarterly or semi-annual interest for a period of approximately five years, with interest and principal repayments secured against the assets of the company.

Note that the definition specifically excludes a number of fundraising activities. Principal among them, and often used in residential securitisation programmes, is an undertaking to pay money under a promissory note that has a face value of at least $50,000. A second exception is an undertaking by a body to repay a loan if made in the ordinary course of

Market in Participation—Current Issues in International Finance' (1990*) Malaya Law Review* 308. Subsequently, in *Bellah v First National Bank of Hereford* 495 F2D 1109 (5th Cir 1974), the court ruled that notes issued in the context of a commercial loan did *not* constitute "securities" for the purpose of the Act. However, since *Reves v Ernst and Young* US 110 S Ct 945,108 L Ed 2d 47 (21 February 1990), the courts have presumed that all notes, including promissory notes, are "securities", unless this presumption can be rebutted—for example, by showing that the note bears a "family resemblance" to one of the specified instruments in the Act because:

1. It is sold as an investment instrument.
2. There is a plan of distribution.
3. There is a reasonable expectation of the investing public that the note is a security.
4. There are other regulatory schemes, which reduce the risk of the instruments, including collateral and insurance support.

If this definition were accepted in Australia, most RMBSs would be classified as "securities" for the purpose of the fundraising provisions of Ch. 6D of the Australian *Corporations Act*. However, the manner and extent to which the *Corporations Act* applies, depends on the characteristics of the debt instruments and the underlying assets, as set out below.

[50] The intention of the definition is to focus on the legal right to repayment of the debt, rather than on the piece of paper evidencing the debt (the development of which has been so effective in facilitating primary and secondary trading in debentures). For readers without a legal background, a "chose in action" is a right that is enforceable by legal action.

business of the lender, and if the borrower receives the money in the ordinary course of carrying on a business that neither comprises nor forms part of the business of borrowing money and providing finance. This exclusion has had an impact on RMBS issues in practice. Typically, RMBSs are initially acquired by professional dealers, many of whom lend money in their ordinary course of business. Moreover, an SPV that issues RMBSs will invariably not be in the business of "providing finance". Such RMBS will therefore not be categorised as "debentures" and so will not be regulated under the *Corporations Act*, unless they fall within the definition of "managed investment scheme".

Debentures are generally understood to mean documents that acknowledge or create a debt owed by the company that issues them. At common law, it is clear that there is no unanimity on the definition of a debenture. The traditional view was that to be a debenture, a document would have to acknowledge or evidence an existing specific debt as distinct from providing security for a debt or an acknowledgement of general indebtedness. To rule out the risk that promoters may market their debt instruments legalistically as "debentures" to unsophisticated investors who assume that the instruments are secured when they are not,[51] Ch. 2 L of the *Corporations*

[51] *Burns Phillip Trustee Co Ltd v Commissioner of Stamp Duties* (1983) 83 ATC 4477; *Handevel Pty Ltd v Comptroller of Stamps* (Vic) (1985) 62 ALR 204, 216–217.

Historically, the expression "debenture" has applied not to the indebtedness but to the paper, which is the evidence of the debt: this was certainly the meaning in the previous *Corporations Law*. The meaning of debenture usually quoted is "a document, which either creates a debt or acknowledges it, and any document, which fulfils either of these conditions is a "debenture"": *Levy v Abercorris Slate and Slab Co* (1887) 37 Ch D 260, 264 per Chitty J. See also R. Tomasic, J. Jackson and R. Woellner, *Corporations Law: Principles, Policy and Process* (4th edition, Sydney: Butterworths, 2002) paragraph 9.8; H. A. J. Ford, et al., *Ford's Principles of Corporations Law* (10th edition, Chatswood: Butterworths, 2001) and D. Janet, *Company Law* (London: Palgrave, 2001) 66–68. In *Broad v CSD (NSW)* (1980) 11 ATR 59, Lee J held that debenture for the purpose of New South Wales loan security duty provisions only applies to debentures issued by bodies corporate and hence does not apply to securities given by an individual, as was the situation in that case. In *Handevel Pty Ltd v CS* (Vic) (1985) 16 ATR 1044, 1055, the High Court accepted that one essential characteristic of a debenture is that "it is issued by a company." It has been held, in a stamp duty context, that a debenture differs from a mortgage in that there is no need for any charge on any property to be contained in it: *British India Steam Navigation Co v IRC* (1881) 7 QBD 165, 172; *Lemon v Austin Friars Trust Ltd* [1926] Ch 1; *Edmonds v Blaina Furnaces Co* (1887) 36 Ch D 215, 219; *Re Shipman Boxboards Ltd* [1942] 2 DLR 781; *Handevel v CS* (Vic) 1985) 16 ATR 1044.

The possibility of a debenture evidencing a future debt was raised in *Handevel's* case (1985) 62 ALR 204, 217, where the High Court stated that:

Act provides a statutory "gloss" or qualification to the broad definition of "debenture" in section 9 of the Act. In particular, section 283BH regulates whether a given debt security is legally allowed to be promoted as a "debenture". Section 283BH (3) prevents a borrower from describing a document evidencing a debt as a "debenture", unless repayment of the money deposited or lent is secured by a charge in favour of the trustee for debenture holders over the tangible property of the borrower. Where the security is a first mortgage over land, the debentures may be described as "mortgage debentures": section 283BH (2). If the loan is unsecured, the document must be described as an "unsecured note" or an "unsecured deposit note": section 283BH(1).

> [I]n Burns Philip Trustee Co Ltd v Commissioner of Stamp Duties… Hunt J stated that in order to constitute a debenture the debt which is acknowledged or created must be, existing not a future debt… however, the statement needs to be qualified to allow for a document which makes provision for the repayment of a loan to be made thereafter.

It is unclear whether it is the loan or the repayment, which is "to be made thereafter". If it is the loan, then the contingent future debts may be covered. In England, Lloyd J in *NV Slavenburg's Bank v International Natural Resources Ltd* [1980] 1 All ER 955, 976 was prepared to go even a step further and rejected a proposition that a document relating to a future unspecified debt could not be a debenture. This suggestion made by a single judge was *obiter* and conflicts with a number of cases interpreting stamp duty provisions similar to those in the *Corporations Act*, which requires an acknowledgement or creation of a specific debt: *Associated Broadcasting Services Ltd v Comptroller of Stamps (Vic)* (1988) 88 ATC 4359, 4363; *Commissioner of Stamp Duties (NSW) v Board* (1980) 11 ATR 59, 69.

However, the suggestion that the definition of debenture may cover future debts adds some weight to that interpretation of *Handevel's* case. Significantly, *Handevel's* case and Burns Philip both dealt with a definition of debenture, which referred to "debentures, stock and other securities", but the definition in the previous provisions of the *Corporations Act* included a reference to "money that is or may be deposited with or lent to the body". See also *Association Broadcasting Services and Humes Ltd v Comptroller of Stamps (Vic)* (1989) 89 ATC 4,646. *Handevel's* case opens up the possibility that contingent debts and possibly general indebtedness may constitute a "debenture". This gives greater weight to an argument that the previous *Corporations Law* definition of debenture extended to future debts.

It is conceptually difficult to understand how a document can acknowledge or evidence a debt (the essential requirements of the previous *Corporation Law*), which may never come into existence. This difficulty is exacerbated when the amount of the debt will be determined in the future depending, for instance, on how much is drawn down by the borrower. The *CLERP Act* 1999 (Cth) has replaced the previous debenture definition with a new provision excluding those words "money that may be lent to the body", which should eliminate the uncertainties associated with the definition of "debenture" in corporations legislation in the past.

Plainly the bonds issued under RMBS programmes could well, and in practice are generally designed to, fall within the ambit of the definition of "debenture" in Ch. 2 L of the *Corporations Act*.[52]

Managed Investment Scheme Provisions and RMBSs

Section 9 of the *Corporations Act* provides that a managed investment scheme includes the following features:

- People contribute money or money's worth as consideration to acquire rights (interests) to benefits produced by the scheme.
- Any of the contributions can be pooled, or used in a common enterprise, to produce financial rights or benefits arising out of rights or interests in property, for the people (the members) who hold interests in the scheme. Members can hold interests either by way of contribution or by acquiring an interest from another member.
- The members do not have day-to-day control over the operation of the scheme; however, they may have the right to be consulted or to give directions.

The debt instruments that cannot be characterised as "debentures" under the *Corporations Act* fall within the ambit of the Managed Investment Scheme ("MIS") provisions in Ch. 5C of the Act,[53] which regulate the creation and operation of MISs having at least 20 members, or which are promoted by a person who is in the business of promoting MISs.

An MIS must be operated by a single "responsible entity" that is a public company holding a dealer's licence. If the public company holds scheme property, it must act as trustee for the scheme members: section 601FA. A person who seeks to register an MIS must lodge an application with ASIC;

[52] See, for example, the bonds issued as RMBSs by Macquarie Securitisation Ltd in *Master Information Memorandum, PUMA Fund P-7*.

[53] The MIS is a statutory creation originally derived from the recommendations of the English Anderson Committee on Fixed Trusts (1936) and the current legislation is based on those recommendations: see *Prevention of Fraud (Investment) Act* 1939 (UK). The definition of an MIS is extremely wide, to a degree which is "barbarous" according to Jones J. in *W.A. Pines Pty Ltd v Hamilton* (1981) WAR 225, commenting on the definition of "prescribed interest". See also the judgement of Mason J. in *Australian Softwood Forests Pty Ltd v Attorney General for New South Wales* (1981) 6 ACLR 45. Many forms of securitisation are likely to constitute managed investment schemes for purposes of the *Corporations Act*. For example, a unit in a unit trust constitutes a "managed investment" for the purposes of the *Corporations Act*: see *Attorney General of NSW v Australian Fixed Trusts* [1974] ACLC 40–100, in which it was held that a unit in a unit trust constituted a "prescribed interest" for MIS purposes.

it must be accompanied by a copy of the scheme's constitution, the scheme's compliance plan, and a statement signed by the responsible entity's directors certifying that those documents comply with relevant provisions: sections 601GA, 601GB. Sections 295 and 301 require a registered scheme to prepare financial reports and have them audited at the end of each financial year and, pursuant to section 314, to send a copy of the auditor's report to the members of the scheme.

A mortgage securitisation programme based on bills of exchange or promissory notes [illegible] regulated as MISs. In general, all MISs to which Ch. 5C applies must be registered with ASIC: section 601ED(1). Under section 601ED(2), an MIS need not be registered with ASIC if none of the security issues made under the scheme require Product Disclosure Statements to investors in terms of Div 2 of Pt. 7.9 of the *Corporations Act*. This means, for example, that securities in MISs offered to up to 20 persons every 12 months, and which did not raise $2 million or more, need not be registered. Similarly, issues of securities in MISs to investors who do not need disclosure under section 708 of the Act (e.g. so-called sophisticated investors) need not be registered with ASIC.

Regulation of the Trust Deed[54]

As per the section 283AA of the *Corporations Act*, a company—including, in this context, the corporate trustee of an SPV—offering "debentures" (in practice, this includes RMBSs) to the public for subscription must execute a trust deed, which comprises covenants relating to[55]:

- The proper and efficient conduct of the borrowing company's business.
- The security trustee's duty to exercise reasonable diligence to ascertain whether the property of the borrower will be sufficient to repay the amount of debt.
- The provision of relevant information by it to the security trustee.
- The setting of a limit to the amount borrowed.[56]

[54] As noted earlier, the repayment obligations under the initial housing loans are generally secured in favour of a security trustee, who serves under the terms of the trust deed. The provisions of the trust deed are, of course, regulated not only by the *Corporations Act*, but as noted earlier, also by the *Trusts Act* 1973 (Qld).

[55] See Ch. 2 L.4, sections 283DA–283 DC.

[56] This requirement is also set out in the Listing Rules of the Australian Stock Exchange (ASX).

- Meetings, which are requisitioned by not fewer than 10% of bondholders, to consider the company's latest accounts and, where necessary, direct the security trustee to exercise its power of sale over the relevant security properties.

Section 283AB provides that even if these covenants are not expressly set out in the trust deed, they are implied by statute. They relate primarily to undertakings by the borrowing company to use its best endeavours in the conduct of its business, and to provide proper accounting of its activities.

In addition to these requirements under the *Corporations Act*, the trust deed will invariably in practice include many other clauses designed to provide some "code of rights" for bondholders as between themselves; to give the trustee power to act against the borrowing company and its guarantors; and to set out the rights and liabilities of the trustee, as well as any discretionary powers which may bind the bondholders: sections 283BA–283BI.

6.3.2 Disclosure Requirements Relevant to RMBSs

Fundraising Provisions for Issue of RMBSs

Introduction of the *CLERP Act* 1999 largely overhauled the *Corporations Act* by inserting a new Ch. 6D (sections 700–741), replacing the previous prospectus provisions.[57] However, these provisions were subsequently revised as a result of amendments made by the *Financial Services Reform Act* 2001 (Cth) (FSRA).[58] The fundraising provisions also regulate

[57] For a detailed discussion, see N. Calleja, 'Current Issues relating to Prospectus Advertising and Securities Hawking' (2000) 18 *Companies and Securities Law Journal* 23.

[58] For example, the *Corporations Act* no longer requires that there be an "offer to the public" to determine the circumstances in which a prospectus must be registered with the ASIC. Instead, there is a general prohibition—that is, a person is prohibited from making an offer or distributing an application form for an offer of securities that needs disclosure unless a disclosure document for the offer has been lodged with the ASIC: section 727(1). Prior to the amendments made by the *CLERP Act* 1999 (Cth), prospectuses had to be both lodged, and in most cases, registered with the ASIC before being distributed to investors. The registration process was designed to give ASIC opportunity to pre-vet prospectuses to ensure they complied with the prospectus content requirements and did not contain any misleading statements or material misrepresentations. While sections 718 and 727(1) insist that disclosure documents must still be lodged with ASIC, the *CLERP Act* has removed the previous

investments in "securities". This is due to the fact that debentures are included within the definition of "securities" in sections 700(1) and 716A of the Act, RMBSs are clearly regulated by Ch. 6D.[59] As per the provisions of the *Corporations Act*, any attempt to raise funds by the issue of securities[60] must be accompanied by a "disclosure document", a copy of which must be lodged with ASIC: sections 706, and 727(1).

Even though the word "disclosure" itself is not defined in the act, a "disclosure document" for an offer of securities[61] is defined in section 9 as:

- A prospectus for the offer
- A "short form" prospectus
- A profile statement for the offer
- An offer information statement for the offer[62]

Since the definition for "securities" section 9 includes both debentures and MISs, the disclosure provisions of Ch. 6D and Pt. 7.9 apply to securitisation issues unless a suitable exemption is available. In most cases, the Information Memoranda used by the mortgage securitisation industry satisfy the criteria for "prospectuses" in any event, notwithstanding the fact that many of the industry's Information Memoranda are marketed to investors who fall within the ambit of the statutory exemptions from the disclosure requirements under the Act. In RMBS programmes, the securities themselves are generally marketed using an Information Memorandum, which contains a comprehensive compilation of the parties' rights and responsibilities, and their legal risks and liabilities in the case of non-performance. While the quality and quantity of the disclosures in Information Memoranda vary somewhat

requirement of ASIC registration. The FSRA amendments also shifted the disclosure requirements applicable to managed investment schemes from Ch. 6 D of the *Corporations Act.* to the financial product disclosure provisions of Pt 7.9 of the *Corporations Act.*

[59] See, for example, *Master Information Memorandum-PUMA Fund P7,* 2000, paragraph 1.11 and *PUMA Sub-Fund Series* 2014, pp 8–9, 83.

[60] "Issue" is defined in section 9 of the Act to include "circulate, distribute and disseminate".

[61] "Offer" is now generally accepted as having broad meaning. The law will regard an "offer" as also including the distribution of material that would encourage an investor to enter into a course of negotiations calculated to result in the issue or sale of securities: *Attorney General for NSW v Australian Fixed Trusts Ltd* [1974] 1 NSWLR 110; *Australian Softwood Forests Pty Ltd v A-G for NSW* (1981) CLC 40–734.

[62] Which type of disclosure document is appropriate for a particular issue of securities is determined by the nature of the prospective investors in the issue, and the level of disclosure required by the Act: see section 705.

across the industry, an Information Memorandum plays a role, which is essentially analogous to that of a prospectus in the fundraising provisions of the *Corporations Act*.

Content of Prospectus or Disclosure Documents

The *Corporations Act* prescribes the form and content of various types of disclosure documents necessary for offer of securities. Additional information must be set out in a prospectus, which is ought to be a full-disclosure document, in contrast to the other types of disclosure documents. The *Corporations Act* enforces a general disclosure test for the contents of a prospectus as well as specific disclosure obligations. Under section 710(1), a prospectus must contain all the information that investors and their professional advisers would reasonably require, to make an informed assessment of the matters set out in that section. A prospectus must contain this information only to the extent that it is reasonable for investors and their professional advisers to expect to find such information in the prospectus, and only if the information is actually known, or in the circumstances ought reasonably have been known (e.g. by making inquiries).

Section 710(1) of the *Corporations Act* identifies a general disclosure test substantially similar to its predecessor; it was slightly reworded by the *CLERP Act* 1999 to ensure that information is not included in a prospectus merely because it had been included in the past, or was contained in other prospectuses.[63] In deciding what information should be included under the general disclosure test, section 710(2) specifies that regard must be had to:

- The nature of the securities.
- The nature of the body.
- If the securities are in a managed investment scheme—the nature of the scheme.
- The matters that likely investors may reasonably be expected to know.
- The fact that certain matters may reasonably be expected to be known to their professional advisers.[64]

[63] Section 710 (1) specifies that the following information must be disclosed in relation to an offer to issue shares, debentures, or interests in an MIS:

- The rights and liabilities attaching to the securities offered.
- The assets and liabilities, financial position and performance, profits and losses, and prospects of the body that is to issue the shares, debentures, or interests.

[64] In general terms, the more complex the securities being offered, the greater the level of disclosure required: see, for example, the Corporations and Securities Panel's decision in *Re Email Ltd* (2000) 18 ACLC 708.

Exclusions to Disclosure Requirements
Disclosure requirements identified in Ch. 6D suggests that an RMBS issue involves an expensive, lengthy, and fairly inflexible process. However, section 708 identifies several exceptions for such disclosure requirements. Accordingly, there are number of situations in which disclosure to prospective investors is not required in respect of security offerings.[65]

Sophisticated Investors Section 708(8) defines a sophisticated investor. Such investors are deemed not to need the protection of the disclosure requirements because they are experienced, financially sophisticated, or wealthy investors. For example, under the so-called Licensed Dealer Exemption, offers of securities made through a licensed dealer to experienced investors do not need disclosure: section 708(10)(d). The dealer must be satisfied on reasonable grounds that the investor has previous experience in investing in securities that allows them to assess such matters as the merits of the offer, the value of the securities, the risks involved in accepting the offer, and the adequacy of the information given by the person making the offer. In the case of so-called Large Offers, the "sophisticated investor" exception under section 708(8)(a) refers to offers of securities in which the minimum amount payable on acceptance of the offer is at least $500,000. Neither is disclosure to investors required where the investor accepts an offer of $500,000 or more payable by instalments over a period of time, or where the investor seeks only to "top up" a previously accepted large offer: section 708(8)(b). Judging from the wording of these provisions of the *Corporations Act,* Parliament has taken the view that such investors have sufficient means to obtain the relevant information themselves, and that mandating disclosure would be unnecessary.[66]

Professional Investors Section 708(11) lists "professional" investment persons and bodies to whom disclosure is not required when making an offer of securities. These include:

[65] See generally, P. Hanrahan, I. Ramsay and G. Stapledon (eds.), *Commercial Applications of Company Law* (Sydney: CCH, 2003) 25–110.

[66] The Policy Paper *Corporate Disclosure: Strengthening the Financial Reporting Framework* (CLERP 9) 2002 proposed that the sophisticated investor exemption be harmonised with the similar "wholesale clients" exemption that applies to product disclosure statements for financial products.

- Licensed or exempt dealers or investment advisors who are acting as principal.
- Persons who control at least $10 million for the purpose of investment in securities (including amounts held by an associate or held in a trust that the person manages).
- Bodies or friendly societies registered under the *Life Insurance Act* 1995.
- Certain regulated superannuation funds and approved deposit funds.

In relation to the professional investor exemption, a caution needs to be sounded. An issuer of securitised debt instruments could inadvertently breach the disclosure provisions of Ch. 6D if it offers securities to an investor who appears, or purports, to satisfy the requirements contained in section 708(11) mentioned earlier, but who in fact does not. In these circumstances, the issuer will not be entitled to the exclusion in this section for the benefit of it is not based on the investor appearing to satisfy the requirement; the investor and its associates must in fact control not less than $10 million in investments. If the investor does not, then the issuer of RMBS could be liable for failing to lodge its disclosure documents with the ASIC in accordance with section 727(1) of the Corporations Act. Contravention of section 727 is a criminal offence punishable by a fine of $20,000 or five years imprisonment or both: section 1311 and Schedule 3.

Debentures of Certain Bodies Nor is disclosure required in the case of an offer of a company's debentures where the company is an Australian Authorised Deposit-taking Institutions (ADI) or registered under the *Life Insurance Act* 1995.[67]

Most residential mortgage securitisation programmes in Australia employ structures that come within the ambit of one or more of these exemptions from the Corporations Act's disclosure requirements.[68] For example, paragraph 1.8 of Macquarie Securitisation Ltd's *PUMA Sub-Fund Series* 2014 refers to "Distribution to Professional Investors Only" and states that:

[67] See section 708(19). An Australian ADI is defined in section 9 as an authorised deposit-taking institution within the meaning of the *Banking Act* 1959(Cth) and a person who carries on State banking within the meaning of paragraph 51(xiii) of the Constitution.

[68] A. Finch, (1995) 247, 267; Clayton Utz, *A Guide to the Law of Securitisation* (Sydney: Clayton Utz, 2004).

> This Master Information Memorandum and each Series Supplement has been prepared … for institutions whose ordinary business includes the buying and selling of securities.… and are not intended for, should not be distributed to,… as an offer or invitation to, any other person.[69]

Paragraph 1.10 of the Information Memorandum, *Master Fund P-7*, refers to an "Excluded Offer or Invitation" and states that:

> Each offer for purchase or invitation to buy Bonds under this Master Information Memorandum…, will be an excluded offer for the purposes of the Corporations Act as the amount payable by each person to whom the offer is made or the invitation is issued is at least A$500,000. Accordingly, neither this Master Information Memorandum nor any Series Supplement is required to be lodged with, or registered by, the Australian Securities and Investment Commission.

In a similar vein, Securities Pacific Australia Ltd's Information Memorandum states that "…the securities are issued pursuant to a private placement and may only be sold to a person whose ordinary business is to buy or sell securities in accordance with the relevant provisions of the Corporations Act."[70] Likewise, MGICA Securities Limited's issue of MGICA Mortgage Securities (MMSs) states that MMSs will be offered only to selected institutions whose ordinary business includes the buying and selling of securities, and that the MMSs will not be offered to the public or any section of the public.

It is not beyond the realms of possibility that if the market for RMBSs in Australia expands substantially in the foreseeable future, RMBS issue of securities of less than $500,000 could be sold to retail investors ("Mum and Dad"), as distinct from the higher face value securities currently marketed to "sophisticated" institutional investors. If this were to become the case, new provisions in the *Corporations Act*, or possibly an entirely separate new regulatory regime embodied in "stand-alone" legislation, may become necessary. The *Investment Company Act 1940* (US) could serve as a useful model in this regard, which is discussed in Chap. 8.

[69] See *Master Information Memorandum*, P-7 and *Master Information Memorandum PUMA Sub-Fund Series* 2014, p 9.

[70] B. Salter, (1993) 5.

Information Memoranda: Misstatements and Omissions

Both statute and the common law recognise liability for misstatements and omissions in Information Memoranda, even if the securities are marketed by way of Information Memorandum to investors who fall within the exemptions from the *Corporations Act's* disclosure requirements (i.e. investors to whom disclosure need not be made anyway). It may be argued that section 728, which exclusively concerns misstatements in a disclosure document, does not apply to an "exempt offer" of RMBSs. However, this does not mean that section 728 can be ignored. It continues to be relevant in determining whether an omission from an Information Memorandum can lead to civil liability. In such cases, an issuer may be liable for misleading and deceptive conduct under section 1041H. In terms of statutory liability, the *CLERP Act* 1999 introduced new provisions dealing with liability for misstatement and omissions in disclosure documents into Pt. 6D.3 of the *Corporations Act*, replacing the previous fundraising liability provisions in section 996 of the former *Corporations Law*.

In a broad sense, Pt. 6D.3 and Ch. 7 attempt to ensure that all information pertinent to the investment decision is disclosed to an investor: sections 710–713. Sections 728 and 1041H of the *Corporations Act* provide the two principal provisions that give effect to that objective, which apply to all disclosure documents.

Section 728(1) provides that a person must not offer securities under a disclosure document if:

- There is misleading or deceptive statement in either the disclosure document, any application form accompanying the disclosure document.
- There is an omission from the disclosure document of material required by the fundraising provisions: (sections 710–715), for example, contents of prospectuses, profile statements, and offer information statements.
- A new circumstance has arisen since the disclosure document was lodged and it would have been required by the fundraising provisions to have been included in the disclosure document.

Legal provisions of section 728 prohibits a securitiser from offering RMBSs under a disclosure document if it contains a misleading or deceptive statement or omits information required by the fundraising provisions.[71] The idea behind the prohibition in section 728 is to place the responsibility for compliance with the content-setting rules for disclosure documents directly on the issuer of securities, and to make non-compliance actionable at the suit of investors who suffer loss or damage because of that non-compliance.

Breach of section 728(1) amounts to a criminal offence provided there is a misleading or deceptive statement in the disclosure document (e g the Information Memorandum), or if the misstatement or omission in a disclosure document is "materially adverse"[72] from an investor's point of view.

Concept of "Materiality" and "Materially Adverse"

The concept of materiality in the context of misstatements and omissions in disclosure documents is not defined in the *Corporations Act.* Materiality, as interpreted in the US securities context, means whether the matter judged to be material would have been significant to the decision-making process of reasonable investors. The test of material omission in disclosure documents has received extensive judicial comment in the United States. In *TSC Industries Inc v Northway Inc*, the US Supreme Court characterised the nature of the standard of materiality, as "a mixed question of law and fact, involving as it does the application of a legal standard to a particular set of facts". This means that it is the decision for the tribunal of law, not of fact.[73]

[71] Section 728 is broadly similar to its predecessor, section 996, but there are some important differences. First, while section 996 was concerned with those who authorised or caused the issue of prospectus, the statutory duty imposed by section 728(1) is placed upon the person offering the securities under a disclosure document. In the case of an offer to issue mortgage-backed securities in a securitisation programme, the person is the issuing body, which is the trustee of the securitisation fund. Second, while section 996 was confined to a disclosure defect in the prospectus, section 728(1) applies to a misstatement in the disclosure document or any offer document.

[72] Section 728(3).

[73] 426 US 438, 450 (1976). The United States has a long history of judicial analysis of the meaning of "material": see, for example, *Escott v Barchris Construction Corp* (283 F Supp 544, 1968, 1967–1969) CCH December, 92, 179 ("Material" means the facts which have an important bearing upon the nature or condition of the issuing corporation or its business); *Feit v Leasco Data Equipment Corp* (332 F Supp 544 1971*); Ross v Warner* (SD NY Dec 11 1980) 1980 CCH December, 97,735 (A fact is material if there is a substantial likelihood that, under all the circumstances, a reasonable investor would consider it important in reaching an investment decision). The essence of this history has been codified in the SEC's regulations as follows:

The *Securities Act* 1993 (US) and Securities and Exchange Commission's Rules (see e.g. sections 11 and 12) refer to the word "material" in several key provisions which have a similar operation to the provisions in Ch. 6D of the *Corporations Act.* Section 728 has been based on section 11(a) of the *Securities Act* 1933 (US), which provides as follows:

> [I]n case any part of the registration statement... omitted to state a material fact required to be stated therein or necessary to make the statements therein not misleading, the person acquiring such security (unless it is proved that at the time of such acquisition he knew of such untruth or omission) may, either at law or in equity, in any court of competent jurisdiction, sue ...

Section 728 provides for an omission of material that should have been included in the disclosure document under sections 710–715, not to be misleading. Section 728(1) provides direct guidance as to the nature of the matters that need to be disclosed in order for issuers to satisfy its requirements. The current Australian provision is, therefore, potentially less limited in its application than its counterpart in the United States.

In *Cackett v Keswick*, the UK courts examined the scope of the concept of a "material omission", and the application of a statutory provision requiring the disclosure of all "material contracts" as follows:

> The test must be, is the omission material? And if the Court sees that the fact omitted is of such a nature that it might be reasonably deter, or tend to deter, the ordinary investor from entering into the contract, this is sufficient. It is in great measure an inference of fact to be drawn by the Court or a jury from the circumstances of the case. If a material fact is omitted from a statement put forward to induce a person to enter into a contract, and he does enter into the contract on the faith of that statement, it is a fair inference that he would not have contracted if he had known of the fact, in that in this sense the omission induced the contract.[74]

"The term "material" when used to qualify a requirement for the furnishing of information as to any subject, limits the information required to those matters as to which an average prudent investor ought reasonably to be informed before purchasing the security registered": see (1968) CFR 230.405(1): H. Saban (1994) 82; P. von Nessen, 'The Americanisation of Australian Corporate Law' (1999) 26 *Syracuse Journal of International Law and Commerce* 239.

[74](1902) 2 Ch 456, 460.

The concepts expressed in these extracts are similar to those contained in section 728(1) of the *Corporation Act*. The decision in *NatWest Australia Bank Ltd Tricontinental Corporation Ltd*[75] indicates that the following factors may be taken into account in determining whether an omission from an Information Memorandum constitutes a breach of section 12DA and 1041H:

- The relationship between the parties
- The nature of the commercial enterprise
- Whether information was "material and important" to the decision
- The knowledge and expertise of the parties

The phrase "materially adverse" is not defined in the *Corporations Act*. In the case of *Re BTR PLC and BTR Nylex Ltd*, the Full Federal Court commented that whether a matter is materially adverse reflects, to an extent, its effect on the price of the securities.[76] The only person facing primary criminal liability is the entity making the offer of securities in question (e.g. the issuer or trustee in a securitisation programme). In other words, directors of a company will not face primary criminal liability.[77] In addition, an investor who suffers damage as a result of a breach of the requirement set out in section 728(1) will have a right to seek compensation from the person liable for the misstatement or omission in the Information Memorandum: section 729(1). This civil liability will exist for a period of six years from the date the cause of action arose: section 729(3). Section 729(1) sets out the range of people potentially liable for compensation and the extent of their liability. The issuer of a disclosure document, its directors, and underwriters are responsible for the disclosure document as a whole. Other people, such as experts, named with their consent in the disclosure document are liable only for their own statements in the disclosure document. Compensation can be sought against a person regardless of whether that person has been convicted of

[75] (unreported, Supreme Court of Victoria, No. 2493 of 1990). The approach of the court in Tricontinental involved an assessment of whether the relevant omitted information was material. This was also adopted by the Full Court in *Fraser v NRMA Holdings* (1995) 13 ACLC 132–133.

[76] (1989) 23 FCR 553.

[77] However, section 176 of the Crimes Act 1900 (NSW) and section 191 of the Crimes Act 1958 (Vic) impose primary criminal liability on directors and officers for a misstatement in a prospectus.

an offence in respect of the contravention, as this provision (section 729) operates independently of the offence provision (section 728(3)). Breach of section 728(1) carries a maximum penalty of 200 penalty units, imprisonment for five years, or both: section 1311 and Schedule 3.

Section 729(1) lists other people who are potentially liable for misstatements in, or omissions from, the disclosure documents, including directors of the issuing body, underwriters, and any person named in the disclosure document.[78] Under section 730, a person referred to in section 729 must notify the person making the offer "as soon as practicable" if they become aware of certain deficiencies in the disclosure document, or a "material new circumstance" has arisen.

The phrase "as soon as practicable" is not defined in the Act. It seems likely that it is designed to impose a reasonably practical time limit after the person becomes aware of the deficiencies for issuing the appropriate notice. What is reasonably practical is a question of fact and must vary according to the circumstances. In addition, the phrase "material new circumstances" is not defined in the Act. A matter has been held to be material, in the context of the takeover provisions, if it might reasonable affect, the decision of the ordinary investor whether or not to accept the offer in the particular circumstances of the bid.[79]

In section 1041H, Parliament seeks to ensure that all relevant information is disclosed to investors is, which operates as a "catch all" provision. Other statutory provisions which give rise to civil liability in relation to defective Information Memoranda are section 12DA of the *Australian Securities and Investment Act* 2001 (*ASIC Act*) and, if neither sections 1041H or 12DA apply, section 18 of the *Competition and Consumer Act* 2010 (Cth)

[78] Section 769C(1) also provides that representations about *future* matters will be considered misleading if they are not made with reasonable grounds.

[79] *Cackett v Keswick* [1902] 2 Ch 456, 464. Thus, a matter is material in this context if its disclosure is necessary to enable an investor to make an informed assessment of the offer: *Australian Consolidated Investments Ltd v Rossington Holdings Pty Ltd* (1992) 35 FCR 226.

Finally, section 729(4) states that Pt. 6D.3 does not affect any liability that a person has under any other law. Presumably this includes professional negligence or negligent misstatement on the part of an issuer, director, or manager of a securitisation programme: R. Sammonds, 'Directors' Negligent Misstatement Liability in a Scheme of Securities Regulation' (1979) *Ottawa Law Review* 633; M. Rajacic, P. Rajapakse and E. Webb, 'The Impact of the *Trade Practices Act* 1974 (Cth) on the Auditors' Liability' (2000) 19 *University of Tasmania Law Review* 205, 226–227. Cases such as *Al-Nakib Investments (Jersey) Ltd v Longcroft* [1990] 3 All ER 321 have also held that prospectuses of company are capable of sustaining a cause of action for negligence for the offerees.

(CCA) (formerly section 52 of the *Trade Practices Act* 1974 (Cth)). Both sections 1041H and 12DA are modelled on section 18 of the CCA.[80]

Section 1041H provides that "a person shall not, engage in conduct, in relation to a financial product or a financial service that is misleading or deceptive or is likely to mislead or deceive." Section 1041H(2) relates to the publication of notices (e.g. advertisements), and to negotiations and arrangements preparatory to or related to an issue of RMBSs.[81] The section imposes strict liability, so that it applies even where no disclosure document has been lodged with ASIC (e.g. because one of the section 708 exemptions applies).[82]

Section 12DA of the *ASIC Act* prohibits a person, in trade or commerce, from engaging in relation to financial services, in misleading or deceptive conduct. It is likely that almost every Information Memorandum used in RMBS programmes could be regarded as being "in relation to financial services" for the purpose of attracting the application of section 12DA of the *ASIC Act*. The *Explanatory Memorandum* to the *Financial Services Reform Bill* 1998, which introduced section 12DA into the *ASIC Act*, indicates that the intention was to replicate the CCA's consumer protection provisions in the *ASIC Act*. Whilst section 12DA appears in a division headed "Consumer Protection", however, it is not limited to consumer protection and has general application, including to the wholesale and retail security markets.

The result is that two prohibitions—that is, those in sections 1041H of the *Corporations Act* and 12DA of the *ASIC Act*—apply to an Information Memorandum in RMBS programmes. Why this duplication was considered

[80] *Cleary and Ors v Australian Co-operative Foods Ltd* (1999) ACSR 701; Explanatory Memorandum, *Financial Sector Reform Bill* 1998, paragraph 4.12.

[81] Section 1041H(2) states that "engaging in conduct in relation to a financial product" includes (but is not limited to) any of the following:

(a) Dealing in a financial product
(b) Without limiting paragraph (a)

  (i) Issuing a financial product
  (ii) Publishing a notice in relation to a financial product

[82] Section 1041H is based on the former section 995 of the *Corporations Act*. The *Corporations Act* provides its own definitions of "financial product", "financial services", and "dealing" for the purposes of section 1041H. Broadly, these are the same as the equivalent definitions in the *ASIC Act* for section 12DA: see definitions provided in sections 12BAA; 12BAA(7); 12BAA(8); 12BAB(7) of the *ASIC Act*.

necessary remains unclear, particularly as both sections were drafted in almost identical terms.

These terms "misleading conduct" and "deceptive conduct" are not defined in the *Corporations Act* or the *ASIC Act*. However, these concepts have, in effect, created their own jurisprudence, particularly in the area of trade practices.

As noted earlier, sections 1041H and 12DA are modelled on section 18 of the *Competition and Consumer Act 2010 (Cth)* (CCA). It seems likely that the courts' interpretation of these concepts in the context of section 18 of the CCA would also be applicable to sections 1041H and 12DA.[83] For instance, the term "likely to mislead or deceive" has been judicially defined in relation to section 52 of the TPA (currently section 18 of the CCA) to mean "a real and not remote chance of misleading or deceiving".[84] In *ASC v Nomura International Plc*,[85] the same meaning was held to apply to that term in section 995 (the predecessor of section 1041H).[86] It is also clear from the policy behind the introduction of section 12DA that it is intended to cover, in relation to financial services, the same conduct as section 52 (currently section 18 of CCA).[87]

A number of principles can be drawn from the section 18 cases that are relevant to the manner in which sections 12DA and 1041H apply to disclosure documents or Information Memoranda in RMBS programmes:

- Whether conduct is misleading or deceptive will be determined objectively in the context in which it occurs. An intention to mislead is irrelevant. An issuer can therefore breach sections 12DA and 1041H unwittingly.[88]

[83] The relevance of section 18 of CCA case law to the former section 995 of the *Corporations Act* was recognised in *Fame Decorator Agencies Pty Ltd v Jeffries Industries Ltd and Ors* (1998) 16 ACLC 1235; *Fraser v NRMA Holdings Ltd* (1995) 15 ACSR 590; C. Lockhart, *The Law of Misleading and Deceptive Conduct*, (Sydney: Butterworths, 1998); D. Crocker, *Prospectus Liability Under the Corporations Act* (Melbourne: Centre for Corporate Law and Securities Regulation, 1998) Ch. 8.

[84] *Global Sportsman v Mirror Newspapers* (1984) ATPR 40–463, 45,343.

[85] (1999) 17 ACLC 55.

[86] See also *Winpar Holdings Ltd v Goldfields Kalgoorlie Ltd* (2000) 18 ACLC 665, 668.

[87] Explanatory Memorandum, *Financial Sector Reform Bill* 1998, paragraphs 4.12 and 4.13.

[88] See generally, *Annand and Thompson Pty Ltd v TPC* (1979) ATPR 40–116, 18,272; *Sterling v TPC* (1981) ATPR 40–212, 42,918; *Snoid v Handley* (198) ATPR 40–219.

- Silence on an issue of securities will be considered to be misleading and deceptive if the facts give rise to a reasonable expectation that the matter would have been disclosed.[89] For example, in the case of *Fraser and Anor v NRMA Holdings Ltd and Ors*,[90] on appeal, the Full Court made the following statements concerning omissions:

> Where the contravention of section 52 [of the Trade Practices Act 1974] allegedly involves a failure to make a full and fair disclosure of information, the applicant carries the onus of establishing how or in what manner that which was said involved error or how that which was left unsaid had the potential to mislead or deceive. Errors and omissions that have that potential must be relevant to the topic about which it is said that the respondents' conduct is likely to mislead or deceive.[91]

It is arguable, therefore, that because issuers of RMBS are under an obligation under section 728(1) to disclose all information, a failure to do so could constitute misleading or deceptive conduct for the purpose of sections 1041H and 12DA. The test of whether an omission from an Information Memorandum constitutes a breach of sections 12DA and 1041H depends upon whether an investor had a "reasonable expectation" that the omitted material would be disclosed. Although the sections do not create an independent duty of disclosure, they have the practical result through the "reasonable expectation" test of setting the standard of disclosure in an Information Memorandum. If that standard is not met, then those responsible are exposed to potential liability for breach of the sections. Where it is alleged that an issuer did not disclose a vital piece of information, investors have an incentive to plead sections 1041H, 12DA, and 728(1) in the alternative.

[89] *Warners v Elders Rural Finance Ltd* (1993) 41 FCR 399; *Demagogue Pty Ltd v Ramensky* (1992) 39 FCR 31, 32.

[90] (1995) ATPR 41-374. See also *NRMA Ltd and Ors v Morgan* (1999) 17 ACLC 1029, 1045; *Commonwealth Bank of Australia v Mehta* (1990) ATPR 52,598; *Warner v Elders Rural Finance Ltd* (1993) 41 FCR 399; and *Demagogue Pty Ltd v Ramensky* (1992) 39 FCR 31.

[91] See *Demagogue Pty Ltd v Ramensky* (1992) 39 FCR 31, 40; and *Fraser v NRMA Holdings* (1995) 13 ACLC 132, 141].

- In *Wiestman v Katies Ltd*,[92] it was held that, in order to evaluate whether or not certain conduct was impermissible, the court must first identify the "audience" at which the conduct was aimed, and then judge whether that particular audience would have found the conduct misleading or deceptive. For the purposes of section 728(1), it will generally be relatively easy to identify this "audience", simply by inquiring as to the class of investors at whom the relevant Information Memoranda was targeted (e.g. were subscriptions being solicited from members of the public at large, or from only selected institutional investors?).[93]

Once the relevant audience has been identified, a court will attribute a standard of perception or knowledge to the audience against which the conduct in question will be assessed. Under the CCA, courts have applied various standards. Some cases apply a very low standard encompassing all those that come within the audience (including the ignorant, the unthinking, and the credulous); others focus on the standard of a person, not particularly intelligent nor well informed, but of somewhat less than average intelligence or background knowledge.

In the context of more sophisticated dealings such as those typically involving securitisation, the courts may well incline to this last view, on the basis that commercial investors should take reasonable care of their own interests. Generally, a reasonable level of commercial experience would be attributed to such an audience. Thus, in the context of an Information Memoranda, the courts will judge whether the impugned disclosure (or absence of it) constitutes conduct that is "misleading or deceptive or is likely to mislead or deceive", in the context of the financial sophistication of the target group at which the issuer was aiming for subscriptions. The more sophisticated the audience, the less likely that a conclusion against the issuer will be arrived at by the court (i.e. it is more likely that the court would believe that the audience would not have been misled or deceived—for example, because it had at its disposal access to information that would have put a proper perspective on statements which might otherwise be misleading or deceptive).

[92] (1977) ATPR 40-041, 17,441-17,443; see also *Paula Brock v The Terrace Times Pty Ltd* (1982) ATPR 40-267, 43,412.

[93] See, for example, *Puxu Pty Ltd v Parkdale Custom Built Furniture Pty Ltd* (1980) ATPR 40-171, 42,360; *World Series Cricket v Parish* (1977) ATPR 40-040, 17,437; and the comprehensive discussion contained in *CCH's Australian Trade Practices Reporter*.

Whether an omission from an Information Memorandum constitutes a breach of sections 1041H and 12DA depends on whether an investor in the target "audience" had a "reasonable expectation" that the omitted material would be disclosed. Although the sections do not create an independent duty of disclosure, they have the practical result, through the "reasonable expectation" test, of setting a standard of disclosure in an Information Memorandum. If that standard is not met, then those responsible (e.g. the issuers and fund managers involved in preparing Information Memoranda) are exposed to potential liability under the sections. Accordingly, the information that an investor would expect to be disclosed in an Information Memorandum is similar to that set out in section 710(1) and (2) of the *Corporations Act* for a prospectus—that is, all information that an investor would reasonably require and reasonably expect for the purpose of making an informed assessment of the issuer and the relevant securities.

Both sections 1041I of the *Corporations Act* and 12GF of the ASIC Act impose civil liability on the person whose "conduct" constituted the contravention and on any other person "involved in the contravention". A contravention of section 12DA does not constitute an offence: section 12GB(1) ASIC Act. However, persons aggrieved can claim for their loss by way of civil action pursuant to section 12GF ASIC Act. These remedies are similar to those in CCA for a breach of section 18 of that Act.[94] Similarly, section 1311 of the *Corporations Act* specifically provides that a breach of section 1041H is not an offence. Instead, the consequence of a breach is potential civil liability under section 1041I of the *Corporations Act*, which is also based on section 236 of CCA. Section 52 of the *Corporations Act* also provides that "a reference to doing an act … includes a reference to causing, permitting or authorising the act or thing to be done". In other words, a party who authorises the issue of an Information Memorandum will probably be deemed to have engaged in the relevant conduct to the extent that the Information Memorandum comprises any misleading or deceptive conduct.

Defences for Misleading or Deceptive Statements

Two main defences are available to persons against whom civil or criminal liability under sections 729 or 728(3) respectively of the *Corporations Act* is alleged. These are the so-called due diligence and reasonable reliance defences.

[94] See sections 224, 236, and 237 of CCA.

(a) *The "Due Diligence" Defence*

In the case of misleading or deceptive statement or an omission appearing in a prospectus, a person does not commit an offence against section 728(3) (concerning materially adverse misstatements and omissions) and is not liable under section 729 (recovery for loss or damage due to contravention) for a contravention of section 728(1) if the person proves under section 731 that he or she:

- Made all inquiries that were reasonable in the circumstances—This element of section 731 concerns the process of inquiry. It concerns the situation before the prospectus is issued, and it fastens on the operation of the prospectus. In the context of an RMBS issue, it means that the fund manager and its officers should have undertaken an active and critical process of inquiry in relation to the statements included in the Information Memorandum in order to tease out anything that is misleading or deceptive. For this element to be made out, the defendant should also be able to point to the inquiries that were in fact made. In evidentiary terms, it would plainly be prudent for the fund manager and its officers to keep records of an appropriate "paper trail" of their inquiries.
- After doing so, believed on reasonable grounds that the statement was not misleading or deceptive—The second element provides that anyone relying on the "due diligence" defence must first make reasonable enquiries before they can form a belief based on reasonable grounds that the relevant statement is not misleading and deceptive. In establishing these "reasonable grounds", the defendant must establish as a matter of evidence that he or she held the belief that there was no misstatement.[95]
- After doing so, believed on reasonable grounds that there was no omission from the prospectus in relation to that matter.[96]

[95] See, *Adams v Thrift* [1915] 1 Ch 557. The words "reasonable grounds" require a consideration of objective criteria and an assessment as to reasonableness: *Group Four Industries Pty Ltd v Brosnan and Anor* (1991) 9 ACLC 1181, 1184. Those grounds must be objective and verifiable, well founded, and bona fide.

[96] See section 731. This third element deals with omissions instead of statements. The comments made in relation to the previous two elements apply equally in the context of this third element.

The "due diligence" defence in section 731 applies only in relation to prospectuses, and not all disclosure documents. However, there is little doubt, based on the foregoing argument, that, in appropriate circumstances, the defence could be available in respect of Information Memoranda in RMBS issues, provided the due diligence has taken place in a bona fide fashion.[97]

(b) *Defence of Reasonable Reliance*

Under the provision of section 700(1) of the *Corporations Act*, persons responsible for misleading or deceptive statements or omissions in disclosure documents can claim defence, if they reasonably relied on information given to them by others,[98] or if the document becomes misleading or deceptive because of new circumstances of which they were unaware.

As per the section 733(2), at the time when disclosure documents are prepared, much of the information they contain is likely to come from outside experts and professional advisers.[99] For example, in the context of the *Master Information Memorandum, PUMA* Sub-Fund Series 2014, the

The text of section 731 is quite different from the former "due diligence" defence under then-section 1011 of the *Corporations Law*, and to the current "due diligence" defence under section 85(1)(c)(ii) of the *Trade Practices Act*, which the courts have interpreted to mean a "proper system to provide against contravention of the Act and that it had provided adequate supervision to ensure that the system was properly carried out": *Universal Telecasters (Qld) Ltd v Guthrie* (1978) 18 ALR 531, 534. The former section 1011 had provided that "a person who authorised ... the issue of prospectus is not liable ... if it is proved that the false or misleading statement or omission (a) was due to a reasonable mistake; (b) was due to a reasonable reliance on information supplied by another person; or (c) was due to the act or default of another person, to an accident or to some other cause beyond the defendant's control."

[97] In *Adams v Eta Foods Ltd* [1987] ATPR 40–831, the court held that the "due diligence" defence was not available in the case of the former sections 995 and 996 (to which sections 1041H and 728(1) respectively are now functionally almost equivalent), where the "diligence" activities had been approached in an ad hoc fashion, or where the defence was effectively an ex post facto rationalisation of the true facts.

[98] For the "reasonable reliance" defence to succeed, the person relied upon must be someone other than a director, employee, or agent: section 733(1). It is not clear how this defence interacts with directors' general duty to act with skill, care, and diligence. For example, as was held in the decision in *Daniels v Anderson* (1995) 13 ACLC 614, a director is obliged to actively monitor delegated activities, and is under a duty to make further enquiries if he or she has suspicions concerning the adequacy of disclosure, or where a prudent person could be concerned about a matter.

[99] See, *Master Information Memorandum, PUMA Sub-Fund Series 2014*, p 57.

Fund Manager prepares the Information Memorandum and the Series Supplement for each Series of Bonds issued with the advice and assistance of the legal counsel. Such information includes the programme parameters; the terms and conditions of each bond issue; and the procedures, guidelines, and lending criteria for the residential housing loans that form part of the mortgage pool. As a matter of policy, it seems reasonable that the issuer should be able to rely on the expertise of external experts and professional advisers, since this is why professional advisers are engaged in the first place.

For the purposes of section 733, the "reliance", which the SPV and fund managers place on others, ought to be reasonable. This essentially is an objective test and is measured against what other people would do when placed in similar circumstances. In the case of *Rovell v American National Bank*[100] in a US context, the court held that "reasonable reliance" was driven by the facts of each case. The Australian courts have been more specific. For example, in interpreting the "reasonable reliance" defence in section 85(1)(b) of the former Australian *Trade Practices Act* 1974 (Cth), the court in *Gilmore v Pool-Blunden and Ors*[101] pointed out that the defence was available where an issuer relied on legal opinion given by counsel, which can be "information" for the purposes of the defence. Certainly, from a legal risk management perspective, the usual strategy adopted by Australian securitisers is to seek legal and other professional advice concerning compliance with the fundraising regime, and to sue those advisers if the advice turns out in hindsight to have been negligent.[102]

The defences "due diligence" and "reasonable reliance" make it obvious that if an issuer and its officers in an RMBS programme are to avoid criminal or civil liability for potential breaches of Ch. 6D, they must show that they have been duly diligent in ensuring that all information disclosed in an Information Memorandum is up-to-date and accurate, and that it contains all information relevant to an investor for making an informed decision about whether or not to invest in those particular mortgage-backed securities.

[100] (Unreported, 21 October 1999: 7th Cir 1999).

[101] (1999) SASC 186.

[102] See, for example, *NRMA Ltd v Morgan* (1999) 17 ACLC 1029. It is also likely, as a matter of the proper construction of section 733, that the "reasonable reliance" defence implies some element of causation, in a somewhat similar fashion to the law's approach to liability for negligence: *Duke Group Ltd (on liquidation) v Palmer and Ors* (1999) SASC 97.

Common Law Liability

The common law on the other hand provides investors with rights where they have been misled or deceived by a prospectus. Common law liability in this context is primarily fault-based, allowing damages for deceit or negligent misrepresentation.[103] Financial advisers and independent experts have been held to owe a duty of care to those who retain them and consequently to be liable for reasonably foreseeable losses resulting from negligent preparation of their reports.[104] However, any misrepresentation that becomes a term of a contract gives rise, in a sense, to strict liability.[105] The remedy of rescission is also generally available where an SPV which, even without fault of its own part, issues a misleading prospectus.

Information Memoranda and Use of Disclaimers

Usually Information Memoranda in securitisation programmes include an extensive disclaimer or exclusion of liability in relation to representations contained in them. The disclaimers usually appear in the Important Notice section at the front of the Information Memorandum.[106] The disclaimers are generally in broad terms and usually contain an express denial of liability in respect of representations or statements contained in the Information Memorandum and a direction to investors to make and rely upon their own enquiries in relation to the securities on offer.

Knowing the nature and purpose of an Information Memorandum, there must be some doubt as to how effective any disclaimer can be, given that paragraph (a) above (The "Due Diligence" Defence) appears to conflict with the basic philosophy and operation of section 18 of the CCA (and, it would seem, sections 12DA of *ASIC Act* and 1041H of the *Corporations Act*). Section 18 cannot be contracted out, irrespective of the sophistication or desire of the parties.[107] In addition, the direction noted in paragraph (b) above (Defence of Reasonable Reliance) is not one that

[103] Based on the seminal case of *Hedley Byrne and Co. Ltd. v Heller and Partners Ltd* [1974] AC 465.

[104] *Esanda Finance Corporation Ltd v Peat Marwick Hungerfords* (1997) 188 CLR 241; *Hill v Van Erp* (1997) 188 CLR 159; and *Duke Group Ltd (in liquidation) v Palmer* (1991) 31 ACSR 213.

[105] *Heilbut, Symons and Co v Buckleton* [1913] AC 30.

[106] See, for example, *Master Information Memorandum, PUMA Sub-Fund Series 2014*, p 7.

[107] *M.K. Hutchence and Ors (Trading as "INXS") v South Sea Bubble Co Pty Ltd* (1986) 8 ATPR 40–667 (These cases are based on section 52 of TPA); and A. Terry, 'Disclaimers and Deceptive Conduct' (1986) *Australian Business Law Review* 478, 479.

an investor will usually be in a position to comply with in any meaningful way. It seeks to eliminate the causal connection between the misleading statements or omissions in a deceptive Information Memorandum and the resultant damage, by advising investors that they must not rely on the Information Memorandum. These obvious difficulties are borne out by the case law that has developed in relation to disclaimers.[108] For example, in *Pappas v Soulac Pty Ltd*,[109] the courts stated that disclaimers may sometimes be used in Information Memoranda in an effort to prove that investors have not relied on any inducement or representation by the fund manager when investing in the RMBSs. However, as noted by French J in *Kewside Pty Ltd v Warman International Ltd*,[110] the success of a disclaimer in eliminating reliance will be a question of evidence, not a question of law. Even where a plaintiff has signed an acknowledgement that he or she has not relied on any inducement or representation by the defendant (e.g. a fund manager, in the present context), this may not be enough to show that the plaintiff did not in fact rely on the inducement or representation. The comments of Wilcox J in Collins *Marrickville Pty Ltd v Henjo Investments Pty Ltd* are instructive on this point: "If in fact the misleading conduct of a respondent has induced an applicant to enter into an agreement, that inducement is not negated because, in the agreement itself, the applicant says to the contrary."[111]

However, in *Keen Mar Corporation Pty Ltd v Labrador Park Shopping Centre Pty Ltd*,[112] disclaimers have been upheld on the basis that the plaintiff's acknowledgement of the disclaimer and its own non-reliance were sufficiently specific and contemporaneous with the representations or statements for the court to find in favour of the defendant. In *Khalaf Agalby v Darlington Commodities Ltd*,[113] the court provides a convenient list of some factors that will help to preclude reliance by investors on any representations by an issuer or its agents. In that case, the defendant had taken the precaution of:

[108] The provisions giving rise to civil liability for misleading or deceptive conduct in an Information Memorandum (section 12GF of the *ASIC Act* and section 1041I of the *Corporations Act*) each require that the applicant establish its reliance upon that conduct in incurring the damages claimed. The two sections are based on section 82 of the CCA.

[109] (1983) 50 ALR 231, 238.

[110] (1990) ATPR 40–050.

[111] (1987) ATPR 40–782. Similar comments were given by Heerey J in *Karmot Auto Spares Pty Ltd v Dominelli Ford (Hurstville) Pty Ltd* (1992) ATPR 41–175, and McDonald J in *NatWest Australia v Tricontinental Corporation Ltd* (cited earlier).

[112] (1989) ATPR 46–048.

[113] (1985) ATPR 40–535.

(a) Obtaining from the investor a "Client's Declaration of Understanding of Risk", which comprised a list of printed questions requiring individual handwritten answers by the investor. The tenor of the various questions asked was "Do you understand the risks associated with the investments you are about to make?"
(b) Including in the agreement further acknowledgements by the investor of the risks involved, together with express disclaimers by the defendant in relation to any loss or damage suffered by the investor as a result of any of a number of specifically identified causes.

While the court did not find that the investor had established any evidentiary foundation for assertions of misleading conduct, it went on to say that the investor "would still face the formidable hurdle of the operation of the 'Client's Declaration of Understanding of Risk'" and other disclaimers. The Keen Mar case cited earlier indicates that a pro forma disclaimer could well be worthless and that a disclaimer will be ineffective if the party intended to be bound by it is in some way misled into accepting it. That case also shows that it may be useful to specify what factors have been relied upon by a potential investor when purchasing securities.

The status of disclaimers and exclusion clauses in relation to section 52 of the former *Trade Practices Act* (section 18 of CCA, and presumably sections 12DA and 1041H) was well summarised by French J in *Kewside Pty Ltd v Warman International Ltd* as follows:

> To the extent that [disclaimer or exclusion] provisions relied upon have contractual effect, they cannot prevail against the provisions of section 52, or the cause of action created by section 82 of the Act. A disclaimer or exclusion clause will affect liability for misleading or deceptive conduct only if it deprives the conduct of that quality or breaks the causal connection between conduct and loss. Whether it has that effect in a given case is a question of evidence and not a question of law.[114]

The intention of the party engaging in relevant conduct is not an element of a contravention. If, notwithstanding the disclaimer, statements made in an Information Memorandum were capable of being misleading or deceptive in the sense outlined earlier, the disclaimer would probably not protect the parties responsible for the Information Memorandum

[114] (1990) ATPR 46–050, 53,222.

from a breach of section 52 of the TPA (currently, section 18 of the CCA or presumably sections 12DA and 1041H). This is acknowledged in such cases such as *Petera Pty Ltd v E A J Pty Ltd*,[115] *Benlist Pty Ltd v Olivetti Australia Pty Ltd*[116] and *NatWest Australia v Tricontinental* (referred to earlier). More particularly, the courts are reluctant to give effect to attempts "to evade liability for the known and contemplated consequences" of conduct.[117]

For these reasons, a disclaimer, in itself, is unlikely to be effective as a means of avoiding contravention.

Effectiveness of Sections 12DA and 1041H

From a law reform perspective, an interesting question arises as to whether the *Corporations Act* itself advantages investors in RMBSs, relative to investors in other corporate securities, who wish to sue the SPV or its agents (e.g. the fund manager) on the basis that they were induced to invest because of false or misleading Information Memoranda.

As far as the current legislation is considered, if investors in other corporate securities sue under sections 728 and 729 for loss because of a misleading or deceptive statement in a disclosure document, their claim can be defeated if the defendant can prove the defences in sections 731–733.[118]

[115] (1985) ATPR 40-605.

[116] (1990) ATPR 40-043.

[117] *Mackman v Stengold Pty Ltd* (1991) ATPR 41-105.

[118] The objective of securities regulation is to seek a balance between the interests of investors and those responsible for the preparation of a prospectus. Thus, for registered prospectuses, civil liability is imposed on those who are responsible for the preparation of the prospectus for any misleading or deceptive statements and any omission from the standard of disclosure: sections 710, 728, and 729. However, the balance is achieved by extending to the class of section 729 persons, the benefit of the defences in sections 731–733. Section 12DA of *ASIC Act* on the other hand, is essentially a consumer protection device. It favours consumers at the expense of the company. The *Corporations Law Simplification Task Force* recommended exempting registered prospectuses from the operation of section 18 of the CCA and 995 of the *Corporations Law* (the predecessor of section 1041H) on grounds that "Despite taking every possible precaution to comply with the requirements of the Corporations Law, business is likely to remain exposed to liability because it is not able to rely on the defences. The result is to increase the cost of fundraising by Australian business": see M. Legg 'Misleading and Deceptive Conduct in Prospectuses' (1996) 14 *Corporations and Securities Law Journal* 47, 48; and *Corporations Law* Simplification Task Force, Report on Fundraising, Attorney General's Department, 1995, 18–20. Logically, if sections 52 of former TPA and the former section 995 of the *Corporations Law* were inappropriate for the

However, liability under sections 12DA and 1041H[119] is strict, so that an investor's claims in relation to a misleading Information Memorandum would not be able to be met by any defences. This is despite the fact that most investors in RMBS issues are so-called sophisticated investors, for the purposes of the disclosure provisions. This implies that sophisticated investors in the RMBS markets have greater likelihood of recovery than investors in other corporate securities in the financial markets

6.3.3 *The Regulation of Industry Participants*

The Wallis Committee Report of the Financial System Inquiry (FSI)[120] in 1997 identified a number of core factors affecting the financial system in Australia.[121] The *Financial Services Reform Act* (FSRA) was implemented in 2001 after the release of CLERP 6. Chapters 7 and 8 of the *Corporations Act* was replaced by a new Ch. 7 of the FSRA, as well as some related amendments.

Section 911A(1) of the *Corporations Act* requires that a person who carries on a financial services business in Australia hold an Australian Financial Services Licence (AFSL) covering the supply of those financial services. The essential elements of carrying on a business of supplying financial services are that:

business because they disturbed the balance between the interests of investors and securities issuers and impeded the raising of capital, then this must also be the case for mortgage securitisation markets.

[119] Albeit subject to section 1041I of the Act.

[120] In June 1996, the Financial System Inquiry, also known as the Wallis Inquiry after its Chairman Mr Stan Wallis, was commissioned to provide a stocktake of the results of the financial deregulation of the Australian financial system since the early 1980s. The FSI's main aim was to recommend further improvements to the regulatory arrangements governing Australia's financial system.

[121] Following the FSI, many of the recommendations were implemented; establishing two different regulators—one focusing on market conduct and disclosure and the other on prudential issues. For instance, the Australian Securities and Investments Commission (ASIC) and the Australian Prudential Regulation Authority (APRA) were created. Many of the recommendations of the FSI were engulfed in a set of reforms of the *Corporations Law* known as the *Corporate Law Economic Reform Program* (CLERP). The financial services reform aspect became known as "CLERP 6". In March 1999, the CLERP 6 Consultative Paper "Financial Products, Service Providers, and Markets—An Integrated Framework" was issued, providing a regulatory framework for the licensing of financial product markets and service providers, and disclosure requirements for such service providers and their representatives; and financial product disclosure.

- The business is in relation to a "financial product"
- The "financial product" be provided in the manner as set out in Division 4 of Pt. 7.1 of the Corporations Act

Under section 911D, a person carries on a financial services business in Australia, if, in the course of their carrying on the business, that person engages in conduct that is:

- Intended to induce people in Australia to use the financial services which the person provides
- Likely to have that effect

It might be thought that trustee-issuers of RMBSs are required, under the legislation, to obtain an (AFSL) in order to market their bonds. Certainly, the usual prerequisites to a licence requirement must be satisfied. RMBSs are plainly "financial products"[122] under Ch. 7, and the issuers of RMBSs are plainly providing "financial services".[123] In general, if an

[122] The definition of "financial product" under Ch. 7 of the *Corporations Act* is broad, and presumably designed to "cover the field" of financial products and instruments in practice. Section 763A provides that a "financial product" is a facility through which, or through the acquisition of which, a person:

- Makes a financial investment
- Manages a financial risk
- Makes non-cash payments

A detailed list of "financial products", which includes "debentures" (a term which, as noted earlier, in practice invariably encompasses RMBSs issued in Australia), is provided by section 764.

[123] As with the definition of financial product, "financial services" are defined very broadly. Section 766A of the *Corporations Act* provides five limbs for defining a "financial service":

1. Providing financial product advice (section 766B). The provision of "financial product advice", "dealing in a financial product", and "providing a custodial or depository service" are plainly of relevance for participants in RMBS programmes. Under section 766B, "financial product advice" is defined as:

   [A] recommendation, statement of opinion or report on either of the above, that is intended to influence a person/section in making a decision in relation to a particular financial product or class of financial products; or could reasonably be regarded as being intended to have such an influence.

2. Dealing in financial product (section 766C).
3. Making a market for a financial product (section 766D).

investor gives money to a financial product provider (e.g. a representative of a trustee-issuer for RMBSs) with the intention that the provider will use the funds invested to generate a financial return or other benefit for the investor, the product will be caught under this definition: section 763B.

Financial product advice is usually provided in an RMBS programme in the form of investment banks, which structure the RMBS transactions for a fee, providing advice to any intermediary selling the bonds; the SPV or the licensed dealers and originators providing advice to potential investors in RMBSs; and an Information Memorandum, prepared by the issuer or fund manager for distribution to potential investors in RMBSs, which may contain advice.

The definition of "dealing" is provided in section 766C of the *Corporations Act,* which includes "applying for or acquiring a financial product, issuing a financial product, underwriting the securities or interests, varying a financial product or disposing of a financial product". Arranging for a person to do any of these activities is also dealing in a financial product: section 766C(2). Most of the participants in an RMBS transaction will be involved in "dealing" in financial products, including persons (normally investment banks) who arrange for others to deal in the RMBSs and therefore require an AFSL; persons (normally investment banks) who sell RMBS to wholesale investors, who then arrange for others to deal in the bonds, and therefore require an AFSL; persons (normally banks and insurance companies) who provide support facilities such as swaps, loans, and mortgage insurance to the SPV, and who may therefore be "dealing" in relation to these services; trustees of SPVs, who deal with RMBSs in their capacity as trustees; and managers of SPVs who deal in RMBSs in their capacity as managers. Trustees are not able to rely on the "self-dealing" exception in the same way as the issuer can, and the Australian Securitisation Forum has suggested that securitisation trusts,

4. Providing a custodial or depository service (section 766E); generally, a person provides a custodial or depository service to a client if they have an arrangement with the client to hold a financial product or a beneficial interest in a financial product in trust for, or on behalf of the client: section 766E. An RMBS transaction normally involves custodial or depository services in the context of the trustee providing such a service to the sponsoring bank or IMP. Such services might also be provided by the security trustee to the bondholders, in the event that a default occurs and their security is enforced.
5. Operating a registered scheme: section 766A(1)(d). See generally, Australian Securitisation Forum, *Submission to the ASIC: Licensing Relief for Securitisation Structures,* 23 October 2003, http://www.securitisation.com.au/asf.

such as RMBS trusts, should be able to rely on this exception.[124] A person is not deemed to be "dealing" if all they do is to deal on their own behalf: section 766C(3). This encompasses principals who apply for, vary, dispose of, or otherwise deal in a financial product on their own behalf (such an individual who applies for a managed investment product for themselves); but it applies only to the principal, and not someone engaged in dealing on the principal's behalf.

However, Ch. 7 of the *Corporations Act* does not trespass on other prudential regulation of financial products and services. Section 911A(2)(g) of the Act specifically exempts Australian Prudential Regulation Authority (APRA)-regulated providers and services marketed only to wholesale clients[125] from the need to hold an AFSL.[126] Because, as noted in previous chapters, the issuers and other providers of RMBSs meet these requirements,[127] there is no need for them to

[124] See generally, Australian Securitisation Forum, Submission to the ASIC: *Licensing Relief for Securitisation Structures,* 23 October 2003, http://www.securitisation.com.au/asf.

[125] More generally, the importance of the distinction between wholesale and retail clients in relation to various types of financial products is fleshed out in Ch. 7, Pt. 7.1, Division 2 of the Regulations. The extent of the legislative-style detail in these Regulations is somewhat surprising—the Regulations contain the types of provisions that would normally be found in legislation that has been passed through Parliament, rather than subordinated legislation promulgated by the bureaucracy. The question arises as to whether the legislation, replete with significant logical gaps and lacking in detail, was hurriedly passed through Parliament for political purposes, with the bureaucracy left to fill in the detail after it was passed.

[126] Besides the providers of APRA-regulated services to wholesale clients, other people who are exempted by section 911A(2) from the need to hold an AFSL include representatives of entities who are already licensees; issues that are the subject of an "intermediary authorisation"; operators whose services are provided within an already-licensed market; general advice in the media; overseas-regulated entities; entities who provide financial services only to related companies; self-managed superannuation trustees; and providers of services that have been specifically exempted in writing by ASIC and gazetted as such.

[127] To remove any doubt, section 761G of the legislation makes a distinction between "retail" and "wholesale" clients, with all of the following clients being "wholesale" clients: (a) clients who purchase a product whose price or value is at least $500,000 (see Regulations 7.1.18–7.1.27); (b) clients who purchase a product for use in connection with a business that is not a small business; (c) individuals purchasing the product for non-business use who meet the minimum asset or income requirements in the Regulation 7.1.28 (i.e. currently $2.5 million in net assets, or gross income of at least $250,000 over both of the last two years); or professional investors. In a sense, therefore, the test in section 716G of the *Corporations Act* is somewhat similar to that in section 708, which mandates the provision of prospectus or other disclosure documents in respect of an issue of securities. The effect of this "wholesale" client status is set out in Regulation 7.1.27. As noted earlier, historically in practice in

hold an AFSL. The APRA-based regulation of RMBS providers has already been discussed in depth in Chap. 5.

A related issue is whether banks or other financial institutions that engage in hedging activities (e.g. providing interest rate swaps to assist the fund manager with the risk management aspects of RMBSs) are also required to hold an AFSL. Again, by a similar process of reasoning, because these providers and their wholesale activities are regulated by APRA and in practice market RMBSs only to professional investors, they would appear to be exempted by sections 761G and 911A(2)(g) from the need to hold an AFSL.

6.4 Contractual Issues in RMBS Programmes

Prima facie, a housing loan, perhaps at its most fundamental, can be viewed as a contract between lender and borrower. From a perspective not only of (social) economic efficiency in neoclassical microeconomic theory but also of ethical theory, transparency and informed choice in contracting are generally regarded as desirable, at least to the point where the benefits of additional information equal the costs at the relevant margin.[128]

Kirby P in *Canham v Australian Guarantee Corporation Ltd* highlighted the importance of borrowers making informed decisions when assessing loan contracts:

> The ultimate truth behind the philosophy of truth in lending…is that disclosure…will help to ensure honesty and integrity in the relationship (where one party is normally disadvantaged or even vulnerable); promote informed choices by consumers; and allow the market for financial services to operate effectively.[129]

Australia, RMBSs have invariably been marketed only to professional investors in the wholesale markets. In essence, the FSRA (now Ch. 7 of the Act) and the attendant Regulations have not changed this market practice. Regulations 7.1.18 and 7.1.20 specify that clients who pay more than $500,000 for a financial product are "wholesale" clients in respect of that product.

[128] There is a plethora of economic theory to this effect. See, for instance, A. Koutsoyiannis, *Modern Microeconomics* (2nd edition, N.Y.: Macmillan, 1979) 257, 393–394; and R. A. Posner, *Economic Analysis of Law* (6th edition, N. Y.: Aspen Law and Business, 2002). In the context of ethical theory, see for instance, J. Rachels, *The Elements of Moral Philosophy, with Dictionary of Philosophical Terms* (4th edition, Boston: McGraw Hill, 2002) Ch. 14.

[129] (1993) 31 NSWLR 246, 254; (1993) ASC 56–227, 58,354.

6.4.1 Notice to Borrowers

Based on our previous discussion, securitisation via RMBS programmes entails the risk that borrowers might find their homes sold by financial intermediaries downstream who have "purchased" their bank's or IMP's mortgagee rights, not due to a failure to pay on the part of the borrowers, but as a result of some act or omission by a downstream financial intermediary in the supply chain. This raises the concern whether most home loan borrowers are aware of this risk at the time of taking out their loans. Experience would indicate that most are not, and nor is it specifically brought to their attention.

The loan contract invariably states, from a bank's or IMP's point of view, albeit in fine print amongst many thousands of words, that the housing loan may be assigned. Typically, the clause in most contemporary mortgage documents is to the effect that the bank or IMP "may assign or otherwise deal with [its] rights under this mortgage or any secured agreement in any way [it] considers appropriate". If the banks are to take mortgage security over residential properties, they can and should be expected to explain at least the major clauses in their mortgage documents to borrowers—and the deceptively simple assignment clause is certainly one with potentially major consequences for borrowers, as the law now stands. So that they can make an informed decision about their choice of financier, most borrowers would wish to be made aware—and indeed would expect their banks to tell them—of any risk that they could lose their homes, whether through mortgage assignment or any other cause. On the other hand, the banks and IMPs would rely on such clauses to avoid liability in the event of proceedings instituted by borrowers for loss of their homes.

Furthermore, the banks can and should advise their customers to obtain independent legal advice about the effects of clauses in their mortgage documents. The problem with banks completely relying on advising customers to obtain independent legal advice is that currently, in practice, solicitors are not commenting on assignment programmes in mortgages because they do not fully understand them and sometimes have continuing conflicts of interest from acting on behalf of banks or other parties in past transactions.

However, it is unclear whether such clauses would be effective from a legal perspective, or whether they even ought to be upheld from an economic or ethical perspective. The mere fact that a loan agreement contains a clause, amongst many others, to the effect that the loan may be assigned is surely not a basis for an informed choice on the part of the borrower about the consequences of assignment, if the risks are not communicated to the borrower (or, if communicated, are expressed in such a way that the borrower understands, and is able to make an informed decision about whether or not to sign the loan agreement).

Almost 50 years ago, admittedly in the context of exclusion clauses, the courts propounded the fundamental principle that the more unreasonable a clause, the greater the notice which must be given of it. Denning LJ in the English Court of Appeal expressed the principle eloquently in a well-known dictum, observing that:

> *Some clauses, which I have seen, would need to be printed in red ink on the face of the document, with a red hand pointing to it before the notice could be held to be sufficient* [emphasis added].[130]

It seems difficult to argue convincingly that this principle should not apply equally to bringing the risks of securitisation to the attention of home loan borrowers today. In the event of litigation (e.g. if borrowers' homes were sold through no fault of their own), their banks or IMPs would presumably seek to rely on the assignment clauses in their loan contracts as a means of avoiding liability, in the same way as other commercial firms seek to rely on exclusion clauses in their contracts.

Such clauses are generally construed against the interests of the persons who drafted the clause (*contra proferentem*), with the *proferens* (in this context, the originating bank or assignor) being required to take reasonable steps to give notice of the existence and contents of the clause to those against whom it is intended to be used. In practice, this generally means that the clause must be presented clearly and unambiguously in such a way that a reasonable person would become aware of it[131] and realise that it could have an impact on his or her rights and liabilities under the contract.[132] The steps that are reasonably required to bring the clause to the attention of the other party (in this context, the mortgagor) must

[130] *Spurling (J) Ltd v Bradshaw* [1956] 1 WLR 461, 466; [1956] 3 All E.R. 121, 125 per Denning LJ (as he then was).

[131] *Thompson v London, Midland and Scottish Railway Co* [1930] 1 KB 41; *Thornton v Shoe Lane Parking Ltd* [1971] 2 QB 163; *White v Blackmore* [1972] 2 QB 651, 664 (per Lord Denning MR): P. S. Latimer, *Australian Business Law* (Sydney: CCH, 2004) paragraphs 5.190 and 6.220.

[132] *Mendelssohn v Normand Ltd* [1969] 3 WLR 139, 143, per Lord Denning MR.

be taken before or at the time the contract is entered into. A clause brought to the attention of a party after the contract has been entered into will not be effective.[133]

Silence on the part of the bank or IMP at the time of the home loan interview might not protect the financier if the borrower were to bring proceedings under the CCA, rather than the contract. Under section 18 of the CCA (formerly section 52 of the TPA), silence in respect of the contract and its clauses may amount to misleading or deceptive conduct.[134]

The risk that the banks and IMPs run, if they do not bring the risks of their participation in RMBS programmes to the attention of home loan borrowers, is that they could ultimately face a wave of litigation similar to that precipitated by the foreign currency loan scandals of the mid-to-late 1980s. In essence, all of that litigation arose, not from the complicated nature of then-"novel" financing arrangements but from the banks' failures to notify borrowers of the risks involved—in those cases, the risk that borrowers could ultimately have their mortgaged properties sold not through any conscious default on their part, but because of adverse exchange rate fluctuations over which they had no control.[135]

[133] *White v Blackmore* [1972] 2 QB 651, 664 as per Lord Denning MR; *Olley v Marlborough Court* [1949] 1 KB 532; *Oceanic Sun Line Special Shipping Co Inc v Fay* (1988) 165 CLR 197.

[134] See the decision of the Full Court of the Federal Court of Australia in *Henjo Investments Pty Ltd v Collins Marrickville Pty Ltd* (No 1) (1988) 39 FCR 546, 556–557 per Lockhart J; *Demagogue Pty Ltd v Ramensky* (1992) 39 FCR 31, 32, per Black CJ; and *Kimberley NZI Finance Ltd v Torero Pty Ltd* (1989) ATPR (Digest) 46–054, 53,195 per French J. Cf. At common law, silence is not generally regarded as a misrepresentation. As noted in *Smith v Hughes* (1871) L R 6 QB 597,604, "The general rule, both of law and equity, in respect to concealment, is that mere silence with regard to a material fact, which there is no legal obligation to divulge, will not avoid the contract, although it operates as an injury to the party from whom it is concealed."

[135] See, for example, *Clenae Pty Ltd and Ors v ANZ Banking Group Ltd* [1999] VSCA 35 (9 April 1999); *David Securities Ltd and Ors v Commonwealth Bank and Ors*, unreported, Full Federal Court, per Lockhart, Beaumont and Gummow JJ, 10 May 1990; the same case at first instance in the Federal Court of Australia per Hill J, 11 May 1989; *Chiarabaglio v Westpac Banking Corporation* (1989) ATPR 40–971; and *Leitch and Ors v Natwest Australia Bank Ltd and Anor*, unreported, 12 October 1995, Federal Court of Australia, per Cooper J. See also, A. Tyree, *Banking Law in Australia* (4th edition, Sydney: Butterworths, 2002); W. S. Weerasooriya, *Banking Law and the Financial System in Australia* (Sydney: Butterworths, 2001).

The banks' exposure in the late 1980s was increased by the fact that many (and perhaps most) of their own managers and loans officers were unaware of the consequences of currency fluctuations and so could not, even if they had wished to, have informed borrowers of the risks. In a similar vein today, experience suggests that many (and again, perhaps most) bank managers and loans officers are just as unaware of the risks inherent in RMBS transactions now (and the consequences for borrowers) as their counterparts were in regard to the risks to foreign currency loan borrowers in the mid to late 1980s.

The precedents provided by the foreign currency loan cases of the early 1990s[136] may provide some protection for housing loan borrowers facing the risk of losing their homes because of the risks inherent in today's RMBS transactions. These cases reaffirm that the banks and IMPs plainly owe their customers a duty to exercise reasonable skill in fulfilling their obligations under the loan contract.[137]

Furthermore, if they adopt novel financing arrangements that may impact on the borrower, the banks and IMPs *may* have a duty to explain the technical aspects of the arrangements to their borrowers[138]—however, this is by no means certain, and probably depends on the circumstances[139] (e.g. whether

[136] See generally, B. Marshall, 'Loans, Losses and Liability: Lessons from Foreign Currency Litigation in Australia' (2000) 11 *Journal of Banking and Finance Law and Practice* 175.

[137] *Selangor United Rubber Estates v Cradock* (No. 3) [1968] 1 WLR 1555; *Bank of Baroda Ltd v Punjab National Bank Ltd* [1944] AC 176; and *Riedell v Commercial Bank of Australia Ltd* [1931] VLR 362.

[138] In the view of Tadgell J in *Abound Catering Conventions and Receptions Pty Ltd v National Australia Bank Ltd,* there was a duty on the bank to take reasonable care to explain all the technical aspects of the loan, and it was reasonable to provide some explanation of the way that (in that context) an overseas loan is obtained by the bank, and the risks (e.g. because of currency fluctuations) inherent in that type of financing: see *Abound Catering Conventions and Receptions Pty Ltd* (unreported VSC 26 October 1989), 26.

[139] Issues that arose in the foreign currency loan cases, and which would be likely to arise in the context of any litigation involving home loan borrowers and RMBSs, include:

- Whether a duty to advise even arises and, if it does, what the nature of that duty owed by the lender to the borrower is, in a situation of extraordinary risk: see *David Securities Ltd v Commonwealth Bank of Australia* (1990) 23 FCR 1; *Commonwealth Bank of Australia v Mehta* (1991) 23 NSWLR 84.
- Whether, if the banks owe a duty of disclosure, that duty is higher than in more "normal" commercial transactions.
- The degree to which any information, recommendation, or advice provided must be complete and unequivocal: see *Westpac Banking Corporation v Potts* (1992) Aust Torts Reports 81.

the customer is even likely to understand the explanation given). If they were to give an explanation or advice, the banks and IMPs would of course need to exercise reasonable care and skill in giving that explanation or advice.[140]

Having said this, it is likely that such cases could be easily distinguished in the event of litigation over RMBS programmes, precisely because they involve foreign currency risk and may on that account be able to be distinguished in judicial minds from the risk to borrowers in RMBS transactions.

This risk to housing loan borrowers that they might lose their homes through no fault of their own; the uncertainty of whether, at common law, the banks and IMPs even owe a duty to explain that risk and other technical aspects of RMBSs to their home loan borrowers; and the risk that many (perhaps most) bank managers, loans officers, and independent lawyers are themselves unaware of that risk, are compounded by the fact that, at present, there is no specific legislation requiring the banks or IMPs to bring those risks to the attention of home loan borrowers. While it is true that borrowers may be protected (arguably) by section 18 of the CCA, and equivalent provisions in the *Corporations Act*, this is by no means clear and unequivocal. In the longer term, there remains the risk of moral hazard, and the extent to which appropriate regulation may be needed to correct for this.

6.4.2 Hedging Agreements[141]

In an RMBS programme, the interest component of the mortgage loan repayments received by the trustee-issuer may be based on a fixed or a variable interest rate. A mismatch will arise if either:

- Whether, if a duty is owed, that duty is not just to warn of the risk inherent in the particular financing arrangement, but to articulate that risk as a type of "gamble": see *Commonwealth Bank of Australia v Mehta* (1993) 23 NSWLR 84; and *Abound Catering Conventions and Receptions Pty Ltd* (unreported, Victorian Supreme Court, 26 October 1989).

[140] *Potts v Westpac Banking Corporation* [1993] 1 QdR 135, 138; *Commonwealth Bank of Australia v Smith* (1991) 102 ALR 453, 475; *Cornish v Midland Bank* [1985] All ER 513.

[141] For a more comprehensive discussion of hedging agreements, see T. Valentine, G. Ford and R. Copp, *Financial Markets and Institutions* (Sydney: Pearson Education, 2003) Ch. 14–15; B. Hunt and C. Terry, *Financial Markets and Institutions* (3rd edition, Melbourne: Thomson Publishing, 2002) Ch. 17–21; and S. L. Schwarcz, *Structured Finance: A Guide to Principles of Asset Securitisation* (N.Y.: Practicing Law Institute, 1993) 13–15.

(a) Variable-rate home loan interest is received, but the interest payable on the bonds is at a fixed rate.
(b) Fixed rate home loan interest is received, but the interest payable on the bonds is at a variable rate.
(c) There is a timing mismatch between the cash flows received and the cash flows payable (e.g. if the home loan repayments are received on a monthly basis, but the bond interest is payable semi-annually).

In order to manage the financial risks inherent in such mismatches, the trustee (or more usually, its fund manager) will enter into hedging agreements, such as interest rate futures and options, and interest rate swap contracts.[142] In effect, interest rate futures fix a variable rate, so that the fund manager knows precisely what rate it earns or must pay; interest rate options give the fund manager the option to fix the interest rate if it chooses; and interest rate swap contracts enable variable-rate interest to be converted to fixed rate interest, or fixed rate interest to be converted to variable-rate interest.[143]

It might be thought that notice should be given to home loan borrowers not only that their loans may be assigned to SPVs as part of an RMBS transaction, but that those SPVs will almost certainly use financial derivatives—such as futures, options, and swaps—to manage some of the risks involved.

However, there is a fundamental point of difference between the two types of notice. The argument in favour of notifying home loan borrowers that the assignees of their housing loans will almost certainly use financial derivatives to help manage the risks involved is generally a moot one: if hedging agreements are properly managed, there is no risk to home loan borrowers of losing their homes, through no fault of their own. That risk will generally arise for other reasons. On the other hand, if the fund

[142] For example, in the case of Macquarie Bank's PUMA Fund, the relevant interest rate swap providers include Deutsche Bank, J P Morgan Chase Bank, Commonwealth Bank of Australia, and UBS Australia Ltd. The interest rate swap agreements are governed by the terms of the standard form International Swap and Derivatives Association (ISDA) Master Agreement.

[143] See for instance, *Master Information Memorandum, PUMA Fund P-7*, paragraph 5.7 and *Master Information Memorandum, PUMA Sub-Fund Series* 2014, pp 33 and 115.

managers do not properly manage their hedging arrangements,[144] there are already well-established causes of action, such as negligence, of which aggrieved bondholders can avail themselves.

6.5 Summary

Even if RMBS issues can in theory be based on debt and equity instruments, the only equity issue in Australia to date has been the FANMAC issue in the late 1980s, which the NSW government used to fund a highly publicised social housing scheme with fixed rate mortgages for low-income borrowers, known as the "HomeFund" scheme. Ultimately, this programme failed due to lack of servicing capacity on the part of borrowers under the scheme, and the NSW government was forced to step in to compensate both borrowers and investors.[145] There is also some evidence that the former Insurance and Superannuation Commission (now subsumed into APRA) historically discriminated against equity securities in favour of debt securities.[146]

Conceivably, partially due to the failure of the HomeFund issue, as well as the fact that many institutional investors have historically preferred debt instruments whose market yields can be readily compared with those of semi-government note stock for portfolio management purposes, all RMBS issues since the late 1980s in Australia have been confined to debt instruments. Under the current *Corporations Act*, these debt securities underlying RMBS issues are in practice characterised as "debentures", pursuant to sections 9 and 92 of the Act.

Under the same Act, companies (including banks) that offer "debentures" such as RMBSs to the public for subscription must do so within the framework of a trust, and SPVs in Australia invariably operate as trusts in practice. Debt instruments that cannot be characterised as "debentures" under the *Corporations Act* automatically fall within the ambit of the Managed Investment Scheme ("MIS") provisions of the Act.

[144] For example, if an interest rate swap provider fails to perform its obligations under the agreement, or the interest rate swaps are terminated, the bondholders may be subject to losses from interest rate fluctuations. The security trustee, on behalf of the bondholders, could claim against the fund manager for any failure to provide financial advice and information about the risks, and the fund manager's (and probably the swap counterparty's) failure to perform their obligations under the hedge contract.

[145] See, for example, R. Bruce et al., (1997) 257.

[146] See A. Finch, (1995) 272.

Issuing debt instruments that are structured as "debentures" saves transactions costs. It is true that the SPV incurs the costs of complying with the reporting, record keeping, and other requirements pursuant to Ch. 2 L of the *Corporations Act*,[147] subject to a right of indemnity from the trust assets, and these costs will be reflected in the pricing of the overall transaction. However, those costs are significantly less, across all stakeholders in the issue, than the regulatory compliance costs that would result if the underlying securities were subject to the MIS provisions.

Furthermore, the underlying debt securities in virtually all RMBS issues in practice are generally exempt from the disclosure requirements in Ch. 6D.2 of the *Corporations Act* because they are sold only to institutional and other "sophisticated" investors under section 708(8) of the Act. This also saves transactions costs across all stakeholders in the issue.

On the "down side", securitisation via RMBS programmes involves the risk that borrowers might find their homes sold by downstream financial intermediaries who have "purchased" their bank's or IMP's mortgagee rights, not due to a failure to pay on the part of the borrowers, but as a result of the insolvency of, or some act or omission by, downstream financial intermediary in the supply chain. This begs the question of whether most home loan borrowers are aware of this risk at the time of taking out their loans. Experience would indicate that most are not, and nor is it specifically brought to their attention.

Bibliography

Books and Book Chapters

Baker, P. V., *Snell's Equity*, London: Sweet & Maxwell, 1990.

Bruce, R., McKern, B., Pollard, I. and Skully, M., *Handbook of Australian Corporate Finance*, 5th edition, Sydney: Butterworths, 1997.

Clayton Utz, *A Guide to the Law of Securitisation in Australia*, Sydney: Clayton Utz, 2004.

Ferran, E., *Mortgage Securitisation: Legal Aspects*, London: Butterworths, 1992.

Ford, H. A. J. and Lee, W. A., *Principles of the Law of Trusts*, Sydney: Law Book Company, 2004.

Ford, H. A. J., Austin, R. P. and Ramsay, I. M., *Ford's Principles of Corporations Law*, 10th edition, Chatswood: Butterworths, 2001.

[147]And licensing requirements, where relevant: see Regulation 7.6.01(1)(r) of the *Corporations Regulations*.

Glennie, D. and Bouter, E., *Securitisation*, London: Kluwer Law International, 1998.

Hanrahan, P., Ramsay, I. and Stapledon, G. (eds.), *Commercial Applications of Company Law*, Sydney: CCH, 2002.

Hunt, B. and Terry, C., *Financial Institutions and Markets*, 3rd edition, Melbourne: Thomson Learning, 2002.

Janet, D., *Company Law*, London: Palgrave, 2001.

Koutsoyiannis, A., *Modern Microeconomics*, 2nd edition, N.Y.: Macmillan, 1979.

Latimer, P. S., *Australian Business Law*, Sydney: CCH, 2004.

Meagher, R. P., Gummow, W. M. C. and Lehane, J. R. F., *Equity: Doctrines and Remedies*, 4th edition, Sydney: Butterworths, 2002.

Posner, R. A., *Economic Analysis of Law*, 6th edition, N.Y.: Aspen Law and Business, 2002.

Rachels, J., *The Elements of Moral Philosophy, with Dictionary of Philosophical Terms*, 4th edition, Boston: McGraw Hill, 2002.

Rajapakse, P., 'Corporations Law and Trust Aspects of Asset Securitisation in Australia' in D. Campbell (ed.), *International Asset Securitization and Other Financing Tools*, N.Y.: Transnational Publishers Inc, 2000.

Saban, H., *Corporate Debt Securitisation*, Singapore: Butterworths, 1994.

Schwarcz, S. L. and Ford, A. D., *Structured Finance: A Guide to the Principles of Asset Securitization*, N.Y.: Practising Law Institute, 2002 (Loose-Leaf Service).

Tomasic, R., Jackson, J. and Woellner, R., *Corporations Law: Principles, Policy and Process*, 4th edition, Sydney: Butterworths, 2002.

Tyree, A., *Banking Law in Australia,* 4th edition, Sydney: Butterworths, 2002.

Valentine, T., Ford, G. and Copp, R., *Financial Markets and Institutions in Australia*, Sydney: Pearson Education Australia, 2003.

Weerasooriya, W. S., *Banking Law and the Financial System in Australia,* Sydney: Butterworths, 2001.

Journal Articles

Ayers, K. R., 'Limiting Trustee Liability to Lenders' (1996) *New Zealand Law Journal* 181.

Calleja, N., 'Current Issues Relating to Prospectus Advertising and Securities Hawking' (2000) 18 *Companies and Securities Law Journal* 23.

Carver, J. P., 'The Market in Participation–Current Issues in International Finance' (1990) *Malaya Law Review*, 308.

Ellis, R. D., 'Securitization Vehicles, Fiduciary Duties, and Bondholders' Rights' (1999) 24 (2) *The Journal of Corporation Law* 295.

Finch, A., 'Securitisation' (1995) 6 (4) *Journal of Banking and Finance Law and Practice* 247.

Frankel, T., 'The Legal Infrastructure of Markets: The Role of Contract and Property Law' (1993) 73 *Boston University Law Review* 389.

Hughes, R., 'The Right of a Trustee who Carries on Business to Indemnify out of Trust Property' (1991) *Australian Business Law Review* 5.

Jones, P., 'Delegation by Trustees: A Reappraisal' (1990) 22 *The Modern Law Review* 381.

Legg, M., 'Misleading and Deceptive Conduct in Prospectuses' (1996) 14 *Corporations and Securities Law Journal* 47.

Marshall, B., 'Loans, Losses and Liability: Lessons from Foreign Currency Litigation in Australia' ([illegible]) [illegible] *Journal of Banking and Finance Law and Practice* 175.

Rajacic, M., Rajapakse, P. and Webb, E., 'The Impact of *the Trade Practices Act* 1974 (Cth) on the Auditors' Liability' (2000) 19 *University of Tasmania Law Review* 205.

Sammonds, R., 'Directors' Negligent Misstatement Liability in a Scheme of Securities Regulation' (1979) *Ottawa Law Review* 633.

Senarath, S., 'Securitisation and the global financial crisis: can risk retention prevent another crisis?' (2017) 18 *International Journal of Business and Globalisation* 153.

Taylor, B., 'The Enforceability of Debt Securities Issued by Trustees in Securitisation Programs' (1998) 9 (4) *Journal of Banking and Finance Law and Practice* 261.

Terry, A., 'Disclaimers and Deceptive Conduct' (1986) 14 *Australian Business Law Review* 478.

Tevis, J. B., 'Asset-Backed Securities: Secondary Market Implications and Regulation' (1991) 23 *Pacific Law Journal* 135.

Von Nessen, P., 'The Americanization of Australian Corporate Law' (1999) 26 *Syracuse Journal of International Law and Commerce* 239.

Working Papers, Magazines, Newspapers and Reports

Australian Securitisation Forum, Submission to the ASIC: Licensing Relief for Securitisation Structures, 23 October 2003, http://www.securitisation.com.au/asf (12 December 2003).

Boyd, A., 'Securitisation Market Shrank 14% Last Year', *Australian Financial Review*, 24 February 1994, 30.

Collinson, P., 'Trustee Investments Status for Mortgage-Backed Securities', *Conference on Impediments to the Securitisation of Housing Mortgages Proceedings*, Canberra: AGPS, 1988.

Corporations Law Simplification Task Force, *Report on Fundraising*, Attorney General's Department, Canberra, 1995.

Macquarie Securitisation Ltd, *The PUMA Fund P-7: Master Information Memorandum*, Sydney, February, 2000.

Macquarie Securitisation Ltd, *The PUMA Sub-Fund Series – 2014: Master Information Memorandum*, Sydney, July 2014.

McWilliams, B., 'Companies and Securities Impediments to Mortgage Securitisation', *Conference on Impediments to the Securitisation of Housing Mortgages, Proceedings and Conference Papers,* Canberra: AGPS, 1988.

Salter, B., *Changes to the Law Relating to Securitisation*, Discussion Paper, Sydney: Clayton Utz, 1993.

Senarath, S. 'The Dodd-Frank Act doesn't solve the principal-agent problem in asset securitisation' (2017) *blogs.lse.ac.uk* (11 November 2018) http://blogs.lse.ac.uk/businessreview/2017/04/21/the-dodd-frank-act-doesnt-solve-the-principal-agent-problem-in-asset-securitisation/

Senarath, S., Not so "Bankruptcy-Remote': An insight into Sri Lankan Securitization Practices in a Post_GFC Context' (Paper presented at the MAC-MME conference 2016, Prague, Czech Republic).

Standard and Poor's, 'Credit Ratings on Mortgage-Backed Securities', *Structured Finance Australia and New Zealand*, Melbourne, 1998.

Standard and Poor's, 'RMBS, CDO Activity Lead Australian Securitisation Issuance Growth in 2003', *Credit Ratings Commentary and News,* July 2003.

Standard and Poor's, *Credit Review: International Structured Finance*, Melbourne, April 1991.

CHAPTER 7

Insolvency Considerations Pertaining to Trustee-Issuer and Mortgage Originator

7.1 Introduction

As discussed in Chap. 1, residential mortgage-backed security (RMBS) programmes inherently entail the risk that borrowers may find their homes sold by downstream financial intermediaries who have acquired their bank's (or independent mortgage provider's [IMP]) mortgagee rights. This essentially is not due to a failure to pay on the part of the borrowers but as a result of the insolvency of downstream financial intermediary in the supply chain.

This chapter investigates the probable impacts on other stakeholders in the RMBS programme, including home loan borrowers, if either the originator or the trustee-issuer were to[1] become insolvent. Hence, this includes an investigation into the types of transactions which may be considered void or voidable as a result of such insolvencies; the potential impacts on secured creditors, mortgage indemnity providers, pool insurers, and the fund manager, or administrator. This chapter will also include a discussion of how best to structure an insolvency-remote issuer.

[1] The insolvency event is expressed throughout this chapter in the past subjunctive and modal auxiliary forms since, to the author's knowledge at least, no bank, IMP, or trustee-issuer involved in an RMBS programme in Australia has as yet gone into insolvency. See P. Roberts, *Understanding Grammar* (N.Y.: Harper, 1954) 165, 169–170 and 176.

P. Rajapakse, S. Senarath, *Commercial Law Aspects of Residential Mortgage Securitisation in Australia*,
https://doi.org/10.1007/978-3-030-00605-1_7

7.1.1 *Insolvency and Bondholders*

Section 95A of the *Corporations Act* provides that "a person is solvent if, and only if, the person is able to pay all the person's debts, as and when they become due and payable."[2]

If the special purpose vehicle (SPV) fails to repay their debts to secured creditors (i.e. bondholders), the typical remedy would be the appointment of a receiver to the trust fund, under the terms of their charge.[3] The significance of such an appointment is that the security trustee on behalf of the bondholders would exercise its right of sale in respect of the residential mortgages assigned by the originator to the SPV.

Based on the composition of the mortgage pool, a security trustee would exercise its right of sale in respect of the mortgages,[4] and determine the requirements of bondholders. As identified earlier, if for some reason the bondholders are not being paid their interest and/or principal, they may well direct the security trustee to sell the charged assets, in the same manner as any mortgagee or charge may choose to exercise its power of sale in appropriate circumstances. This would be entirely possible in an economic downturn or recession and could happen through no fault of individual borrowers.

Ceteris paribus, apparently most borrowers could do as against the security trustee is to temporarily enjoin it (e.g. as a third party) from selling the charged assets (i.e. the borrowers' homes). The bank or SPV are more likely to be sued by borrowers, either individually or by way of a class action, for negligence, misrepresentation, a breach of section 18 of the *Australian Competition and Consumer Act 2010* (Cth), or a similar cause of action. This is how housing loan borrowers might, in the foreseeable future, find their homes sold out from them through no fault of their own.

There are some alternatives that exist for unsecured creditors, and for secured creditors, such as bondholders, who are still owed money after the

[2] Less usefully, section 95A goes on to state, that "A person who is not solvent is insolvent."

[3] The relevant clauses are set out in the *Master Information Memorandum, PUMA Fund—P 7*, at paragraphs 6.2, 4.1 and 1.12 and *PUMA Sub-Fund Series* 2014, p 80. Also, refer to the discussion in Chap. 6 of the book.

[4] It means the composition of the portfolio in terms of "good mortgages", in other words, mortgages where there is a stable cash flow and a relatively low risk and "poor mortgages", where there is a substantial risk of default in respect of those mortgages. A bank would be better off disposing the poor mortgages, and retaining the good ones, in terms of maximising their overall returns.

security trustee has exercised its right of sale in respect of those properties comprising the mortgage pool (effectively making them unsecured creditors to the extent of any shortfall).

Eventually, if a company (e.g. an originating bank or IMP, or a trustee-issuer) becomes insolvent,[5] the court may order that it be wound up on the application of any of a number of persons, including the company itself, a director of the company, or a creditor of the company even if the creditor is a secured creditor, or is only a contingent or prospective creditor.

On the other hand, perhaps usually, there is some likelihood that the company might trade out of difficulty prior to reaching this point. Hence an administrator would be appointed (e.g. under a voluntary administration or "VA" procedure) to manage the affairs of the company until the creditors determine how best to recoup the debts owed to them. An administrator may be appointed by the company itself; its liquidator or provisional liquidator; or a person who is entitled to enforce a charge on the whole, or substantially the whole, of a company's property.[6] There are essentially three options open to creditors at this stage. They may:

(a) Execute a deed of company arrangement, under which they basically agree to be paid a specified proportion of the debts owed to them.
(b) Agree to wind up the company.
(c) Terminate the administrator's appointment and hand the day-to-day control of the company back to the directors.[7]

The VA procedure under Pt. 5.3A of the Act can be discussed in the context of an originating bank—however, it could equally apply to an

[5] A company will be considered insolvent if, despite the fact that its assets significantly outweigh its liabilities, these assets are illiquid and are unable to be utilised to meet the company's liabilities as and when they fall due and become payable. Insolvency may be established by a company failing to comply with, or dispute, within 21 days of a statutory demand being served on the company by a creditor: section 459C(2). Other evidence that have been considered to prove solvency of a company include failure to disclose assets: *Garseabo Nominees Pty Ltd v Taub Pty Ltd* (unreported, Supreme Court Qld, No. 2425, 1979, 9 June 1979), maintenance of cash flow: *Molnar Engineering Pty Ltd v The Herald and Weekly Times Ltd and E J Burns* (1984) 1 FCR 455, net asset position: *Fat-sel Pty Ltd v Brambles Holdings Ltd* (1985) 61 ALR 531: see S. Colbran, 'Security for Costs against Corporations: section 1335 of the *Corporations Law*' (1993) 11 (5) *Company and Securities Law Journal* 273, 276–277.

[6] Sections 436, 436A, 436B, and 436C of the *Corporations Act*.

[7] Section 439C of the *Corporations Act*.

originating IMP or the trustee-issuer of the RMBS programme (in relation to its unsecured creditors). Once appointed, the administrator's main objective would be to convene meetings of the originating bank's creditors. An initial meeting must be held within 5 days of the administrator's appointment, with another later meeting being held to report to creditors on the originating bank's position and prospects, so that the creditors can decide the bank's future. In general, this second meeting to decide the originating bank's future must occur within 5 business days after the end of the "convening period" (i.e. 21 days from the date of appointment). Section 439A(6) gives the court discretion to extend the convening period.

However, it does not go on to suggest the circumstances in which this discretion should be exercised. Given the potential complexity of the matters requiring consideration by the administrator and the originating bank's creditors, the statutory period of 21 days can prove very tight, and applications for an extension are reasonably common. If granted, the extension also prolongs the freeze on assets described later. Pending a resolution of the originating bank's creditors terminating the administration, Pt. 5.3A would put the assets and affairs of the originating bank in the control of the administrator and seek, with certain exceptions, to freeze those assets and suspend any enforcement action in relation to them. This effective "moratorium" would have several impacts in relation to RMBS programmes:

- In relation to property generally of the originating bank—Section 437D would render void any transaction affecting the originating bank's property while it is under administration, unless the administrator either consented to that transaction or the transaction had been entered into under an order of the court.
- In relation to charges over the whole or substantially the whole of the originating bank's property—provided it obtains the administrator's consent or the leave of the court under sections 437D(2) and 440B, a chargee over the whole or substantially the whole of the originating bank's property may enforce the charge during the "decision period", which runs from the date that chargee receives notice of the administrator's appointment (assuming the chargee did not itself appoint the administrator) through to the tenth business day after that date. This is conditional on the chargee enforcing its charge in relation to all of the originating bank's property that is subject to the charge. If

the chargee were to do this, then the general moratorium would not apply to assets the subject of that charge, and the administrator's powers and functions would be subject to those of the chargee (or the chargee's receiver or other agent appointed to enforce the charge: section 441A). If the chargee did not enforce its security in that manner before or during the decision period, then that chargee would be bound by the general moratorium.

Furthermore, the general moratorium would not apply to property subject to a charge if enforcement action under section 441B (e.g. entering into possession, agreeing to sell, or arranging for a sale or invitation to tender) were taken before the administrator's appointment.

- In relation to debts secured over substantially less than all the assets of the originating bank—in this case, enforcement would almost certainly be slowed down by the moratorium, unless the trustee under the RMBS programme was able to pre-empt the appointment of the administrator and commence enforcement beforehand, within the meaning of section 441B. Of course, secured creditors have an extra element of protection, in that they are not bound by a deed of company arrangement unless they themselves voted in favour of it. In contrast, an unsecured creditor could be in the minority, but nevertheless become bound to accept a compromise that is disadvantageous to it.

7.2 Originator's Insolvency

Essentially for three reasons, financial distress (and ultimately, insolvency) on the part of the mortgage originator could threaten the existence of an RMBS programme[8]:

(i) In the process of securitisation, mortgages and related insurance policies are generally transferred by way of equitable assignment to the trustee-issuer. The originator residues the legal owner of the

[8] Nor is this a mere academic or hypothetical risk. Prudential regulation by APRA is generally very good by international standards, but as the recent high-profile case of HIH shows, APRA's prudential regulation is by no means a guaranteed prophylactic against the risk of insolvency.

mortgages, and so far as mortgagors are concerned, there is generally little or no suggestion that their mortgages have been sold. This position would almost certainly change substantially, however, if the originator is subjected to severe financial difficulties.

(ii) An originator facing financial agony would be less likely to be in a position to compete for new mortgage business. This originator's capacity to offer new mortgages for use as substitutes in the securitised pool might be considerably reduced, and the securitisation brought to a premature end. This problem could be aggravated if uneasy existing borrowers refinance elsewhere, rather than incur the risk that their originating bank's interest rates or enforcement policies get too far out of line with those of rival banks or IMPs. If borrowers attempted to refinance, a separate question also arises as to whether other banks or IMPs would be willing to refinance them, once these other banks or IMPs became aware that their mortgages had already been equitably assigned to an SPV.

(iii) Under the voidable transactions provisions of the *Corporations Act*[9] (e.g. as insolvent or voidable transactions,[10] uncommercial transactions,[11] or unfair preferences[12]),[13] if the transfers of its mortgagee rights to an SPV occurred in the six months prior to insolvency, and if a mortgage originator became insolvent and winding-up of proceedings commenced,[14] there would be a risk that transfers of its mortgagee rights to an SPV might be "clawed back".

[9] See Pt. 5.7B, Division 2 of the *Corporations Act*.

[10] See sections 588FC and 588 FE respectively. Transactions may even become voidable up to two years after they are effected, if they fall within section 588FE(3) and the originator becomes insolvent within that time.

[11] See R. Tomasic et al., *Corporations Law Principles, Policy and Process* (Sydney: Butterworths, 2002) [15.43].

[12] See section 588FA.

[13] For example, section 588FJ of the *Corporations Act* provides that, in relation to a company being wound up in insolvency, a floating charge created on property of the company during the six months ending on the relation-back day (or between the relation-back day and the start of the winding-up) is, unless the court otherwise orders, void. The winding-up would be deemed to have commenced at the time of the presentation of the petition for winding-up: see section 9.

[14] While the voidable transactions provisions apply only where a company is winding up, an administrator must nevertheless make an estimate of the possible monies that could be "clawed back" under the voidable transactions provisions *if* the company were to be wound up. In this sense, the voidable transactions provisions relate to both the winding-up and administration stages of insolvency.

On another relevant note, circumstances might arise in which an originator has transferred mortgages to an issuer (e.g. substitute mortgages in replacement for others that have been redeemed) at about the time that a winding-up order has been presented against the originator. However, these transfers would not necessarily be void under section 588FJ if the agreement to transfer the mortgages "straddled" the date of presentation of the winding-up petition. In *Re French's (Wine Bar) Ltd*,[15] it was held that where, a company had entered into a specifically enforceable unconditional contract for the sale of property before the presentation of a winding-up petition, the completion of the contract after the petition had been presented would not constitute a disposition within the meaning of section 127 of the *Insolvency Act* 1986 (UK), which is similar to section 588FJ of the *Corporations Act*.

For a court to determine that the transfer of mortgages to an issuer of mortgage-backed securities is liable to be adjusted under section 588FB as an uncommercial transaction, it would have to be established that the transaction had taken place at a time when the company was insolvent (section 588FC) and that the value of the consideration received by the originator was significantly less than the value of the consideration which it provided to the issuer:

In addition, the originator must, at the time of the transaction, have been unable to pay its debts within the meaning of section 95A of the *Corporations Act*, or have become so unable as a consequence of the transaction to do so. Inability to pay debts as they fall due can be inferred from a failure to pay a debt which is due and undisputed.[16] The burden of proof as to these requirements is always on the liquidator or administrator, as the case may be, and it would be very difficult to discharge in the context of an RMBS programme, because the portfolio of mortgages transferred to the trustee-issuer is generally in practice sold at a price equal to the present value of the principal amount of the loans comprising that pool.

Second, the directors of the originator are usually required to certify that the originator is able to pay its debts at the time of the transfer and will not become unable to do so as a result of transferring these mortgages. Third, the court would be precluded from voiding the transaction if it were not an unfair loan; the SPV acted in good faith and has changed

[15] [1987] BCLC 499.

[16] *Taylors Industrial Flooring Ltd v M and H Plant Hire (Manchester)* (1990) BCLC 216; *Re DKG Contractors Ltd.* [1990] BCC 903.

its position in reliance on the transfer; and at the time of the transfer, the SPV had no reasonable grounds for suspecting that the assigning bank or IMP was insolvent: section 588FG(2).

During the life of the issue, some mortgages may have to be released from the trustee's security and transferred back to the originator (e.g. where a mortgagor wants to refinance). In practice, such mortgages can be sold back to the originator for cash or, for so long as is permitted, in exchange for new mortgages.[17] It is not possible for RMBS documentation to restrict such substitutions to circumstances where the directors of the originator can certify its secure financial position, since, if a borrower wants to redeem his or her mortgage in accordance with the mortgage terms, the originator is bound to ensure that he is able to do so by retrieving the mortgage from the securitised pool. Having said this, it would presumably be rare in practice that a re-transfer of mortgages would constitute an uncommercial transaction, since the relevant documentation generally seeks to ensure that the value of any re-purchased mortgages is not "significantly less" than the value of the substitute assets provided by the originator (although ultimately this would be a question of fact for a court).[18]

Any subordinated loan facilities provided to the issuer by the originator at the outset of the securitisation might also come under scrutiny under section 588FB. However, where, as is usually the case, the provision of such funding is conditional upon the directors of the originator certifying that the company is able (and will continue to be able) to pay its debts, the requirements as to a time when the company was insolvent would generally not be satisfied (assuming the accuracy of the certificates).

In practice, the problem of unfair preferences would appear to be more theoretical than real. In theory, a transaction could be vulnerable as a preference if, in the event of the originator's insolvency, it had the effect of putting the trustee-issuer in a better position than it would have been in without the transaction. This transaction would generally need to have taken place within six months prior to the appointment of an administrator. In *Re MC Bacon Ltd*, the English courts have held that such a transaction would not be a preference unless (in the present context) the originator positively wished to improve the trustee-issuer's position, and this positive influenced its decision to proceed with the transaction. Having said this, the court

[17] See, for example, Master Information Memorandum, PUMA Fund P-7, paragraph 4.7.3.

[18] *Re MC Bacon Ltd* [1990] BCLC 324, 340.

made it clear that this positive wish need not be the only influencing factor, nor even the one which "tipped the scales" in making the decision to transact.[19] Moreover, in practice, it is unlikely that the transfer of mortgages to the trustee-issuer would have the required effect of placing the issuer in a better position than it would have been otherwise. This could generally only happen if the mortgages were transferred at an under-value and, in practice, the mortgages are usually sold to the trustee-issuer at the present value of their aggregate outstanding principal amount, with the directors of the originator being required to certify the originator's solvency at that time. Assuming this practice is followed and the directors' certificates are correct, no problem of unfair preferences should arise in practice.

If an administrator or a liquidator were to establish that the transactions between the originator and the issuer were vulnerable as unfair preferences, the court's powers to rectify the situation would be the same as those in respect of section 588FB and the same limitations would apply: section 588FG(2).

For the reason of these risks, RMBS programmes are designed in an "insolvency-remote" approach with the view of minimising the effects that originator insolvency would have on the trustee-issuer, by guaranteeing that all necessities constituting the true valid transfer of mortgage rights to the trustee-issuer are achieved. Largely the terms of sale force the originator to complete the transfer of mortgages to the trustee-issuer (including effecting registration of the issuer as the legal owner of the mortgages)[20] if the trustee considers that the security is under threat.

7.3 Trustee-Issuer's Insolvency

7.3.1 *Trustee-Issuer's Insolvency as the Trustee*

If there was just one investor with one originator, there would not be a need for an SPV, since the required assets can be transferred to the investor. However, when there are multiple investors, the SPV works as a conduit between the investors and the originators. Investors thus have an undivided interest in the assets of the SPV. All investors are collectively the beneficial owners of the receivables.[21]

[19] [1990] BCLC 324.

[20] D. Glennie and E. Bouter, *Securitisation* (London: Kluwer Law International, 1998) 5.

[21] Kothari, Vinod, *Securitization: The Financial Instrument of the Future* (John Wiley & Sons, 2006) 663.

From a technical point of view, trusts practically cannot turn out to be insolvent. This is due to the fact that trusts do not have any detached legal capacity. Hence trusts cannot sue or be sued; they cannot have liquidators or administrators appointed to them. In a sense, when a trust incurs a liability, it is the trustee that actually incurs the liability (e.g. when an SPV issues bonds from a securitisation programme to an investor). In other words, for debt securities issued by the trust, the trustee will be personally liable. Hence, the trustee will be entitled to be indemnified from the assets of the trust against the liability and will have a lien over the assets of the trust to secure its rights under the indemnity, provided that the liability was incurred for the purposes of the trust and in accordance with the provisions of the trust deed; and if on the other hand indemnity from the assets of trust is inadequate, unless otherwise agreed, the trustee will have to meet its liabilities with respect to the trust from its own assets. In RMBS programmes which have trustee-issuers, the obligations of the trustee to bondholders and other creditors will invariably be limited to the assets of the trust out of which the trustee is indemnified for the liability (in the absence of fraud, negligence, or wilful default on the part of the trustee). However, this limitation does not affect the nature of the liability. The liability is the trustee's liability—even though one which is limited by reference to the trustee's indemnity from the assets of the trust.[22]

In this manner, a reference to a trust being insolvent in fact suggests that the obligations, which the trustee has properly incurred as trustee of the trust cannot be met from the earnings of the trustee's indemnity from the assets of the trust. The consequences would be that if the trustee has not limited its liability, the trustee must meet those obligations from its own assets, and if it is unable to do so, the trustee will itself be insolvent. If the trustee has limited its liability in the manner so described, the trustee's liability in respect of the obligations will be reduced to the amount available to meet those obligations from the assets of the trust, and neither "the trust" nor the trustee will be insolvent.[23] In this second scenario, even though the trustee's liability has been reduced, the trustee's failure to meet its obligations in full may have other consequences under

[22] See, for instance, *Master Information Memorandum, PUMA Fund—P-7*, paragraphs 1.12, and 7.9 and *PUMA Sub-Fund Series 2014*, p 122.

[23] See generally, B. Taylor, 'The Enforceability of Debt Securities Issued by Trustees in Securitisation Programs' (1998) 26 *Journal of Banking and Finance Law and Practice* 261.

the agreement between the trustee-issuer and bondholders, including the accelerated repayment of principal to investors, and the triggering of the enforcement of security given by the trustee.

Nevertheless, trustee insolvency may arise due to the trustee being unable to meet liabilities unconnected with the trust or the RMBS programme, or as a result of a failure by the trustee to otherwise properly perform its duties as trustee. In general, the trustee companies who act as issuers in RMBS programmes are also trustees of hundreds of other trusts. A failure by the trustee company to perform its obligations in relation to any one of these trusts could lead to the trustee incurring some personal liability and, conceivably, to its insolvency.[24]

Typically, the insolvency of the trustee-issuer in the capacity of trustee does not present a serious risk to RMBS programmes due to following reasons.

- First, assets of a specific trust will not be utilised in order to encounter the trustee's compulsions to its general creditors. The same principle applies for creditors of other trusts for whom the trustee-issuer acts in the capacity of the trustee.
- Second, the trust deed customarily provides provisions such that the trustee will be replaced if it becomes insolvent, and for all the assets of the trust to vest in the new trustee, who (usually) will be appointed by the fund manager of the programme.[25]

In addition, in the Australian context, RMBS programmes comprise trusts that naturally take a charge over assets and hold them for the benefit of investors who purchase the bonds issued, although trusts may hold other assets, which are relatively small packages of liquid assets such as government bonds. Apart from such assets, there will be no other major assets. Voluntary administration or liquidation, in this manner, would not be economically feasible for an RMBS programme in Australia. Thus, we can suggest that, in the event of insolvency, it would be better for bondholders to exercise their rights under the mortgages and related insurance contracts in the Australian context.

[24]Taylor above n 23 272–273. See generally, J. Chen, 'Asset Securitisation and the Singapore Insolvency Regime' (2001) 16 (8/9) *Journal of International Banking Law* 198.

[25]See, for instance, *Master Information Memorandum*, *PUMA Fund—P-7*, paragraph 7.1 and *PUMA Sub-Fund Series 2014*, p 101.

7.3.2 *Insolvency of the SPV in the Capacity of the Issuer*[26]

Minimising Risk to the Investor

As we have already noted, securities issued by trustee (where the issuer is a trustee company) will be the obligation of the trustee in the capacity of the issuer, which investors rely upon. Trustee-issuer should be able to indemnify her payment obligations from the underlying trust assets. If the trust assets are not sufficient to meet the debt obligations, this will essentially pose a risk to the investors.[27] The risk that the trust assets will not be sufficient to meet the obligations incurred by the trustee-issuer in relation to the trust is minimised by a number of ways. Accordingly, the trustee-issuer may require to grant a charge over the trust assets to an independent security trusty, who will hold such mortgages in favour of holders of securities. In this manner, the trustee-issuer's right of indemnity will be "avoided". Hence the security trustee may independently enforce the mortgage over the trust assets and apply the proceeds of sale to meet the payment,[28] in case the trustee does not make a payment in full on the securities. If the liabilities are to be met,[29] a provision requiring an order of priority would also act as a means of minimising risks to the investor. Lastly, strengthening the indemnity clause in the trust deed in a way such that the trustee-issuer may indemnify itself to the extent necessary to meet payments on the securities, nevertheless any other breach of trust it may have committed.

Redemption in a Typical Securitisation Programme

A securitisation scheme provides room and procedure for redemption of the underlying assets, if required. If a default takes place, essentially, security will become enforceable. In general security trust deed defines events of default. However, in general there are a number of such events.[30] Accordingly, a default in payments (due), to bondholders, which may

[26] It is assumed throughout the following discussion that the trustee-issuer has validly acquired the mortgages from the originator and that the transfer or assignment is not liable to be set aside or adjusted.

[27] Pelma Rajapakse, Richard Copp and J Gardner, 'Insolvency Issues in Residential Mortgage Securitisation' (2008) 34 *Monash University Law Review* 30.

[28] See, *Master Information Memorandum, PUMA Fund—P 7*, paragraph 6.2 and *PUMA Sub-Fund Series 2014*, p 108.

[29] *Master Information Memorandum, PUMA Fund—P7*, paragraph 4.6.

[30] Id, paragraph 6.2.; H. A. J. Ford, R. P. Austin and I. M. Ramsay, *Ford's Principles of Corporations Law* (10th edition, Chatswood: Butterworths, 2001) [25.060].

include payments of interest or repayment of principal which is not paid within a specified period, failure by the issuer (or the originator or any agent) to perform other responsibilities, and finally, (likely) cessation of the issuer's business.[31]

The latter two categories of events may be subjected to the condition that they will create events of default only if the security trustee confirms to the trustee-issuer that, in its opinion, their occurrence is destructive to the interests of the bondholders. In general security trust deeds provide requirements necessitating the issuer to notify the security trustee (in writing) if a default takes place, as soon as issuer becomes conscious of it.[32]

In general, the security trustee is authorised to issue a notice to the issuer announcing the mortgage-backed securities to be due and payable, in its discretion, in an event of default. Typically, an issuer is also equipped with provisions such that it can take such steps upon the request of a certain proportion of the bondholders or upon the passing of an extraordinary resolution at a meeting of bondholders. Such enforcement notice will result in making the bonds immediately due and repayable at their principal amount together with accrued interest.

Usually a provision would be included in the terms, stating that in the event of the service of an enforcement notice, any floating charge in the package will thereupon automatically crystallise. Hence the charge essentially converts into a fixed charge.[33] The consequences of this decision would be on persons who are dealings with an issuer company. Such persons are ignorant of the fact that a floating charge over its assets has crystallised in this way (this has already been addressed at length in the literature,[34] and need not be repeated here).

[31] This may include the passing of a resolution or the making of an order for the winding-up of the issuer, the presentation of a petition for an administration order in respect of the issuer or the taking, by a third party, of significant enforcement proceedings against the issuer.

[32] *Master Information Memorandum, PUMA Fund—P7*, paragraph 6.2.

[33] See *Re Brightlife Ltd* [1987] Ch 200 [1986] 3 All ER 673, in which Hoffmann J held that the service of a notice of crystallisation was effective to cause a floating charge to crystallise into a fixed charge. See also *Re Permanent House (Holding) Ltd* (1989) 5 BCC 151.

[34] For example, an automatic crystallisation may occur without the knowledge of either the company or the secured bondholder. The result might be prejudicial to third parties, who have given credit to the company. Third party unsecured creditors might find that all the company's assets, including goods that they have delivered on credit, had been swept up by the secured creditors. The public interest requires balancing of the advantages to the economy of facilitating the borrowing of money against the possibility of injustice to unsecured

Security trust deed determines the order of application of funds received by the security trustee after its security becomes enforceable. Remuneration, costs, and expenses of the trustee, chargers pertaining to any receiver appointed to realise the security, would be first tier. The next tier would be the payment of all other outgoings in relation to the trust assets as the receiver thinks fit.[35] Then comes those claims of secured bondholders. If there are multiple series of bonds that have been issued, the senior and fast prepayment bondholders will be prioritised within the tier.

Security and Its Validity

Despite the borrower's (issuer's) financial difficulties, one of the principal concerns of a secured lender to an insolvent borrower (in this context, an insolvent issuer of RMBSs) is that its security should remain valid. Under the *Corporations Act,* certain securities are void as against specified persons, including liquidators and administrators, if the securities have not been registered with the ASIC: section 266. Under section 266 of the *Corporations Act*, liquidators and administrators can apply to the court in order to have securities created by the companies to which they are appointed set aside in certain circumstances.

An RMBS programme is generally structured in a way such that it gives the trustee-issuer a power to obstruct the appointment of an administrator. If an issuer of mortgage-backed securities were to encounter severe financial difficulties, it is fair to anticipate that the security it has given to the security trustee would be challenged by a liquidator than by an administrator.

As per the provision of section 436A of the *Corporations Act,* a petition for the appointment of an administrator by the court could be presented by the trustee company, its board, or any of its creditors. However, if the creditor who had appointed a receiver opposes, no administrator could be

creditors: See R.M. Good, *Legal Problems of Credit and Security* (London: Sweet & Maxwell, 1982) 70–73; and R. Pennington, 'Loans to Companies; the Development of the Law' in B. G. Pettet (ed.), *Company Law in Change* (London: Stephens, 1987) 103–107. A. J. Boyle, 'The Validity of Automatic Crystallisation Clauses' (1979) *Journal of Business Law* 231. Boyle has suggested that automatic crystallisation should be prohibited on grounds of public policy.

[35] See, for example, *Master Information Memorandum, PUMA Fund—P 7,* paragraph. 6.2; *Master Information Memorandum, PUMA Sub-Fund Series 2014,* p 111.

appointed[36] before the petition was heard at a creditors' meeting. If the security held by the security trustee includes a floating charge over the whole of the issuer's assets, the security trustee will have the power to appoint a receiver and, if it does so, will accordingly be able to obstruct the appointment of an administrator. In order to ensure that the security trustee is entitled to exercise its power to appoint a receiver at the appropriate time, the presentation of a petition for an administration order must be included as a "default event" in the trust deed and documentation (e.g. information memorandum) to the RMBS issue.

In practice, it is not possible to structure an RMBS scheme with no possibility that the issuer may run into liquidation. In certain cases, certain creditors of the issuer together with the originator may require to grant a guarantee to the issuer, ensuring that they will not enforce their rights against the SPV, if they have not been paid in respect of the transfer of the underlying mortgages. However, certain creditors, such as the tax authorities, may not be required to restrict their conduct. Under the provisions of the section 459 of the *Corporations Act*, if a creditor of an issuer were to have the issuer put into compulsory liquidation, this would not, of itself, prevent the security trustee from enforcing its security. However, a typical liquidator would be customarily examining the security package carefully in order to assure that the mechanism is not vulnerable in this respect.

Is the Security Void or Voidable?

An apparently valid security might be found by the courts to be void or voidable, under a number of ways, in the event of an issuer's liquidation. First, as we discussed earlier, a charge may be exclusively or partially void against a liquidator if it is a registrable charge. However, the relevant registration requirements have not been fully complied with.[37]

If the issuer becomes insolvent, the security might be at risk, given the provisions of sections 588FA, 588FB, 588FD, or 588FJ.[38] As noted earlier, section 588FA is concerned with unfair preferences. Broadly, a company gives a preference if it does something which has the effect of putting

[36] A receiver is broadly defined within the meaning of section 90 of the Act as a receiver and manager of the whole (or substantially the whole) of a company's property appointed by or on behalf of the holder of a debenture secured by a charge. See P. Hanrahan et al., *Commercial Applications of Company Law* (Sydney: CCH, 2002) [23–100].

[37] Section 266 *Corporations Act*.

[38] This section deals with floating charges created within six months before the relation-back day.

one of its creditors, guarantors, or sureties into a position which, in the event of the company going into insolvent liquidation, will be better than the position he would have been in if that thing had not been done. Subject to satisfaction of certain other conditions specified in section 588FA (some of which are discussed further later), the court can set aside a preference at the request of a liquidator by making such order as it thinks fit for restoring the position to what it would have been if the preference had not been given

In the United Kingdom, the courts have decided that the creation of security can constitute the giving of a preference, but in order for that security to be caught by section 239 of the *Insolvency Act* 1986 (UK) relating to voidable preference, the person in whose favour the charge is created must be an existing creditor, guarantor, or surety of the charger at the time of its creation and the charge must be given in respect of past indebtedness, and not in consideration for the injection of new funds.[39] In other words, a preference, it is generally thought, should involve some element of improvement to the position of the person preferred. If this view is correct, security created by an issuer of mortgage-backed securities in favour of the security trustee to the issue should not be vulnerable as a preference since the charge is created in return for new money. Moreover, the funds are advanced to the issuer only on the basis that they will be secured, and the creation of the charge merely gives effect to the parties' agreement that the security trustee's position is to be a secured creditor of the issuer and does not in any way improve it.

In *Re MC Bacon Ltd*, however, Millett J took a different view. In his opinion, it would be virtually impossible to uphold the validity of a security taken in exchange for the injection of fresh funds into a company, were it not for the fact that voidable preference provision in section 239 of the *Insolvency Act* 1986 (UK), which is analogous to section 588FA of the Australian *Corporations Act*, required that the company must have intended to prefer the creditor in question. This requirement would not be satisfied where the company was actuated only by proper commercial considerations, such as where the granting of the security was an unavoidable price of obtaining the funding. On this basis, the security would not

[39] See *Re Blackpool Motor Car Co Ltd, Hamilton v Blackpool Motor Car Co Ltd* [1901] 1 Ch 77; *Re MC Bacon Ltd* (1990) BCLC 324; and *Re Softley, ex parte Hodgkin* (1875) LR 20 Eq 746; and *Re F and E Stanton* [1929] 1 Ch 160, 192 respectively. H. Saban, *Corporate Debt Securitisation* (Singapore: Butterworths, 1994) 71–72.

be impeachable as an unfair preference if the issuer were obliged to give it in order to get the funding and does not act out of a desire to prefer the security trustee.[40]

Pt. 5.7B of the *Corporations Act* provides that a transaction may be set aside by the court if it is an uncommercial transaction within the meaning of section 588FB and is also an insolvent transaction under section 588FC. An insolvent transaction is an "unfair preference" or an "uncommercial transaction" which:

- Was entered into or given effect to at a time when the company was insolvent.
- Caused or contributed to the company's insolvency.[41] However, a court is not allowed to make an order materially prejudicing a right or interest of a party to an uncommercial transaction and unfair preference if it is proved that.
- The person became a party to the transaction in good faith.
- At the time when the person became a party to the transaction, they had no reasonable grounds for suspecting that the company was or would become insolvent, and a reasonable person in their circumstances would have become insolvent.
- The person provided valuable consideration under the transaction or changed their position relying on the transaction.

Section 588FG provides a measure of protection to investors against subsequent winding-up of any party to a transaction in a securitisation programme. However, rating agencies are nevertheless concerned to ensure that the transactions in a mortgage securitisation programme are commercial and, in particular, that any sale of assets to the issuer is a true sale for full value.

Under section 588FD (1), a loan to a company is unfair if the interest on it or the charges relating to it are extortionate. Such transactions may be set aside under Pt. 5.7B of the *Corporations Act*.[42] There have been no reported Australian cases that have considered the meaning of the term "extortion-

[40](1990) BCLC 324.

[41]See, for example, R. Tomasic, (2002) [15.43]; [15.47].

[42]P. Lipton and A. Herzberg, Understanding Company Law (Sydney: Law Book Company, 2003) 703.

ate" in the context of this section. It is generally the case, however, that interest rates on bonds issued, or on funds borrowed under a liquidity facility, in an RMBS programme are determined with reference to prevailing market rates. It is unlikely that interest rates determined in this manner would be regarded by the courts as extortionate.

In the context of an RMBS programme, all these provisions would be applicable upon the winding up of the issuer, any seller of assets to the issuer, or any other person who provides rights to the issuer in part of the RMBS programme.

Subordination and Insolvency

In a typical RMBS programme, an issuer of RMBSs in Australia issues multiple tranches. Hence, bonds are usually issued in a subordinated basis, with multiple tranches. In this manner, if the issuer becomes insolvent resulting in subsequent enforcement proceedings, subordinated bonds will be paid after senior bonds.[43]

7.4 Risk Minimisation for Stakeholders

Two basic factors are taken into consideration when rating MBSs. They are creditworthiness of the underlying mortgage pool, which is allocated to secure the securities, and the creditworthiness of the seller/originator or borrower. Rating agencies typically require certain measures to be included in the trust deed (also in other documents, to the extent such provisions are applicable) to ensure that the SPV is "bankruptcy-remote", and hence the SPV is unlikely to be dragged into voluntary or involuntary insolvency proceedings.[44]

[43] See, for example, *Master Information Memorandum, PUMA Fund P-7*, paragraphs 2 and 4.4 and *PUMA Sub-Fund Series* 2014, pp 55–56. These bonds are still generally secured, in favour of the security trustee on behalf of the bondholders. Cf. the claims of the unsecured creditors of an insolvent entity rank equally, without preference (*pari passu*), and in the event of there being insufficient funds to pay all of them, they will be paid proportionately: section 555 of the *Corporations Act*. However, debts that are validly secured against the insolvent entity's property are not subject to the above *pari passu* principle, and rank in priority in the event of a winding-up.

[44] See generally, V. Kothari, *Securitisation, the Financial Instrument of the New Millennium*, (Calcutta: Academy of Financial Services, 2003) Ch. 6; Standard and Poor's, *Structured Finance Australia and New Zealand* (Melbourne, 2000) 92; R. B. True, 'Risk and Insolvency Issues in Japanese Asset Securitization' (1996) 28 *New York University Journal of International Law and Politics* 505.

7.4.1 Limits on Powers and Objects of the SPV

Reducing the risk of insolvency of the SPV is crucial when it comes to risk minimisation for stakeholders. Hence, there should be a mechanism where SPV will be protected, or perhaps prohibited, from businesses unrelated to its core objectives of mortgage securitisation and issuance of RMBSs.[45] Thus, limiting objects and powers of the SPV (allowing room for those barest activities necessary to effect the RMBS transaction) would be a practical solution.

For that reason, the trust documentation typically includes an objects clause that defines the purpose of the SPV[46] and constrains the SPV from carrying on those activities needed to ensure the sufficiency of cash flow to pay its RMBSs and to powers incidental to that purpose. For example, if a trustee were prohibited by the terms of the trust deed from engaging employees in its capacity as trustee and then if, in breach of the trust deed, the trustee purported to engage employees in its capacity as trustee, neither the trustee nor those employees (in their capacity as agents) would be entitled to be indemnified for unpaid wages and the like from the trust assets. The trustee-issuer is generally not given powers to carry on any other activity. In this manner, by way of restraining the trustee-issuer's powers, potential for creditors will not be able to claim SPV's assets through subrogation to the trustee's right of indemnity.

It would be risky for the SPV to engage in unrelated business activities unless the parties to a transaction were willing to allow the rating to reflect the effect of those activities on the entity's resources, cash flows, and the SPV's ability to pay its obligations in a timely manner, even if the objects and powers of an SPV were not restricted in this manner.

7.4.2 Limitations on Debts

It is customary for a trust deed of a typical RMBS programme to provide room for the SPV to issue multiple classes of securities. However, all such

[45] It might be thought that since the trustee-issuer is generally a company, it is not restricted in terms of its objects and powers: see sections 124–129 of the *Corporations Act*. However, the SPV is primarily a trust vehicle, albeit generally with a corporate trustee. In such a context, sections 124–129 of the *Corporations Act* are not really applicable.

[46] E.g. to hold the mortgage receivables; collect them, pass them on, reinvest them etc.

classes of securities should gain the same credit rating.[47] Such regulation is a must, provided the fact that the holder of supplementary bonds would be incapable to disturb the creditworthiness of the trust or bring about the winding-up of the same.

The SPV may be able to issue subordinated non-recourse debt, provided the trust deed and related documentation allow it. In this context, "recourse" refers to the obligation of the issuer to pay for those mortgage receivables that run into default. Normally, in an RMBS transaction, there is a right of recourse, but it is limited to the cash collateral (and any over collateralisation) placed by the originator, and to the underlying assets securing the bond issue. Bondholders and other secured creditors, such as swap providers in the case of the SPV's unpaid swap obligations, therefore have no recourse to any other assets of the issuer for satisfaction of the issuer's obligations under the related bonds,[48] and their rights are subordinated to those of existing bondholders.

In any additional debt issue, the risk to the SPV should be no larger than that originally vested on the initial RMBS issue. In practice, creditors are at times requested to execute an agreement with the trust ensuring that they will not file an involuntary petition against the SPV until at least one year after the RMBSs have been repaid.[49] The idea is to reduce the risk of involuntary liquidation or other insolvency proceedings against the trust.

7.4.3 *Role of the Directors as Corporate Trustee-Issuers*

For some RMBS structures, for example, typically bank assignment programmes, the corporate issuer is established by a sponsoring bank. In such a situation, directors of the bank would serve on the board of the corporate issuer (SPV). On the other hand, the SPV's directors most likely would be officers of the originating bank or of support providers.

Conflicts of interest can arise due to such inter-relationships. For example, if the sponsor was to become insolvent but the SPV was performing adequately, the sponsor might have an incentive to seek to liquidate the

[47] See, for example, the multiple series of bonds issued by the PUMA Fund in *Master Information Memorandum, P-7,* paragraph 2.

[48] See, for example, *Master Information Memorandum, PUMA Fund, P-7,* paragraphs 3.3, 4.8.4 and 5.2.

[49] It should be noted, however, that even if they do execute such agreements, the legal efficacy of this "contracting out" procedure remains uncertain.

SPV and consolidate its assets with those of the sponsor. Due to concerns about potential conflicts, rating agencies frequently require that the SPV's board be employed with independent directors. Arguably, for example, the risk of the SPV going into liquidation is lessened if the corporate issuer has at least some directors who are independent of the sponsoring bank and other facility providers, assuming of course that these directors' votes are required in any motion to liquidate the SPV or amend its constitution to more easily facilitate liquidation of the SPV, and they decide to vote against it. However, this is an ongoing concern regarding corporate governance and independent directors in current literature.[50]

7.4.4 *Separateness Covenants*

Separateness of agreement, perhaps we could call it separateness of covenants, is generally included in the documentation pertaining to the ongoing operations of the programme. Apart from this, the SPV's existence, separate and distinct from that of the originator, is also reflected in the structure of the RMBS programme.

An SPV should be, and should appear to be, an independent entity from its sponsor or the originator. Separateness covenants helps to guarantee that the SPV is perceived to be an entity that is truly independent of its sponsoring entity. However, if the SPV is not, or at least does not appear to be, independent, the courts may decide to consider assets of the SPV as part of the sponsoring entity in case such entity becomes insolvent. Separateness covenants generally include a number of obligations that may include[51] requirements to maintain books, accounts, and records part from those of any other entity; prohibiting commingling its assets with those of any other entity; not to provide guarantee or become obligated for the debts of any other entity, or hold out its credit as being available to satisfy the obligations of others; not to acquire obligations or securities of its members or shareholders; not to pledge its assets for the benefit of any other entity, or make any loans or advances to any other entity; not to create or permit any encumbrances over any of the underlying securities to the RMBS issue, other than those by which its RMBS issue is secured;

[50] A detailed discussion of this debate is beyond the scope of this book. For a summary of the debate, see L.C. Keong (ed.), *Corporate Governance: An Asia-Pacific Critique* (Hong Kong: Sweet & Maxwell Asia, 2002).

[51] See, for example, Standard and Poor's, (2000) 93.

prohibit discharging any person from his obligations under any of the agreements that form part of the trustee's security, except in certain specified circumstances (e.g. repayment of the loan amount); and not to have any subsidiaries other than those specifically contemplated by the programme documentation.

As noted earlier, with respect to the commingling of assets, where the mortgage originator in an RMBS programme is also the servicer, the cash collected by the originator may at times (whether deliberately or not) become co-mingled with the cash collected by the originator in the capacity of servicer. The result is that the cash collected by the SPV cannot be clearly identified so that, in the event of insolvency, such cash could become part of the originator's asset pool, and not be available to the SPV, even though it strictly belongs to the SPV. Plainly, in order to avoid uncertainty, such commingling of assets should be avoided. This is particularly important in the context of practice in Australia, where the issuer is invariably a trustee. In such cases, the assets of the trust must be distinguishable from, and not mixed in with, any other assets of the issuer, or the assets of any other trust of which the issuer is a trustee. If the assets do become mixed, they may lose their characterisation as property of the trust and consequently their protection from claims by any general creditors of the trustee.

Another situation that might arise is that, as noted earlier, the trust deed governing the SPV normally allows the SPV to issue multiple classes of debt, provided those classes of securities all have the same credit rating. Again, in order to avoid complications, any commingling of assets should be avoided.

In some overseas jurisdictions (e.g. in the United States) where issuers may be companies or trusts, it is common for corporate issuers to market segregated series of securities. These are separate series of bonds, which are backed by different types or qualities of assets, and which are rated independently by the rating agencies. Segregated series of bonds may have different ratings. Because of this, the asset backing for each bond series must be kept separate so that the security for one series may be enforced without impacting on the continued operation of another series.

7.4.5 *Tax Liability of the Issuer*

A tax liability, perhaps an unexpected tax liability, on the issuer may result in the issuer being forced into insolvency. On the other hand, such proceeding will result in a premature termination of the RMBS programme, in which trustee (or perhaps court proceedings) may enforce the security held on behalf of the investors and other secured creditors. Structuring the issuer such that it is "tax neutral" is a one way of "avoiding" the risk of tax. In other words, the issuer manages its tax liabilities so that its revenue (assessable income) is offset by an equal amount of deductions or exemptions. RMBS programmes in Australia are often structured in this manner.

7.4.6 Limited Recourse of Creditors

Limited recourse provisions are employed in RMBS issues in order to ensure that the SPV is bankruptcy-remote. Such provisions are phrased in a way such that provisions would sustain even in the event of the issuer's insolvency.[52] As noted earlier, in an RMBS transaction, there is normally a right of recourse, which is limited to the cash collateral (and any over-collateralisation) placed by the originator, and to the underlying assets securing the bond issue. Bondholders and other secured creditors, such as swap providers in the case of the SPV's unpaid swap obligations, therefore have no recourse to any other assets of the issuer for satisfaction of the issuer's obligations under the related bonds. However, bondholders may be entitled to have their debts paid from liquidating issuer's assets, if bond series were issued without competent limited recourse provisions.

In case of a default, it is likely that bondholders may commence insolvency proceedings, with the view of accessing assets of the issuer. Even if such an attempt did not succeed, say, for example, because of the first priority fixed charges granted to a security trustee for the benefit of the other bondholders, yet it may prevent judicious payments of amounts due to the other bondholders. From a rating agency's point of view, limiting the recourse of creditors of a trustee-issuer is not a matter of a momentous concern, since the insolvency of the trustee should not of itself result in termination of the RMBS programme. However, it is, naturally, a significant issue from the trustee's perspective, and in terms of the rights of creditors against trustee-issuers.

[52] See, for example, *Master Information Memorandum, PUMA Fund, P-7*, paragraphs 3.3, 4.8.4 and 5.2 and *PUMA Sub-Fund Series 2014*, pp 66–69.

7.5 Summary

Smooth functioning of an RMBS programme will heavily depend on the risk of insolvency of the mortgage originator and, perhaps to a lesser extent, the risk of the trustee-issuer being insolvent. Considering a typical insolvency proceeding, in both cases, a "stay" would be imposed on all creditors' actions against the entity. This may include actions related to the collateral. A stay would result in setbacks in payments to creditors. Typically, the originator would continue to receive and transfer borrowers' repayments on a regular basis. In certain cases, the originator may transfer additional mortgage assets to the asset pool in order to "top up" the security pool. Prima facie, there is a risk that liquidator may claim trust assets if the originator becomes insolvent. Thus, it is supreme important that the SPV is structured "bankruptcy-remote".

In the Australian context, prudential regulations of Australian Prudential Regulation Authority (APRA) minimise the insolvency risk pertaining to both originators and trustee-issuers. Yet, as experience in recent years has shown, prudential regulators in Australia—and APRA, in particular[53]—are hardly omniscient in terms of identifying corporate distress in those institutions they oversee.

The situation is worsened since, in practice, most Australian home owners (borrowers) are uninformed, and thus unaware, about the fact that their houses could be sold by financial intermediaries downstream who have "purchased" the originator's mortgagee rights. This is not because of any default on the borrower's side, but because of default, loss, or insolvency on the part of the financial intermediary, or others in the supply chain.

Bibliography

Books and Book Chapters

Boyle, A. J., 'The Validity of Automatic Crystallisation Clauses' (1979) *Journal of Business Law* 231.

Ford, H. A. J., Austin, R. P. and Ramsay, I. M., *Ford's Principles of Corporations Law*, 10th edition, Chatswood: Butterworths, 2001.

Glennie, D. and Bouter, E., *Securitisation*, London: Kluwer Law International, 1998.

[53] Recall the collapse in 2001 of HIH Insurance Limited, the largest collapse in Australian corporate history: see R. Baxt, 'The HIH Litigation' (2002) 30 *Australian Business Law Review* 145.

Hanrahan, P., Ramsay, I. and Stapledon, G. (eds.), *Commercial Applications of Company Law*, Sydney: CCH, 2002.
Keong, L. C. (ed.), *Corporate Governance: An Asia-Pacific Critique*, Hong Kong: Sweet & Maxwell Asia, 2002.
Kothari, V., *Securitisation: The Financial Instrument of the New Millennium*, Calcutta: Academy of Financial Services, 2003.
Kothari, Vinod, Securitization*: The Financial Instrument of the Future* (John Wiley & Sons, 2006).
Roberts, P., *Understanding Grammar*, N.Y.: Harper, 1954.
True, R. B., 'Risk and Insolvency Issues in Japanese Asset Securitization' (1996) 28 *New York University Journal of International Law and Politics* 505.

Journal Articles

Baxt, R., 'The HIH Litigation' (2002) 30 *Australian Business Law Review* 145.
Chen, J., 'Asset Securitisation and the Singapore Insolvency Regime' (2001) 16 (8/9) *Journal of International Banking Law* 198.
Colbran, S., 'Security for Costs against Corporations: Section 1335 of the *Corporations Law*' (1993) 11 (5) *Company and Securities Law Journal* 273.
Rajapakse, Pelma, Richard Copp and J Gardner, 'Insolvency Issues in Residential Mortgage Securitisation' (2008) 34 *Monash University Law Review* 30.
Taylor, B., 'Assignment of Securities in Corporate Refinancing' (1998) 13 (10) *Australian Banking and Finance Law Bulletin* 141.

Working Papers, Magazines, Newspapers and Reports

Macquarie Securitisation Ltd, *The PUMA Fund P-7: Master Information Memorandum*, Sydney, February, 2000.
Macquarie Securitisation Ltd, *The PUMA Sub-Fund Series – 2014: Master Information Memorandum*, Sydney, July 2014.
Standard and Poor's, 'Credit Ratings on Mortgage-Backed Securities', *Structured Finance Australia and New Zealand*, Melbourne, 1998.

CHAPTER 8

Assessment of Current Regulation and Practice of RMBS Programmes

8.1 Introduction

As stated in Chap. 1, the book seeks to examine the aspects of relevant law and regulation, which facilitate and hinder the development of residential mortgage-backed security (RMBS) market in Australia, and to suggest some legal reforms. In order to achieve these goals, an analysis of the different stages of the RMBS process in Australia was undertaken in Chaps. 4, 5, 6, and 7 based on a contractarian framework—a subset of microeconomic theory. This framework, discussed in Chap. 2, outlined the RMBS process and the incentives for and conflicts of interest among participants in this process. Chapter 3 set the stage for the analysis in Chaps. 4, 5, 6, and 7 in terms of a more detailed discussion of the relevant institutional features of RMBS. In this chapter (i.e. Chap. 8), the results from the analysis are brought together and used as a basis in examining the current legislative and regulatory provisions governing RMBS in order to identify those relevant aspects of law and regulation, which facilitate or impede the growth of the RMBS industry. The "public benefit test" framework is used as a guide in this examination. As expounded in Chap. 2, this framework is based on the principles of social cost-benefit analysis and is used to identify an optimal RMBS legal and regulatory regime that would provide a resolution to the conflicting interests of participants in the RMBS process. As also mentioned in Chap. 2, the "public benefit test" is similar to that used to evaluate the introduction of Commonwealth and State legislation pursuant

P. Rajapakse, S. Senarath, *Commercial Law Aspects of Residential Mortgage Securitisation in Australia*,
https://doi.org/10.1007/978-3-030-00605-1_8

to the *Statutory Instruments Act* 1992 (Qld) and the Commonwealth-State *Competition Principles Agreement* 1995.[1]

The assessment is undertaken within a framework that reflects the functional stages of an RMBS programme—namely, the origination process, the transfer of mortgagee rights to the special purpose vehicle (SPV), the issuance of mortgage-backed securities, and insolvency and financial risks for the originator and issuer, based on the discussion in Chaps. 3, 4, 5, 6, and 7.

8.1.1 Review of Chapters

Chapters 1 and 2 set out the process for a typical RMBS programme and identified the role of each of the stages in the process and the objectives that participants in an RMBS programme intend to achieve. The mortgage securitisation process can be summarised as follows.[2] A mortgage lender or originating bank with a substantial pool of mortgage loans sells or transfers a portfolio of its mortgages to an SPV. This SPV is a trust, established separately from the originating bank or IMP. The transfer is intended to separate the mortgages from risks associated with the originator. For this reason, the originating bank must structure the transfer so that it constitutes a "true sale", that is sufficient under insolvency law to remove the mortgages from the originating bank's asset pool.

To raise the funds to purchase these mortgages, the SPV issues RMBSs to professional (mainly institutional) investors in the capital markets. The interest and principal from these RMBSs are paid for from collections or repayments on the housing loan mortgages purchased by the SPV. The investors of the RMBSs therefore look to the cash flow from the mortgages, and not necessarily to the credit of the originating bank for repayment. The SPV must be structured in such a way as to be insolvency-remote, in order to gain acceptance in the market as an issuer of RMBSs. "Insolvency-remote" in this context means that the SPV is unlikely to be adversely affected in the event that the originating bank or independent mortgage provider (IMP) becomes insolvent.

The trustee of the SPV (which in practice in Australia is invariably structured as a trust) is entitled to all repayments received from home loan borrowers/mortgagors. In order to cover the possibility that the

[1] As noted in Chap. 1, any legislation that is likely to impose appreciable costs on the community, or a section of it, is subjected to a Regulatory Impact Statement to determine whether the legislation is likely to be for the benefit of the public.

[2] See Fig. 1.2 in Chap. 1.

mortgage pool will not provide sufficient income to enable payment of the bond interest when it falls due (e.g. as a result of borrowers' failure to pay), some form of credit enhancement is also provided. Generally this includes mortgage insurance, the division of the bond issues into senior and subordinated bonds, and a cash reserve.

After obtaining credit enhancement, the issuer usually has the RMBSs rated by a rating agency such as Standard and Poor's Ratings Group or Moody's Investor Services. The originator of the mortgages normally continues to service the loans, communicating with borrowers, collecting payments, and earning a fee for doing so. When all principal payments have been made and the RMBSs have matured, the SPV is extinguished, and any remaining mortgage assets including cash are returned to the originating bank.

The goal of mortgage securitisation is to obtain low-cost capital market funding by separating the originator's mortgage receivables from the risks associated with that originator. The objectives for Australian deposit-taking institutions (ADIs)—originating banks and independent mortgage providers—include off-balance sheet financing for accounting purposes; the earning of fee income; an enhanced ability to transform illiquid assets (i.e. home mortgage loans) into tradable securities; the transfer of risk; additional liquidity for the bank or IMP; and the ability to improve asset and liability management, and to reduce costs through economies of scale and scope. For institutional investors, RMBS programmes provide additional opportunities for diversification; an investment that is tailored to investor preferences; an investment that is secured, over real property; and an investment at yields that tend to be attractive, by comparison with those of other debt instruments of similar risk.[3] Chapters 4, 5, 6, and 7 examined, in detail, the commercial law and regulatory aspects of various stages of an RMBS programme.

To aid this investigation, this chapter recapitulates the key stages of the RMBS process and then assesses the impacts of the relevant law and regulation governing RMBSs in terms of the public benefit guidelines set out in the *Statutory Instruments Act* 1992 (Qld) and the Commonwealth-State *Competition Principles Agreement* 1995. Within this framework, the chapter qualitatively investigates the extent to which the current law and regulation hinders or facilitates the achievement of those objectives at each functional stage of the RMBS process. The analysis in this chapter provides the basis for the recommendations for legislative reforms outlined in Chap. 9.

[3] These objectives are among the most important. Of course, the priority accorded to particular objectives will vary with the individual originator and investor.

8.2 Assessment of the Mortgage Origination Process

The mortgage origination process involves the following. The borrower initially makes a loan application to a bank or mortgage originator (an independent mortgage provider—IMP)[4] that is reviewed for approval by the bank management or a fund manager; the mortgaged property is valued by an approved valuer appointed by the fund manager or the originator; the loan application is then approved by the relevant home loan insurer; the solicitors then prepare the mortgage documentation and settle the mortgage loan, subject to the requirements of the *National Credit Code* (NCC).[5] After the mortgage is executed, funds are advanced and the security interest of the originator is perfected.[6] The payment by the mortgagor to the originator of the principal and interest instalments under the loan may commence afterwards. In return for a service fee, the originator collects the mortgage repayments on behalf of the SPV.

8.2.1 Objectives of the Mortgage Origination Process

In order for the mortgage origination process to work effectively, the following must be achieved:

- Acquisition of good quality mortgage loans for securitisation: Mortgage securitisation is primarily meant to create a security (RMBS) out of a basic asset (the mortgage loans). The originator expects the security to stand on its own worth, and hence, to make the credit rating of the originator insignificant. This would mean the mortgage loans being securitised should be of high quality.[7] This is accomplished by complying with the law of contract, the property legislation, and the rating agency's lending criteria for mortgage pool selection. The cash flow

[4] An IMP acts as "spotter" for the larger banks, and earns an origination fee in the form of a "spotter's fee".

[5] The impact of the *National Credit Code* in securitised mortgages will be discussed later in this chapter. See also Chap. 5.

[6] The mortgagor transfers his/her rights over the security property to the originator, as mortgagee, (the right to sell the security property and recoup any outstanding debt owed by the mortgagor).

[7] If the asset has any collateral protection, such as guarantees, title, or right over an asset, backing it, it adds up to the quality of the assets.

produced by the mortgage loan is used as the source of funds for the payments to be made to the purchasers of RMBS (bondholders).

- Lowering financing costs for originators: a well-regarded pool of mortgages owned by a bank can be used to structure an RMBS of higher credit quality and, therefore, of lower market cost than the bank or corporate entity could itself issue.
- Reduction in regulatory capital: For a banking originator that faces regulatory capital requirements, a securitisation transaction that qualifies as a sale of assets for bank-regulatory purposes reduces the need for holding adequate capital to meet their credit risks.[8]
- Retention of servicing revenue: The originating bank normally continues as servicer, retaining the servicing fee, which is the excess of the SPV's revenue over costs and surplus income from the mortgage receivables once the RMBSs are fully paid back to investors.

8.2.2 *Impact of the Regulation for Facilitating the Mortgage Origination Process*[9]

The following section assesses the extent to which these objectives of the origination process are achieved by the current regulations and practices in the market.

Rights and Obligations of the Originator and the Borrower Under Property Legislation

Under the Torrens system of land holding, the mortgages comprising the mortgage pool are registered on each property's certificate of title. This gives the originating mortgagee a statutory charge over the security property for the right to repayment of the loan. The borrower or mortgagor is obliged, under the terms of the mortgage, to repay the principal and interest on the loan, and comply with various covenants. Thus, the law relating to mortgages facilitates the origination process, where the borrowers are obligated to make regular payment on the loans, which would enhance the cash flow for payment to investors in the RMBS.

In the context of mortgage origination in Australia, the originator is typically noted on the certificate of title as the holder of the registered

[8] The capital adequacy requirements are discussed under "origination process" in Chap. 4 of the book.

[9] The analysis throughout this chapter assumes that other factors remain equal or constant (*ceteris paribus*).

mortgage, and any subsequent (equitable) assignees, such as the trustee-issuer of the SPV, are equitable mortgagees. If the initial borrowers default, the mortgagee has the right to exercise its power of sale, as well as the rights to foreclose, appoint a receiver, and enter into possession, and the right to sue personally to enforce the borrower's loan contract. Priority contests between mortgagees in the context of an RMBS programme are unlikely to occur under the current Torrens system, unless both security interests were unregistered. Under the Torrens system, an earlier registered first mortgage is recorded on the certificate of title to the security property, and hence, the second registered mortgagee would be aware of the first registered mortgage, which would take priority over the later registered mortgage. This system of registration effectively facilitates a clear transfer of assets from the originator to the SPV.

8.2.3 Regulations That Impede the Mortgage Origination Process[10]

Risk-Weighting of RMBS at 100%

As discussed in Chap. 4, under the Australian Prudential Regulation Authority's APRA) prudential standards, an originator's portfolio of residential mortgages are risk-weighted at 50% for capital adequacy purposes, but an issue of RMBS that is backed by those same mortgages is weighted at 100%. Consequently, an ADI would need to allocate twice as much capital for the RMBSs as it would for loans secured by the same mortgages. Thus, on balance, it can be said that the current capital adequacy guidelines arguably create a commercial incentive for institutions not to invest in the RMBSs issued.

Therefore, it is important for the residential mortgage securitisation industry that the risk-weightings applied to highly rated RMBS be revised and that APRA amend the capital adequacy guidelines to reflect the important distinctions between investing in a 100% risk-weighted entity and highly rated, senior ranking RMBS backed by 50% risk-weighted residential mortgages.

Under the current capital adequacy guidelines issued by APRA, Guidance Note 112.1—*Risk-Weighted On-Balance Sheet Credit Exposures* (September 2000), the RMBS is allocated a 100% risk-weighting for

[10] The analysis throughout this chapter assumes that other factors remain equal.

capital requirement purposes.[11] This risk-weighting will not support the growth of residential mortgage securitisation in Australia. The industry groups have made submissions to APRA to reduce the risk-weighting applied to highly rated RMBS.[12]

Moreover, the Bank for International Settlements (BIS) on 29 April 2003 issued a revised proposal for capital requirements for securitisation—namely, the *Third Consultative Paper on the Treatment of Asset Securitisation*.[13] Under these new proposals, mortgage loans with credit rating from AAA to AA- would be risk weighted at 20%, while those rated A+ to A- will be risk weighted 50% and so on, down to B+ or below, after which the full value of a mortgage loan will be deducted from the bank's capital.

The new risk-weightings would appear to offer a credit arbitrage for Australian banks, based on the fact that a typical Australian RMBS issue has no tranche rated lower than AA-. A bank can securitise a pool of mortgage loans and the whole RMBS issue will be risk-weighted at a lower rate of 20%, compared to the higher rate 50% allocated for mortgage loans that secure the same issue; under the Basel Accord I, the BIS 2003 proposals for capital requirements would benefit the RMBS market by giving banks a greater incentive to remove residential mortgage loans from their balance sheets. A 20% or 50% risk-weighting for RMBS would also encourage investment in RMBS and provide investors with greater opportunities to diversify their mortgage portfolios.

Additional reasons for recommending that highly rated RMBS be risk-weighted at (say) 20%–50% include that:

- Holders of RMBS are, in essence, purchasing a direct interest in the income and principal cash flows generated by the underlying assets.
- The underlying assets are typically a pool of housing loans fully secured by a registered mortgage over residential property which would (if kept on balance sheet) be risk-weighted at 50%.

[11] This requires a thorough economic analysis which the present book does not address. For an alternative approach into risk-weighting, see Senarath, 'Securitisation and the global financial crisis: can risk retention prevent another crisis?', (2017) 18 *International Journal of Business and Globalisation*, 153.

[12] Australian Securitisation Forum, *Submission to APRA in response to APS 120—Fund Management and Securitisation*, 14 June 2000, http://www.securitisation.com.au/asf.

[13] BIS Home Page http://www.bis.org.

- The process of securitising the underlying assets includes a rigorous due diligence on those assets by a third-party global rating agency, which imposes stringent parameters on the vehicle issuing the RMBS.
- To achieve the necessary ratings on the senior RMBS, structural and/or third-party facilities are put in place to enhance the underlying assets, which effectively ensure that the securitised underlying assets carry less risk than equivalent on-balance-sheet assets.

Implications

The (opportunity) cost of maintaining capital to cover assets for regulatory purposes plainly represents an economic cost to a regulated ADI. If costs increase, ADIs and sponsors who wish to maintain their profit margins may increase revenue by raising interest rates and/or bank fees to borrowers, to the extent permitted by prevailing regulation.

If an ADI initiates or sponsors an RMBS issue for which it cannot secure regulatory capital relief, initial borrowers may bear some or all of the additional cost for the ADI of providing 100% capital cover in respect of the issue, in the form of higher interest rates or charges.

The Australian Securitisation Forum has commented that investor demand in the domestic RMBS market would be adversely affected, relative to offshore markets, as investors who are APRA-regulated ADIs must risk weight RMBS at 100% (instead of 50%, as is the case in other major international regulatory environments such as the United States, Japan, and the United Kingdom).[14] This will serve in part to reduce the liquidity of the domestic market.[15]

Overseas-licensed ADIs would be able to purchase RMBS at yields prevalent in Australia while allocating the risk-weighting imposed by their own regulatory jurisdictions. This will create a competitive advantage to overseas-licensed ADIs, which will achieve a better return on capital than Australian-licensed ADIs.

[14] E. J. Park, 'Allowing Japanese Banks to Engage in Securitization: Potential Benefits, Regulatory Obstacles, and Theories for Reform' (1996) 17 *University of Pennsylvania Journal of International Law* 723, 745; I. Falconer 'Securitisation in the United Kingdom' (1989) *Butterworth Journal of International Banking and Finance Law* 105, 109. See also, Senarath (2016), Not so "'Bankruptcy-Remote': An insight into Sri Lankan Securitization Practices in a Post_GFC Context" (Paper presented at the MAC-MME conference, Prague, Czech Republic); Senarath, S. 'The Dodd-Frank Act doesn't solve the principal-agent problem in asset securitisation' (2017) *blogs.lse.ac.uk* (11 November 2018).

[15] Australian Securitisation Forum, *Submission to APRA Regarding Risk Weighting of Mortgage-Backed Securities*, 24 July 2002, http://www.securitisation.com.au/asf, 2–3.

Hence, a reduced risk-weighting will enable regional ADIs, as investors, to diversify their mortgage portfolios, creating greater opportunities for spreading risk exposures within the market. This would facilitate the growth of the RMBS market for the benefit of the investing public.

In June 1999, the Bank for International Settlements issued a Consultative Paper entitled *New Capital Adequacy Framework* (Basel Accord II), which provides that a bank's minimum capital requirements should be based on its overall risk profile.[16] In general APRA has accepted the need to revise the risk-weighting for RMBS. However, changes to prudential standards have been postponed by APRA in the expectation that this issue would be dealt with as part of the implementation of Basel II.[17]

The benefits, which would be obtained from a change to the 50% risk-weighting for RMBS, should not be delayed. The need to amend the APRA Guidance Note 112.1 to give effect to a 50% risk-weighting for RMBS has been widely recognised by the industry. It is suggested that risk-weighting for RMBS should not be 100% but rather should be something less than that—perhaps 50% or 75%. It certainly should not be weighted at 100% as a mandatory rule.

These recommendations would, if implemented, help to ensure that financial institutions are not penalised for their involvement in RMBS transactions as sponsors, issuers, or investors. Further, the implementation of these recommendations would help to bring the Australian market into line with other major overseas RMBS markets.

8.3 The Transfer of Mortgagee's Rights to the Special Purpose Vehicle

One of the key steps in a mortgage securitisation process is for the SPV to acquire, from the originator, the mortgagee rights in the loans which form the backing for the RMBSs. The rights transferred to the SPV include the lender's right to receive principal and interest repayments from the borrower; the lender's right to exercise its power of sale under the terms of the residential mortgage; and the lender's right to any mortgage insurance payout in the event of default by the borrower. In practice, the transfer of

[16] P. Jackson, 'Bank Capital Standards: The New Basel Accord' (2001) *Bank of England Quarterly Bulletin* 55.

[17] APRA, Media Release 11 November 2004, http://www.apra.gov.au; G. Gunning, 'Basel II: A Capital Idea But Still Hurdles to Jump' *Standard and Poor's Inaugural Financial Market Conference*, Sydney, October 2002, 2.

mortgagee rights is effected by an equitable assignment. In an equitable assignment, the SPV acquires an equitable title to the mortgages, but the originator remains the legal owner and holds the legal title on trust for the SPV-assignee.[18] The mortgagor is not a party to the sale agreement and is not notified of its existence. In an RMBS issue, the mortgages are usually transferred to the SPV by way of an equitable assignment, with provision made for the transfer to be perfected or completed in certain circumstances. The circumstances in which the SPV will call for the completion of the transfer of the mortgages typically include the originator being in persistent default in the performance of its obligations relating to the securitisation, or it being in insolvency administration.

The assignment or transfer is structured so as to be "bankruptcy-remote" to gain investor acceptance in the capital market securities. In general, this is achieved by ensuring that the assignment or transfer constitutes a "true sale" by the originator to the SPV.

8.3.1 Objectives of the Transfer of Mortgagee Rights to the SPV

These include the:

- Off-balance sheet treatment of assets: If structured as a sale of mortgage receivables, securitisation can allow the originator to remove its assets from the balance sheet, reduce its assets and its debts, thereby increasing its scope for borrowing. In effect, mortgage securitisation allows an ADI to achieve greater leverage.
- Making the SPV "insolvency-remote": The SPV must be insulated, to the extent practicable, from a possible insolvency of the originator.
- Separating the source of payment: that is, mortgage receivables from the originator in the event the originator becomes insolvent. The SPV must be "ringfenced" from the originating bank or mortgage originator. That is, the SPV structure must be legally separated from the originating lender and its management.
- Bringing into effect a "true sale" of the mortgages.
- Reduction in the cost of funds for originators and issuers: RMBS issues may alleviate the agency costs of primary debt lending by lowering the costs of monitoring borrower behaviour. RMBSs are also rated more highly than normal corporate bonds by rating agencies,

[18] In a legal assignment, the legal title to the mortgage is vested in the SPV absolutely.

because of the isolation of mortgages in an "insolvency-remote" entity, thus reducing the cost of funds to the originator when compared to other traditional forms of financing. In addition, assigning its rights as mortgage lender or originator reduces the bank's or IMP's regulatory compliance costs, and its overall cost of funds.

- Opportunity for risk management afforded to originators. For example, credit risk and interest rate risk are the key uncertainties that concern ADI lenders. By passing on these risks to investors, or to third parties when credit enhancements are involved, ADIs are better able to manage their risk exposures.

8.3.2 *Impact of the Regulation for Facilitating the Transfer of Mortgagee Rights to the SPV*

This section provides a qualitative assessment of the extent to which the existing law and regulation relating to the transfer of mortgagee rights to the SPV impedes or facilitates the achievement of these objectives and criteria in RMBS issues in practice.

Property Legislation

Mortgage securitisation involves transfer of a lender's right to receive principal and interest repayments on the mortgage—it is a transfer of a right to the assignee (SPV). It is therefore required that the law of property or the contract between the parties should not prohibit the right to assign mortgages to a third party in equity at the minimal cost to the assignor and assignee. If the underlying mortgage contract has an obligation on the part of the issuer, which cannot be divested from the rights of the originator, then the rights cannot be transferred independent of the obligations. Hence, the risks associated with the assets cannot be eliminated, in which case mortgage securitisation cannot function.

SPV Trust Structure

In Australia, the use of a trust as an SPV in residential mortgage securitisations facilitates an off-balance sheet treatment of assets for accounting purposes, where the trustee company is not related to or a subsidiary of the originator for the purposes of the Australian accounting standard on consolidation.[19] The "insolvency-remoteness" of the SPV is accomplished by

[19] Australian Accounting Standard, AASB 1024, *Consolidated Accounts*, May 1992, paragraphs xxi–xxiii. See further discussion in Chap. 5.

establishing the SPVs as master trusts, which cannot be insolvent or become subject of a bankruptcy case. This is because trusts do not have any legal capacity separate from the trustee or beneficiaries. In practice, the SPVs comprise two classes of trust funds—warehouse funds and sub-funds. The assets of the master trust cannot be used to meet the liabilities of any other trusts, and none of the assets of other trusts are available to meet the liabilities of the master trust fund.[20] Such a structure provides comfort to investors that they are investing in a pool of mortgages, which is not subject to any subsequent deterioration in the credit quality of the originator. In this way a separation of the originating bank and the SPV is achieved.

The transfer of the originating bank's rights to a legally separate trust alleviates the agency costs of primary debt lending, by lowering the costs of monitoring borrower behaviour.[21] Separation of the originating bank from the mortgage loans in the pool themselves can enable the originator to raise funds at less cost, through the RMBSs issued by the SPV, than if it raised funds through securities issued directly. For example, the RMBS issued by the SPV, depending upon the structure of the transaction, may have a higher investment rating than securities issued directly by the originator (particularly if the originator is a regional bank or an IMP) and, therefore, would typically bear a lower interest rate than the originator might be able to obtain for its own securities. Accordingly, the use of a trust structure in the RMBS programmes ensures insolvency-remoteness of the SPV, and off-balance-sheet financing for the originator (for accounting purposes) in a manner that would appear to be in the stakeholders' interest and for the public benefit.

APRA's Guidelines for Achieving a "Clean Sale"

Having accomplished a separation of the originator and the SPV, the stakeholders must ensure that the ownership of the mortgages, together with the attendant risks and rewards in respect of the assets, are effectively transferred to the SPV. This is necessary in order to justify a finding that a "true sale" or "clean sale" of the mortgagee's rights has occurred. APRA has issued prudential guidelines setting out the criteria for a "true sale" that should be complied by the ADIs and SPVs.[22] These guidelines assist originators in the

[20] See, for example, *Master Information Memorandum, PUMA Fund P-7,* paragraphs 4.17, 7.4. and discussion in Chap. 5. See also, *Master Information Memorandum, PUMA Sub-Fund Series 2014,* p 58.

[21] See B. Minton, T. Opler and S. Stanton, 'Asset Securitisation Among Industrial Firms', *Working Paper,* Fisher College of Business, Ohio State University, Columbus Ohio, November 1997.

[22] These criteria were examined in detail in Chap. 5.

sense of providing clear criteria for achieving a clean transfer of the assets and therefore capital relief for capital adequacy purposes. In ensuring that these criteria are achieved in an RMBS issue, the key considerations are the method of transfer of the mortgage assets and the so-called moral risks retained by the originating bank. A "true sale" will not be effected if, for example, the originator retains a right to share in any profits of the SPV, or investors in the RMBSs have any recourse back to the originating bank.

National Credit Code Disclosure Requirements, and Legibility of Credit Contract Documents

The *National Credit Code* requires that certain information be incorporated into the mortgage documents and the related contractual documentation. Section 184 of the Code provides that a credit contract, mortgage, or guarantee, or a notice given by a credit provider must be easily legible and clearly expressed. Legibility of this information in home loan contracts facilitates securitisation of these loans.

Two limbs of the Code are aimed at ensuring that a debtor is informed of all important terms of a proposed credit contract in an understandable form. They are (a) disclosure requirements and (b) the mandatory provision of documentation in plain English.

- *Disclosure Requirements*

Sections 16 and 17 of the Code stipulate that:

(i) A credit contract document must disclose the matters set out in section 17.
(ii) There must be both a pre-contractual statement setting out all the same matters as are referred to in section 16 (the statement can take the form of a copy of the proposed contract) and an information statement in a form prescribed by the regulations detailing the debtor's statutory rights and obligations.

Credit providers who fail to disclose these key requirements are potentially liable for a civil fine of up to $500,000 for each non-disclosure. To protect against this potential liability, issuers in practice typically need to obtain additional credit support of up to a $500,000.

Importantly, the matters that need to be disclosed under section 16 in the pre-contractual statement and the credit contract include the commissions to be paid by, or to, the credit provider (section 17(14)), which includes any amounts payable to mortgage originators.

Disclosure of all the key requirements, which include terms and cost of the credit contract, will enable the prospective borrowers to make a fully informed decision as to borrowing and their rights and obligations relating to the credit contract. Pre-contractual disclosure can contribute to informational efficiency and ultimately to social welfare by enabling lenders, borrowers, and investors to gather information at a reduced cost. This will result in a borrower becoming increasingly aware of their rights under the Code, and (in the absence of market imperfections) a correspondingly greater incentive on mortgage originators to comply with the Code to avoid penalties.[23]

The disclosure requirements under sections 16 and 17 also help to ensure that all credit contracts provide the same type of information to borrowers. This does not mean that each lender must grant credit according to the same criteria but means rather that each lender must provide the same key information to all borrowers, making it easier for borrowers to compare loans originated by different lenders.[24]

Impact of Section 188 of the Code

Under many RMBS programmes, the initial credit provider for the housing loan is the originator of the loans for the programme. As discussed in Chap. 5, under section 188 of the Code, the originating bank or IMP remains the credit provider so long as it continues to receive repayments from the mortgagors, but once that ceases, the trustee-issuer of the SPV effectively becomes the credit provider, and assumes the attendant responsibilities under the Code.

In a securitisation programme, trustees act as a bare trustee or mortgagee of record for mortgages on behalf of the lending institutions who may contract the mortgage origination process to mortgage originators. The Trustee's duty is to hold the legal interest on their behalf. Whether the Trustee becomes the credit provider for the purpose of the Code following the assignment of the loan and supporting security from the originator to the Trustee depends on whether the originator continues to

[23] The increased uniformity and clarity of the Codes throughout Australia may, other things being equal, help to produce a more informed generation of borrowers. On the other hand, this may have the potential for more disputes to arise regarding the credit contract.

[24] Cf. If credit contracts were allowed to contain different sets of information, it would be more difficult for investors to evaluate loans originated by one lender against loans originated by another lender.

receive payments from the borrowers following the assignment. However, trustees' responsibilities are to their lender beneficiaries, to bondholders, and not to borrowers or mortgagors. Trustees do not have any day-to-day involvement in the origination, provision of funds for the housing loan, management, or enforcement of mortgage loans. Instead, these functions are undertaken by the fund manager and/or by specialist mortgage originators appointed pursuant to a trust deed.

One of the inadvertent effects of the *National Credit Code*, prior to introduction of section 188, was that if the fund manager or the mortgage originator committed a breach of the Code, they were not responsible for the consequences under the Code. Instead, these were borne by the Trustee, as it becomes the "credit provider" for the purposes of the Code. This was an inequitable outcome, as it exposed the Trustee to civil and criminal penalties as a result of the actions of third parties over which it had no control. In addition, the Trustee was not entitled to be indemnified by any third party, or out of the assets of the trust fund, for any criminal, or the majority of the civil consequences, as a result of a breach of the Code. Because of this, the Trustee Corporations Association of Australia (TCA) made a detailed submission on this issue to the Ministerial Council on Consumer Affairs in 1996.[25] In that submission, TCA recommended that the Code be amended, to clarify that the trustee in a mortgage securitisation programme is not the credit provider for the purposes of the Code and, instead, it is the fund manager or mortgage originator named in the relevant credit contract as the credit provider. Further, the TCA suggested that the regulation should allow the parties within a given securitisation programme to negotiate indemnities between themselves to reflect the agreed risk profiles under the Code.

In addition, the consumer credit regulation should give certainty in terms of whom the debtor or guarantor can sue under the Code for breaches of it. The TCA argued compellingly that professional corporate trustee who normally acts as the trustee of an RMBS programme should not need to expose its personal assets to the civil and criminal consequences for a breach of the Code where it was not actually responsible for that breach.

On the basis of the TCA's submissions, the former *Consumer Credit Code* was amended to include section 169A (currently section 188 of NCC). The section allows any stakeholder who is potentially liable under the Code to obtain an indemnity from another person, who may themselves in turn obtain an indemnity from anyone except the borrower or guarantor. The

[25] See Trustee Corporations Association of Australia, Submission to the Financial System Inquiry (Wallis Committee), December 1996.

liabilities to which section 188 applies include both civil and criminal penalties, a payment in settlement of a liability or alleged liability under the Code and a liability under another indemnity for any liability under the Code. A court or tribunal order may be made under section 77 in relation to unjust loan contracts, and it would be imprudent of trustees not to obtain an indemnity from the credit provider against such liability. Nevertheless, such indemnities are justified on the basis that if they were not given, the trustee-issuer of the SPV would not be obtaining "clean" mortgagee rights, for which it gave good consideration when those rights were assigned to it in equity. Overall, the amendment under section 188 has the effect that the person responsible for carrying out the functions regulated by the Code is required to comply with the Code and be legally liable for its breach. These amendments to the Code are likely to substantially encourage the development of the RMBS market in Australia and facilitate the delivery of the benefits of mortgage securitisation to programme participants.

There would appear to be room for further amendment to the Code, in order to clarify the meaning of the "nominated credit provider" within an RMBS programme. The Code should, to remove any doubt, provide that the mortgage originator or fund manager named in the credit contract is the "nominated credit provider" for the purposes of the Code.[26]

8.3.3 Regulations That Impede the Transfer of Mortgages to SPV

The common law requirements or criteria for establishing a "true securitisation" are less stringent than those from an accounting standards perspective.[27] In considering these issues concerning whether a "true sale" has taken place, the courts have not developed a definitive formula or set of factors to distinguish, in a securitisation context, between a true sale and a secured financing arrangement. It is possible for a court to come to a conclusion that the real intent of the securitisation transaction was not to legally or equitably transfer the mortgages to the SPV, but

[26] This again assumes no information asymmetry between the parties, and that existing market power regulation, such as the *Trade Practices Act* 1974 (Cth), is sufficient to deal with any imbalances in market power between the parties.

[27] See I. Plater, 'Accounting and Tax for Off-Balance Sheet Financing' *IIR Conference*, Sydney, September 1992, 6–12; C. Wheeler, 'Accounting Aspects of Securitisation' in, C. A. Stone, A. Zissu and J. Lederman (eds.), *Asset Securitisation Theory and Practice in Europe* (London: Euromoney Publications, 1991) Ch. 40.

rather that it simply comprises an alternative financing arrangement. In the United States, there have been cases where securitisations of loans receivables have been re-characterised by the courts as financing transactions, rather than effective transfers of mortgagee rights to the SPV.

If the originator becomes insolvent and the mortgages are owned in equity by an SPV, then the SPV would also be entitled to the repayments on the mortgages. Assuming the mortgages were paid, the SPV then would have sufficient cash to pay its securities without defaulting, which would be beneficial to investors in RMBS. If the transfer were held not to be a true sale, it would be deemed to be an advance of funds by the SPV to the originator, secured by the mortgages. This has significant consequences for, amongst other things, a financial institution's capital adequacy and taxation obligations. If the originator's rights have not been transferred to the SPV, it may aggravate the agency cost of primary debt lending by increasing the cost of monitoring borrower behaviour. The SPV would then be a creditor of the originator and have security interest, but not an equitable interest, in the mortgages. In such a case, the originator's insolvency would automatically result in a stay of all actions by creditors to foreclose on or otherwise obtain property of the originator. If the courts treat the transaction as a substantive borrowing, the investors would be worse off than a secured lender, as they would not even hold a perfected security interest.

Ascertaining whether a "true sale" has occurred in Australia is made more difficult by the fact that there is no Australian case in point, and the few cases that have been decided overseas are somewhat inconsistent. Various courts have considered whether a given transfer of loan receivables constitutes a true sale or secured borrowing. The facts of the decided cases have not, for the most part, been representative of securitised transactions. It has been argued that the approach of the UK courts contrasts sharply to the approach that was taken in UK Accounting Standards Board's statement—FRS 5 *Accounting for Securitisation*. The English courts are more inclined to honour the expressed intention of the parties than read an implied intention into the circumstances. However, the US courts have delivered several decisions ignoring the body of an agreement and regarding a securitisation programme as a financial transaction (i.e. essentially, as a secured loan). Accordingly, the cases are not easily harmonised, and which factors are relevant and which should be given greater weight are open to interpretation. In these circumstances, it is arguable that this gap in the existing law and regulation impedes the growth of the RMBS market in Australia.

Notice of Assignment

In RMBS programmes in practice, when mortgages are equitably assigned to the SPV, the mortgagors are generally not notified that the mortgagee rights to their loans have been assigned to the SPV-issuer, and they are not parties to the contract, in a legal sense. The risks of not notifying home loan borrowers impacts on RMBS programmes in Australia in various ways. By informing the borrowers of the assignment of mortgages, the SPV would have an opportunity to obtain an acknowledgement from each of the borrowers as to the amount of his or her outstanding indebtedness. Each borrower would thereafter generally be estopped from claiming that, in fact, a lesser sum was due.[28] Since the borrowers are not informed of the equitable sales or transfers of their mortgages, the issuers would only be able to claim from them the amount actually due on the mortgages, and borrowers would not be estopped from bringing claims for greater amounts. There is, of course, a theoretical risk of a mortgage being sold to an SPV on the basis of incorrect information as to the amount of the mortgage debt. However, in practice, the originator would be required to give a warranty as to the accuracy and truth of the particulars of the portfolio for the purpose of securitisation.[29]

As discussed in Chap. 2, the banks' and the IMPs' failure to give notice to home loan borrowers that the mortgagee rights to their loans have been assigned, could create a moral hazard problem and have implications for economic efficiency. In addition, neglecting or deliberately failing to notify borrowers of a risk that their houses could be sold through no fault of their own would seem at the least to be unconscionable and potentially in breach of consumer credit and trade practices legislation.

The SPV-assignee of a mortgage transferred under an equitable assignment is in a less secure position than it would have been, if that mortgage had been transferred under a legal assignment. While it is important for an SPV-assignee to minimise all unnecessary legal risks, this must be balanced against the cost of the administrative inconvenience involved in providing the extra comfort of a legal assignment or complete transfer. Where the cost of this protection is excessive relative to the degree of risk involved, the rating agencies are likely (and in practice, frequently do) to accept an equitable assignment of mortgages, provided the credit quality of the

[28] *Dixon v Winch* [1900] 1 Ch 736 (CA); *Turner v Smith* [1901] 1 Ch 213.

[29] *Master Information Memorandum, PUMA—P7*, paragraph 5.3

originator is good and, where necessary, alternative protection is provided through appropriate insurance policies.[30]

It seems trite to suggest that where mortgage rights have been or are about to be equitably assigned, legislation ought to require the bank or IMP, on the grounds of fairness as well as economic efficiency, to inform its borrowers of the sale and the identity of the new payee (assignee). Upon receipt of this notice, borrowers might well choose to continue to pay the SPV-assignee. However, if they elect to continue to pay the originator-assignor, legislation should be introduced to ensure that their loan could not be discharged, avoided, or repudiated. Plainly, such a statutory requirement for notification would be costly for the banks and IMPs. However, not to do so would be patently unfair for borrowers who discover too late that the power of sale over their mortgages has been exercised, through no fault of their own and without their knowledge.

In terms of the notice to borrowers, it might even be economically efficient to require under legislation that any assignments of mortgagee rights under RMBS programmes be notified on the title deeds to the particular properties, so that the borrowers or the potential buyers of those properties are aware that the mortgage rights have been assigned to an SPV. This might be a relatively straightforward way of ensuring appropriate disclosure in a way that provides a demonstrable net public benefit.[31]

Such legislation might also require the fine print in mortgage documents that relates to notice to borrowers to be drawn to the attention of the borrowers, with the implications of it being spelled out to borrowers in plain English. In the words of Lord Denning M.R. in *Thornton v Shoe Lane Parking Ltd*,[32] such clauses "should be printed in red ink with a red hand pointing to" them. Further, the effect of any assignment—namely, that borrowers could lose their houses through no fault of their own—should be printed in big bold letters.[33] Once borrowers were alerted to

[30] Standard and Poor's, 'Credit Ratings on Mortgage-Backed Securities' *Structured Finance Australia and New Zealand*, 1998, 8.

[31] Plainly, a rigorous "public benefit test", perhaps along the lines of a social cost-benefit analysis, would need to be conducted to determine whether the social benefits outweigh the social costs.

[32] [1971] 2 QB 163, 169.

[33] This would help to ensure clear communication and a "meeting of minds" between all of the parties and stakeholders concerned. The RMBS process is essentially a nexus of contracts. In an equitable environment, this "meeting of minds" is one way to ensure that those contracts, and the points at which they interface, are mutually beneficial to the parties and other stakeholders.

this risk and impart the information to others, the current information "gap" between borrowers and originating lenders is likely to reduce. It could be argued that this may discourage the ADIs securitising the mortgages, and that the only reason that they are involved in securitisation programmes is that their borrowers are unaware about these risks.

Set-off Issues Between the Lenders and Borrowers

As discussed in Chap. 5, the assignee of a debt that is secured by a mortgage accepts the debt subject to any equities, such as a right of set-off, that arise before it gives notice of the transfer to the original borrower. The risk of an SPV-assignee not receiving all of the anticipated income because of a right of set-off exercised by a borrower against the original mortgage lender is, in practice, minimised by a provision in the mortgage documentation, in which each borrower contractually agrees not to exercise any right of set-off it may have against the original lender under the general law. A contract to such effect would generally be valid until a mortgagor became bankrupt, although thereafter, set-off would be governed by the rights of set-off under bankruptcy law. The operation of these bankruptcy set-off rules could result in a reduction of the trustee-issuer's income with respect to a particular mortgage.

Impediments Under the National Credit Code (NCC)

Lack of a Monetary Ceiling

A monetary ceiling is precise and at least on one criterion (value) would enable credit providers (including securitisers) to identify, without the risk of error, potential situations that would be regulated by the Code and those that would not. This in turn would allow securitisers to set parameters to ensure that the Code did not apply to securitised credit contracts, so that they could avoid the risk to them of unenforceability or a breach under the Code.

A monetary ceiling would also represent an attempt to distinguish between those transactions which require the benefit of the Code and other larger financings where the policy reasons for legislative intervention are less pressing. With the latter, as the amount of credit increases, one could expect debtors to be increasingly sophisticated (e.g. in the sense used in the *Corporations Act*), or to have the resources to be able to afford financial and legal advice.

Mortgage Prepayment

In drafting the terms of housing mortgage loan agreements, lenders are constrained by a range of consumer protection provisions in the Code. For investors, these protections create risk and uncertainty, which, in turn, raise the costs of securitisation or increase the costs of capital for issuers. From a policy perspective, the Code must balance the competing needs for consumer protection and investor protection.

The rates of principal and interest payments in mortgage loan pools vary between pools, and are influenced by economic, legal, and demographic factors such as prevailing market interest rates for housing loans, and the terms and conditions of loans. There is no guarantee as to the actual rates of prepayment on the mortgage loans comprising the pools. Issuers usually have the right to "call" (repay) the bonds they issue.[34] Borrowers typically prepay their fixed rate loans when interest rates fall, and that is precisely the time when investors would not welcome their money back. Thus, the rate and timing of principal and interest payments and the ability to redraw principal or request a further advance on a housing loan affect the rate and timing of payments on RMBSs, which in turn would affect the yields on the bondholders' investment. Overall, for investors, there will typically be a mismatch in terms of timing and structure of cash flow, which to them represents a cost.

The problem has not been resolved by property laws that stipulate the right of mortgagors to prepay without penalty. Risks to investors from prepayments are typically addressed by structuring SPVs so that the risks of prepayments are shifted and allocated between bondholder classes by distinguishing between the holders of senior and subordinated bonds.[35] This nonetheless presumably increases the cost of capital, because investors in the riskier series of RMBSs are likely to demand compensation from the SPV for their higher risks. Establishment fees also represent a cost for borrowers. From the ADIs' perspective, credit providers are at risk in relation to their establishment fees or charges by virtue of section 72(1), which permits a court to annul or reduce an establishment charge if it is "unconscionable". Pursuant to section 72(3), in determining whether an establishment charge is "unconscionable", a court is to have regard to whether the amount of the charge "is equal to the credit pro-

[34] See, for example, *Master Information Memorandum, PUMA Fund—P 7*, paragraph 4.10; *Master Information Memorandum, PUMA Sub-Fund Series 2014*, p 33–34.

[35] In addition, investors' market risks from falling interest rates may be addressed in practice—albeit at a cost—by derivative contracts, such as swaps.

vider's reasonable costs of determining an application for credit and initial administrative costs for providing the credit or is equal to the credit provider's average reasonable costs of those things in respect of that class of contract". Plainly, this is useful for borrowers.

However, the restriction has a special impact in the context of RMBS programmes. It is quite commonplace in many programmes that an originator obtains a substantial part of its revenue for procuring the settlement of a mortgage through the payment of an establishment fee by the debtor/mortgagor. Section 72 in effect prohibits this and generally requires RMBS programmes to restructure the means by which originators are remunerated for introducing mortgages. The implication is that the RMBS programme must either account to the originator on an ongoing basis for a share of the interest accrued in respect of the credit provided or alternatively pay an upfront fee to the originator out of the programme's own funds and absorb that cost over time. Under both these techniques, the ultimate cost of the originator's remuneration is passed on to borrowers. Bearing in mind that the amount and nature of any establishment fee or charge must be fully disclosed in a pre-contractual statement as well as in the contract document itself (sections 16 and 17), so that the debtor will always be aware of the amount of the establishment fee before entering into the credit contract, it is questionable whether this impact of section 72 was unintended by Parliament.

Mitigation of Risks Under Sections 72 and 76

- *"Hardship Risk"*

Additional liquidity risk would be introduced to mortgage-backed securities programmes as a result of the application of section 72 of the Code, which deals with borrower hardship. The programmes may need to provide additional structural enhancements to mitigate the risk: that is, an additional amount of cash collateral will generally be needed to provide sufficient reserves to cover any temporary payment relief granted to borrowers, and the maturity date of the RMBSs will require extension beyond the maturity date of the underlying mortgages. In addition, the programmes must ensure whether the mortgage insurance will explicitly insure the lender against the risk introduced where the loan contracts are varied by either the credit provider or the courts. If the mortgage insurance policies do not cover these risks, the programmes will need to incorporate additional credit enhancement into the RMBS structure. Such enhancement can add a significant cost to the transaction and, depending on the circumstances, may make it uneconomic.

- *"Unjust Contract" Risk*

Under section 76 of the Code, the credit tribunal has the power to reopen unjust credit contracts, mortgages, and guarantees where unfair tactics have been employed in the origination of these credit contracts; the credit provider should have known that the borrower could not afford the loan; or where the terms of the contract could only be met with some financial hardship. Substantial delays may result in enforcing the credit contracts and security held; the risks and costs of mortgage defaults, the means by which rating agencies assess the default, compliance, and recovery risk/options have changed enormously[36]; and the process of evaluating, auditing, and compliance for RMBS programmes would be prohibitive in terms of logistics and cost.

As a result of the operation of this section, additional credit support may need to be included in RMBS programmes to mitigate the effects of credit risk for investors in RMBSs. Credit providers will also need to obtain professional indemnity insurance to cover the liability created by a breach of section 76.

Home Visits

Section 156 prohibits a credit provider from visiting a place of residence for the purpose of inducing a person to apply for or obtain credit, except at the unsolicited invitation of the person concerned. Any resulting credit contract is unenforceable against the debtor. The effect is that mortgage originators who do not have a branch network, or offer to visit potential customers at home as part of their general marketing campaign, will be prohibited from continuing to do so.

Implications

As can be seen, some of the provisions of the Code are likely to have a prejudicial effect on the residential mortgage securitisation industry as a whole. Industry representative bodies such as Mortgage Industry Association of

[36] See generally, Standard and Poor's, 'Uniform Consumer Credit Code—Implications for the Rating Process' *Structured Finance Australia and New Zealand* (Melbourne, 1998) 72–73.

Australia and the industry participants should voice their industry's concerns to the Ministerial Council of Consumer Affairs. The rating agencies have expressed concerns about the potential financial burden of penalties meted out pursuant to the Code for inadvertent violations.[37] The cost of additional enhancement by mortgage securitisers to offset these concerns would generally be passed on to consumers in terms of higher interest rates or charges.

8.4 Issuance of RMBSs by the SPV

After the mortgage originator transfers its mortgagee rights to the SPV, the trustee-issuer issues bonds to investors. Most bonds (RMBSs) issued under RMBS programmes fall within the *Corporations Act* definition of "debenture" and are bound by the trust deed requirements of the Act. Those bonds are paid from the loan repayments made by the borrowers on the mortgages, purchased by the SPV. The proceeds of the RMBS issue are used to pay for the pool of mortgages acquired by the SPV. The great majority of RMBSs are purchased by authorised deposit-taking institutions (ADIs), and insurance and superannuation funds seeking short-to-long-term debt investments. These investors are classified as sophisticated investors under the *Corporations Act*. Because of their greater experience and expertise, issuers of securities to sophisticated investors are not subject to the same onerous disclosure requirements under the *Corporations Act* as are issuers of securities to "public" individual investors. An information memorandum plays a role analogous to that of a prospectus in the "public" investor market, although it is true that the quality and number of the disclosures in information memoranda and other disclosure documents vary tremendously in practice.

8.4.1 Objectives and Criteria for Issuance of MBSs

In order for the issuance process to work effectively, it must be capable of:

- Transforming mortgage loans to tradable securities, and the transfer of risk: that is, the creation of a marketable security based on the cash flows of the originator's assets. To make as a marketable instrument, the RMBSs should be packaged as homogenous lots affordable to various investors.

[37] These penalties arise under general State Government regulations. See also, Standard and Poor's, *Structured Finance Australia and New Zealand* (Melbourne, 1999) 65.

- Providing an investment tailored to investor preferences: RMBSs are formally rated and structured with great flexibility to match the investment objectives of the investors looking for a safe high-grade investment. For example, the bonds are issued as senior and subordinate classes providing different rates of return to investors.[38]
- Ensuring accurate information is disclosed to investors so as to enable them to make an informed decision in relation to investment in RMBSs. The form and content of disclosure documents should be particularly focused on helping investors evaluate credit risk and prepayment risk.
- Increasing investor confidence in RMBS transactions.
- Avoiding any liability for breach of the disclosure requirements in relation to issues of debt securities under the *Corporations Act*.
- Achieving a high credit rating for the RMBS issue and reducing information costs for investors.
- Compliance with Australian Financial Services licensing requirements, where necessary, under the *Corporations Act*.

8.4.2 Regulation That Facilitate the Issuance of MBSs in the Market

The impact of the law and regulatory requirements on the making and issuance of RMBS in Australia is substantial. This is because most originating lenders, insurers of the loans, and investors in RMBS are regulated institutions. The main laws governing standards of these regulated institutions are the prudential standards and guidelines issued by the APRA, *Corporation Act* 2001 (Cth), and *Financial Services Reform Act* 2001 (Cth). The following section examines whether the corporation and financial services regulations facilitate or hinder the achievement of the above objectives in the issuance of RMBS.

As discussed in Chap. 6, the majority of securities issued by the residential mortgage securitisation programmes in Australia have been debentures or other forms of debt securities. Issuing debt instruments that are structured as "debentures" saves transactions costs.[39] It is true that the

[38] *Master Information Memorandum, PUMA Fund P-7* paragraphs 4–7; *Master Information Memorandum, PUMA Sub-Fund Series 2014*, pp 16–17.

[39] It has been said that "the essential legal problem in creating a capital market product is to devise a means by which the debt obligations arising from the initial borrowing can be transferred between the investors in a manner that, without increasing the risks to the investor,

SPV incurs the costs of complying with the reporting, record keeping, and other requirements pursuant to Ch. 2 L of the *Corporations Act*,[40] subject to a right of indemnity from the trust assets, and that these costs will be reflected in the pricing of the overall transaction. However, those costs are significantly less across all stakeholders in the issue than the regulatory compliance costs that would result if the underlying securities were subject to the Managed Investment Scheme provisions.

Excluded Offers

To date, RMBS issues have been "excluded offers" largely due to the economics of issuance to institutional (rather than retail) and professional investors,[41] and the inefficiencies for securitisation created by the corporations' legislation. An offer of RMBSs to the retail market would require compliance with disclosure obligations under the fundraising provisions in Ch. 6D, sections 700–741 of the *Corporations Act*. Under these provisions, a company is prohibited from making an offer of securities to retail investors, unless a disclosure document (e.g. a prospectus) for the offer has been lodged with the Australian Securities and Investment Commission: section 721(1). The compliance with the disclosure requirements in Ch. 6D of the *Corporations Act* for an RMBS issue involves an expensive, lengthy, and fairly inflexible process.

Some relief from these comprehensive disclosure requirements is offered by section 708, which sets out a number of situations in which disclosure to prospective investors is not required in respect of security offerings. Accordingly, most residential mortgage securitisation programmes in Australia employ structures that come within the ambit of one or more of these exemptions from the *Corporations Act's* disclosure requirements, which would have an impact upon reducing the cost of structuring the issue.

Investor acceptability is a key objective that needs to be ensured in the issue of RMBS and for the development of the RMBS market. Currently, the market has been limited to institutional and professional investors,

reduces as far as possible the costs to the issuer and the investor": Mallesons Stephen Jaques, *Australian Finance Law* (3rd edition, Melbourne: Longman Professional, 1994) 109.

[40] And licensing requirements, where relevant: see Regulation 7.6.01(1)(r) of the Corporations Regulations.

[41] The majority of securitisation programmes that are currently available by way of excluded offer are assigned the highest possible ratings by Standard and Poor's Ratings Group and Moody's Investors Service: M. Johnson, 'Australian Market Gets Bigger and Better' (April 2000) *Asiamoney* 1, 4.; A. Finch, 'Securitisation' (1995) 6 *Journal of Banking and Finance Law and Practice* 247.

although eventually, it may have to attract the participation of retail investors. In such an event, considering the novelty of the securitisation concept, it is imperative that investors are able to identify and comprehend the various risks associated with investing in RMBSs and make an informed investment decision. Investor acceptability would be driven by the extent to which such risks are disclosed and explained.

The aim of the fundraising provisions is to balance the needs for investor protection with the objective of maintaining an efficient and effective capital market. Accordingly, the disclosure requirements under the *Corporation Act* facilitate investor protection objective. It aims to ensure that a minimum amount of relevant, accurate information is disclosed to investors so as to enable them to make an informed decision whether or not to accept an offer of RMBS. With the prospects of securitisation developing greatly as a result of consumer demand, it is appropriate that the retail investor market be considered. Likewise, the availability of highly rated, fixed interest-type securities offered by securitisation provides additional investment opportunities for retail investors, smaller superannuation funds, and charities.

Licensing of Participants in the Mortgage Securitisation Industry

As noted in Chap. 6, the residential mortgage securitisation industry operates almost entirely in the wholesale market. Under the *Financial Services Reform* legislation, some participants in the wholesale financial services market need to obtain an Australian financial services licence, while others are not strictly required to, but do so for the sake of prudence. The Australian Securitisation Forum (ASF) and other industry participants[42] have suggested that the number of licences required for a single securitisation transaction be limited.[43] Because of the nature of securitisation transactions (as explained in Chap. 6), any licensing regime would have an ongoing and negative impact on the RMBS industry.

The ASF has noted that where the end product of a securitisation transaction, a bond (RMBS or unit in a trust), is sold to institutional investors

[42] Industry participants who have contributed to the submission include Macquarie Securitisation Ltd, ABN Amro Australia Ltd, Australian Mortgage Securities Ltd, Clayton Utz solicitors, RAMS Home Loans Pty Ltd, Perpetual Trustees Australia Ltd, Standard and Poor's Australia Pty Ltd, Moody's Investors Services Pty Ltd, and Trustee Corporations of Australia.

[43] Australian Securitisation Forum, *Submission to ASIC: Licensing Relief for Securitisation Structures*, 23 October 2003, http://www.asic.gov.au.

by a person who has a licence, there should be no need for each entity (e.g. SPV or fund manager) in a securitisation transaction to also hold a licence.

If the SPV is a corporate entity,[44] it does not require a licence as it acquires the mortgages, and acts on its own behalf. Therefore, the SPVs have the benefit of the self-dealing exemption in section 766C(3) of the *Financial Services Reform Act*[45] and issue bonds through licensed dealers.

If the SPV is the trustee of a trust, it is acting as a trustee and it is not acting on its own behalf and cannot obtain the benefit of the "self dealing" exemption in section 766C(3). The industry groups have suggested that an appropriate exemption be made available as the trustee is acting as principal and not agent. Similarly it will also need a licence to provide custodial or depository services. The custodial and depository services provided by the trustee are incidental to the primary purpose of the trust, which is segregation of mortgage assets, and therefore the ASF has argued that the trustee would not require a licence for providing this service.

ASIC's Proposals for Ongoing Licensing Relief for SPVs

In August 2004, on the basis of the industry groups' submissions, ASIC issued proposals to grant ongoing AFS licensing relief for SPV-issuers in securitisation programmes.[46] The proposed relief applied to those SPVs issuing securitisation products, derivatives, and providing custodial services, dealing in the underlying assets of the trust and the carrying on of business in relation to a particular securitisation transaction. According to ASIC, the basis for relief is that an SPV is created for the sole purpose of effecting a particular single securitisation. Further, the securitisation process is largely a predetermined one where the documentation provides for only very limited ongoing functions and discretions for the SPV. ASIC believes that in these circumstances, requiring SPVs to hold an AFS licence may impose an unreasonable burden.

The licensing relief does not apply to issuers that are not SPVs but carry on business only as trustee of a securitisation trusts. Neither do the proposed conditions of the relief affect services provided to retail clients.

[44] Corporate SPVs are off-balance sheet companies established to acquire assets and issue bonds to investors.

[45] See generally, Clayton Utz, *The Essential Guide to Financial Services Reform Act* (Sydney: CCH, 2002) paragraph 2–370.

[46] Australian Securities and Investment Commission, 'Licensing: Securitisation' *Consultation Paper*, August 2004, http://www.asic.gov.au.

Implications

It could be argued that the objective in securitisation is to release risk-based capital and/or achieve a lower cost of funds for the securitised asset. If all the participants in a securitisation programme are subject to licensing requirements, compliance with these requirements may increase its funding costs to an extent that renders it economically unsustainable.

Sophisticated investors such as insurance and superannuation funds do not need investor protection in the same way that, for example, average pensioners do, who do not really possess the bargaining power or the information or knowledge need that protection. One of the forms of protection provided for under the *Corporations Act* is licensing of the investment advisors and the people who sell these securities to the investing public or retail clients. Fundamentally, the law would take the view that sophisticated investors have sufficient bargaining power, and information or knowledge about the securities that they are buying and do not need protection. That means in the context of licensing of these suppliers of these securities, those sophisticated investors therefore do not need the suppliers who supply these securities to them to be licensed. In practice, the sponsoring banks and ADIS market these RMBS only to sophisticated investors and those sophisticated investors who by definition do not require the sponsoring banks and ADIs and SPVs to be licensed. This is reflected in the *Corporations Act*. There is an exclusion given for securities that are marketed to sophisticated investors under the assumption that these sophisticated investors have sufficient bargaining power, information, or knowledge about the securities sufficient to not warrant any investor protection.[47] However, on one argument, it might still be prudent for the industry to seek regulatory licensing relief on a commercial basis, and if they do not get it, to apply for the licences anyway, even though, strictly speaking, under corporations law, SPVs and ADIs do not need to obtain an Australian Financial Services Licence (AFSL).[48]

The current law however tends to treat all sophisticated investors equally. In other words, it assumes that provided that every sophisticated investor has at least as much information or bargaining power as the financial institutions who are selling the RMBS to it. It is possible that different investors might still be sophisticated as defined by the legislation but still have different degrees of knowledge or information or bargaining power about the securities as between themselves. Therefore, the question arises

[47] There is an exclusion given for securities that are marketed to sophisticated investors: see section 911A (2) of the *Corporations Act*.

[48] Refer to discussion in Chap. 6 regarding regulation of participants.

as to whether in fact the current regulation which seems to take "one shoe fits all" approach to sophisticated investors is appropriate. Should the regulation in fact make allowances for different sophisticated investors having different degrees of bargaining positions and knowledge about the product relative to the financial institutions supplying RMBS to them?

There are two main approaches to this problem. One is that there is a different regulatory solution for all sophisticated investors that is typically catered for in regulation by giving the regulatory decision maker some discretion as to what level of protection is appropriate to each particular sophisticated investor. The other main approach, which is costly, could be to define the sophistication of each investor with reference to some minimum level of knowledge or information about the product and the processes, and also some minimum level of bargaining power. Anybody above that minimum level would not need investor protection, although they might require different regulatory solutions. The extent to which this is a problem, and the formulation of appropriate solutions to it, would be a fruitful area for further research.

8.4.3 *Regulation That Impede the Issuance of MBSs in the Market*

Managed Investment Schemes

- *Compliance and Cost Issues*

If RMBSs were to be marketed to unsophisticated retail investors, they would be likely to be issued under the Managed Investment Schemes provisions of the *Corporations Act*. The current requirements of the Managed Investment Schemes, particularly those requiring a majority of its board of directors independent of any other participants in the securitisation programme, enhance investor protection. These structures are usually a unit with the trustee being an independent statutory trustee. An independent security trustee usually holds a charge over the assets of the trustee-issuer and may also be required to carry out certain custodial duties.

Every registered Managed Investment Scheme must have responsible entity, being the person who operates the scheme and performs the functions, which are conferred upon the scheme by its constitution and the *Corporations Act*. There would be additional costs, which these requirements would impose upon the responsible entity both in terms of implementation and ongoing compliance. A possible impact of these requirements is that residential mortgage securitisation programmes may be inhibited from offering securities to the public.

The current requirements of the Managed Investment Schemes dealing with the role of the independent custodian will impose onerous obligations on the custodian and, as a practical matter, have the effect that the custodian is a *de facto* trustee (but without the right of indemnification given to a trustee out of the trust fund). The role and the duties of the custodian will require careful review to ensure effective investor protection is achieved, which will affect the day-to-day operations of the RMBS programmes and the costs associated with them.

An Alternative Structure

The United States has regulated the securitisation industry separately from the managed fund industry. In 1992, the Securities and Exchange Commission of the United States adopted a new Rule 3a-7 under the *Investment Company Act* of 1940. It excluded issuers, pool income-producing assets, and securities backed by those assets from the definition of "investment company" subject to them complying with the following conditions[49]:

1. Securities issued are based on underlying cash flows of the structure.
2. The securities are rated, at the time of initial sale, in one of the four highest long-term debt categories (or equivalent short-term categories) with at least one internationally recognised rating agency. Any securities not meeting this test can only be sold to qualified institutional investors (Rule 144A of the *Securities Act* 1933).
3. The issuer is required to substantially hold all eligible assets to maturity and there are restrictions on the acquisition of additional assets (that is, the regulation contemplates a passively managed structure).
4. The appointment of an independent trustee to hold either a perfected security interest or an ownership interest in the assets that generates the cash flow, which is valid against third parties.

The Rule 3a-7 permits structured financings and securitisations to offer their securities publicly in the United States without registering under the

[49] CCH, Federal Securities Law Reports, *New SEC Rulings: Structured Financing Exclusion* (N.Y.: CCH, 1992) paragraph 85,062. B. Salter, 'Legal Changes Affecting the Structure of Securitisation Programs' *Discussion Paper*, Clayton Utz, 1993, 5.

Investment Company Act and complying with the Act's substantive requirements. The rule has removed unnecessary and unintended barriers to the use of structured financings in all sectors of the economy, including the small business sector. This approach could represent a suitable model for the Australian RMBS market.

Recommendation

It is suggested that the *Corporations Act* be amended to regulate the public offer of interests in RMBS programmes to unsophisticated retail investors. As residential mortgage securitisation develops, it will be necessary for RMBS issues to be made to a wider investor group rather than only the institutional wholesale market, which has funded programmes to date through "excluded issues" under the *Corporations Act*. This would also meet the demand of retail investors for a highly rated, fixed-interest type product in the absence of a major private corporate bond market in Australia, as well as the diminishing supply of government and semi-government fixed rate notes.[50]

It is also suggested that an alternative structure—similar to that in the United States—be considered to enable the issues by residential mortgage securitisation industry to be regulated separately from the managed funds industry. Consideration should be given to establishing a separate and distinct chapter or division of the *Corporations Act* to regulate the offering of interests in securitisation programmes. The securities issued, irrespective of whether they are structured by debt or equity, should comply with the above condition. It is suggested that the provisions of the mutual fund industry in the United States would provide a useful comparison for this purpose.

Disclosure Obligations

The most commonly stated rationales for disclosure under information memoranda are the protection of investors by alleviating information asymmetry and to make securities markets efficient—that is, to help market participants to determine prices for securities that accurately reflect all available information.[51] Thus, disclosure would contribute to

[50] R. O'Connor, 'The Australian Model' (May 2001) *Mortgage Banking* 56, 60.

[51] See generally, P. G. Mahoney, 'Mandatory Disclosure as a Solution to Agency Problem' (1995) 62 *The University of Chicago Law Review* 1047; F. H. Easterbrook, 'Mandatory Disclosure and the Protection of Investors' (1984) 70 *Vanderbilt Law Review* 669; E. W. Kitch, *Regulation of the Securities Market* (University of Virginia Law School, 1999), http://www.helsinki.fi/oik/tdk.html.

informational efficiency (and ultimately to social welfare) by enabling investors to gather information at a reduced cost.[52]

As discussed in Chap. 6, civil liability is imposed under sections 1041H of the *Corporations Act* and section 12DA of the ASIC Act, in relation to an information memorandum used in an RMBS issue. The issuers are obligated under section 728(1) to disclose all information, and a failure to do so could constitute misleading or deceptive conduct for the purpose of sections 1041H and 12DA. The test of whether an omission from an information memorandum constitutes a breach of section 1041H and 12DA(1) depends, therefore, upon whether an investor had a reasonable expectation that the omitted material would be disclosed.[53] Traditionally, a material fact has been defined as a fact that would assume actual significance to the holder of a security, that is, that would affect the decision to buy or sell the security.[54] Depending on the facts, there might be uncertainty about what the *Corporations Act* would require in the way of disclosure for RMBS representing an interest in a pool of loans to home loan borrowers. For example, would disclosures about individual borrowers be required if a large number of loans were securitised? Any requirement to make borrower specific disclosure could make the securitisation effort unpalatable to both lender and borrower. The problem would be aggravated if the pool of borrowers were able to change, because continuous updates could be needed.

Although the sections do not create an independent duty of disclosure, they have the practical outcome—setting a standard of disclosure in an information memorandum through the reasonable expectation test. If the standard is not met, then those responsible are exposed to potential liability for a breach of the sections.[55] It is therefore important for those involved in the preparation of an information memorandum to be able to

[52] M. Kahan, 'Securities Laws and the Social Costs of Inaccurate Stock Prices' (1992) 41 *Duke Law Journal* 977, 999.

[53] *Demagogue Pty Ltd v Ramensky* (1992) 39 FCR 31, 32; *Kimberley NZI Finance Ltd v Torero Pty Ltd* (1989) ATPR 46–054.

[54] R. Rosenberg and J. Kravitt, 'How Feasible is the Securitization of Loans to Small and Medium Sized Businesses?' (Fall 1993) *Commercial Lending Review* 4, 14.

[55] See, for example, ASIC Media Release, 'ASIC Acts to Ensure Fundraising Documents Provide Sufficient Information for Investors' 17 April 2003: ASIC placed an interim stop order on prospectus of Gold Bullion, due to concerns the prospectus contained potentially misleading or deceptive statements, and omitted material information. Gold Bullion is Melbourne-based, listed company that securitised gold through the issue of redeemable preference shares. This involved the offer of "Gold Bullion Securities", which enabled investors

assess precisely the type of information that a court would be likely to consider that should be disclosed in an issue of RMBSs.

Investors typically do not have access to all information relating to the mortgage-backed securities. An information memorandum, therefore, performs a function similar to that of a prospectus by providing investors with all the material information required to make an investment decision. Accordingly, the material that an investor would expect to be disclosed in an information memorandum is similar to the standard set out in section 710 of the *Corporations Act*, that is, all information that investors and their professional advisors would reasonably require to make an informed assessment of the RMBS issue.

There are shortcomings in relation to the application of section 12DA and 1041H to an information memorandum in an RMBS programme. These include the uncertainty posed by the "reasonable expectation" test, which sets the standard of disclosure in an information memorandum and the uncertainty regarding the class of persons liable under the sections. The liability under sections 12DA and 1041H is strict (subject to section 1041I (3)), rendering a sophisticated investor's claim on a defective information memorandum unable to be met by any defence. Whilst defences such as "due diligence" are applicable for registered prospectuses issued for average individual investors, those who prepare an information memorandum do not have the benefit of these. Effectively, therefore, sophisticated investors have greater rights of recovery than members of the public. These sections are essentially consumer remedies and lack the necessary balance between the interests of investors and those responsible for the preparation of an information memorandum. Issuers and investors may face competing or inconsistent incentives, which in contractarian theory are resolved by achieving an equilibrium or "balance" between the various competing interests.[56] The precise point of this balance or equilibrium position depends directly upon the bargaining power of the various competing stakeholders.

Section 733(1) of the *Corporations Act* provides a defence for issuers who prepare an information memorandum, in circumstances where they

to purchase an interest in physical gold bullion, and to buy and sell that interest through the ASX. The offer was not underwritten and had no minimum subscription.

[56] In entering into contracts, an agency problem arises between corporate managers and investors, and between lenders and borrowers, because of the conflicting interests of the parties: see generally F. H. Easterbrook and D. R. Fischel, 'Corporate Control Transactions' (1982) 91 *Yale Law Journal* 698, 700. See further discussion in Chap. 2.

reasonably relied on information given to them by others,[57] or if the document has become misleading or deceptive because of new circumstances of which they were unaware. When information memoranda are prepared, issuers obtain professional advice for information such as setting programme parameters; the terms and conditions of each bond issue; and the procedures, guidelines, and lending criteria for the residential housing loans that form part of the mortgage pool. Thus, the provision of a defence that the issuer would be able to rely on the expertise of external experts and professional advisers, protects issuers' with the right to sue those advisers if the advice turns out to be negligent, and would minimise the legal risks.

Lack of Separate Disclosure Standards for Issuance of Mortgage-Backed Securities

Currently, there are no disclosure items under the *Corporations Act* specifically tailored to RMBSs. Disclosure items in information memoranda issued in the RMBS programmes are based on the market-driven disclosures that appear in practice. Thus, through the industry practice, informal disclosure practices have developed. These practices may not be fully transparent to issuers and investors. The existing disclosure standards may not adequately capture certain categories of information that may be material to an RMBS transaction, such as the background, experience, performance, and roles of various transaction parties, including the sponsor, the servicing entity that administers or services the mortgage assets and the trustee.

It is suggested that the disclosure items relating to these entities need to be designed to elicit more useful information in these areas. In Australia, experiences such as First Australian National Mortgage Acceptance Corporation (FANMAC)—HomeFund have highlighted the need for improved disclosures as well as attention to servicing practices.[58] As

[57] For the "reasonable reliance" defence to succeed, the person relied upon must be someone other than a director, employee, or agent: section 733(1). It is not clear how this defence interacts with directors' general duty to act with skill, care, and diligence. For example, as was held in the decision in *Daniels v Anderson* (1995) 13 ACLC 614, a director is obliged to actively monitor delegated activities, and is under a duty to make further enquiries if he or she has suspicions concerning the adequacy of disclosure, or where a prudent person could be concerned about a matter.

[58] See discussion in Sect. 6.3.1 of Chap. 6. See generally, A. Boyd, 'Securitisation Market Shrank 14% Last Year' *Australian Financial Review* 24 February 1994, 30; B. Salter, 'Civil Liability for Errors and Omissions in Information Memoranda in Wholesale Debt Capital Markets' (2003) 14 *Journal of Banking and Finance Law Practice* 61–80.

discussed in Chap. 6, it would be appropriate to clarify the regulatory requirements for RMBS under the *Corporations Act*, in order to increase market efficiency and transparency and to provide more certainty for the overall RMBS market and its investors and other participants.

Some of the key information requirements that must be disclosed in the offer documents and provided under the corporations' regulation include the following:

- Terms of the residential mortgage loan[59]
- Property information[60]
- Borrower information[61]
- Terms of the offer of RMBS
- Description of the issuer (SPV) and originator
- Transaction structure
- Statement of risk factors relating to investing in RMBS
- Information related to other risks (asset risk, third-party credit enhancer risk, legal risk, and cash flow risk)
- Disclaimers of the trustee, originator, servicer, and SPV
- Continuing disclosure throughout the life of the issue

The US Securities and Exchange Commission (SEC) proposed new rules and forms to address disclosure and reporting requirements for asset-backed securities under the *Securities Act* of 1933 and the *Securities Exchange Act* of 1934. Principally, the SEC proposed to provide tailored disclosure guidance and filing requirements for asset-backed securities offerings under the *Securities Act* and *Securities Exchange Act*; and streamline and codify existing regulation relating to registered offering of asset-backed securities in addition to the statutory registration statement prospectus.[62]

[59] For example, coupon or interest rates on underlying loans, loan maturity dates and loan age, loan size, points paid at settlement.

[60] These include geographic distribution, property types, occupancy types, loan-to-valuation ratio.

[61] These include credit scores, loan documentation, loan purpose, borrower debt-to-equity ratios.

[62] Securities and Exchange Commission, '*Proposed Rule: Asset- Backed Securities*', Release No 33–849, June 2004, http://www.sec.gov.

In addition, the disclosure documents need to be prepared in response to the "plain English" initiative, in that even the most complex structures must be described clearly and accurately without resorting to overly legalistic presentations.

Many compliance issues may be mitigated and potential problems avoided through clearer and more transparent regulatory requirements. Establishing clear and transparent requirements would also reduce costs to entry into the market. This would lower the overall costs of complying with the securities laws under the *Corporations Act*.

Such proposals would improve investors' ability to make informed investment decisions about RMBS issues as well as help increase investor confidence in the servicing of RMBS transactions. This would be likely to promote investor confidence and market efficiency by decreasing information asymmetries between investors and originators, and promoting more efficient pricing and valuation of the securities. This would in turn lead to increased efficiency and competitiveness of the Australian capital markets. Increased market efficiency and investor confidence would also tend to encourage more efficient capital formation.

The proposal for a separate disclosure regime may have certain indirect negative effects. For example, enhancement of disclosure will increase transaction costs and have an impact upon the prices of the RMBSs. In addition, disclosures will increase transparency regarding a sponsor's or servicer's business practices. However, all such parties would be required to disclose such information equally, and the increased disclosures are designed to facilitate information to investors to improve their ability to make informed investment decisions.

8.5 Financial and Insolvency Risks

Broadly, the risks inherent in mortgage securitisation can be divided into insolvency and financial risks.[63] A number of investor risks are associated with securitised mortgages. Additionally, risks exist within the RMBS structure. RMBS issues are usually structured so as to attract a triple A rating. Technically this rating is assigned to the RMBS issue rather than to the issuer since the likelihood of default in an RMBS programme depends on the quality of the mortgage pool and related credit enhancements and not on the issuer's general creditworthiness. Triple A rating is the highest possible

[63] Within each of these broad groupings, there is a substantial overlap of risks.

rating and it is not given unless the rating agency is convinced as to the financial integrity of the issue. The structure of the mortgage securitisation must therefore be designed to ensure that the issuer will be in a position to pay its debts throughout the life of the issue and that its financial security will not be undermined by the insolvency of the originating bank or any other party to the transaction. Thus, the sponsor of a mortgage securitisation must be able to minimise and appropriately allocate these risks efficiently.

8.5.1 *Objectives and Criteria*

- Developing an insolvency risk-remote legal structure and managing the financial risks such as asset risks, credit risks, liquidity risk, prepayment risk, and interest rate risk are the two biggest challenges or objectives in structuring an RMBS issue.
- Protecting the financial security of issuers.
- Protecting the issuer's exposure to third-party insolvency. Third parties include originator/servicer, mortgage insurers, and junior or subordinate bondholders.

8.5.2 *Law and Regulation That Facilitate Growth in the Market*

Measures Used for Minimising Risks

As noted in Chap. 2, mortgage securitisation reduces the role of intermediaries and more efficiently allocates the risks inherent in the underlying mortgages with those willing to bear that risk, and thus, improves the efficiency of the overall financial system. The following measures are used in practice to minimise those risks.

The risk of issuer insolvency is minimised by making that entity a special purpose vehicle (trust), which is legally separated from the originating bank (ringfenced), has little or no other business, has strict borrowing limits, and has enough cash from the outset to meet fees, and other costs. An independent trustee company is appointed to act as trustee-issuer of securities. These measures are in fact provided under APRA's prudential regulations, which facilitate for the isolation of risks from the originating bank.[64]

[64] APRA, *Fund Management and Securitisation*—APS 120 (September 2000).

One of the major factors that contribute to the financial security of issuers and to the protection of investors is the quality of the mortgage pool and collateral security. In a typical case, this will comprise mortgages which have been selected as high-quality assets in respect of which perceived risk of default or delayed payments is low. The lending criteria that mortgages have to satisfy in order to be included in a typical securitisation were discussed in Chap. 3.[65] In the transfer of mortgagee rights to the SPV, the originator is usually required to give representations and warranties on various matters including satisfaction of the applicable lending criteria, the status of the mortgages as registered first legal mortgages and compliance with applicable registration requirements; the valuations, and the existence of accompanying insurance policies. The transfer of mortgages usually also specifies that, in the event any warranty proving to be incorrect, the originator is required to repurchase the mortgages in question.[66]

Various credit facilities are also usually made available to the issuer in order to ensure that it is able to meet its payment obligations fully and promptly. These include subordinated loans from the originator (or sometimes from a third party), the purpose of which is to meet initial costs and expenses and often to provide it with some initial capital. The sums advanced are fully subordinated, which means that the loan is not repaid until all principal and interest payments due on the bonds are paid in full.[67]

To reduce the insolvency and financial risks associated with the borrower/mortgagor, several credit enhancement techniques are used. The most common method of addressing credit risk in issues of RMBS is to obtain mortgage pool insurance. The obligations of the individual borrowers are the subject of insurance policies, which guarantee payment of principal and interest. One disadvantage of this form of credit enhancement is that if the paying ability of the insurer is downgraded, this can threaten the rating of the RMBS unless the risk is re-insured elsewhere.

The second means of addressing credit and liquidity risks is the creation of senior/subordinated tranches of RMBSs, wherein default and prepayment risks substantially lie. The senior bonds receive preferential sequential

[65] See also, Standard and Poor's, 'Mortgage-Backed Criteria' *Structured Finance—Australia and New Zealand* (Melbourne, 1998) 15–17.

[66] See, for example, *Master Information Memorandum, PUMA Fund P-7*, paragraph 5.2.

[67] Id, paragraph 7.2. See also, *Master Information Memorandum, PUMA Sub-Fund Series 2014*, pp 42–43.

payment of principal and interest, with payment on more junior or subordinated bonds dependent on complete payment of the senior bonds.[68] Although secured on the same mortgage pool, the subordinated bonds rank behind the senior bonds in point of security, and in the event of enforcement, no sums are paid in respect of the interest and principal due on the subordinated bonds unless the interest and principal due on the senior bonds are repaid in full. In the event of the issuer's insolvency, the subordination of the bonds in this way would be effective, since the secured lenders rank for payment in accordance with their positions on the priority ladder.

A third way of addressing credit and liquidity risks is over collateralisation.[69] This basically involves assigning with values exceeding the value of RMBSs issued to the mortgage pool. A "reserve" of assets is held to cover the risk of borrower insolvency and default. The "reserve" also creates a buffer against large unanticipated prepayments.

One of the measures used to mitigate the interest rate differential risk[70] is to adjust the rate of interest on the mortgages.[71] For an originator who wants to remain an active participant in the RMBS programmes, charging significantly higher interest rates than those prevailing generally is unlikely to be an attractive policy in view of the adverse impact it would be likely to have on its ability to attract new business. In addition to commercial constraints, there may also be legal restrictions, which preclude adjusting mortgage interest rates deal with interest rate risks. Legal restrictions may arise from the terms of the securitised mortgages. Even though RMBS are usually (but not invariably) backed by variable rate, rather than fixed rate mortgages, it does not necessarily mean that the interest rate can be varied entirely at the lender's discretion. Under the *National Credit Code*, the courts have the power to strike out mortgage terms, which they consider to be unconscionable and a mortgage may be re-opened under section 72 of the Code, if it constitutes an unfair or unjust credit bargain.

Interest rate risk can also be addressed by means of an interest rate swap structured so as to ensure that the issuer has funds available to it, which is sufficient to make the payments due on the bonds.[72] Structuring an interest rate swap facility allows investors to receive a market-based interest rate.

[68] *Master Information Memorandum, PUMA Fund P-7*, paragraph 4.5. See further discussion in Chap. 3.

[69] This has been already discussed in Chap. 3.

[70] That is the risk that the rate of interest being paid by borrowers will be insufficient to enable the issuer to make payments due on the RMBSs.

[71] See generally, *Master Information Memorandum, PUMA Fund P-7*, paragraph 5.7.

[72] Id, paragraph 9.4.

The terms of redemption of the bonds are also drafted so as to minimise the issuer's exposure to liquidity risk in respect of principal repayments. The provisions for compulsory redemption are usually included in the trust deed, which require the issuer to redeem bonds out of the proceeds of mortgage redemptions, or sale or enforcement proceeds that the issuer is able to obtain.[73]

8.5.3 *Law and Regulation That Impede Growth in the Market*

As discussed in Chap. 7 of the book, the effects of insolvency of the originator and issuer of the securitisation programme are crucial to an assessment of the risks for investors who acquire RMBSs.

Risks in Investment in RMBSs

Regardless of the form of the SPV (corporate or trust), the issuer poses potential risks of losses for investors if the originator of the loans becomes insolvent, if the borrowers under the loans become insolvent, or if the issuers become insolvent. Where the issuer is acting as the trustee of a trust, two possible insolvencies can occur—the insolvency of the trust and the insolvency of the trustee. If the trust is insolvent, one of the major problems that arise is whether the assets of the trust will be distributed in the manner intended by the securitisation transaction documents. If the trustee, but not the trust, is insolvent, it is important that the insolvency of the trustee has a minimal impact on the operation of the trust and payments under the RMBSs. It must be possible to replace the trustee-issuer and ensure that the assets of the trust are not available for the general creditors of the insolvent trustee-issuer.

In an RMBS programme, the bonds issued are debt obligations of the trustee-issuer only in its capacity as trustee of the trust. The bonds do not represent an obligation of the trustee-issuer in its individual capacity or any of the other parties to the securitisation transaction. The assets of the trust will be the sole source of payments on the RMBSs. However, if the trustee-issuer is negligent, commits a fraud, or fails to comply with an obligation imposed upon it under the trust deed, the trustee-issuer's assets will be used to make payments on the RMBSs. Therefore, if the assets of the trust are insufficient to pay the interest and principal on the bonds

[73] Id, paragraph 8.8.

when due, there will be no other source from which to receive these payments and investors may not recover their entire investment or achieve the yield they expect to receive.

There is a risk in RMBS programmes that the originator may become insolvent. Unless the assignment of the mortgages to the SPV is structured to be a true sale, and not a secured loan, the mortgages may be clawed back into the originator's assets. Such structuring is not difficult to achieve, but substance should be adopted to the extent possible over form.[74] The risk that underlying cash flows could suffer or be fragmented as a result of originator insolvency may be higher when equitable assignment only is used in transferring the mortgages to the SPV.[75] As mentioned previously, equitable assignment is used primarily when the originator remains to service the loan; the relationship between the borrowers is maintained by the façade of legal ownership. If the originator of the mortgages becomes insolvent, the originator's trustee in bankruptcy may claim the loans for the originator's creditors. Therefore, even if the mortgage loans are of the highest quality, if the originator's financial position is weak, investors in these RMBS are vulnerable.

The insolvency laws and the laws governing the foreclosure of collateral (mortgages) are somewhat diverse and cumbersome. When an entity enters into voluntary administration, be it the issuer, originator, or the borrowers, "a stay" is imposed on all the creditors' actions against the insolvent entity, including actions related to the collateral, except in limited circumstances.[76] A stay can cause delay in payments to creditors and prevent them from liquidating the collateral in their possession. If the originator fails, a stay may also adversely affect the mortgage pool and the bondholders. Usually, the originator continues to service the loans, receiving payments from the borrowers for transfer to the mortgage pool and sometimes the originator is obligated to transfer more mortgage assets to the pool. In these cases, the stay may prevent him from making transfers to the mortgage pool.

If the borrowers become insolvent or fail to make payments of interest and principal under the mortgage loans when due, and the credit enhancement is not enough to protect bondholders from the borrower's failure to pay, the bondholders would suffer losses.

[74] See e.g. *Re Lovegrove* [1935] Ch 464, 495 per Maugham LJ.

[75] Moody's Investor Service, *Structured Finance—Special Report* (Melbourne, February 1994) 2–3.

[76] Sections 440 and 441A of the *Corporations Act*.

A variety of legal, economic, and tax factors could affect the performance of borrowers in making payments under the mortgage loans. Under the *National Credit Code,* among other remedies, a court may order a mortgage loan to be varied on the grounds of hardship.[77] Any such variance would reduce the principal or interest payable under a particular mortgage loan. In particular, if interest rates increased significantly, borrowers could experience distress and default rates on the mortgage loans would increase.

Generally, the mortgage insurance policies are subject to exclusion clauses from coverage.[78] Therefore, borrowers' payments may then not be covered because of these exclusions. Moreover, mortgage insurance providers may be unable to perform obligations under the policy or the mortgage insurance policy may be held unenforceable under the *Insurance Contract Act* 1984 (Cth). If such circumstances arise, the bondholders may not receive full repayment of principal and interest on the bonds.

The trustee-issuer may, at a cost, enter into interest rate swaps to manage the mismatch between the variable rate of interest on the mortgage loans and the floating rate of interest payable on the RMBS. If the interest rate swap agreement is terminated or the swap provider fails to perform its obligations, the investors may be exposed to the risk that interest payable on the RMBS will be greater than the variable rate of interest charged on the mortgage loans, which may cause losses to investors.

Priority Rights and Enforcement of Security Trust Deed

If the security provided by a mortgage is enforced and the proceeds of the sale of a mortgaged property, net of liquidation expenses, are less than the amount due under the related mortgage loan, losses to bondholders could result, to the extent where the difference was not covered under a mortgage insurance policy.

Where the RMBSs are issued under a senior/subordinated structure, the holders of senior (Class A) bonds are entitled to principal and interest payments before the subordinate (Class B) bonds, following enforcement of the charge under the security trust deed. Consequently, Class B bondholders would not receive full repayment of principal or payment of interest on the Class B bonds. Prior to enforcement of the charge under the

[77] See discussion in Chap. 5.

[78] See, for example, *Master Information Memorandum, PUMA Fund P.7*, paragraph 6.1; *Master Information Memorandum, PUMA Sub-Fund Series 2014*, pp 80–81.

security trust deed, if an amount is outstanding under a redraw facility or liquidity facility, repayment of those outstanding amounts will be ranked ahead of the Class B bonds.[79]

If the security trustee were to enforce the security interest on the assets of the trust after an event of default under the security trust deed, there would be no assurance that the market value of the assets of the trust will be equal to or greater than the outstanding principal and interest due on the bonds, or whether the security trustee would be able to realise the full value of the assets of the trust.

According to the order of priorities under the security trust deed, the fees and expenses owed to the trustee-issuer, the security trustee, and the receiver would generally be paid from the proceeds of the sale of assets of the trust, prior to payment on the bonds. Consequently, the proceeds from the sale of the assets of the trust after an event of default under a security trust deed may be insufficient to pay the amounts due to bondholders.

In addition, the trustee-issuer would be subject to the penalties and compensation provisions of the *National Credit Code*. The trustee-issuer normally has a limited indemnity from the fund manager in respect of such liabilities.[80] If the trustee-issuer was unable to recover any such liabilities under the *National Credit Code* from the fund manager, the assets of the trust would normally be used to indemnify the trustee-issuer prior to payments to the bondholders. This could delay or decrease the amount of collections available to make payments to bondholders.

8.6 Conclusion

The RMBS market in Australia is unlikely to develop, let alone flourish, without a legal infrastructure that provides uniform, predictable, stable rules in relation to the institutional features of, and participants' conduct in, the market.[81] The process requires a legally binding assignment of mortgage assets to an insolvency-remote, special purpose vehicle, a developed securities market, and a regulatory system to support it, as well as regulated intermediaries that inspire investor confidence.

[79] Id, paragraph 6.2.

[80] Id, paragraph 5.8.

[81] *See* R. D. Cooter, 'Decentralised Law for a Complex Economy: The Structural Approach to Adjudicating the New Law Merchant' (1996) 144 *University of Pennsylvania Law Review* 1643, 1673; T. Frankel, 'The Legal Infrastructure of Markets: The Role of Contract and Property Law' (1993) 73 *Boston University Law Review* 389.

The results of the investigation reveal that certain aspects of the current law and regulatory practices facilitate the development of residential mortgage securitisation in Australia. These include:

- Rights and obligations of the originator and the borrower under relevant contract law and property legislation, which enhance the cash flow for payment to investors in the RMBS.
- That the Torrens system of land registration facilitates mortgage origination and clear transfer of mortgagee's rights from the originator to the SPV; and the law of property permits the right to assign mortgages to a third party in equity, at minimal cost to the assignor and assignee.
- That use of an SPV trust structure facilitates an off-balance sheet treatment of an originator's assets for accounting purposes.
- A "true sale" of assets allows an originator to recognise an accounting gain (or loss) derived from the assets. If structured as a true sale, the issuer is allowed, under the existing prudential regulation, to reduce its assets and its debts, thereby increasing its scope for borrowing.
- An equitable assignment of mortgages does not require registration, thus reducing the total costs of administration.
- The *National Credit Code*'s key requirements for disclosure, plain English documentation, and standardisation of credit contracts contribute to informational efficiency and reduce information costs for lenders, borrowers, and investors.
- Amendments under section 188 of the Code relieve the trustee from being personally liable for the civil and criminal consequences for breach of the Code. If the fund manager or mortgage originator were to commit a breach of the Code, the trustee would not be responsible for consequences under the Code.
- Variation of mortgage loan contracts on the grounds of hardship allows borrowers to change the method of repayment during financial hardships.
- Issuance of RMBSs structured as "debentures" saves transactions costs, relative to what the costs would be if the issue was via a Managed Investment Scheme.
- Issuance of RMBSs as "excluded offers" (i.e. issues that are exempted from the disclosure requirements under section 708 of the *Corporations Act*) provides for less costly issuance for issuers.

- Strict liability and the lack of a due diligence defence under sections 12DA and 1041H provide sophisticated investors with greater rights of recovery than retail clients.
- Use of an SPV transfers risk from the originating bank to an insolvency-remote vehicle.
- Subordinated debt facilities and credit enhancement techniques help to ensure that investors are repaid their bond principal and interest; that default and prepayment risks for investors are minimised, and that the creditworthiness of the SPV is enhanced; and that minimal credit risk to the Issuer would result in the event of a default by a home loan borrower.
- Priority rights in relation to the enforcement of investors' rights under the security trust deed help to ensure repayment to bondholders and third-party liquidity facility providers.

The results of the investigation also reveal a number of aspects of the law and regulatory provisions that act as impediments to the growth of the RMBS market in Australia. These include:

- The regulatory capital requirements and the risk-weighting criteria in relation to RMBSs which, under APRA's system of prudential regulation, effectively discourage ADIs from converting on-balance sheet assets to off-balance sheet assets, and risk-weighting RMBSs at 100%, rather than (for example) 50% in line with international proposals, keeps the amount of capital needed to maintain RMBSs at unnecessarily high levels. Furthermore, if this cost is passed on to investors by way of higher prices and lower yields, this discourages investment in the RMBSs issued, and is likely to increase interest rates and charges for borrowers.
- Inconsistent definitions of "true sale" by different courts do not assist in determining whether for legal purposes, a transaction should be given on-balance-sheet or off-balance-sheet treatment. The distinction is important because if the transfer is held not to be a true sale, the integrity of the entire RMBS programme is jeopardised.
- Under equitable assignments of mortgages, as they are presently organised in practice in Australia, the originator remains the lender of record, and hence, it runs the risk of being joined in any action relating to the mortgages.

- Lack of notice of the assignments to borrowers may create a moral hazard problem and have implications not only for economic efficiency, but perhaps for liability for unconscionable conduct under the trade practices legislation.
- Key requirements and the performance of statutory responsibilities under the *National Credit Code* may increase costs for securitisers (such as re-drafting of existing loan contracts).
- Failure by the "credit provider" to perform its responsibilities under section 188 of the Code can involve civil and criminal liability.
- Mortgage prepayments may create mismatches in terms of the timing and structure of cash flow for the investors, increasing the SPV's cost of capital, so that investors in subordinated bonds may demand additional compensation for such timing risks.
- Establishment fees charged marginally increase costs for borrowers.
- Compliance requirements under the Managed Investment Scheme provisions of the *Corporations Act* impose significant costs for the issuance of RMBSs.
- Where the originator or trustee-issuer files for administration or liquidation, a stay is imposed on all creditors' actions against the insolvent entity. If the assets of the trust are insufficient to pay the bonds as and when they fall due, investors may not recoup all of their investment.
- Insolvency on the part of the originator could cause delay in payment, or non-payment to creditors. Moreover, the originator's liquidator could potentially claw back any payments to the originator's creditors within six months of the date of his or her appointment, and attack any priority rights of the trustee-issuer to the SPV's mortgage asset pool.
- If the issuer were to become insolvent, bondholders could suffer losses if the credit enhancements were insufficient, or if the proceeds of any property sales were less than the outstanding amount of the loans.

Based on this assessment of the current law and regulatory practices in relation to RMBSs, a number of legislative changes are recommended as being for the public benefit, within the meaning of the *Statutory Instruments Act* 1992 (Qld) and the Commonwealth-State *Competition Principles Agreement* 1995:

- In general, from a commercial law—as opposed to an economic—perspective, the current regulation of RMBSs seems to be appropriate. However, as the market develops, it is likely that, at some point in the foreseeable future (the timing of which will depend on economic and political considerations), the regulation of the market may need to be amended to include:
  - New provisions, or possibly a separate regime, in the *Corporations Act* dealing with RMBS issues of securities of less than $500,000 sold to retail ("Mum and Dad") investors, as distinct from the higher value securities presently marketed to "sophisticated" institutional investors. The *Investment Company Act* 1940 (US) could serve as a useful model in this regard.[82]
  - New provisions protecting housing loan borrowers who are currently unaware that their residences could be sold by the trustee-issuer or SPV—exercising its rights as assignee mortgagee, not because of any default on the borrower's part, but because of default or loss on the part of the trustee-issuer, the SPV, the mortgage originator, the fund manager, or any other downstream provider in the supply chain. So that borrowers are fully informed about this risk when they enter into housing loan contracts, new legislative provisions should specifically require lenders to:

    (i) Bring the relevant clauses in the loan contracts, and their implications, to the notice of the borrower and make sure that they understand the implications.

    (ii) In the case of new mortgages, give the borrowers notice of any proposed assignments before the mortgage is completed and the opportunity to refuse to allow the transfer.

    In this way, borrowers can make an informed decision about whether they wish to incur the risk of losing their homes, accordingly being free to contract with the originating bank or go elsewhere. Some borrowers may be prepared to accept the risk of possibly losing their property in exchange for a significantly lower interest rate and/or bank charges;

[82] In the United States, RMBS issues are regulated separately from the managed funds industry. Consideration could be given in Australia to establishing a separate division of the *Corporations Act* to regulate any future offering of RMBS issues to the public (as distinct from institutional investors).

others will not be prepared to bear such risks and in consequence will pay a higher interest rate and/or bank charges.[83]

Alternatively, section 18 of the *Competition and Consumer Act* 2010 (Cth) could be amended to explicitly provide that "silence may be a misrepresentation".[84] The courts would have discretion as to whether the bank's silence in particular circumstances would amount to misrepresentation (Such an amendment could also be mirrored in the *National Credit Codes*—for example, in return for a greater share of GST revenue from the Commonwealth).

(iii) In the case of existing mortgages, by individual approach to the mortgagors concerned, give each borrower a reasonable opportunity to refuse to give their consent to the transfers and, if necessary, unwind any transfers that have already been made.[85]

In the latter two cases—(ii) and (iii), the legislation could, for the sake of economic efficiency as well as fairness, allow mortgage originators to charge a premium in relation to those housing loans in which the borrowers have refused to consent to the assignment. *However, any premium could be subject to prices oversight by the regulatory authorities* (e.g. *Australian Competition and Consumer Commission, or APRA).*

Legislative amendments regarding information disclosure to borrowers of the assignment of mortgages should be drafted in such a way that they are consistent with economic efficiency. For example, if the originators and issuers of RMBSs have information (e.g. concerning the sale of mortgages to the SPV)

[83] As noted earlier, the point of this book is not that RMBS programmes are bad as such; merely that borrowers should be given the ability to make an informed decision about whether they wish to incur the risks inherent in such a scheme. Any legislation should simply ensure that borrowers are given the freedom to contract on an *informed* basis. This need not imply that borrowers ought to be deluged with information overload about RMBS issues; it merely implies that they should be made aware of the potential risks—for example, of losing their homes through no fault of their own, in exchange for a significantly lower interest rate or lower fees.

[84] Pursuant to such an amendment, the banks could perhaps even bear the onus to provide sufficient relevant information to prospective borrowers, or risk being held liable for damages from misrepresentation.

[85] The point is not that banks and IMPs should be precluded from involvement in RMBS programmes. The point is that there is an appreciable risk to borrowers if they do, and borrowers (not banks or IMPs) should be the ones who decide whether borrowers are prepared to bear that risk. At present, it would appear that most borrowers in practice are not even aware that the risk exists.

not available to borrowers, the pricing of mortgages as well as those of the securities being issued out of these would not necessarily reflect this risk. If so, the whole securitisation process could be characterised by mis-pricing and (other things being equal) whenever mis-pricing arises, resources become inefficiently allocated. In addition, neglecting or intentionally failing to notify borrowers of a risk that their houses could be sold through no fault of their own would seem at the least to be unconscionable and potentially in breach of consumer credit and trade practices legislation.

It might even be economically efficient to require under legislation that any assignment of mortgagee rights be notified on the title deeds to the particular properties. This might be an appropriate way of ensuring information disclosure in a way that provides a net public benefit.

Such regulatory amendments regarding information disclosure would improve borrowers' ability to make informed decisions about purchasing properties, as well as help to increase borrower confidence in housing loan contracts. Other things being equal, this would be likely to promote market efficiency by decreasing information asymmetries between borrowers and originators, as well as promote more efficient pricing of home mortgage loans, and lead to increased efficiency and competitiveness in the Australian housing loan market.

– Improved, timely disclosure requirements, perhaps on a pool (aggregate) basis.[86] Plainly this would need to be subject to a rigorous public benefit test under the *Statutory Instruments Act* 1992 (Qld) and the Commonwealth-State *Competition Principles Agreement*. Nevertheless, improved information disclosure could assist fund managers to assess the prepayment risk of RMBSs, and

[86] A recent study undertaken by the US Securities and Exchange Commission has identified several items for enhanced disclosure in the mortgage-backed securities market. These include the purpose of the loan (e.g. whether it is a purchase or refinance); the original loan-to-value (LTV) ratio; any standardised credit scores of borrowers; the details of servicers for the pool (this need not always be the originator); the occupancy status of the security property (e.g. owner-occupied or rented); the property type (e.g. stand-alone house, detached dwelling, or apartment). For more detail, see Securities and Exchange Commission (US), *Staff Report of the Task Force on Mortgage-Backed Securities Disclosure*, January 2003, http://www.sec.gov.

investors with their investment decisions; improve efficiency, pricing, and market confidence; and (arguably) lower risk.[87]

- In the light of the recent Basel II proposals, the Commonwealth Government should instigate an investigation by APRA, perhaps in conjunction with the Reserve Bank of Australia, into whether the current risk-weighting of RMBSs for capital adequacy purposes should be reduced from 100% to some lower figure.
- Finally, that a panel of independent experts on RMBSs be established (after the manner of the Monopolies and Mergers Commission Panel in the United Kingdom), so that the industry regulators such as APRA and ASIC have access to expert advice in relation to complex matters involving RMBSs.

In order to facilitate the growth in the RMBS market in Australia to the point where it is demonstrably for the public benefit, there needs to be an appropriate regulatory balance between the interest of investors and the liability of the participants in the securitisation industry. If an appropriate balance is not struck, the development of the RMBS market may be impeded, by either jeopardising the integrity of the market as a source of funds, or by making it too costly and burdensome for Australian banks and other financial institutions to source their debt funds from the RMBS market.

Bibliography

Books and Book Chapters

Clayton Utz, *The Essential Guide to Financial Services Reform Act*, Sydney: CCH, 2002.

Mallesons Stephen Jaques, *Australian Finance Law*, 3rd edition, Melbourne: Longman Professional, 1994.

Park, E. J., 'Allowing Japanese Banks to Engage in Securitization: Potential Benefits, Regulatory Obstacles, and Theories for Reform' (1996) 17 *University of Pennsylvania Journal of International Economic Law* 723.

Wheeler, C., 'The Accounting Aspects of Securitisation in the United Kingdom' in C. A. Stone, A. Zissu, and J. Lederman, (eds.), *Asset Securitisation Theory and Practice in Europe*, London: Euromoney Publications, 1991.

[87] To remove any doubt, it would also be useful if the *National Credit Codes* were amended to clarify whether the originator or the SPV is the "nominated credit provider" for the RMBS issue, with all of the attendant legal risks and responsibilities, which that designation confers.

Journal Articles

Boyd, A., 'Securitisation Market Shrank 14% Last Year', *Australian Financial Review*, 24 February 1994, 30.

Cooter, R. D., 'Decentralized Law for a Complex Economy: The Structural Approach to Adjudicating the New Law Merchant', (1996) 144 (5) *University of Pennsylvania Law Review* 1643.

Easterbrook, F. H. and Fischel, D. R., 'Corporate Control Transactions' (1982) 91 *Yale Law Journal* 698.

Falconer, I., 'Securitisation in the United Kingdom' (1989) *Butterworth Journal of International Banking and Finance Law* 105.

[illegible], A., 'Securitisation' (1995) 6 (4) *Journal of Banking and Finance Law and Practice* 247.

Frankel, T., 'The Legal Infrastructure of Markets: The Role of Contract and Property Law' (1993) 73 *Boston University Law Review* 389.

Jackson, P., 'Bank Capital Standards: The New Basel Accord' (2001) *Bank of England Quarterly Bulletin* 55.

Johnson, M., 'Australian Market Gets Bigger and Better' (April 2000) *Asiamoney* 1.

Kahan, M., 'Securities Laws and the Social Costs of Inaccurate Stock Prices' (1992) 41 *Duke Law Journal* 977.

Mahoney, P. G., 'Mandatory Disclosure as a Solution to the Agency Problem' (1995) 62 *The University of Chicago Law Review* 1047.

Pollsen, R., Hu, J. and Elengical, J., 'A Record Year for Residential MBS' (April 2002) *Mortgage Banking* (Washington) 36.

Rosenberg, R. and Kravitt, J., 'How Feasible is the Securitization of Loans to Small and Medium Sized Businesses?' (Fall 1993) *Commercial Lending Review* 4.

Salter, B., 'Civil Liability for Errors and Omissions in Information Memoranda in Wholesale Debt Capital Markets' (2003) 14 *Journal of Banking and Finance Law and Practice* 61.

Salter, B., 'Privacy Legislation Update' (1993) 4 (2) *Journal of Banking and Finance Law and Practice* 113.

Senarath, S., 'Securitisation and the global financial crisis: can risk retention prevent another crisis?' (2017) 18 *International Journal of Business and Globalisation* 153.

Working Papers, Magazines, Newspapers and Reports

Australian Securities and Investment Commission, *Licensing: Securitisation*, Consultation Paper, August 2004, http://www.asic.gov.au

Australian Securitisation Forum, *Submission to APRA Regarding Risk Weighting of Mortgage-Backed Securities*, 24 July 2002, http://www.securitisation.com.au/asf

Australian Securitisation Forum, *Submission to the ASIC: Licensing Relief for Securitisation Structures*, 23 October 2003, http://www.securitisation.com.au/asf

Australian Securitisation Forum, *Submission to the Australian Prudential Regulation Authority in Response to APS 120 – Fund Management and Securitisation*, 14 June 2000, http://www.securitisation.com.au/asf

CCH, *Federal Securities Law Reports, New SEC Rulings: Structured Financing Exclusion*, N.Y.: CCH, 1992.

Gunning, G., 'Basel II: A Capital Idea but Still Hurdles to Jump', *Standard and Poor's Inaugural Financial Market Conference*, Sydney, October 2002.

Kitch, E. W., 'Regulation of the Securities Market', University of Virginia Law School, 1999, http://www.helsinki.fi/oik/tdk.html

Macquarie Securitisation Ltd, *The PUMA Fund P-7: Master Information Memorandum*, Sydney, February 2000.

Macquarie Securitisation Ltd, *Master Information Memorandum, PUMA Sub-Fund Series 2014*, Sydney, July 2014.

Minton, B., Opler, T. and Stanton, S., *Asset Securitization Among Industrial Firms*, Working Paper, Fisher College of Business, Ohio State University, Columbus Ohio, November 1997.

Moody's Investor Service, *Structured Finance – Special Report* (Melbourne, February 1994).

Plater, I., 'Accounting and Tax for Off-Balance Sheet Financing', *IIR Conference*, Sydney, September 1992.

Securities and Exchange Commission (U.S.), *Proposed Rule: Asset- Backed Securities; Release No 33–849*, June 2004, http://www.sec.gov

Securities and Exchange Commission (U.S.), *Staff Report of the Task Force on Mortgage-Backed Securities Disclosure*, January 2003, http://www.sec.gov

Senarath, S. 'The Dodd-Frank Act doesn't solve the principal-agent problem in asset securitisation' (2017) *blogs.lse.ac.uk* (11 November 2018) http://blogs.lse.ac.uk/businessreview/2017/04/21/the-dodd-frank-act-doesnt-solve-the-principal-agent-problem-in-asset-securitisation/

Senarath, S., Not so "Bankruptcy-Remote': An insight into Sri Lankan Securitization Practices in a Post_GFC Context' (Paper presented at the MAC-MME conference 2016, Prague, Czech Republic).

Standard and Poor's, 'Credit Ratings on Mortgage-Backed Securities', *Structured Finance Australia and New Zealand*, Melbourne, 1998.

Standard and Poor's, 'Mortgage-Backed Criteria', *Structured Finance Australia and New Zealand*, Melbourne, 1999.

Standard and Poor's, 'Uniform Consumer Credit Code – Implications for the Rating Process', *Structured Finance Australia and New Zealand*, Melbourne, 1998.

Trustee Corporations Association of Australia, *Submission to the Financial System Inquiry*, (Wallis Committee) December 1996.

Web Sites

BIS Home Page, http://www.bis.org
APRA Home Page, http://www.apra.gov.au
ASIC Home Page, http://www.asic.gov.au
AASB Home Page, http://www.aasb.com.au

CHAPTER 9

Summary of Conclusions

9.1 Introduction

The aim of the book is to identify the features of the existing law and regulation, which facilitate and hinder the development of the market for residential mortgage-backed security (RMBS) in Australia and to suggest some key areas in which the current law and regulation relating to RMBS in Australia could be reformed. In order to achieve these aims, an assessment of the current law and regulation relating to various stages of an RMBS process was undertaken in Chaps. 4, 5, 6, and 7 based on a contractarian framework, which was discussed in Chap. 2. From the results of these analyses, Chap. 8 examined the aspects of law and regulation that facilitate and impede the growth of the RMBS programme using the "public benefit test" framework, which was also discussed in Chap. 2. Based on the results of this examination, the book now, in this chapter, provides a number of specific recommendations for the reform of relevant legislation and current practice relating to RMBS issues, and offers a range of areas for future research in law and economics. As a starting point, an account of the summary of the findings and main conclusions of the book is provided.

P. Rajapakse, S. Senarath, *Commercial Law Aspects of Residential Mortgage Securitisation in Australia*,
https://doi.org/10.1007/978-3-030-00605-1_9

9.2 Summary and Main Conclusions

From a commercial point of view, the securitisation process can be characterised as a series of contracts or agreements, which are motivated by each participant's desire for financial gain or profit.[1] Contractarian theory, which encompasses the agency theory often cited in the accounting and financial economic literatures, provides a framework within which to analyse the incentives of the various stakeholders at each stage of, or contract in, the overall securitisation process. In terms of economic efficiency, this contracting process will be privately and socially optimal, provided there are no external or public goods effects. Of these, there is at least the potential for external effects, the chief externality being driven by moral hazard. In this context, moral hazard would relate to the potential for banks or independent mortgage providers (IMPs) approving loans too easily, in the belief that they can transfer the risk (including the risk of liability for breach of contract)[2] to other legal entities.

This potential for moral hazard is compounded by information asymmetry. In a theoretical world of perfect information, any information asymmetry between stakeholders would, other things being equal, be reflected in the contract prices at each stage of the process. However, in practice, most borrowers are currently unaware that their residences could be sold by downstream financial intermediaries who have "purchased" the bank's (or IMP's) mortgagee rights, not because of any default on the borrower's part, but because of default, loss, or insolvency on the part of the financial intermediary, or others in the supply chain.

Once some borrowers become aware of this risk and communicate it to others (thereby narrowing the information asymmetry between borrowers and lenders), there is the potential for a significant public goods effect. Specifically, no stakeholder can claim the property rights to this information, which is—or becomes—a public good.

It is an economic question whether these risks are efficiently priced into all contracts included in the securitisation process, and in any case, such an investigation is plainly beyond the scope of a legal book and best left to others with economic expertise. However, if they are not, the result could

[1] In a broad sense, this even applies to the borrowers, who anticipate that ultimately the value of the property they have borrowed to purchase increases sufficiently to more than compensate them for their investment outlay and net borrowing costs.

[2] As noted earlier, this would not necessarily relieve the bank or IMP of any liability in tort. However, for the reasons outlined earlier, a detailed discussion of the bank's or IMP's liability in tort is beyond the scope of the book.

be an external cost which ultimately impacts on the community (or at least that part of the community that borrows housing loans to finance the purchase of residences).[3]

It is impossible to predict, with any precision, the nature or timing of any new regulatory framework for RMBSs. Nevertheless, some useful comment can still be made concerning a legal assessment of the current regulation, and the general form that any new regulation is likely to take.

9.2.1 Current Regulation

The crucial management-strategic issues (as distinct from the more basic regulatory compliance issues) concerning the commercial aspects of RMBS regulation centre on key provisions of the *Corporations Act* and the *National Credit Code*; whether there has been a "true sale" of the mortgagee's rights to the special purpose vehicle (SPV) in assignments; and the appropriate risk-weighting of RMBSs for capital adequacy purposes.

Although RMBS issues can in theory be based on debt and equity instruments, the only equity issue in Australia to date has been the First Australian National Mortgage Acceptance Corporation (FANMAC) issue in the late 1980s, which the NSW government used to fund a highly publicised social housing scheme with fixed rate mortgages for low-income borrowers, known as the "HomeFund" scheme.[4] This issue ultimately failed because of a lack of servicing capacity on the part of borrowers under the scheme, and the NSW government was forced to step in to compensate both borrowers and investors.[5]

Perhaps in part because of the failure of the HomeFund issue, as well as the fact that institutional investors have historically preferred debt instruments whose market yields can be readily compared with those of semi-government note stock for portfolio management purposes,[6] all RMBS issues since the late 1980s in Australia have been confined to debt instruments.

[3] From a social perspective, an interesting research question would be how the courts or the legislature will (or should) allocate these risks or, rather, the liability that flows from them. It is possible that the industry needs to be re-regulated, at some future stage of its development, in order to achieve economically efficient and "just" outcomes across all stakeholders and the community.

[4] A. Finch, 'Securitisation' (1995) *Journal of Banking and Finance Law and Practice* 247, 258.

[5] See, for example, see R. Bruce, B. McKern, I. Pollard and M. Skully, *Handbook of Australian Corporate Finance* (5th edition, Sydney: Butterworths, 1997) 257.

[6] See Standard and Poor's, *Structured Finance in Australia and New Zealand* (Melbourne, 1999) 5.

Under the current *Corporations Act*, the debt securities underlying RMBS issues are characterised as "debentures", pursuant to sections 9 and 92 of the Act. Debt instruments that cannot be characterised as "debentures" under the Act automatically fall within the ambit of the Managed Investment Scheme ("MIS") provisions of the Act.

Issuing debt instruments that are structured so as to fall within the statutory definition of "debentures" saves transactions costs for issuers. It is true that the SPV incurs the costs of complying with the reporting, record keeping, and other requirements pursuant to Ch. 2 L of the *Corporations Act*,[7] subject to a right of indemnity from the trust assets, and these costs will be reflected in the pricing of the overall transaction. However, those costs are significantly less, across all stakeholders in the issue, than the regulatory compliance costs that would result if the underlying securities were subject to the MIS provisions.

Furthermore, the underlying debt securities in virtually all RMBS issues in practice are generally exempt from the disclosure requirements in Ch. 6D.2 of the *Corporations Act* because they are sold only to institutional and other "sophisticated" investors under section 708(8) of the Act. This also saves transactions costs across all stakeholders in the issue.

Some of the Information Memoranda used to promote the sale of such RMBSs in practice run a real risk of being perceived to be "financial product advices" under Ch. 7—and specifically, section 766A—of the Act. There may sometimes be a "fine line" in practice between mere puffery[8] and running foul of the "misleading or deceptive conduct" provisions in sections 1041E, 1041H, and 769C of the Act.

From a private or self-interest perspective, the incentives to structure the issue as "debentures" under the *Corporations Act* are understandable, because they ultimately result in lower transactions costs across all participants in the issue. However, this begs the question of whether, because of the current wording of the *Corporations Act*, some RMBS issues that are currently structured as "debentures" to minimise regulatory compliance costs should, from a public interest perspective, be subject to more or different regulation in order to protect investors and creditors. In general, it would be surprising if the current legislation were found to be inadequate, given the current state of the market (including the absence of financial distress and corporate failure in the market).

[7] And licensing requirements, where relevant: see Regulations 7.6.01(1)(r) of the *Corporations Regulations*.

[8] See, for example, *Carlill v Carbolic Smokeball Co* [1893] 1 QB 256; and *Lambert v Lewis* [1982] AC 225.

Growth of RMBSs and Macroeconomic Implications on the Market
RMBSs have increased substantially in recent years as a popular source of credit, drawing more attention of the Reserve Bank of Australia (RBA) on consequences of these developments on monetary policy. More importantly, the expansion in RMBS market occurred through expansion in the volume of financing by asset-backed securities which are entirely of non-conforming loans or low-documentation loans. This is a concern to the RBA as it could create an increased risk of having too much easy finance being available, leading to inflation and asset bubbles. Thus, there is need to keep a close eye on the development of the RMBS market in order to avoid additional pressure on inflation and interest rates that can arise from it.

9.2.2 Towards a New Regulatory Framework?

Nevertheless, even if a different regulatory regime were not necessary in the current market, it may become necessary in the future. For example, as the market develops in terms of demand, and the volume and value of transactions, financiers may find it profitable to market RMBS issues comprising securities of less than $500,000 sold to retail ("Mum and Dad") investors, as distinct from the higher value securities presently marketed to "sophisticated" institutional investors.[9]

If or when the market develops to this extent, it may become useful to include a separate regime for mortgage-based securities, including RMBSs in the *Corporations Act*, which is distinct from the regimes for debentures and MISs. Such a regime, based on the US model, would be an appropriate method for the Australian RMBS programmes.[10] Alternatively, the existing fundraising and disclosure provisions of the *Corporations Act* could be amended to include new provisions regulating the issue of RMBSs.

It may also be useful for industry regulators such as ASIC and Australian Prudential Regulation Authority (APRA) to have access to a formalised

[9] There may even be scope for increased government involvement in the industry. For example, in the United States, the mortgage-backed securities markets consist primarily of securities issued or guaranteed by two government-sponsored agencies, Fannie Mae and Freddie Mac, and one US-owned corporation, Ginnie Mae. Mortgage-backed securities are also issued by private institutional issuers. The government-sponsored entities and Ginnie Mae guarantee timely payments on their respective bonds. Any proposal for increased government involvement in the industry in Australia would need to be scrutinised carefully, however, particularly in the light of the Home Fund scandal discussed earlier.

[10] See further discussion in Sect. 8.4.3 of Chap. 8.

revolving panel of recognised, independent experts on RMBSs, on which the regulator (or ultimately the Minister) could draw for advice and expertise in relation to complex matters involving the RMBS industry. While an examination of this nature is plainly beyond the scope of a legal book, it provides an interesting and useful area for future (economic or economic-analysis-of law) research.

As part of the structure of an RMBS programme, the mortgage originator's (e.g. lender's) rights are assigned, or sold at a price, to the SPV. This means that, assuming the assignment is comprehensive and effective, the lender is able to "wash its hands" of any liability as a credit provider to the initial housing loan borrowers under the *National Credit Code*, leaving all liability with the downstream SPV. Not surprisingly, in light of their experience with litigation, as with the foreign currency lawsuits of the early 1990s,[11] the major bank lenders in particular therefore face an incentive, other things being equal, to securitise their home loans using RMBS programmes in this way.

A crucial strategic issue for management in RMBS programmes is whether there has been a "true sale" of the mortgagee's rights to the SPV. As the relevant regulator, one of APRA's key concerns in relation to securitisation programmes is whether sufficient risk and reward have been transferred from the originating bank to the SPV in order to justify a finding that a true sale of the mortgagee's rights has occurred. It will not be if, for example, the originating bank retains influence over the setting of interest rates, the way in which delinquent assets are followed up, or the right to share in any profits of the SPV; or if investors in the RMBSs have any recourse back to the originating bank.

If a "true sale" has not been effected, the mortgaged loans unsuccessfully assigned will lose their off-balance sheet status, and will be re-characterised as normal on-balance sheet secured loans. This plainly has significant consequences for, amongst other things, the ADIs' capital adequacy and taxation obligations. APRA's task as the regulator is made more difficult by the fact that there is no Australian case on point, and the few cases that have been decided overseas are inconsistent.

[11] See, for example, *Clenae Pty Ltd and Ors v ANZ Banking Group Ltd* [1999] VSCA 35 (9 April 1999); *David Securities Ltd and Ors v Commonwealth Bank and Ors*, (unreported, Full Federal Court, 10 May 1990) per Lockhart, Beaumont and Gummow JJ; the same case at first instance in the Federal Court of Australia per Hill J, 11 May 1989; *Chiarabaglio v Westpac Banking Corporation* (1989) ATPR 40–971; and *Leitch and Ors v Natwest Australia Bank Ltd and Anor*, (unreported, 12 October 1995, Federal Court of Australia) per Cooper J.

From a public interest perspective, there may also be a moral hazard problem[12] inherent in RMBS programmes, in that ADIs may have an incentive to lend housing loans to their customers too easily, if they know they can assign their rights and responsibilities under the loans to an SPV and believe that, as a result, they will not be held responsible if downstream participants in the issue default or become insolvent. One useful avenue for future research would be an investigation of the extent of this problem in a social and political context and, if it needs to be rectified, the best means of doing so. If a significant moral hazard problem exists, it may be useful for government to legislate to compel ADIs to accept their "fair share" of responsibility (e.g. in tortious actions) for failures of their RMBS programmes. In this context, increasing tort liability means making the banks more accountable for the risks they incur, which may adversely affect many of their customers. In truth, however, the bank's tortious liability is not being increased at all; it is simply not being recognised because of the complexity of the transactions involving RMBS programmes. As discussed in Chap. 6 earlier, if bank officers and independent lawyers better understood the nature of RMBS programmes, it is entirely possible that some of the banks at least, could be sued in tort for deceit (or something similar). In short, the problem is one of information asymmetry, a breach of the *Competition and Consumer Act*, not expanded liability in tort.

For capital adequacy purposes, normal residential mortgage loans are risk-weighted at 50%. If they have been securitised and APRA has granted regulatory capital relief, then the RMBSs themselves are effectively risk-weighted at zero (i.e. the bank or regulated financial institution need hold no capital against them for capital adequacy purposes). However, if APRA has withheld regulatory capital relief, the RMBSs themselves are weighted at 100% for capital adequacy purposes. The extent of this disparity in the risk-weightings may be seen as somewhat surprising, particularly in the light of the recent Basel III proposals, as well as the fact that investors in RMBSs have the protection of mortgage insurance in addition to that of the residential mortgages themselves, and the fact that, in similar circumstances, regulators overseas weight RMBSs at around 50%. Moreover, the disparity would seem to create commercial incentives, purely because of the current regulation, for Australian Deposit-taking Institutions (ADIs) to use their residential mortgage loans to issue RMBSs, and for some institutions not to invest in the RMBSs issued.

[12] See, for example, *Locker and Woolf Ltd v Western Australian Insurance Co Ltd* [1936] 1 KB 408; and *Jester-Barnes v Licenses and General Insurance Co Ltd* (1939) 49 Ll L Rep 231.

It is suggested that, even if the Australian authorities do not weight RMBSs at 50% in line with the underlying residential mortgage loans, they would do well to at least consider reducing the risk-weighting for RMBSs. A detailed and precise estimation of the appropriate weighting for RMBSs is a statistical exercise and well beyond the scope of a legal book—however, such an examination would plainly be a useful avenue for future (economic or finance) research.

9.3 Recommendations

The findings of the book give rise to several policy recommendations. A number of legislative changes are recommended to help narrow the information asymmetry between borrowers and securitisers, and minimise potential moral hazard problems in Australian RMBS programmes. The main recommendations of the book are:

- In general, from a commercial law—as opposed to an economic—perspective, the current regulation of RMBSs seems to be appropriate. However, as the market develops, it is likely that, at some point in the foreseeable future (the timing of which will depend on economic and political considerations), the regulation of the market may need to be amended to include:
  - New provisions, or possibly a separate regime, in the *Corporations Act* dealing with RMBS issues of securities of less than $500,000 sold to retail ("Mum and Dad") investors, as distinct from the higher value securities presently marketed to "sophisticated" institutional investors. The *Investment Company Act* 1940 (US) could serve as a useful model in this regard.[13]
  - New provisions protecting housing loan borrowers who are currently unaware that their residences could be sold by the trustee issuer or SPV exercising its rights as assignee mortgagee, not because of any default on the borrower's part, but because of default or loss on the part of the trustee issuer, the SPV, the mortgage originator, the fund manager, or any other downstream

[13] In the United States, RMBS issues are regulated separately from the managed funds industry. Consideration could be given in Australia to establishing a separate division of the *Corporations Act* to regulate any future offering of RMBS issues to the public (as distinct from institutional investors).

provider in the supply chain. So that borrowers are fully informed about this risk when they enter into housing loan contracts, new legislative provisions should specifically require lenders to:

(i) Bring the relevant clauses in the loan contracts, and their implications, to the notice of the borrower and make sure that he or she understands the implications.
(ii) In the case of new mortgages, give the borrowers notice of any proposed assignments before the mortgage is completed and the opportunity to refuse to allow the transfer.
(iii) In the case of existing mortgages, by individual approach to the mortgagors concerned, give each borrower a reasonable opportunity to refuse to give their consent to the transfers and, if necessary, unwind any transfers that have already been made.[14]

In the latter two cases, the legislation could, for the sake of economic efficiency as well as fairness, allow mortgage originators to charge a premium in relation to those housing loans in which the borrowers have refused to consent to the assignment.[15] However, any premium could be subject to prices oversight by the regulatory authorities (e.g. Australian Competition and Consumer Commission and APRA).

- Improved, timely disclosure requirements, perhaps on a pool (aggregate) basis.[16] Plainly this would need to be subject to a rigorous public benefit test under the *Statutory Instruments Act*

[14]The point is not that banks and IMPs should be precluded from involvement in RMBS programmes. The point is that there is an appreciable risk to borrowers if they do, and borrowers (not banks or IMPs) should be the ones who decide whether borrowers are prepared to bear that risk. At present, it would appear that most borrowers in practice are not even aware that the risk exists.

[15]If the banks have lower costs because of securitising, they can (assuming a highly competitive environment) have lower interest rates and charges. The premium is built into the bank's pricing via the competitive process in the market.

[16]A recent study undertaken by the US Securities and Exchange Commission has identified several items for enhanced disclosure in the mortgage-backed securities market. These include the purpose of the loan (e.g. whether it is a purchase or refinance); the original loan-to-value (LTV) ratio; any standardised credit scores of borrowers; the details of servicers for the pool (this need not always be the originator); the occupancy status of the security property (e.g. owner-occupied or rented); the property type (e.g. stand-alone house, detached dwelling, or apartment). For more detail, see Securities and Exchange Commission (US), *Staff Report of the Task Force on Mortgage-Backed Securities Disclosure*, January 2003, http://www.sec.gov.

1992 (Qld) and the Commonwealth-State *Competition Principles Agreement*. Nevertheless, improved information disclosure could assist fund managers to assess the prepayment risk of RMBSs, and investors with their investment decisions; improve efficiency, pricing, and market confidence; and (arguably) lower risk.

- In the light of the recent Basel III proposals, the Commonwealth Government should instigate an investigation by APRA, perhaps in conjunction with the Reserve Bank of Australia, into whether the current risk-weighting of RMBSs for capital adequacy purposes should be reduced from 100% to some lower figure.
- Finally, that a panel of independent experts on RMBSs be established (after the manner of the Monopolies and Mergers Commission Panel in the United Kingdom), so that the industry regulators such as APRA and ASIC have access to expert advice in relation to complex matters involving RMBSs.

9.4 Suggestions for Further Research

A number of suggestions for further research, in both law and commerce, are made throughout the book.

In terms of legal research, a detailed investigation of the income tax aspects of RMBS issues would prove useful for practitioners in the industry. Similar research could be conducted into the indirect tax consequences of RMBS transactions relating to GST, stamp duty, land tax, and other transaction taxes including bank account debits tax and financial institutions duty.

Second, the legal researchers could focus on the impact of the recently enacted reforms to the privacy legislation on borrowers who are unaware that their loans have been securitised in the form of RMBS issues and, in the same context, the extent to which the ADIs' duty of confidentiality has been compromised by such securitisations. To the extent that borrowers do not expressly consent to the disclosure to an SPV of private information concerning them,[17] the privacy legislation remains a real concern, which is worthy of further, more detailed investigation.

[17] That is, in terms of Part IIIA of the *Privacy Act* 1988 (Cth)—in particular, sections 18 L(4), (4A) and (6), and 18 N(1)(b), (1)(bg)(i) and (1)(bh), and 18 N(1A), (1B) and (5).

Third, legal researchers could examine the impact, in terms of insurance law and practice, on mortgage insurers and their customers, of negligence on the part of the ADI, SPV, or mortgage manager in carrying out their duties in relation to mortgage securitisations.

The book also has a number of implications for economic and accounting research.

For example, further research could investigate whether, from an economic point of view, different regulation is required for RMBS issues, or whether the current regulatory regime as it applies to "debentures" in the *Corporations Act* is sufficient and effective from a public interest perspective.

A second avenue for future economic research could be an investigation of the extent and social cost of the moral hazard problem inherent in assignment or "bank" programmes, namely that ADIs may have an incentive to lend housing loans to their customers too easily, if they know they can assign their rights and responsibilities to an SPV and not be held responsible if the issue subsequently goes awry. For example, a social cost-benefit study could be conducted to determine whether the problem needs to be rectified from an economic point of view, and if so, the best means of doing so.

A third area for future finance research would be the detailed and precise statistical estimation of an appropriate weighting for RMBSs for capital adequacy purposes, in order to determine whether RMBSs in Australia, currently risk-weighted at 100%, should be weighted at some lower percentage. Such research would have potentially profound implications for the day-to-day management of bank assets and liabilities.

Fourth, accounting researchers could fruitfully investigate the appropriate reporting requirements of the various on-balance sheet and off-balance sheet transactions in RMBS issues.

Finally, at the time of writing, there is no generally accepted Australian accounting standard for securitisation. This is somewhat surprising, since such accounting standards are used overseas—for example, in the United Kingdom and the United States. Accounting researchers could usefully investigate the appropriateness of introducing similar standards for use in Australia.

Bibliography

Books and Book Chapters

Bruce, R., McKern, B., Pollard, I. and Skully, M., *Handbook of Australian Corporate Finance*, 5th edition, Sydney: Butterworths, 1997.

Journal Articles

Finch, A., 'Securitisation' (1995) 6 (4) *Journal of Banking and Finance Law and Practice* 247.

Senarath, S., 'Securitisation and the global financial crisis: can risk retention prevent another crisis?' (2017) 18 *International Journal of Business and Globalisation* 153.

Working Papers, Magazines, Newspapers and Reports

Securities and Exchange Commission (U.S.), *Staff Report of the Task Force on Mortgage-Backed Securities Disclosure*, January 2003, http://www.sec.gov

Senarath, S. 'The Dodd-Frank Act doesn't solve the principal-agent problem in asset securitisation' (2017) *blogs.lse.ac.uk* (11 November 2018).

Standard and Poor's, 'Credit Ratings on Mortgage-Backed Securities', *Structured Finance Australia and New Zealand*, Melbourne, 1998.

Glossary

Assignment A mode of transferring assets which involves the actual transfer of the title to the receivables. In relation to a mortgage, it would mean the transfer of a mortgage by the mortgagee (lender) to the mortgagor (borrower and occupier).

Bankruptcy remoteness A technique used for isolating assets or loans from the bankruptcy risk of the company selling them (originator). The originator finances its loans by transferring them to a special purpose vehicle (SPV) which issues securities backed by the loans. The transfer of the loans to the SPV is designed to be a "true sale", which removes the loans from the originator's balance sheet. This places the loans outside the originator's bankruptcy estate in case it goes into bankruptcy. In addition, the SPV is established in such a way that it is independent from the originator.

Capital adequacy Regulations that require authorised deposit-taking institutions (ADIs), for example banks to maintain minimum amount of capital relative to the assets of the bank. Generally these requirements are set in accordance with the framework promoted by the Bank for International Settlements (BIS).

P. Rajapakse, S. Senarath, *Commercial Law Aspects of Residential Mortgage Securitisation in Australia*,
https://doi.org/10.1007/978-3-030-00605-1

Collateral Assets are serving as security for a loan. The underlying security, mortgage, or asset are for the purposes of securitisation. In the case of a mortgage loan secured by collateral, if the borrower fails to make required payments, the lender has the right to seize and sell the collateral to recover the defaulted amount.

Conduit In securitisations, this means an entity (a trust or a company) formed to hold assets transferred by the originator on behalf of the investors. It issues securities backed by assets purchased by the SPV from the originator.

Credit enhancement Techniques used in a securitisation structure to improve the credit quality of a security or a bond so that it can obtain high rating, for example by providing a cash collateral or third party guarantee etc. Most securitisations use credit enhancements to allow their securities to obtain a triple-A ("AAA") ratings.

Credit risk The risk that an issuer of debt securities or a borrower may default on its obligations.

Delinquency A condition of having failed to make one or more scheduled payment on a debt obligation. A borrower may be considered delinquent on its debt as soon as the due date of payment has passed.

Equitable assignment An assignment of receivables that does not complete the legal requirements for an assignment, for example a formal stamped instrument or a notice to borrowers etc. The common law recognises equitable assignment as creating an equity between the assignor and the assignee, though it cannot have any standing in relation to either the borrower or any third parties.

Interest rate risk The risk that a security's value will change due to a change in interest rates. For example, a bond price drops as interest rates rise. For a depository institution, also called a funding risk, the risk that spreads income will suffer because of a change in interest rates.

Interest rate swap A contract between two parties to swap a fixed rate of interest for a floating rate of interest, or different bases for a floating rate of interest.

Liquidity risk The risk that arises from the difficulty of selling an asset in a timely manner. It can be thought of as the difference between the "true value" of the asset and the likely price, less commissions.

Loan-to-valuation ratio (LTV) The principal amount of a loan outstanding as a percentage of the valuation of the property forming the collateral for the loan.

Mortgage A creation of security interest, normally over real property, in order to secure a loan or debt obligation.

Mortgage pool A group of mortgages with similar class, interest rate, and maturity characteristics.

Mortgage-backed securities (MBS) This is a broad term which encompasses securities backed by a pool of mortgage loans. MBS are further classified into residential mortgage-backed securities and commercial mortgage-backed securities. Commercial mortgage-backed securities represent securities backed by mortgage loans for commercial properties such as multi-family dwelling, shops, restaurants, and showrooms.

Mortgagee The lender of a loan secured by a property.

Mortgagor The borrower of a loan secured by property.

Off balance sheet A debt or asset, which does not show up on the balance sheet of the entity that originated the asset or debt. In a securitisation transaction, if the transaction qualifies for a true sale, the assets transferred by the originator are off the balance sheet of the originator, and so is the amount received on account of such transfer.

Originator An institution which originates loans. In a securitisation transaction, the originator sells the loans to a trust or SPV, but typically retains the role as a servicer.

Over-collateralisation The provision of security for a loan or debt issue which is in the amount owing so as to offer protection to the lender or investor in the event of a fall in the collateral value.

Pass through It refers to a securitisation structure where the SPV makes payments on the securities to the investors, on the same periods, and subject to the same fluctuations, as are there in the underlying assets. That is to say, amount collected every month is passed through to investors, after deducting fees and expenses.

Pay through A form of debt security where the payments to the investors are paid through the SPV who does not strictly pay the investors only when the receivables are collected by it, but keeps paying on the stipulated dates irrespective of the collection dates.

Prepayment Payment of principal on a loan before its due date.

Prepayment risk The risk that borrowers prepay their mortgage loans. Mortgage loan prepayments tend to increase when interest rates fall and home-owners have the opportunity to refinance their loans at lower interest rates. In turn, prepayments return a substantial portion of invested principal to the MBS investors. Investors who receive a return principal may be forced to reinvest at lower yields. Hence, prepayment is viewed as a risk in securitisation.

Securitisation In a securitisation transaction, a company raises money by issuing securities that are backed by specific assets. In most cases, the underlying assets are loans such as mortgage loans, accounts receivables, or auto loans. The cash flow from the underlying assets usually is the source of funds for the issuer to make payments on the securities.

Servicer An entity that collects payments on securitised assets and that administers securitisation transaction. Administrative duties including processing payment to investors and transmitting periodic reports to investors and rating agencies. Often an originator of securitised assets acts as the servicer

Special purpose vehicle (SPV) An entity established with the sole (special) purpose of purchasing assets and issuing securities backed by these assets to finance the purchase. Frequently, the SPV serves as a trust or a corporation. In relation to securitisation, it means the entity which would hold the legal rights over the assets transferred by the originator.

True sale In a securitisation transaction, the originator of assets transfers the assets to the SPV in a transaction designed to be a true sale. An example of a transaction that is not a true sale is a pledge of collateral to secure a debt. In securitisations, achieving a true sale is an important aspect of bankruptcy remoteness.

Index

P. Rajapakse, S. Senarath, *Commercial Law Aspects of Residential Mortgage Securitisation in Australia*,
https://doi.org/10.1007/978-3-030-00605-1

The manufacturer's authorised representative in the EU is Springer Nature Customer Service Centre GmbH, Europaplatz 3, 69115 Heidelberg, Germany. If you have any concerns regarding our products, please contact ProductSafety@springernature.com

Printed and bound by CPI Group (UK) Ltd, Croydon, CR0 4YY

30/09/2026

02225216-0012